AMERICAN CRISIS

William Ellery: A Rhode Island Politico and Lord of Admiralty

Rebels Under Sail: The American Navy in the Revolution

The American Revolution: Changing Perspectives (coeditor)

The Baron of Beacon Hill: A Biography of John Hancock

Jack Tars and Commodores: The American Navy, 1783–1815

Under Two Flags: The Navy in the Civil War

Silas Talbot: Captain of Old Ironsides

Samuel Adams: Radical Puritan

America and the Sea: A Maritime History (coauthor)

Empires at War: The French and Indian War and
the Struggle for North America, 1754–1763

America and the Sea: Treasures from the Collections of
Mystic Seaport (coauthor)

AMERICAN CRISIS

George Washington and the Dangerous Two Years
After Yorktown, 1781–1783

WILLIAM M. FOWLER JR.

WALKER & COMPANY
New York

Published by Walker Publishing Company, Inc., New York
A Division of Bloomsbury Publishing

ISBN: 978-0-8027-1706-1

Printed in the U.S.A.

Book Club Edition

To the staff of Snell Library at Northeastern University.
My partners in teaching and scholarship.

CONTENTS

Maps   ix

Introduction   1

Chapter One   3

Chapter Two   14

Chapter Three   35

Chapter Four   53

Chapter Five   68

Chapter Six   86

Chapter Seven   109

Chapter Eight   129

Chapter Nine   145

Chapter Ten   159

Chapter Eleven   174

Chapter Twelve   189

Chapter Thirteen   208

Chapter Fourteen   222

Epilogue   241

Acknowledgments   249

Appendix 1. Newburgh Address   251

Appendix 2. A Circular Letter   257

Notes   267

Bibliography   319

Index   331

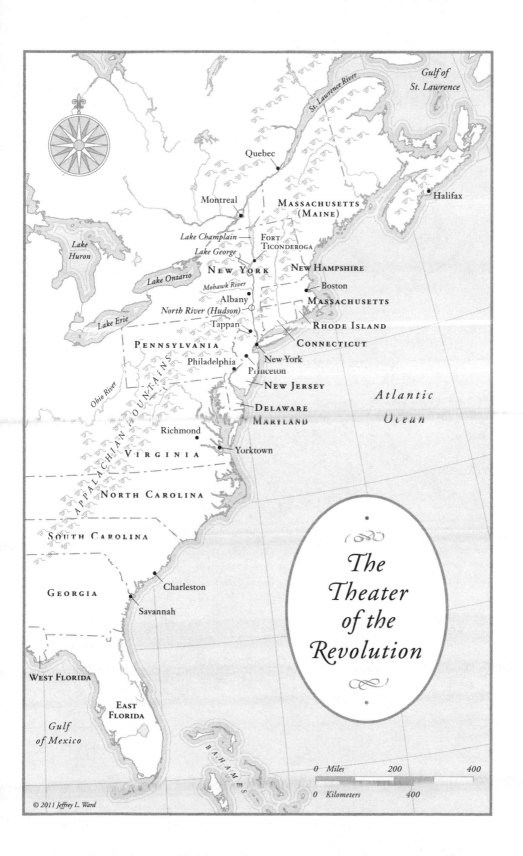

The
Theater
of the
Revolution

© 2011 Jeffrey L. Ward

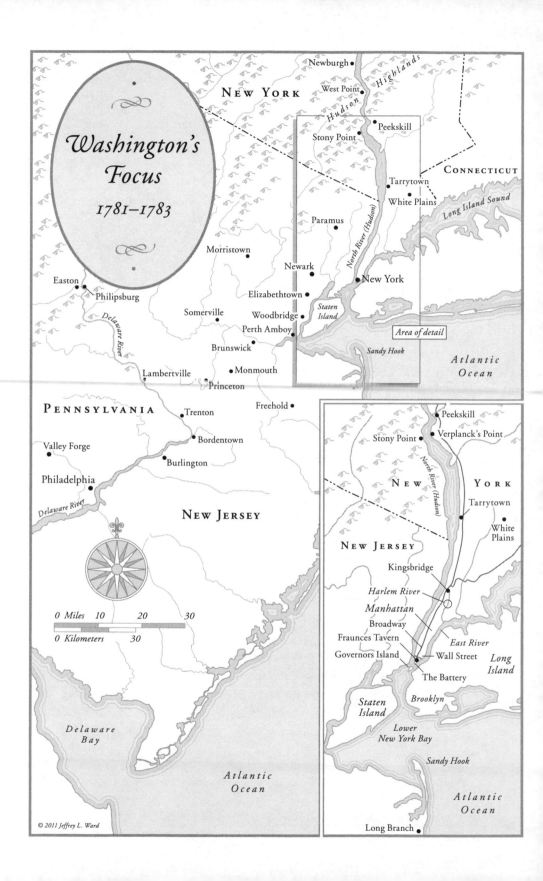

Washington's
Focus
1781–1783

NEW YORK

Newburgh
West Point
Hudson Highlands
Peekskill
Stony Point
Tarrytown
White Plains
CONNECTICUT
Long Island Sound
Paramus
Morristown
Newark
New York
Easton
Philipsburg
Elizabethtown
Staten Island
Somerville
Woodbridge
Perth Amboy
Brunswick
Sandy Hook
Atlantic Ocean
Lambertville
Monmouth
Princeton
Freehold
Area of detail
PENNSYLVANIA
Trenton
Bordentown
Valley Forge
Burlington
Philadelphia
NEW JERSEY
Delaware River
Delaware River

0 Miles 10 20 30
0 Kilometers 30

Delaware Bay

Atlantic Ocean

Peekskill
Stony Point
Verplanck's Point
North River (Hudson)
NEW YORK
Tarrytown
White Plains
NEW JERSEY
Kingsbridge
Harlem River
Manhattan
Broadway
East River
Fraunces Tavern
Governors Island
Wall Street
Long Island
The Battery
Staten Island
Brooklyn
Lower New York Bay
Sandy Hook
Atlantic Ocean
Long Branch

© 2011 Jeffrey L. Ward

INTRODUCTION

O N THE MORNING of January 6, 1783, the doors of the Continental Congress in Philadelphia opened to admit Major General Alexander McDougall, Colonel John Brooks, and Colonel Matthias Ogden.
These officers bore an urgent message from the American army encamped
at Newburgh, New York. The army, they warned, was on the verge of
mutiny. The members were thunderstruck. After eight years of bloody
war the army that had brought the nation so close to victory now stood
as a threat to the very principles for which it had fought. How could this
have happened?

Most Americans in 1783, and many today, believe that the surrender of
the British army under Lord Cornwallis at Yorktown, October 19, 1781,
marked the end of the American Revolution. Even British leaders of the
time shared this view. Lord North, for example, the king's first minister,
upon hearing the news of Yorktown, exclaimed, "O God it is all over."
However, Yorktown did not end the American Revolution. The war for
independence was not over, and no one understood this better than the
American commander in chief.

George Washington had cause to worry. Even after the victory at
Yorktown, the British still held Charleston, Savannah, and New York
City. The distant northern posts of Oswego, Detroit, Michilimackinac,

and Niagara remained in their hands as well, and the Royal Navy, despite the setback in the Battle of the Chesapeake Capes during the Yorktown campaign, continued to dominate the seas. Nor was the stubborn King George III ready to admit defeat.

Enemy intentions and the king's attitude were not Washington's only concerns. Six years of war had put a heavy strain on the new nation. The "Spirit of '76" had waned, and he feared that the good news of victory would work to further weaken American resolve. To Virginia's governor, Thomas Nelson, Washington wrote anxiously that "instead of exciting our exertions," the victory at Yorktown might "produce such a relaxation in the prosecution of the War, as will prolong the calamities of it."[1]

Washington had cause to fret about American firmness. Congress was nearly bankrupt. The states could not agree on a plan for national revenue, and the fabric of the union, never strong, was fraying as Congress divided into bickering factions. In the meantime the French, having financed the war, were balking at providing additional loans while making plans to withdraw their forces from North America. The American army with Washington at its head was the only viable national institution, but it too was under stress as the alarming news from McDougall, Brooks, and Ogden demonstrated dramatically.

With Congress broke and unable to act, some in the body saw opportunity in the crisis. They conspired to use the army as a lever to advance an agenda aimed at strengthening the national government. If not an actual coup d'état, their machinations certainly rose to the level of a plot to challenge civilian authority over the military. Had these men succeeded in their aims, they would have forever broken the trust between the armed forces of the United States and its citizens. That they did not succeed was due to one man, George Washington, who on March 15, 1783, stood before the officers of his army "single and alone" and prevented a mutiny that would have altered the course of American history. This is the story of these "dangerous years" and the commander who, in the words of Thomas Jefferson, "prevented this revolution from being closed as most others have been by a subversion of that liberty it was intended to establish."[2]

CHAPTER ONE

I T WAS FIVE in the afternoon on October 9, 1781, the seventh year of
the American Revolution. All eyes were on the American commander
in chief as he approached the line of cannon, their muzzles aimed toward the British entrenchments at Yorktown. A gunner handed Washington a lit match. The general's hand moved slowly toward the touch
hole, the cannon roared and leaped back on its carriage as hundreds of
other guns, American and French, followed with a thunderous barrage.
General Charles Cornwallis, the British commander who five years before, while pursuing Washington across New Jersey, had boasted that he
would "bag the American fox," was himself brought to ground.

The Revolution had not gone well for the British. Initially a colonial
rebellion, by 1778 it had spilled into a world war with the entry of the
French as American allies. Forced to defend their possessions on a global
scale, the British ministers abandoned any hope of subduing the northern and middle colonies and instead concentrated their forces on retaking
the southern colonies, where they anticipated a surge of loyalist support.[1]
In 1780, while retaining New York City as his principal American base,
the British commander in chief Sir Henry Clinton struck south, taking
Charleston, South Carolina. After securing the city he returned to New
York, leaving General Cornwallis in charge. Soon Cornwallis managed

to move beyond the city and secured a good portion of South Carolina and Georgia.

Had Cornwallis been more cautious and less ambitious, he might well have been satisfied with what he had captured. But after inflicting a humiliating defeat on an American army commanded by General Horatio Gates at Camden, South Carolina, on August 16, 1780, Cornwallis elected to forge north toward North Carolina and Virginia.[2] These colonies, he boasted, "would fall without much resistance and be retained without much difficulty."[3]

Unfortunately for the British, Cornwallis's march into the interior proved costly. He had not taken into account the sapping of his strength by constant attacks from southern partisans like Francis Marion and Thomas Sumter; nor did he appreciate the brilliance of Nathanael Greene, the American commander who replaced General Gates. Described by the British military historian Sir John Fortescue as "a general of patience, resolution, and profound common sense," Greene took Cornwallis on a wild chase through the interior of North Carolina in a campaign dubbed "the Country Dance." Although he never defeated Cornwallis, Greene so weakened and frustrated his enemy that Cornwallis gave up chasing him down and marched his army into Virginia, to search for a secure coastal location where he might either be resupplied or be evacuated by Clinton. Cornwallis eventually chose Yorktown, a small port town on the banks of the York River close by the mouth of Chesapeake Bay. By the end of August 1781 he had assembled his entire army there to await word from General Clinton.[4]

Washington and General Rochambeau, commander of French forces in North America, had been watching Cornwallis's march north with great interest.[5] Having shut himself up in Yorktown, thus putting his back to the river, the general, they knew, was in a vulnerable spot. Salvation for the British depended upon control of the seas. Only by sea could Clinton reenforce or remove the trapped army. Although Clinton did have a naval squadron at New York, and a sizable army, he hesitated to act, fearing that if he should weaken his own position to rescue Cornwallis, the allies might take the opportunity to attack New York City.

As both sides pondered their options, grand news arrived for the allies: the French West Indian fleet under Admiral François-Joseph-Paul de Grasse was sailing north to escape the hurricane season and would be stationed near the Chesapeake Capes until mid-October. Might his fleet, the admiral queried, be usefully employed? Instantly Washington and Rochambeau saw the opportunity for an allied concentration of naval and military forces aimed at Cornwallis.

With impressive speed and coordination the two generals, Washington from the Hudson Valley, Rochambeau from Rhode Island, put their troops on the move toward Virginia, while summoning de Grasse to join them. Clinton was caught unawares. Not until September 2 did he realize the peril of the situation, and by that time the allied armies and the French fleet were both closing on Yorktown. Desperate to prevent the French fleet from rendezvousing with Rochambeau and Washington, Clinton ordered his admirals to take whatever force they could assemble at New York and sail to intercept de Grasse. Six days after clearing Sandy Hook, the British sighted the French. For three days the two fleets tacked about with intermittent engagements. While neither side could gain a decisive advantage, the British finally elected to withdraw, leaving command of the sea to the French. Cornwallis's fate was sealed. By late September the combined armies, with de Grasse standing off shore, had assembled and taken up positions surrounding Yorktown. It was a classic eighteenth-century siege. The besiegers formed a semicircle facing the enemy, French on the left, Americans on the right. Engineers went to work laying out and digging zigzagging trenches. By the ninth all was in readiness as Washington fired the first American shot.

Each day four hundred allied guns fired more than seventeen hundred rounds onto the enemy. The British response was pitiful. At about nine on the morning of October 17, 1781, American sentries caught sight of a young British drummer boy clutching for a hold as he struggled to reach the top of an earthen parapet. His soiled red uniform bespoke days of huddling in damp shelters while iron shot rained down. Unarmed except for a bulky side drum and two sticks, he finally reached the top. For the moment this boy had the most dangerous job in America. Amid the dense and acrid smoke left behind by musket and cannon shot, he beat the "parley." General Cornwallis wished to discuss terms of surrender with Generals Rochambeau and Washington.[6]

Captain Ebenezer Denny of the First Pennsylvania Regiment was among the first to spot the drummer boy. "He might have beaten away til Doomsday if he had not been sighted by the men in the front lines," Denny later recalled. "The constant firing was too much for the sound of the single drum; but when the firing ceased, I thought I had never heard a drum equal to it—the most delightful music to all."[7] Quickly, soldiers passed the order "cease fire." The guns fell silent, and the drummer boy advanced toward the American position. Behind him walked a hatless officer waving a white handkerchief above his head. Together, to the rhythm of the "parley," the soldier and the boy marched slowly across the no-mans-land toward the allied positions. As soon as the party passed safely through the lines, the guns resumed their pounding. While the cannon belched iron, Washington read Cornwallis's message:

> To His Excellency General Washington.
> Sir, I propose a cessation of hostilities for twenty-four hours, and that two officers may be appointed by each side, to meet at Mr. Moore's house, to settle terms for the surrender of the posts at York and Gloucester.[8]

Toward evening the guns stood down again as the drummer boy and the officer returned through the British lines carrying Washington's reply.

> Sir, I have received your Favor of this Morning. Regard to humanity induces me to agree to a suspension of hostilities for two hours that your Lordship may propose the Terms on which you choose to surrender.[9]

For the British it was all over. Cornwallis understood his fate. His only hope was to extract concessions. Washington was unwilling to grant any.

Cornwallis responded to Washington with his terms. Although he had no intention of agreeing to all of Cornwallis's requests, Washington agreed to send commissioners to meet the next day at the Moore House, a spacious home situated near the river about one mile east of the British lines. In the meantime the guns remained silent.

In the morning British Highland pipers called soldiers to duty with the wailing of bagpipes. In answer, the Royal Deux-Ponts regimental band struck up a lively tune. Across the scarred battlefield soldiers and officers, victors and vanquished, stood at the crest of their fortifications, barely a few hundred feet apart, gazing anxiously at one another.

Brigade commander Lieutenant Colonel Thomas Dundas and Cornwallis's aide-de-camp, Major Alexander Ross, were the first to arrive at the Moore House. They were soon joined by Colonel John Laurens, aide-de-camp to General Washington, and Second Colonel Viscount de Noailles of the Regiment Soissonois, the Marquis de Lafayette's brother-in-law. After exchanging pleasantries, the officers took seats in the main room to work out the details. The meeting lasted more than eight long and unpleasant hours.[10]

Washington stood firm. He refused the enemy any honors of war. The British regiments had to march out with colors cased and their bands playing an English or German tune. Although officers might be paroled (that is, allowed to return home to England or Germany), rank and file would be held in America as prisoners of war. Loyalists and deserters who trembled at being left to the tender mercies of the rebels had begged Cornwallis to protect them. To answer their pleas, Cornwallis asked that no one be punished "on account of having joined the British army."[11] Washington refused. However, while he understood that feelings were riding high against those who had taken up arms for the king, the commander in chief had little taste for convening endless courts-martial and ordering multiple executions. To avoid such bloody retribution, Washington declared that the fate of the loyalists was a civil matter to be decided at a later date. As for deserters, he agreed to an oblique solution granting Cornwallis's request to permit the sloop *Bonetta* to sail from Yorktown to New York without inspection. The vessel had ample room for any passengers who might wish to leave Yorktown in a hurry. *Bonetta*'s departure with its cargo gave relief to both sides. After wrapping up a few more details, the officers concluded their work, saluted, and each returned to his general.[12]

Numerous accounts of the surrender ceremony have survived. The Yankee doctor James Thacher of Plymouth, Massachusetts, who had spent six years in the field with the Continental army, relished the chance "to receive as captives that vindictive, haughty commander, and that victorious army, who by their robberies and murders, has so long been a scourge to our brethren of the southern states." From horseback he had a perfect view. He reported that at noon units of American light infantry and French grenadiers occupied the British lines, while the main body marched from camp to form up in a gauntletlike position lining the road leading out of Yorktown. With Americans on the right facing the French, the line extended more than mile. "Mounted on his noble courser," Washington took his station on the right. To his left "was the excellent Count Rochambeau."[13] Behind both lines civilian spectators pressed for a view of this historic occasion.

Not even the soldiers called to attention could resist glancing down the road as a mounted figure emerged from the British lines. Like Thacher, they craned their necks to see Cornwallis humbled. All were disappointed. At the head of the column rode Brigadier General Charles O'Hara, Cornwallis's second in command. General Cornwallis, O'Hara explained, was "indisposed." Thacher was disgusted. "Tis no display of magnanimity when a great commander shrinks from the inevitable misfortunes of war." He had given "himself up entirely to vexation and despair."[14] Cornwallis's pusillanimous behavior disappointed the allies, while insulting the brave soldiers he had led.

As O'Hara neared the end of the line he reined his horse toward Rochambeau, intending to offer his sword to an officer whom he deemed to be of equal rank. To his dismay the French general gestured to the allied commander in chief. As O'Hara approached he was diverted a second time. Washington motioned him to deliver his sword to General Benjamin Lincoln, a subordinate of equal rank to O'Hara.[15] Upon accepting the sword, Lincoln paused and then returned it to O'Hara while gesturing to a nearby field. There French hussars had formed a great circle within which, Lincoln ordered, the British were to lay down their arms.

"Ground arms" was the bellowing command. In a "sullen temper" some soldiers threw their muskets to the ground, hoping to smash the locks and render them useless. Lincoln put a quick stop to that behavior. When the last musket was added to the pile the disarmed soldiers returned to their camp. That evening General O'Hara dined with Washington and Rochambeau.

On Sunday October 21 the American army gathered for divine services conducted by the Reverend Israel Evans of New Hampshire. Evans
began by "offering to the Lord of hosts, the God of battles, grateful hom-
age" for the blessings of victory "with which Divine Providence has seen
fit to crown our efforts."[16] While one army gathered to give thanks, at a
distance the vanquished formed up under guard to begin their march inland to prison camps at Winchester, Virginia, and Frederick, Maryland.

Washington skipped the service. He was aboard the *Ville de Paris*,
Admiral de Grasse's flagship. With Lafayette by his side Washington
paid his respects to the admiral and made a request. Would the French
fleet assist him in an attack on Wilmington, North Carolina? The Americans could provide two thousand troops under Lafayette's command, but
they needed transports and a naval escort. Seeing "endless obstacles" to
the proposal, particularly the king's orders to return to the West Indies
and join the Spanish in an assault on the British islands, the admiral
declined politely. Strategically, any prospect of picking off a few rich
British sugar islands trumped liberating the Carolinas. Disappointed,
but hardly surprised, Washington wished his ally well.[17]

Word of the British defeat at Yorktown spread quickly. As soon as he
had reliable information, Clinton dispatched the fast sloop *Rattlesnake* to
London with the "most melancholy news Great Britain ever received."[18]
A few days later he received Cornwallis's official report. "Sir, I have the
mortification to inform your excellency, that I have been forced to give
up the posts of York and Gloucester, and to surrender the troops under
my command."[19] Having conveyed that dismal news, Cornwallis continued with a long explanation as to why this disaster befell him. In sum,
he blamed Clinton.

Washington was anxious that his dispatches be the first to arrive at
Congress with the good news. To be his herald, Washington honored
one of his aides, Tench Tilghman, an officer he described as "a zealous
servant and slave to the public."[20] Tilghman galloped into Philadelphia
shortly before dawn on October 24 and went immediately to the home of
President Thomas McKean. At ten in the morning, their usual hour
of assembly, members took their seats and sat quietly as the clerk read
Washington's dispatch. Members then rose from their seats. Huzzahs

and cheers filled the chamber. Once order was restored, the members voted to "go in procession to the Dutch Lutheran church, and return thanks to Almighty God."[21]

By November 3 most of the American army, aside from two brigades sent south to join General Nathanael Greene, had been ordered north to resume their encampment along the Hudson. Rochambeau's army remained in Virginia, anticipating a spring departure from North America. Cornwallis left on November 4 for New York City and thence home to England.[22] Having sent the captured soldiers off to prison camps and the paroled officers to New York, Washington felt relieved of this "great encumbrance."[23]

Another "encumbrance" was not so easily managed. As the Americans and French took count of their captives, they discovered a considerable number of deserters who had not had the good fortune to escape. Courts-martial were convened to decide the fate of these men. Some who claimed that they were coerced into serving were acquitted. Others were not so lucky. By a General Order on November 3 Washington confirmed death sentences on nine men. A dozen others received one hundred lashes.[24]

Never a commander to bask in victories, rare though they had been in the war, Washington was troubled. Barely a week following the surrender he confided to Thomas Nelson, governor of Virginia, that "the late important success, instead of exciting our exertions, as it ought to do, should produce such a relaxation in the prosecution of the War, as will prolong the calamities of it."[25] He knew that the war was not over. The enemy still occupied New York City, Charleston, Savannah, and Wilmington. They controlled a large swath of northern New England, and despite the French naval victory at the Capes no one doubted that the Royal Navy still commanded the seas. Added to the naval and military situation was a stubborn King George III, who had made it clear, repeatedly, that under no circumstances would he surrender his colonies. Washington was equally troubled by his own situation. De Grasse had already left, Rochambeau's army was likely to leave in the spring, and the Congress was broke.

While Washington mulled over his nation's precarious condition, his personal life took a tumble. A message arrived that he must come quickly to Eltham, his brother-in-law's plantation. Martha's son Jacky Custis was dying.[26]

George Washington was Martha's second husband. Her first marriage, to Daniel Parke Custis, in 1751 produced four children: Daniel, John, Martha, and Frances. Both Daniel and Frances died before her husband died in 1757. In 1759, when Martha married George, she brought her surviving children, five-year-old John (Jacky) and three-year-old Martha (Patsy), to Mount Vernon, her new husband's estate. Although Washington never officially adopted the children—they would always retain the Custis name—he welcomed them into his home and loved them as his own. Patsy died at Mount Vernon in 1773, when she was barely seventeen. In 1774, on the eve of the Revolution, Jacky married Eleanor "Nelly" Calvert, a member of a distinguished Maryland family. The couple settled at Abingdon, a plantation not far from Mount Vernon. Within the space of five years they had four children.[27]

Success eluded Jacky Custis. He was barely able to manage the estate he inherited from his father. He dabbled in Virginia politics, securing election to burgesses, but legislative duties bored him, and in the fall of 1781 he asked permission of his stepfather to join him at Yorktown. Washington agreed, and Jacky joined the general's military "family" in an unofficial capacity. During the siege Jacky contracted a "fever," most likely typhus. Hoping that he would recover away from the pestilence of camp, Washington sent him to nearby Eltham, home of Jacky's uncle, Burwell Bassett.[28]

Washington hurried to Eltham and there met Martha. Together they sat with Jacky until he died on November 5. Martha Washington had outlived all her children.

Washington had intended to go on to Philadelphia directly from Yorktown. Jacky's death changed his plans. He explained to the president of Congress that his journey to Philadelphia was delayed by "an event very distressing to Mrs. Washington."[29] After remaining a few days at Eltham to tidy up family matters, Martha and Nelly returned to Mount Vernon. He would, he told them, join them in a day or two after he visited with his widowed mother, Mary Ball Washington, whom he had not seen since the war began.

Washington had a strained relationship with his mother. When he arrived at Fredericksburg the town turned out to greet him, but not his mother. She was away "over the Moutins [*sic*]." He left a bit of money for her and departed for Mount Vernon. A few days later she thanked him. She made no mention in her note of Jacky's death; nor did she extend any sympathy to Nelly or Martha.[30]

After so long an absence from home, and in the midst of family distress, Washington's strongest desire was to remain at Mount Vernon. Nonetheless, the war was not over, and he had pressing business with Congress in Philadelphia. On Tuesday morning November 20, Washington began his journey north. Martha joined him, leaving Nelly and the children at home.[31]

Their first stop was Alexandria, where the "arrival was announced by the discharge of cannon" and "acclamations." A few Tories, it was reported, "to expiate their crimes . . . joined in applauding the man, whose late successes had annihilated their hopes." Annapolis and Baltimore gave equally raucous receptions until finally, on Monday afternoon November 26, 1781, the Washingtons entered Philadelphia, where the *Pennsylvania Journal* hailed him as "the Saviour of his Country."[32]

A jubilant crowd followed the Washingtons up Third Street to the home of Benjamin Chew between Walnut and Spruce. Chew, the former chief justice of Pennsylvania and a man suspected of loyalist leanings, had prudently left town and taken refuge in the countryside. Chew had rented the rear of his large home to Francisco Rendon, the unofficial emissary from the court of Spain.[33] The Washingtons occupied the front. Best known for its elegant garden, the house sat next to an even more grandiose home, the Powel House. Samuel and Elizabeth Willing Powel were the city's most fashionable couple. During a previous visit to the city Washington had dined and danced at their home on a memorable evening, January 6, 1779, when he and Martha were celebrating their twentieth wedding anniversary.[34]

Philadelphia was also home to one of America's most entrepreneurial self-promoters: Charles Willson Peale. Born to an ordinary family in Maryland, Peale originally apprenticed as a saddler. That was a short-lived occupation, and Peale eventually moved on to master a variety of skills, becoming a watchmaker, silversmith, jeweler, modeler in clay, and, most famously, a portraitist working in crayon, oils, and miniatures. Peale first met Washington in 1772, when he painted him at Mount Vernon in the uniform of a Virginia militia officer. In the course of the next nine years Peale painted him again more than a dozen times.[35] In Washington's grand arrival Peale saw an opportunity he could not miss. At his home on the corner of Third and Lombard streets, only a few blocks from the Chew House, he crafted an "Illumination." According to the *Pennsylvania Packet*, on the evening of November 27 "people were flocking from all parts of their town to obtain a sight of the beautiful expressions of Mr. Peale's respect and gratitude to the conquering Hero." Peale had spent days painting transparencies on his windows. The light from behind the glass enabled spectators to see,

> at the lower window, a ship with the British colours below the French, and the word CORNWALLIS on the stern. At the middle window, above, the portraits of his Excellency General Washington and Count de Rochambeau, with rays of glory and interlaced civic crowns over their heads, framed with palm and laurel branches, and the words in transparent letters, SHINE VALIANT CHIEFS; the whole encircled with stars and flowers de luce.[36]

Whether Washington left his comfortable quarters in the Chew House and ventured into the chill night air of Philadelphia to view Peale's theatrics is uncertain. Most likely he did not. His time might be better spent preparing for the next day's event: his visit to Congress.

CHAPTER TWO

SINCE HIS APPOINTMENT as commander in chief in June 1775, Washington had attended Congress only once.[1] He was, however, no stranger to the body. In September 1774 the Virginia House of Burgesses, where he had sat for many years, sent him and six others to represent the colony in the First Continental Congress.[2] Although he played a minor role in this first gathering, Washington did draw notice from members who knew his reputation as an officer in the French and Indian War and as a Whig leader in the House of Burgesses. His reputation as soldier and statesman, complemented by his physical stature—standing approximately six-foot-two and weighing a solid two hundred pounds—gave him an imposing presence. A Connecticut delegate, Silas Deane, described him as a man of a "hard" countenance, "yet with a very young look, and an easy, soldier like air and gesture."[3] Although not a particularly good speaker, nor an affable glad-hander, Washington moved easily among his colleagues and impressed them with his determination to defend American rights, offering "to raise and arm one thousand men himself at his own expense for the defense of the country."[4] Small wonder that when he returned to the Second Continental Congress in May 1775, this time sporting his militia uniform, the body elected him commander in chief.[5] More than six years later, his return as the conquering hero of Yorktown was a special event.

Shortly after noon on Wednesday November 28, Congress convened to welcome Washington. Light spilling in through large sash windows gave the room the deceptive appearance of warmth as two fireplaces labored to ward off the chill. The president, John Hanson of Maryland, sat at the front behind a slightly elevated table.[6] To his right the secretary, Charles Thomson, and his assistant sat attentively at a table crowded with documents. On the floor twenty-six delegates, arranged by state, sat in high-backed Windsor chairs. When the commander in chief entered, escorted by two members of the body, all turned to look, but no one stood, as such an act would have shown undue deference. He moved to the front of the room, where the president and secretary sat. As he looked about the chamber many of the faces were new to him. Nearly all of the "old revolutionaries" from the heady days of " '75" were absent. Although this was a moment of high drama, the Congress was in a low mood.[7]

In the early days of the war cascading events had pushed Congress to dramatic and rapid action under hectic conditions. Within weeks the members had fashioned a national government, sought foreign alliances, raised an army and navy, established a post office, collected money, advised states on their internal matters, and set rules for their own conduct. At first democracy ruled. It was a town meeting–like atmosphere with Congress appointing a seemingly endless number of committees, but in the end every decision came back to the full chamber for deliberation and decision. The immediate threat of the king's forces drove members together, and a fair degree of conviviality and consensus had prevailed.

By 1781 much of the early spirit had waned. After six years of struggle Congress found itself overwhelmed with confounding responsibilities. Any issue that came to the floor went almost immediately to committee. Committee reports came back to the body for discussion and action, with each state having a single vote. As factions developed and political schisms widened, the open model of participation that had worked at the beginning of the Revolution began to fail. The notion that everything was everyone's business resulted in delay, neglect, and inaction. In an effort to expedite matters, Congress established standing committees, among them Commerce, Secret Correspondence, and Marine. Such committees channeled work in more rational directions, but they did nothing to lessen the volume of the flow. Members were drowning in work. During the early part of the war, for example, William Ellery, a delegate from Rhode Island, served on thirty-three special and six standing committees.[8] In trying to avoid the Scylla of concentrating power in the hands of too few, Congress was wrecking itself on the Charybdis of legislative committees.[9]

Adding to congressional woes was the reality that as the tempo of work increased, the number of members available for committee assignments and general sessions was declining. Increasingly, members did not show up for sessions either because state legislatures lagged in making appointments or because elected delegates simply never arrived in Philadelphia or went home. Those who stayed were discouraged by the workload and were weighed down by the expense of living in Philadelphia.

Political dissention also played a hand in the decline of Congress. The body had voted unanimously for the appointment of George Washington as commander in chief and for independence. But conflict was inevitable given the nature of Congress itself, which, like any national assembly, represented a wide range of geographic, economic, social, and political viewpoints. In 1778, however, a particularly noxious debate arose, with effects that permanently poisoned the body. The catalyst for the debate was the conduct of Silas Deane.

In the spring of 1776 Congress had sent Deane, a Connecticut delegate, on a secret mission to France with instructions to obtain military supplies. Deane was clever and devious. His activities in Paris included clandestine meetings, bribes, embezzlement, and even murder. He quickly accumulated a legion of enemies in France and in America. Responding to allegations of misconduct, Congress recalled him in 1778. His arrival in Philadelphia ignited a fierce battle in Congress between those who supported Deane and those who condemned him. Never a man to mind his tongue or pen, Deane fanned the flames of controversy and counterattacked with venomous publications and sharp verbal assaults.[10] Among Deane's attackers was the old Virginia revolutionary Arthur Lee, joined by his New England allies, including Samuel Adams. In Silas Deane they saw the personification of a revolution gone astray; cupidity and a loss of public virtue had displaced true and simple republicanism. Deane's supporters rejected the charges against him and accused Lee and others of a vile conspiracy. Whatever the merits of the charges and counter-charges, the Deane affair pushed Congress into partisan warfare. Congress became, as John Adams later recounted, "a theatre of parties and feuds."[11]

This political "theatre" did not play well in the countryside. Bickering, political paralysis, and lack of attendance all contributed to Congress's declining national reputation. State authorities, sensing how little regard their constituents had for the men in Philadelphia, felt at ease reneging on promises to supply money to the body, leaving the assembly increasingly powerless, penniless, and leaderless.[12]

The struggle to locate political power in an increasingly confused galaxy of authority was a natural outcome of the Revolution itself. At a time when thirteen states were rebelling against arbitrary political authority in London, it was natural that they should be wary of passing similar power to men in Philadelphia. Fear of concentrating power in the hands of a select few prevented administrative reform and kept rule by committee intact. Nonetheless, by 1781 the crisis in Congress was too compelling to be ignored.

Since the beginning of the war Congress had functioned without de jure authority, exercising limited power without any formal consent of the governed; nor did the body have a recognized governmental structure such as each colony had enjoyed under the authority of the king. Anxious to legitimize its existence, in November 1777 Congress approved a national frame of government, the Articles of Confederation, which created a weak central government and left most power in the hands of the states. For the moment this was as far as the states were willing to share power, but even then the states took more than three years to ratify the document.[13] In the meantime, in an effort to establish coherent lines of authority, Congress created four executive departments—Foreign Affairs, War, Treasury, and Marine—under individual heads elected by the members of Congress and reporting to them. Robert R. Livingston took the post of secretary of foreign affairs; General Benjamin Lincoln accepted the job at War; Robert Morris took the reins at Treasury (he was better known as the superintendent of finance). Alexander McDougall was offered and then refused the office of secretary of marine. Since there was virtually no navy left in Continental service, McDougall's refusal gave Congress an excuse to relegate what few duties were left in the office to the superintendent of finance.[14]

Notwithstanding ratification of the Articles, and attempts at reform, Congress was sinking lower. National finances in 1781 were in a mess. "Not worth a Continental" was the common expression to describe the popular attitude toward paper money issued by Congress. Inflation was running wild. The news from Yorktown was a welcome tonic, but the victory had done nothing to fill the coffers of Congress or persuade the states to support a national government. In the midst of this gloom Washington's triumphal arrival gave respite from the doldrums and offered a rare occasion for celebration.

President Hanson called for order. He then addressed Washington with words that the general may have found less than comforting. After offering congratulations, he assured the commander that the Congress would exhort "the states in the strongest terms to the most vigorous and timely exertions" to send money and men. For this purpose it had appointed a committee! He asked Washington to remain "for some time in Philadelphia" so that he might confer with these gentlemen. Washington replied with thanks to the gentlemen. With appropriate deference he congratulated the Congress on its promise to "exhort the states." He would, he assured the members, "give every assistance . . . to their committee." On the other hand, the commander in chief was equally clear that his first responsibility was to his army, and he would return to them as soon as "duty calls."[15]

With that brief reply Congress gave permission for him to depart.

Washington understood that in all likelihood "duty" would not call until the spring. Rarely did eighteenth-century armies undertake winter campaigns. With the notable exceptions of his two victories at Trenton (December 26, 1776) and Princeton (January 3, 1777) the American army, like its British counterpart, spent winters encamped and inactive. Having endured winters at Morristown and Valley Forge, the Washingtons would have looked forward to spending the cold months amid the comforts and company of friends in Philadelphia. The commander in chief decided to remain in the city while the army took up winter quarters along the Hudson River.[16]

What might have been less appealing to the general and his wife was facing the steady stream of people who made their way to Chew House. On Thursday November 29, the day following his first visit to Congress, a delegation from the Pennsylvania Assembly, led by Speaker Frederick Augustus Muhlenberg, arrived to present an address.[17] Muhlenberg's visit set a pattern. Over the next several weeks a long train of people and organizations, faculty from the University of Pennsylvania, magistrates of the city, officers of the American Philosophical Society, and others, came to honor the general. In each case Washington returned the favor with remarks prepared by his hardworking aides Jonathan Trumbull Jr. and Tench Tilghman. Evenings too were filled with moments of accolades. The Friendly Sons of St. Patrick saluted him at an elegant dinner held at the City Tavern, and on at least one occasion a theatrical production was performed in his honor. One day, to escape the tedious routine of receiving and replying to addresses, Washington rode a few miles out to Frankford to engage in his favorite pastime, riding on the hunt.[18]

Washington remained in Philadelphia four months (November 26, 1781–March 22, 1782). Only twice during that period did he attend a session of Congress: when he arrived in the city and when he left. His absence from public sessions mattered little, for the real business of governance was being handled in private.

Monday evenings after Congress adjourned for the day, Washington met with the secretary of the Congress, Charles Thomson, Secretary of Foreign Affairs Robert R. Livingston, Secretary at War Benjamin Lincoln, Superintendent of Finance Robert Morris, and his assistant Gouverneur Morris (no relation to Robert) at Robert Morris's elegant home on Market Street. (This house was once occupied by Richard Penn as well as General Sir William Howe during the British occupation.) The stately three-story brick home was only a few blocks from Independence Hall.[19] Their host was, next to Washington, the most powerful man in America. As light as the public purse was, he nonetheless held the strings. Morris was a self-made man. In the prewar years he had been one of Philadelphia's most successful merchants. Although he allied himself early with the patriot cause, he was a cool Whig, among the minority in the Congress who initially sidestepped signing the Declaration of Independence. He waited a month and then added his signature with the following comment: "Although the councils of America have taken a different course from my judgment wishes, I think that the individual who declines the service of his country because its councils are not comfortable to his ideas makes but a bad subject; a good one will follow if he cannot lead."[20]

Morris was a controversial figure. At a time when the line between public and private finance was vague, the superintendent of finance often crossed over between the two worlds and comingled affairs. Just as they had heaped opprobrium on Silas Deane for his machinations, many of the "old revolutionaries" disdained Morris for what they viewed as equally corrupt behavior.

Morris's assistant, Gouverneur Morris, was a wealthy New Yorker. Elected to the Continental Congress, Morris was of enormous assistance to Washington during the Valley Forge encampment in helping to straighten out the army's tangled logistics. At home, however, he fell out of step with his New York constituency when he insisted on the need to enlarge the powers of Congress at the expense of the states. Defeated for reelection in 1779, he opted to remain in Philadelphia, where he entered into a business partnership with Robert Morris. A notorious rake—"I like only the yielding kiss and that from lips I love"—Morris had shattered and lost his leg in 1780 when, according to rumor, he jumped out of a bedroom window to avoid his lover's returning husband.[21] His peg leg did little to restrain him or change his habits. At six feet and plump, he was an imposing figure. The talented and arrogant Morris once boasted that he "never knew the sensations of fear, embarrassment, or inferiority." His congressional colleague, New Hampshire's Josiah Bartlett, agreed, noting that Morris was "for brass equal to any [he was] acquainted with."[22] Morris was a fervent nationalist. In an unguarded moment following the siege at Yorktown, he revealed his sympathies to General Nathanael Greene. He feared peace more than war.

> I say if the War continues for if it does not I have no Hope, No expectation that the Government will acquire Force and I will go

farther I have no Hope that our Union can subsist except in the Form of an absolute Monarchy and this does not seem to consist with the Taste and Temper of the People. The necessary Consequence if I am Right is that a Separation must take Place and consequently Wars, for near Neighbours are very rarely if ever good Neighbours.[23]

Another key figure at the meetings was Charles Thomson. Born in Londonderry, Ulster, he arrived in Philadelphia as a ten-year-old orphan in 1739. Despite his poor beginnings he managed to garner an education and as a young man displayed considerable political skill in the hurly-burly of Pennsylvania politics. During the turmoil leading up to the Revolution he allied himself with Benjamin Franklin and took a leading role in resisting royal authority. John Adams, who knew and admired Thomson, once called him the "Samuel Adams of Philadelphia." Thomson married into a wealthy Quaker family and was a close associate of Robert Morris's. The First Continental Congress elected him secretary, a post he held for the next fifteen years. For its entire existence Thomson was the Continental and Confederation Congress's chief bureaucrat. He knew more about the body, its members, and its workings than any other person in America.

Rounding out the table at the Monday night gatherings was Robert R. Livingston, another wealthy New York lawyer whose family possessed large estates along the Hudson. Notwithstanding his service on the committee that drafted the Declaration of Independence, he left Congress in 1776 to reenter New York politics and became chancellor, the state's highest judicial position. He returned to Congress in 1779 and accepted the post of secretary of foreign affairs in 1781. He favored a strong central government.

Washington and Lincoln were the only military officers at the table. From Hingham, Massachusetts, Lincoln had risen in the local militia ranks and joined the Continental army in 1776. Washington met Lincoln during the siege of Boston and described him as "an abler and more industrious man than his great bulk and his loose jowls would indicate."[24] In 1777 Lincoln was commissioned a major general; in 1781 Congress appointed him secretary at war while also allowing him to keep his commission as major general.[25] Lincoln and Washington had watched their men suffer pain and defeat firsthand. They knew the dangers of a weak Congress. Personal experience made them advocates for strong government.

It was a congenial, convivial, and politically like-minded group. These men were nationalists with a continental vision who were increasingly impatient with a Congress bound tightly by states whose parsimony and parochialism put victory at risk and made their hope of a strong nation increasingly unlikely. The Revolution had taken them to heights from which they could see beyond their own local interests to envision a "rising empire" of united states. Their hopes, however, were tempered by the fear that the centrifugal forces of localism would overcome the centripetal force of revolution. Only a stronger union, cemented by a reinvigorated Congress, could ensure independence and preserve the nation. They understood that in spite of the fact that the recently approved Articles of Confederation gave structure to the new government, now titled "The United States in Congress Assembled," the sinews of power were as feeble as ever. The Articles had done nothing to provide Congress with what it needed most: an independent source of income.[26] The states, Washington insisted, must not "sitt themselves down in quiet."[27] His dinner companions agreed "that to make a good peace you ought to be well prepared to carry on the war."[28]

To do so, Congress desperately needed French aid. Always anxious to wipe away the disgrace of 1776 when he had been driven off Manhattan, Washington pushed for French naval support to launch a joint attack against New York City. "Without a naval force we can do nothing," Washington wrote to Lafayette in November 1781, urging him to use his influence with the French court to provide ships.[29] De Grasse's departure for the West Indies after the battle at Yorktown crushed that plan, and by the New Year hope of French support grew ever dimmer. For both the French and the British, the strategic focus of the war had shifted to the Caribbean, the cockpit of war between these two superpowers. There was no chance that the French would risk their position in islands so rich in sugarcane by diverting squadrons to North America. Hobbled without support from the sea, Washington was stymied but not defeated, for the British were in no position to attack him either. In this parlous moment the greatest danger to the American cause was not from without but from within. The government of the United States was on the verge of financial collapse. The nation might survive without the French navy, but without French gold the weak republic faced bankruptcy.

French support to Congress, albeit in secret, had begun in 1776. A stream of supplies and money that began as a trickle rose to a torrent after the French alliance in 1778, and by 1781, a time when domestic finances had become ruinous, French money was the principal brace preventing a complete economic collapse.

Ironically, while Congress was close to penury, the American nation as a whole was not. To be sure, the war had exacted a heavy toll. The ongoing enemy occupation of the ports of New York City and Charleston laid a dead hand on commerce in those regions, as did the Royal Navy's prowling cruisers and privateers along the coasts and on the high seas. No blockade is ever complete, and imports into America remained remarkably strong, while exports fell into a steep decline, making it increasingly difficult to find remittances to pay foreign debts. Concurrently, shipbuilding had virtually disappeared, fishing was in turmoil, and trade with the Indians in the West had halted.[30]

Yet despite these disruptions, large areas of the colonies were, and had been for a good part of the war, relatively free from enemy attack and occupation. Many ports hit hard by the collapse of exports managed to find prosperity in privateering. Cut off from foreign imports and markets, many communities looked inward and diverted resources to local productions. None of these activities compensated fully for the domestic disruption caused by the war, but at the same time the states did have resources. The problem was they refused to share them with the central government. As the war dragged on and patriotic enthusiasm waned, the problem had grown more acute. State support had dropped off precipitously.[31]

Over imported wine and fine food Robert Morris and his Monday night companions complained about and condemned the behavior of the states. Morris was particularly annoyed. For more than six years Congress had financed the war by authorizing paper money to a sum of more than 200 million dollars. Since Congress had no regular source of income other than requests to the states which often went unanswered, the value of the paper depended entirely on public faith in the Congress. As faith declined, the money collapsed. Morris was doing all that he could to keep the financial ship of state afloat. To do that, he played one creditor off another. Angry creditors literally came to his door insisting on payment. When he refused them admittance they stormed away in "great wrath."[32] Morris's only hope, and the nation's, was more foreign loans. In near desperation Gouverneur Morris wrote to John Jay, the American minister in Spain, asking him to approach the Spanish Court and "for Heaven's sake convince them of the Necessity [of] giving us Money."[33] At the same time Jay's colleague John Adams was at The Hague seeking assistance from the Dutch.[34] It would take a few months, but eventually the burghers agreed to a loan. Jay had no such luck in Madrid. While awaiting news from Adams and Jay, Morris turned to the French.

Banking on the hope that loss of the thirteen colonies would deal a heavy blow to its perpetual enemy Great Britain, France had invested heavily in American independence. It had dispatched money, ships, and soldiers across the Atlantic. By the end of 1781 the war had cost France an immense sum of money, and though the French might take pride in their role in American victories, thus far they had gotten little out of them except the satisfaction of beating the British.

Pleasing the French was vital, and so maintaining a cordial relationship with the Chevalier de la Luzerne, the French minister to America, was critical. Luzerne, along with his secretary and translator, François Barbé-Marbois, had been in America since the fall of 1779, when the pair had traveled across the Atlantic on board the frigate *Sensible*, accompanied by John Adams and his young son John Quincy, bound home from Paris. During the voyage, for the moment at least, Adams set his Francophobia aside and took a liking to Barbé-Marbois, describing him as a "tall genteel man" whose English was fair enough so that he "fell down the stream" of conversation with him "as easily as possible."[35] Luzerne received less notice. His English was as lacking as Adams's French. After arriving in Boston, the two French diplomats took a month to make their way in a leisurely fashion to Philadelphia. En route they spent two days with Washington at his headquarters. Barbé-Marbois practically deified the commander in chief: Washington was "noble," "modest," "well built," "thin," "even tempered," "tranquil," "orderly," and "polite." "He makes no pretentions, and does the honors of his house with dignity, but without pompousness or flattery."[36]

In Congress attention was on Luzerne. His predecessor, Conrad Alexandre Gérard, had left a scent of ill will on his departure. During his tenure in Philadelphia debates in Congress over what the proposed terms of peace ought to be had revealed serious differences between France and America. Gérard had been urgently defending the interests of his nation. Some members of Congress, in particular New Englanders, aligned with Virginia delegates, had become increasingly suspicious of French motives, fearing that European power politics were overwhelming American interests.

Luzerne, a man of considerable charm, did a good deal to erase suspicions between the two allies. Adams, however, who had returned to France late in 1779 as a commissioner to negotiate peace, remained a thorn in the French side. In the eyes of the French he was one of the principal causes of strain between the two allies. Adams, in their opinion, was too independent and free thinking (that is, anti-French). During the spring of 1781, following the instructions of the French foreign minister, the Comte de Vergennes, Luzerne pressured Congress to restrain the obnoxious Adams, who had crossed swords with Vergennes on numerous points. Previously the minister had tried to get him recalled, but that effort failed. If Adams could not be recalled, perhaps he could be marginalized, and so Vergennes ordered Luzerne to do all that he could to undermine Adams and persuade Congress to limit his role.[37] Luzerne played his part with exceptional skill. In June 1781 Congress instructed the American ministers in Paris "to make the most candid and confidential communications upon all subjects to the ministers of our generous ally the king of France; to undertake nothing in the negotiations for peace without their knowledge and concurrence."[38]

Sensing the displeasure of the French, another American commissioner, Benjamin Franklin, warned his colleagues in Philadelphia of France's growing weariness at the Congress's incessant requests for money.[39] Luzerne echoed the message and in private told Robert Morris that the French court ought not to be expected to do for America what the Americans refused to do for themselves. The states, he argued point-edly and correctly, ignored Congress's requests for support. Why should France send money if the states would not?

Morris, whose sympathies in this matter were almost certainly closer to those of Luzerne than to the recalcitrant states, responded to the chevalier with a history lesson. "Taxation requires Time in all Govern-ments and is to be perfected only by long Experience in any Country. America divided as it is into a Society of free States possessing sovereign Power to all domestic purposes, cannot therefore be suddenly brought to pay." He went on to say that whatever the war was costing France, it was clearly less than the financial toll it was taking on the British. The French were, in Morris's estimation, getting good value for their investment.[40]

Morris's riposte did little to assuage Luzerne. He responded almost immediately with an equally testy rejoinder. He told the financier: "[I do not] think my Court will find in [your arguments] sufficient reasons to change their resolution . . . after the great success which has crowned the allied armies, the king has a right to expect some exhausting efforts on the part of the United States."[41] This was no time for subtle diplomatic language. The armies and navies of France were fighting around the world at great cost while America was in a state of inaction.

While a soft answer might have assuaged the chevalier's wrath, it would have also masked the real American crisis. Always in the back of French minds was the concern that Congress might make a sepa-rate peace unfavorable to France. The possibility of financial collapse made that specter seem more real. Morris understood this and decided to take a hard stand. In a tone that can only be termed impertinent, he told Luzerne that while he was sympathetic to the financial cost to France, it was of no consequence to him. "As to the mode in which [support is sent], His Majesty's convenience and the Situation of affairs will best determine it. I wish to receive Pecuniary Aid and when I consider the Importance I am led to expect it."[42]

Morris was not the only person exchanging barbs with Luzerne. In a response to the secretary of foreign affairs Luzerne warned Living-ston "that the expulsion of the enemy from this continent depends in great measure on the exertion of the United States; France would . . . afford . . . very little assistance."[43]

Thus far in the war France had loaned 28 million livres to the United States.[44] The most recent loan in 1781 had credited the American account with 10 million livres. Little of that money, however, came to Morris. Most of it remained in Europe to pay debts already contracted. The financier needed cash in America to pay the army and meet the rising costs of government. When Luzerne suggested that there had been extravagance in the Congress, Morris "with some warmth" replied that he had done all he could to economize.[45] He assured the minister that a new system of contracting had been put in place to supply the army, and he was moving to reduce the number of officers on active duty. He had gone so far as to cut the office budget for the president of the Congress. Even after all of this, he was still desperate for cash. He needed, he told Luzerne, at least 12 million livres.[46]

Since the military gobbled up the lion's share of expenses, Morris placed the army budget in his crosshairs. He did so, however, at the risk of annoying Secretary at War Benjamin Lincoln, Washington, and the entire Continental army. Morris believed that the sinews of war were financial. In his estimation bankruptcy was a greater threat to the nation than the British army. With the French balking at further loans, the states refusing to fulfill their obligations, and continental currency barely worth the paper on which it was printed, Morris hammered on the theme of economy. He took particular notice of the number of officers in the army. There were, he believed, too many.

How to reduce the officer corps without collapsing morale was Morris's challenge. By the fall of 1780 morale among the officer corps had sunk so low, due mostly to lack of pay, that Washington feared a complete dissolution of the corps. Two years before, in May 1778, to encourage them to remain in service, Congress voted to grant those who served for the duration of the war half pay for seven years.[47] It was, as everyone knew, an unfunded obligation that would come due only at the end of the war. If the army were reduced, however, "deranged" officers might legitimately claim their pay. How, Morris wondered, could this promise be fulfilled?

Washington and Lincoln lobbied for the army. The commander in chief wrote, "I am exceedingly impressed with the Necessity of Oeconomizing the public Monies; but we must not spin this Thread so fine as to break it."[48] Morris acknowledged their concerns but remained unwavering in his view that treasury trumped army. Incessant imprecations from officers who insisted on visiting him in person to make their case only hardened his heart. He would not, he said, "give ground to that Clamor which from want of Pay is ready to burst forth in the Army."[49] The army and Congress were on colliding paths.

Money would solve everyone's ills. On past occasions presidents of Congress had dispatched pleas to state authorities that fell on deaf ears. In January 1782 Washington yet again stepped forward to implore the governors to meet their obligations. "You cannot conceive the uneasiness which arises from the total want of so essential an Article as Money," he argued. For the moment Washington reported that the officers were "quiet," but he couldn't answer for the effects of a disappointment. "Enabling the Financier to comply with his Contracts, is a matter of the utmost consequence; the very existence of the Army depends upon it."[50]

Washington actually underestimated the discontent among his officers, some of whom were taking matters into their own hands. In secret a group sought out the talents of Thomas Paine, America's best-known writer and propagandist, to advance their cause.

In the early days of the Revolution Paine, the English radical, had electrified America with his forceful pamphlet *Common Sense*.

> O ye that love mankind! Ye that dare oppose not only the tyranny but the tyrant, stand forth! Every spot of the old world is overrun with oppression. Freedom hath been hunted round the globe. Asia and Africa have long expelled her. Europe treats her like a stranger, and England hath given her warning to depart. O receive the fugitive, and prepare in time an asylum for mankind![51]

Months later during the dark and desperate days of late 1776, he rallied America again in *The Crisis*.

> These are the times that try men's souls. The summer soldier and the sunshine patriot will, in this crisis, shrink from the service of their country; but he that stands it *now*, deserves the love and thanks of

man and woman. Tyranny like hell, is not easily conquered; yet we have this consolation with us, that the harder the conflict, the more glorious the triumph.[52]

On the morning of January 24, 1782, a delegation of officers visited Paine in Philadelphia to ask if he would "draw up a petition for them to General Washington respecting their pay."[53] Paine's response is unrecorded, but that afternoon he revealed the conversation to Morris. It may well be that Paine was seeking Morris's favor, which he had lost a few months prior when he had failed to deliver to the financier an essay on the topic of taxation. Indeed, whether from writer's block or his indolent ways, Paine had not published for more than a year. But by the end of 1781 he, like the Congress, was running out of cash. The officers' proposal was inviting, and the fee would be welcomed, but reconciliation with Morris might be even more profitable.

Morris was grateful to Paine for the information, and he lost no time communicating "directly to the Secretary at War," who, Morris confided to his diary, "will take measures to keep the [officers] quiet."[54] Those "measures" included keeping such petitions away from Washington, who, Morris feared, would only be agitated by this news. Two days later, however, in a personal meeting, Morris informed the commander in chief of "discontent" in his officers' ranks. Washington was thankful that Paine had come to Morris and that the petition had been suppressed. Perhaps the writer's talents might be redirected, he suggested, observing that Paine's "services to the public had rather been neglected."[55] Morris told the commander in chief that although he "had nothing in [his] power at the present to Offer a compensation for his Services Something might turn up."[56]

Some two weeks later, with Washington's support, Morris drew Livingston into a scheme. The secretary of foreign affairs' participation was essential since he could supply secret information from abroad that would be useful ammunition for Paine. On February 10, 1782, Morris, Washington, and Livingston signed a secret contract with Paine. They promised that they would only ask him to espouse "upright measures," mostly revolving around persuading the states "to grant sufficient taxes" to support the confederation and rouse "the People to Spirited Exertion." For this they agreed to pay him eight hundred dollars per year from the secret service account.[57] Secrecy was essential for if the information leaked out that Paine's efforts were a work for hire, the sponsors' motives would be revealed. If that happened, state authorities, fearful about any loss of power to the Congress, would reap a propaganda windfall. The image of three of America's most powerful men conspiring to enhance their own power and using public money to do it would blemish the reputations of nationalists who sought a more powerful Congress. Unfortunately, Thomas Paine was not discreet. The news was soon about Philadelphia that he was a "hireling writer."[58]

Paine fulfilled his contract. Over the next several months he wrote several essays appearing under the title *The Crisis*, urging the states to support the national cause.[59] He dismissed the flood of petitions and resolutions flowing from the states pleading poverty. The nation was not poor. "There are not three millions of people in any part of the universe who live so well or have such a fund of ability as in America." If the states were ever to "lie down in security," they must now pay the cost.[60]

Paine delivered his essays, but the old passion was absent. The heady days of 1776 were gone, and Paine's rhetoric failed to stir the hearts and minds of Americans. Taxation was not among the emotional issues that "try men's souls."[61]

Although Washington sat in the high councils and engaged in discussions over issues of taxation, foreign affairs, and other matters, his true concern was the army and its well-being. He understood that the army had to grow smaller, but since the British still remained in America and showed little inclination to leave, some force needed to be kept. How to advocate for these men with discontent in their ranks was his challenge.

Not only did Washington get little support from Congress; it embarrassed him to boot. He was "astonished," for example, when he discovered that Lincoln, without consulting him, had assigned several officers to be "servants to civil officers."[62] Equally annoying to him were the politics behind promotion. In bitter debate Congress twice, along sectional lines (North in favor, South opposed), refused to promote Henry Knox, Washington's closest adviser, from brigadier to major general.[63] The members gave as their reasons that Knox lacked seniority and the army had too many generals.[64] In November 1781 the Board of War recommended that "no more General Officers be retained in the field than shall be absolutely necessary."[65] A few weeks after Congress rejected Knox's promotion, Ezekiel Cornell of Rhode Island, sponsor of the November resolution, and a representative of the state most vehemently opposed to increasing the powers of Congress, lobbied the commander in chief for the promotion of eleven brigadiers to major general. Washington shot back, "You must recollect that we already have more Major Generals in Commission than we can conveniently employ."[66] Cornell gave up the plan.[67]

Although Washington was often disappointed by the behavior of civilian authorities, both in the Congress and the states, rarely did he express publicly his dismay and despair. In the matter of prisoners of war, however, he was more forthcoming.

By the standards of civilized warfare victors were expected to secure and care for captives. It was an obligation both inconvenient and expensive. To shed it, Europeans had developed elaborate systems of prisoner exchange, ordinarily referred to as cartels. Ironically, while both the Americans and the British were well acquainted with the traditions of prisoner exchange, for the duration of the Revolution they could never manage to agree on terms. Politicians and generals argued while men rotted and died in captivity.

Until the British general John Burgoyne's surrender at Saratoga in 1777, American prisoners in British hands far outnumbered British in American custody. Saratoga tipped the balance in favor of the Americans, prompting the British commander Sir William Howe to open negotiations for an exchange. His proposal was a simple one for one, soldier for soldier and officer for officer.[68] By keeping the arrangement on a commander-to-commander basis, Howe was offering a practical field expedient that sought to avoid the messiness of the king's refusal to recognize the United States. The members of Congress abruptly upset this plan by insisting that Tories be turned over to them and returned to their homes to be tried. Congressional representatives also demanded that in advance of any exchange Howe pay in gold or silver all the expenses Congress had undertaken for the care of British prisoners. The terms were outrageous, and the promise of exchange collapsed. Washington was furious. Not only had Congress undermined his authority, but it had also condemned his soldiers to continued confinement, punishing them and denying him the return of much needed veteran troops.[69] According to Elias Boudinot, commissary of prisoners, Washington "resented" the action of Congress "and said his troops looked up to him as their Protector and that he would not suffer an opportunity to be lost of liberating every Soldier who was then in captivity let the Consequence be what it might."[70]

Congress's unfortunate actions provoked the British to be equally obdurate. Here and there partial exchanges took place, avoiding the official notice of Congress, but no general exchange was ever accomplished during the entire war. However, as a result of the favorable turn in American fortunes, Washington's attitude toward exchanges shifted. With Cornwallis's surrender the ratio of British prisoners in American hands to American prisoners in British confinement exploded to an astounding 24:1.[71] Those numbers gave Washington pause. At a time when British forces in North America had been hollowed out by defeat and potential reinforcements dispatched to other parts of the empire, any exchange of prisoners in America would work to the advantage of the king's forces. Even those Americans who came home were not likely to stay in service. While in captivity many Continental enlistments had expired, and it was highly unlikely those men who had endured so much would rush to reenlist even if they were fit. In a letter to the president of Congress Washington put an unusual gloss on the situation, assuring him that "we have had no reason to complain of the treatment of the Continental land prisoners in New York."[72] In a further shift two weeks later he wrote to Sir Henry Clinton, who had replaced Howe as British commander in chief in 1778, to correct a misunderstanding. From a previous letter to him the British commander had come to believe that Washington was interested in a general exchange. Washington replied that any exchange would have to be part of a financial settlement that reimbursed Congress for the care of British prisoners. Washington understood that this demand, the same one that had precipitated the collapse of previous negotiations, would break the deal. Sensing his own advantage in numbers, and perhaps hoping that Clinton would pay to get his soldiers back, Washington took a harder line with the enemy.[73]

While the commander in chief and Congress drew closer in the matter of prisoners, they were divided in regard to deserters. Section 6, article 1 of the Articles of War, drawn up and approved by Congress in 1775, decreed the death penalty for desertion. Despite the threat of severe punishment, high rates of desertion, 20–25 percent, plagued the American army.[74] Simple desertion usually brought a punishment of one hundred lashes and a return to service. Desertion to the enemy was likely to bring on the hangman or a firing squad. The challenge was catching deserters. By early 1782 several thousand American deserters were on the loose, all subject to arrest and punishment. Without the means to find these men, capture was unlikely to happen. In Washington's view simple deserters comprised a pool of veterans whose skills he needed. To entice them back into service, the commander in chief supported a general amnesty for those who returned voluntarily to their units.[75]

Congress viewed the issue differently: amnesty was not simply a grant of mercy; it was more about politics and money. Local authorities threw deserters into the same execrable pile as Tories, upon whom they took similar revenge: confiscation of property. In more than six years of war considerable property had been taken and sold. Talk of amnesty might endanger ongoing action, to say nothing of calling into question previous seizures. Lincoln advised Washington to back away, and he did.[76]

Spring 1782 brought both hope and worry to Washington. Although it seemed increasingly unlikely, he still anticipated launching a new campaign, and he wanted to be back with his army to get ready for battle. He knew that after a long winter encampment his soldiers were anxious and uneasy. From Fort Pitt came news that the garrison was close to mutiny, and from Virginia arrived word that regimental officers had refused commands to march south to reinforce General Greene. Washington was taken aback by the officers' behavior. He exploded, "What can they expect from their soldiers when they themselves strike at the Root of Authority and discipline."[77] At every post American soldiers, like the rest of America, waited for news whether there was to be peace or war. Their pay was in arrears, and supplies were dwindling. Officers and soldiers awaited word from their commander.[78]

For Washington, the Philadelphia sojourn had been pleasant and restful, but he had grown weary of political jabber and posturing. In Congress he had witnessed weakness and bickering, and sadly, he had come to realize that the army was not a primary concern. It was, however, his first concern, and on March 18 he asked Congress—provided it had "no farther occasion for my stay in this city"—for permission to join the army on the Hudson.[79] By invitation on Wednesday morning March 20, Washington entered the chamber. He was welcomed and told that Congress granted him his request to leave, but, added the president, "[we] have nothing in particular to give you in charge and have appointed this audience only to assure you of [our] esteem and confidence, to recommend you to the protection of Divine Providence, and to wish you happiness and success."[80] Washington offered no response. He left Philadelphia the next day.[81]

CHAPTER THREE

W
HILE WASHINGTON AND HIS WIFE were making their triumphal progress toward Philadelphia, the French frigate *Surveil-*
lante, commanded by Captain Cillart de Villeneuve, scudded before a
brisk fall breeze on a near record crossing from Yorktown to France.
Among the passengers was the Duc de Lauzun, to whom Rochambeau
had given the honor of announcing to the king the glorious news from
America. Lauzun entered the palace at Versailles on November 20, 1781,
just at the moment when the court was celebrating the birth of the Dauphin. They rejoiced doubly.[1]

While the halls of Versailles resounded with joyful noise, George III,
for the moment, was unaware of events in America. Cornwallis made his
report to Clinton, leaving it to Sir Henry to inform his superiors. Rather
than sending a special messenger, Clinton waited to use the regular mail
packet from New York, which did not arrive in Falmouth until November
24. From Falmouth a waiting post rider spurred his mount on the road to
London carrying the glum news. Clinton had addressed the doleful dispatches directly to Lord George Germain, the secretary of state for the
Southern Department, a post which included responsibility for the American colonies.[2]

As such, Germain had charge of the conduct of the war. Although

Lord North, the first minister, was his superior and sat at the head of the cabinet, Germain devised strategy and issued orders on a daily basis.[3] There was no mistaking his unyielding attitude toward the Americans. When Germain took office in November 1775, a moment when reconciliation was still possible, he declared boldly that he would be "decisive, direct, and firm" in dealing with the rebels. He was, according to the court gossip Horace Walpole, "inflexible." Under his administration that inflexibility had escalated a war of colonial resistance into a world war, cost the kingdom two armies and a major naval defeat, and reduced His Majesty's forces in the colonies to toeholds, at Savannah, Charleston, New York, and Penobscot Bay. In Parliament there had been many demands to sack Germain, but such action would have been an admission of failure sufficient to collapse North's government. Furthermore, in a political world where parliamentary debate drew attention North found Germain useful in the House of Commons, where he used his acid tongue to skewer opponents, making it risky for those who dared speak in opposition. "He engrosses all tongues" was Walpole's judgment.[4]

About noon on Sunday November 25, the post rider from Falmouth drew up at Germain's fashionable Pall Mall residence. Germain was at home closeted with Thomas de Grey, Lord Walsingham, his undersecretary. Parliament, which had been in recess since July, was to open the coming Tuesday, November 27. As was the custom, the king would attend to deliver a speech, for the most part prepared by his ministers, including Germain, outlining the government's policies. Following the speech, by tradition both the House of Lords and Commons would offer responses to the king. On this occasion the ministers had chosen Walsingham to answer in Lords. He and Germain were preparing Tuesday's remarks. The news of Yorktown scuttled that speech, as both men recognized immediately the defeat threatened to sink the government. If Lord North teetered, Germain, as the principal architect of the war, would topple. Before informing North, Germain and Walsingham decided to collect their cabinet allies and go in force to Downing Street to stiffen their leader's shaky resolve.

Germain summoned his coach. He and Walsingham bumped along Regent Street to Portland Place, the home of Lord Stormont, the former ambassador to France, who held the position of secretary of state for the

Northern Department, the office responsible for diplomatic relations with Europe.[5] Like Germain and Walsingham, he had been unyielding toward the Americans. From Portland Place the three hurried to Great Russell Street in Bloomsbury, to the house of Edward Thurlow, the lord chancellor infamous for his capacity to browbeat all who disagreed with him. Thurlow was equally inflexible toward the Americans. Determined to hold a hard line despite the news from America, the ministers departed hastily in company to bring the bad news to Lord North, whom they viewed as a weak and ineffective leader who continued in office only because of the king's stubborn support.[6]

In a moment of pique toward his chief Thurlow exclaimed, "Damn him . . . nothing can goad him forward, he is the very clog that loads everything."[7] North lived under the lingering cloud of his predecessor, the great William Pitt, who had brought glorious triumphs in the previous war against France. In private and public the unfortunate North was compared to the Great Commoner, never to his advantage. Everyone poured blame on him, including Germain, who complained bitterly, "Do what you will, nothing will avail till Lord North will adopt a system, pursue it with firmness, and oblige every department of government to act under his direction."[8] Despite their low opinion of him, North's response to the defeat at Yorktown startled the four ministers. According to Germain, he took the news like "a ball in his breast." Germain's account had North opening "his arms, exclaiming wildly, as he paced up and down the apartment, during a few minutes, 'Oh God! It is all over!' Words which he repeated many times, under emotions of the deepest, agitation and distress."[9]

At first shaken by North's loss of control, the ministers recovered quickly as their instincts for political survival overrode their contempt for their chief. They could only survive if he did. Delaying Parliament's opening to provide time to fashion a strategy to fit the new circumstances was impractical, as members had already arrived in London and sending them home would cause an uproar. The king's speech to Lords and Commons, however, now had to be rewritten to account for the disaster in Virginia. Having decided to hold the course, the ministers prepared a dispatch for the king, informing him of the late news from America. They agreed that until they heard from His Majesty the news had to be kept secret. The meeting adjourned with North in anguish.

In contrast to the emotional scene on Downing Street, at the palace in Kew, just outside London, the king received the news with his usual air of tranquillity, a pose he often took in crisis to calm others and to assert his own firm resolution. "I have," he wrote Germain, "received with sentiments of the deepest concern, the communication which Lord George Germain has made me." In a characteristic understatement the king went on to observe, "I particularly lament it, on account of the consequences connected with it, and the difficulties which it may produce." "Lament" he might, but he would not change. An entire field army had been lost at Yorktown, but as far as George III was concerned, "[it does not make] the smallest alteration in those principles of my conduct, which have directed me in past time, and which will always continue to animate me under every event, in the prosecution of the present contest."[10]

On Tuesday morning November 27, the royal procession made its way from St. James's Palace to Westminster. In a ceremony enshrined in history and tradition, and preserved to this day, the king entered Westminster. After putting on the robes of state and donning the imperial state crown, in grand progress he made his way through the royal gallery to the House of Lords. "My Lords, pray be seated" was his command. As the Lords took their seats the lord chamberlain was dispatched to the House of Commons to "command the honourable House to attend His Majesty immediately in the House of Peers." All of this was done in a prescribed ballet designed to recognize the rights and standing of the House as an independent body. Once assembled, the second session of the Fifteenth Parliament in the reign of King George III came to order to pay heed to the words of the king.[11]

In a relatively short address, barely a thousand words, George III spoke of Cornwallis's disaster as simply the "unfortunate loss" of his forces in Virginia.[12] The "late misfortune," he suggested, was only a temporary setback, and he assured the members that in time his "deluded subjects in America" would be restored to a "due obedience to the laws." He went on to celebrate British victories in the East Indies and then concluded with a quick reference to the need to levy additional taxes to support the war.

Whatever his shortcomings, Lord North was a political realist. The king, he knew, was spouting nonsense. Lords and Commons returned to their chambers to launch their assault on North's government. Opposition to the war was hardly new in Commons. Some members, like Edmund Burke, had long opposed it out of principle; others, including the notorious Charles James Fox, were fired by a visceral dislike of the king and his abusive use of power. In the spring of 1780 the royal prerogative had come under especially heavy attack. After several speeches outlining waste and extravagance, Commons resolved famously "that the influence of the Crown has increased, is increasing, and ought to be diminished."[13] Fox and other opposition members railed against "the enormous weight" of influence that North and his cohorts squeezed from the established power of the Crown. The king and his political cronies had at their disposal "the patronage of immense military establishments, and the annual expenditure of upwards of 20 millions of the public money." They were, in sum, able to "buy" the House. But with events in America turning so sour, not even the force of money and position could stem the torrent sweeping down on the ministry. The king's vacuous remarks laid bare a ministry void of ideas and resistant to change.

Within minutes of their return to the House chamber after the king's address the opposition in Commons let loose a barrage on the ministry. Charles James Fox, Edmund Burke, and Isaac Barré filled the chamber with vitriol. Fox assailed the king and his "servile" and "profligate" ministry. He described the king's speech as one that might have come from "some arbitrary, despotic, hard hearted, and unfeeling monarch." As for North and his colleagues, they sought to put "the blame any where, but in the right place . . . their own weakness, obstinacy, inhumanity or treason."[14] The king's supporters cried out against Fox's intemperate language, but the weight of oratory was clearly on the side of the opposition. Following Fox's long speech, Edmund Burke rose to address those who supported the ministry, as recorded in the *Journals of the House of Commons*.

> If there could be a greater misfortune than those we had undergone in the disgraceful contest we were engaged in, it was hearing men rising up in the great assembly of the nation to vindicate such measures; it was the most alarming part of our condition; it was that which froze up his blood, and harrowed up his soul; for if they were not to be taught by experience; if neither calamities could

make them feel, nor the voice of God make them wise, what had this poor fallen, miserable, and undone country to hope for?[15]

Even in Lords the king and his ministers came under brutal attack. Lord Shelburne pronounced the war "ill fated." The Earl of Abingdon declared that the war "was conceived in folly, tyranny, servility and corruption." The Marquis of Rockingham accused the king of following the "fatal and pernicious counsels" of his ministers. North could barely stand the onslaught.[16]

Outside the halls of Westminster reaction came just as quickly and forcefully. The Liveried Companies of London (an eighteenth-century chamber of commerce), whose members had seen their business strangled by the war, hurled an attack on the king: "Your armies are captured; the wonted superiority of your navies is annihilated; your dominions are lost." Petitions to end the war flowed into Parliament, including one from "the Sheriffs of London, the Lord Mayor, Aldermen, and Commons of the City of London" to end "the unfortunate war with America."[17]

Caught between an angry and obstinate king and volcanic opposition, North sought sanctuary in a middle ground. Rather than sharply rejoining the opposition, he took a more moderate tone, assuring the members that while the king and his ministers would continue to assert the rights of Parliament, that did not necessarily mean forcefully subduing the Americans. He even went so far as to admit to the House of Commons that the war was unfortunate but the attacks on his ministry were "unjust."[18] Even Germain, the principal target of an unrelenting assault, struck a tone of moderation. North's government was reeling. Members demanded an explanation for how the ministry had lost two armies, those of Burgoyne and Cornwallis, and why the navy had withdrawn, abandoning Cornwallis to his dire fate. Sir George Young stood in Commons to accuse the Admiralty of wasting vast sums of money. Out of doors the London press was having a field day stinging the government. For more than two weeks North endured. Had it not been for the respite of the Christmas season, which brought the usual long recess, and the stubborn refusal of the king to yield, the government might have fallen before the New Year.

Not even the Christmas spirit could bring a halt to the turmoil. Barely had the members climbed into their carriages for the journey home to enjoy the yuletide when an emotional Henry Seymour Conway, a persistent opponent of the war (he had moved to repeal the Stamp Act in 1766), burst out to a friend, "We are undone as we have long been. [N]othing but peace can save us."[19] What Conway did not appreciate, nor did most members of Parliament, was that peace by itself was no longer sufficient. Americans would never accept peace without independence.

Over the recess more dispatches arrived from America. To the surprise of few, Generals Clinton and Cornwallis filled their dispatch cases with conflicting accounts of who was to blame for the Yorktown disaster. Cornwallis moved first to protect his flank. In his initial message to Clinton, on October 20, he censured his commander for not sending reinforcements. Clinton in turn debited Cornwallis for going to Virginia in the first place, and the Royal Navy for not getting him out of there.[20] The press and others were just as quick to take up cudgels on behalf of their favorites.

In this political scrum Cornwallis was certain to come out ahead of Clinton. The earl was a peer of the realm and extraordinarily well connected. Clinton, on the other hand, was of more modest origins, less well connected, and given to displays of ill grace that managed to offend all but his closest associates. Nor did it help Clinton's cause that Cornwallis, who no longer had a command in America, was able to leave New York before Clinton, arriving at London in late December. "Lord Cornwallis is in great favor, as things are totally misunderstood," wrote Clinton's cousin the Duke of Newcastle to the general. "He seems to me to be supported both by King and ministers, which I own makes my hair stand on end."[21] Clinton, who could not leave his post in America without the king's permission, remained in New York to fume at the injustice.

While the generals battled over reputations, others fought for more immediate stakes, often their lives. American loyalists were in jeopardy. As areas under British control had gradually shrunk to a few coastal enclaves, these "Good Americans" sought safety within the redcoat lines. By far the largest number of refugees holed up in New York City.[22]

William Franklin, the bastard son of Benjamin and the deposed royal governor of New Jersey, was their spokesman and leader. In the spring of 1780 Clinton appointed Franklin president of the newly formed Board of Associated Loyalists.[23] Its benign title masked a more sinister purpose. The association sprang from an order sent by Germain early in 1780 instructing Clinton to arm and organize loyalist refugees. Their mission was to unsettle the rebels with raids into New Jersey, Long Island, and along the coast.[24] For Franklin and the "associators," the war was personal. They embraced the opportunity to wreck vengeance on an enemy that had upended their lives and taken all that they owned.

Under Franklin's direction bands of loyalist partisans, often called "cowboys," ravaged the patriot countryside. They soon found their match, as rebel "skinners" returned tit for tat.[25] Neither side paid much heed to the niceties of war. When they rode, murder and mayhem joined them. Clinton found Franklin's rascals impossible to control. Hedging as usual, he explained, "I neither claim merit from nor do I consider myself as responsible for any of their transactions."[26]

Franklin and his loyalist friends viewed Clinton's equivocation as bordering on betrayal. They were increasingly wary of the faithfulness of their British protectors. A parade of British generals had come and gone from America, each having arrived with the promise of victory and each having sailed home with his reputation tarnished. Clinton and Cornwallis were only the latest to join the roster.

In the aftermath of Yorktown the loyalists' position grew even more precarious. Whatever public bluster flew from generals and politicians about victory over the rebels, Franklin and his friends sensed the ill wind of reconciliation. Any settlement that left power in the hands of the patriots would work against their interests. They saw fresh evidence of British betrayal in article 10 of Cornwallis's capitulation at Yorktown. In his draft of the article Cornwallis proposed that "natives or inhabitants of different parts of this country, at present in York or Gloucester, are not to be punished on account of having joined the British army." Washington rejected it outright, responding that the treatment of such people was a matter for "civil resort." Given a weak central government and thirteen strong state governments, "civil resort" meant that the fate of the loyalists would be left to the states and local authorities. Washington, and by implication the Congress, could offer no protection for the king's friends.[27] At the local level justice and mercy were likely to be in short supply for the loyalists.

That Cornwallis had yielded to the Americans in article 10 suggested a fundamental weakness of British support for the loyalists.

An angry Franklin told Germain that the failure of the king's government to protect the loyalists left them in a status no better than "runaway slaves."[28] Other loyalists joined the chorus. Some threatened to abandon all hope and go over to the rebels—a very unlikely occurrence.[29] Clinton showed little sympathy. When Franklin asked him for leave to go to England to plead the loyalist case, Clinton, already with enough enemies in London, refused, suspecting that the deposed governor would spend as much time stalking the corridors of Whitehall assailing him as he might in defending loyalists.

Ironically, while he blocked Franklin's departure, Clinton was pulling every lever he could to find his own exit out of New York. No one understood the military situation in America better than he, and no one was less sanguine about British prospects. What few rays of hope were left after Yorktown dimmed further in early March when the general received orders from Germain instructing him that, in light of the deteriorating situation in America, reinforcements he had requested would not be sent, and moreover he ought not to undertake any land operations beyond New York City. Having told the general to sit tight and do nothing to antagonize the Americans, the secretary then counseled him to do all that he could to encourage the loyalists and to reassure them that the king continued to hold their interests at heart.[30] Clinton was beside himself, and in the presence of the colony's chief justice, William Smith, he let loose against North, Germain, and the entire ministry. Smith thought that the general was on the verge of collapse. "He is a distressed man, looking for Friends, and suspicious of all mankind."[31] Yet despite all this, Clinton would not abandon his post unless recalled. Two weeks later he got his wish. On March 27 he opened a dispatch from Germain granting permission for him to return home. The next day another dispatch arrived with the additional information that Sir Guy Carleton would be his replacement. Although the king granted him the option to leave immediately, Clinton decided to await Carleton's arrival. His decision to delay his departure was born of spite and bile. He so detested his second in command, Major General James Robertson, that he could not bear the thought of Robertson succeeding him even temporarily. He preferred to hand authority directly to Carleton.[32]

While Clinton stewed in New York, in London the opposition was heaping up political tinder around the feet of the ministry. To no one's surprise, the first minister to be consumed was Germain. Since the news of Yorktown his departure had been a foregone conclusion, though he resisted to the last. At the eleventh hour he proposed to the cabinet yet another plan: continue to hold New York, retake Rhode Island, blockade Delaware and Chesapeake bays, and harass the American coast. These measures would, he argued, force the rebels to give up their obsession with independence and negotiate reentry into the empire. It was too late. Even while still not willing to grant independence, North and his colleagues understood that escalating the war would bear evil consequences. Having exhausted his options, Germain agreed to go but not without reward. Reluctantly, the king bought him off with a peerage. Germain left office bearing the title Viscount Sackville. North, shaken by Germain's fall, replaced him with Welbore Ellis, "a colorless administrative wheel horse."[33]

Germain's enemies had choreographed his exit nicely. His departure opened the door for the reentry of Sir Guy Carleton. For good reason, senior army officers disdained Germain. He had presided over a war that had ruined reputations. Carleton was among the most embittered.

Carleton was born in Ireland into a landed family with roots in the Protestant Ascendancy. His father died when he was about fourteen.[34] After his mother married a not-so-rich Anglican minister, the young Carleton, with limited opportunities at home, left to join the army. It was hardly an unusual tale. The officer ranks of the king's army were full of men, both Anglo-Irish and Scots, who, with few other prospects, opted for an officer's career.

Carleton was both able and lucky. He entered the service in 1742, at a moment when Europe, after a long period of peace, was about to go over the abyss into a series of wars lasting more than a decade that eventually engulfed the entire world.[35] It was a good time to be a soldier. Also working to Carleton's advantage was the fact that he was well connected. Early in his career he had the good fortune to be posted as an aide-de-camp to the Duke of Cumberland, the king's brother and captain general of the army. While serving under the duke, Carleton made the acquaintance of another promising young officer, James Wolfe. Although Wolfe was prickly and prone to incessant complaining, he was also intellectually curious, a trait shared with Carleton. The two became friends, and as Wolfe advanced he used his influence to help Carleton.[36] When William Pitt tapped Wolfe to command the expedition to Quebec in 1758, Wolfe requested that Carleton join him. At first the king, George II, refused. The cranky king had a long and unforgiving memory. Sometime before, Carleton made some disparaging remarks about the quality of Hanoverian mercenaries. In addition to being king of England, the German-born George II was also the ruler of Hanover, and he took personal umbrage at Carleton's remark. Wolfe was equally stubborn and threatened to resign unless Carleton was approved. Afraid that his plans might crumble, Pitt intervened and persuaded the king to grant Wolfe his request.[37]

Carleton stood with Wolfe on the Plains of Abraham to witness the defeat of the French and the tragic death of his commander and friend. Wounded at Quebec, Carleton sailed home in October 1759 but returned to duty in 1762, serving as quartermaster general during the British siege of Havana, where he was wounded a second time.

War is a school for soldiers, but it also trains administrators. By the Treaty of Paris, 1763, Britain took possession of an empire on a scale not seen since the days of Caesar Augustus. Those who were now responsible for this empire faced monumental challenges of defense, finance, and administration. In seeking to find the talent to run this vast new enterprise, king and Parliament often turned to men whose skills in organizing for war might be put to use governing conquered lands. Carleton lobbied hard to be part of this new empire. The young King George III did not share his father's poor opinion of Carleton and instead described him as a "gallant and sensible man."[38] With the king's nod and an assist from friends in Parliament, in 1768 Carleton became captain general and governor in chief of Quebec.

In the tumultuous 1760s and early '70s, when so many of the king's colonial governors were dueling with unruly assemblies and violent mobs, Carleton presided over a remarkably peaceful province. He astutely walked a fine line between the instructions of his superiors in London, who insisted on "anglicizing" Quebec to incorporate and control the French population, and his conviction that all Quebecers deserved to be respected and treated well. To a remarkable degree, Carleton succeeded in satisfying both his superiors and himself.

While Carleton's evenhanded policies did not inspire great warmth toward the Crown, they did at least assure the French population that under the English king's regime they could expect their culture and religion to be respected and tolerated. This resignation to imperial authority proved invaluable to Carleton when the American rebels invaded Canada in 1775–76. As an example of "better the devil you know than the one you don't," Canadians were more suspicious about the motives of invading Protestant Yankees, with whom they had fought for generations, than concerned about an English administration under Carleton that had thus far proved tolerable. As a result, most Canadians remained either loyal or neutral, allowing Carleton to throw back the invading American army and emerge as the savior of Canada.

While Carleton was driving the Americans from Canada, in London Germain was taking the post of secretary of state and becoming Carleton's superior. Germain and Carleton despised each other and made no secret of their feelings. Upon hearing that the king planned to make Carleton a Knight of the Bath, Germain did all he could to prevent the honor from being bestowed. He failed but not before Carleton learned of his machinations. Their hatred flared wildly in 1777 when Germain posted John Burgoyne, an officer junior to Carleton, to command the northern army assigned to invade the colonies from Canada. Ironically, by appointing Burgoyne, Germain did Carleton a favor as Burgoyne's invasion turned into one of the war's great disasters.[39]

As is always the case in the wake of a military disaster, Burgoyne's humiliating defeat unleashed a storm of invective, and finger-pointing. Carleton, who had a reputation for an unbridled pen, leaped into the fray. His acid attacks on Germain reached a point where even the king noted that he was "highly wrong in permitting his pen to convey such asperity to a Secretary of State."[40] Carleton's sharp pen failed to topple Germain. Instead the king recalled Carleton from Canada, and for the next four years the general stewed in political exile on his Hampshire estate.

Germain's fall in February 1782 revived Carleton's career. Despite the calamitous events in America and the rapid erosion of political support at home, the king remained adamant: he would not recognize the independence of the colonies. Indeed he made it clear to his intimates that he would sooner abdicate than see the colonies separate. For his part, North had lost all hope for victory in America. Physically exhausted and abandoned by his political friends, he anticipated his departure from Downing Street.

On February 22, 1782, General Henry Seymour Conway rose in the House of Commons and offered a motion to end the war in America. Debate lasted until two in the morning, and the motion lost by a single vote. Five days later the House reconsidered it. Debate began anew in the afternoon and stretched long into the evening until at one thirty on the morning of February 28 the House reversed itself and "without a division" supported the motion.[41]

Deserted by his former allies, isolated from any realistic appraisal of the situation in America, the king, desperate to keep the colonies, latched on to Carleton, whom he looked upon as his "best officer" and his last hope.[42] In the face of advice to the contrary, George III believed that Carleton would be able to negotiate with the Americans and find reconciliation without granting independence. On March 8 he signed Carleton's commission as commander in chief in North America. He also signed commissions appointing Carleton and Rear Admiral Sir Robert Digby, the senior naval officer in North America, as "Commissioners for Restoring Peace and granting Pardon to the Revolted Provinces in America and the Inhabitants Thereof."[43]

Carleton's royal commission differed little from similar commissions given to previous commanders in chief, including General Sir William Howe and his brother Admiral Lord Richard Howe in 1776. The wording was also essentially the same as the commission carried to America by the Carlisle Commission in 1778, and indeed, the language was even repeated in the commission held by General Clinton. The Americans had consistently dismissed the conditions contained in these documents. Nonetheless, the king had not changed his mind—negotiations and pardons were encouraged, but independence was not acceptable. After a long audience with the king, Carleton took his leave and prepared to depart for his new command.

Having brought Carleton in, the king finally let North out. Unable to muster a sufficient majority to carry on the king's policies, North submitted his resignation on March 18. "Your Majesty is well apprized that in this country the Prince on the Throne cannot with prudence oppose the deliberate resolution of the House of Commons," he advised. For a dozen years North had served his king, but that seemed to count for little in the mind of George III. The following morning the king responded to North's missive with an incredibly petulant letter. He told his longtime faithful minister that he had been "hurt" by North's remarks, and warned him that if he announced his resignation before the king had a chance to find a successor, North would "certainly for ever forfeit [the king's] regard."[44]

On Wednesday March 20, before a packed House, North announced his departure. The next day the king invited the Earl of Shelburne to form a government. George III had no love for the earl, having once referred to him as the "Jesuit of Berkeley Square," but in the end he had little choice. Although Shelburne and his followers lacked sufficient numbers to carry a majority in the House of Commons, they were willing to join a coalition government with factions led by the Marquis of Rockingham and Shelburne's rival, Charles James Fox.

The new government took office on March 27. Thurlow was the sole surviving minister from the old North administration. Rockingham stood at the head of the ministry and took the traditional post as first lord of the treasury. The offices of the secretaries for the Northern and Southern departments were abolished. In their place a new secretaryship was established: secretary of state for home, colonial, and Irish affairs. This was Shelburne's post. The "Jesuit of Berkeley Square" was living up to his reputation. Not only was he consolidating the existing authority in his own hands, but he also gained new power. He was now the chief minister in direct authority over British commanders, both army and navy. Diplomatic duties, which had once been divided between the two secretaries, were consolidated into a new office, the secretary for foreign affairs, to be held by Fox. The reorganization pitted the old rivals Shelburne and Fox in a contest for dominance.[45]

Rockingham's government was a shaky triptych. The king had a long and unhappy political history with him and Fox, he disliked both heart-

ily, and so he most often dealt with Shelburne, making him a shadow
prime minister.[46] Impaired by deteriorating health, Rockingham made
little protest over Shelburne's favored position, but Fox was not inclined
to be so accepting. With an uncertain hand at the reins, the new ministry was torn in a variety of directions as Shelburne and Fox competed
for authority. From Paris, where he had access to a variety of intelligence reports from London, Lafayette wrote to Alexander Hamilton in
April 1782 that "the New Ministers are not much our friends, they are
not friends to each other. They have some Honest Men with little Sense
and some Sensible Men without honesty."[47]

Carleton watched these political shifts with dismay. He had accepted
his post under North's administration, whose American policies he supported. In the new ministry Shelburne, his immediate superior, was the
only member who thus far rejected independence. Rockingham, Fox, and
the others were willing to consider the possibility. They were concerned
with the ongoing costs of a war that seemed increasingly unwinnable.
England was fighting not only the Americans but France, Spain, and the
Dutch as well. A majority in the House of Commons wanted an end to
the war with America on almost any terms, perhaps including independence. The king, however, had made his position clear: he would rather
abdicate than consent to independence.

Steering between continuing the war or conceding independence,
Shelburne devised a clever plan. "Peace with America, and war with the
rest of the Globe" was the way one newspaper wag put it.[48] Commerce
with the colonies animated the minister, and after more than twenty
years in government no one needed to instruct him on the importance of
doing business with America. Shelburne's first goal was to end the trans-
atlantic unpleasantness and reengage the Americans in trade. As he told
Carleton, he believed that by some plan of colonial autonomy, not independence, reconciliation was possible, but this had to be pushed quickly;
for if the war continued, the Americans might be drawn ever more
closely into the French bosom. America and France had to be divided.

In thinking that reconciliation could be had without independence,
Shelburne was making the same error that had dogged British leaders
since the beginning of the war. The pitch at reconciliation had been
made twice before to the Americans, in 1776 by the Howe brothers and

in 1778 by the Earl of Carlisle, and it had been rejected each time. Many in London trusted in the face value of reports, mostly from loyalists, that the Americans were financially exhausted, that the states were quarreling, Congress was weak, and the rebel army was dissolving. However accurate this description, what Shelburne and his predecessors could not grasp was that the traditional measures of war did not apply to a revolutionary uprising. While the Americans were disunited and fractious, they could agree on one point: independence was an absolute condition for peace.

As Carleton prepared to sail, he confided to a friend that in going to New York he intended to take a firm stand with the Americans. He was not simply going "to be employ'd as a mere Inspector of embarkations," a statement reflecting how little he knew of the reality in America or perhaps even the politics in Parliament.[49] The new ministry was committed to ending the war in America, and Carleton's boastful comment also flew in the face of direct orders from Shelburne: "The first object of your attention must be to provide for withdrawing the garrison, artillery, provisions, stores of all kinds, every species of public property, from New York and its dependencies to Halifax. The same steps are to be taken with respect to the garrisons of Charleston and Savannah." Then in an extraordinary instruction that any officer would have found repugnant, Shelburne told Carleton, "In case you should meet with obstructions by any attack . . . so that it will not be in your power to effect the evacuation without great hazard of considerable loss, an early capitulation . . . is thought preferable . . . to an obstinate defense."[50] No matter Carleton's determined notions, the politicians had decided that the war in America must end—even in surrender.[51]

To the dismay of his superiors, Carleton seemed in no hurry to depart England. Anxious to settle matters in America, Shelburne pressed Carleton, and on April 4 the impatient minister directed Carleton to "immediately Embark on the Frigate [*Ceres*] and proceed to New York with all possible expedition."[52] A few days later *Ceres* cleared the Channel and set a course west on a pleasant and quick spring crossing to America. In the evening the captain entertained his passengers at table. All were in uniform except Maurice Morgann, Carleton's secretary, and Brook Watson, the newly appointed commissary general.

Morgann was a familiar figure in London circles and well known to Carleton. He was a close confidant to Shelburne, having served for more than twenty years as his private secretary. In 1767 Shelburne, then secretary of the Southern Department, sent Morgann on a special mission to Quebec, where he met Carleton, who as the newly appointed governor had been struggling with the challenge of melding British and French law. To secure loyalty and maintain harmony, the governor granted considerable latitude to French Canadians in the management of local affairs. Not everyone agreed that such concessions ought to be made to a conquered people, and complaints filtered to London accusing him of undermining the king's authority. Morgann was sent to investigate. He spent several months meeting with officials and reviewing laws before concluding that Carleton's policies were wise and clearly in the best interests of the empire. His report pleased both the governor and Lord Shelburne.[53]

After returning from his mission to Canada, Morgann resumed his post with Shelburne. His less than onerous duties as a private secretary left him ample time to pursue his intellectual interests. He wrote two widely circulated political pamphlets: *An Enquiry Concerning the Nature and End of A National Militia* and *A Letter to My Lords the Bishops On Occasion of the Present Bill for the Prevention of Adultery*. His best-known work, however, was a book titled *An Essay on the Dramatic Character of Sir John Falstaff*, in which he rehabilitated the character of Falstaff from a drunken coward to a courageous soldier. The book went through several editions in the nineteenth century and remained in print into the twentieth. Morgann's unusual interpretation of Falstaff was challenged by the eminent doctor Samuel Johnson when he came to visit Shelburne at Wickham. Not finding the lord at home, Johnson remained and was entertained by Morgann. Long into the night the two sparred over Morgann's Falstaff. In the morning, Johnson, a man not accustomed to losing an argument or retreating gracefully, announced to Morgann at breakfast, "Sir, I have been thinking over our dispute last night—you were in the right."[54] Morgann did have an unfortunate reputation for talking in "a pompous way that seems borrowed from the House of Commons."[55]

Also in company with Carleton was the new commissary general, Brook Watson, charged with overseeing all matters of army supplies.

Born in Plymouth, England, Watson had entered the Royal Navy. His seagoing career was cut short in 1749 due to a stroke of bad luck: while he was bathing in Havana harbor, a shark attacked him, taking off his leg. In 1778 the dramatic event was captured by the Boston-born painter John Singleton Copley in his famous *Watson and the Shark*. Recovering nicely from the loss of his leg, Watson turned to mercantile pursuits, moved to America, and during the Seven Years War served as commissary to the army, where he earned the nickname "the wooden legged commissary." During his duty in America he made the acquaintance of Guy Carleton. After the war he retuned to London but remained active in American trade and Canadian land speculation. Rumors had reached London of financial irregularities in Clinton's New York accounts. Watson was being sent to straighten out the books.[56]

Shelburne had made it abundantly clear to Carleton that the general's prime mission was to negotiate a peace with the Americans that would keep them within the empire, or at least closely associated with it. Independence was still too bitter a pill to be swallowed. Do all that you can, Shelburne urged, to split the Americans from their French allies. The prospect of a continuing transatlantic Franco-American alliance aimed at Britain was too horrible to contemplate. As evidence of British intentions toward America, while he negotiated peace Carleton was also ordered to make preparations to evacuate Charleston, Savannah, and New York, and if necessary St. Augustine. Foreign soldiers (that is, German mercenaries) were to be transported home while the king's regular forces were to be shipped to Nova Scotia and possibly the West Indies depending upon circumstances. He was to attend to the safety and well-being of the loyalists, providing them transportation to England or to Canada, where land grants awaited them. Carleton confronted a Sisyphean task.[57]

HAD SHELBURNE AND CARLETON KNOWN more about the distressing situation of Washington's army, they might have had second thoughts about evacuation. When Washington left his encampment on the Hudson in the summer of 1781 to begin his march to Yorktown, he took with him the "flower of the army," leaving behind mostly militia, invalids, and raw recruits under the command of Major General William Heath.

"Corpulent and bald headed," as he described himself, Heath was not one of the commander in chief's favorite generals.[1] His moment of fame had come and gone more than six years earlier when he commanded the Massachusetts militia that chased the British back to Boston from Concord and Lexington. He remained at his post as commanding general in Massachusetts until the Second Continental Congress adopted the army in June 1775 and commissioned Washington commander in chief. With a Virginian at the head of a Yankee army, Congress thought it wise to give recognition to local officers, and thus commissioned Heath a brigadier general. During the New York campaign in August 1776, Congress promoted him to major general.

A "political general," Heath had only modest military abilities. In January 1777 he bungled an attack on Fort Independence on the Hudson, causing Washington to take the unusual step of issuing a written "censure." Heath's fellow Massachusetts officer, the crusty Timothy Pickering, who rarely had a good word to say about anyone, was particularly harsh toward his comrade, remarking that Heath's conduct was a "disgrace." Nonetheless, Heath's political influence, particularly strong backing from Massachusetts, made it difficult for Washington to be rid of him. It was neither the first nor last time that the commander in chief would face the challenge of where to put an officer so he was likely to do the least harm. Since the British in New York City under Clinton showed no inclination to venture up the Hudson, the Highland forts guarding that river had seemed a reasonably safe place to post him.[2]

As the troops sent north from Yorktown arrived back on the Hudson, Heath dispatched them to various sites, ordering them to prepare for winter. To feed them, he sent out foraging parties to gather up supplies for the coming winter. One "grand forage," carried out by General John Glover's brigade, brought in "two prisoners; a quantity of corn, hay, etc and about 40 swine."[3] Other smaller parties scoured the countryside, returning with considerable booty, much of it purchased with nearly worthless Continental script, but a good portion simply taken, sometimes violently, particularly if the owner was suspected of loyalist leanings. Not even the fertile Hudson Valley, however, could support the locustlike demands of the soldiers. As winter dragged on, food ran short and soldiers sickened. Winter clothing was scarce. Colonel John Crane, an artillery officer, wrote Henry Knox that "the men are exceedingly naked, destitute of pay and not well fed."[4] In early December smallpox swept the camp. Heath ordered inoculation, but several died. As the weather worsened, Heath ordered the men to construct huts.

For most of the time cold, snow, and ice kept the Americans and British confined. Seeking to take advantage of the season and surprise the British, the American commander in Albany, General William Alexander, better known as Lord Stirling, suggested attacking across the border into Canada and Vermont.[5] Thanks to the machinations of the Allen brothers, Ethan and Ira, politics in the Green Mountains were convoluted and fluid. Caught between competing claims for their land by New York and New Hampshire, Vermonters had taken a sometimes ambivalent position on the Revolution. Stirling had heard rumors that the Allens were in conversation with General Frederick Haldimand, the British commander in Canada.[6] A surprise American strike north, Stirling argued, would prevent the Vermonters from going over to the British. Reports of Stirling's plan alarmed Haldimand, but neither Stirling nor Heath could muster the men for a march north.[7]

Unable to undertake any serious action, both sides broke the tedium of camp life by launching raids. Heath sent American light horse into Duchess and Westchester counties, targeting loyalists. Often executed by local patriot militia with old neighborhood grudges to settle, the raids turned into bloody opportunities to visit murder and mayhem on the enemy. Armed bands of loyalists retaliated quickly and with equal violence.

To the dismay of regular commanders on both sides, this irregular warfare turned personal and vicious, and proved nearly impossible to control.[8]

Occasional raids notwithstanding, the boredom of winter gave ample time for grousing among the enlisted ranks as they huddled in their rude huts. Officers were not immune, for like the men they commanded, they had not been paid either. Frustration had reached such a level that even commanders in the highest ranks, including General Henry Knox, the commander at West Point, were grumbling. Knox was particularly angry when his aide-de-camp, Major Samuel Shaw, informed him that the securities Congress had given him in lieu of pay were "little better . . . than so much blank paper."[9] Discontent was rife and spreading. Some senior officers hinted at mutiny. In an usually blunt manner Colonel Henry Jackson warned his commander and friend Knox that the army was "exceedingly uneasy." The "public," he reported, "have no idea of the distressed situation of the Army." He recounted that "from morning to night and from night to morning you will hear some of the best officers and soldiers (that any nation could ever boast of) execrating the very country they are risking their Lives, lands and health to support."[10] Knox agreed.

Rumblings of discontent in the ranks were not confined to the army in the North. From the South General Nathanael Greene sent alarming reports about the mood of his troops, whose pay was also deeply in arrears, and who suffered from congressional neglect. He warned Robert Morris that "the distress of the Officers are great and many of them have drained every private resource in their power. Men may bear their sufferings to a certain degree beyond which it is dangerous to push them nay ruinous. Clouds of discontent hover over our heads from all quarters."[11]

As spring approached and the weather warmed, ice on the Hudson began to break and supplies arrived from Connecticut and Massachusetts. With fresh provisions the men recovered their health. Sanitary conditions, however, remained deplorable. Lice thrived in the cramped filthy condition of the huts. By the end of winter typhus, the "putrid fever," broke out.[12] In such confined quarters respiratory diseases spread with virulence. The weather signaled relief, but not before hospitals were filled and the grave diggers busy.

Better weather meant the return of the commander in chief. Preparations for his arrival needed to be made. Although Washington traveled light compared to his British counterparts, his headquarters command numbered several dozen men, including his personal guard, mess cooks, military aides, and secretaries Martha, too, was joining him. Finding appropriate quarters for the general fell to Quartermaster General Timothy Pickering, who happily delegated the job to his deputy, Colonel Hugh Hughes.

Hughes had a heavy task. During the course of the war Washington had set up his headquarters in 169 different locations, including private homes, taverns, and field tents stretching from Massachusetts to Virginia.[13] Some places such as the Vassal House in Cambridge and the Chew House in Philadelphia were large and elegant; other accommodations were less impressive. At Valley Forge the commander's quarters were cramped and tiny. In the Highlands, prior to the siege at Yorktown, he had kept his headquarters at the home of William Ellison in New Windsor. That house was no longer available, so Hughes had to scout for new quarters.

Hughes needed a place large enough to accommodate Washington and his immediate "family." This meant not only a main building but barracks for soldiers, stables for horses, warehouses for supplies, and a secure magazine for powder and weapons. It was a tall order, and security loomed large. With the British and their loyalist raiders prowling about the country south of West Point, the commander needed to be north of that post, but within close communication. Locating near the river would provide Washington with easy access to water transport both for himself and the supplies necessary for him and his staff. Hughes settled upon a home in Newburgh, just north of the village of New Windsor and fourteen miles upriver from West Point.[14]

Although the house itself was unprepossessing, the location was spectacular. Situated atop a slope reaching gradually down to the Hudson, the stone house offered a view stretching for miles along the river in either direction. Across the river was a hill commanding a view down the river that made it impossible for anyone to approach without detection. The original structure, built in 1725, had been a simple two-story affair; after 1749 it had been enlarged by the new owners, Joseph and Elsie Hasbrouck, to a reasonably spacious farmhouse of eight rooms. Shortly after her husband's death Elsie sold the house to her newly married son, Jonathan, and his wife, Tryntje DuBois. After thirty years in the house Jonathan died in 1780, leaving his widow to occupy the home alone.[15]

She was not alone for long. In late 1781 Quartermaster General Pickering commandeered a portion of the house for himself and his wife, but allowed the widow to remain. This arrangement lasted only a few weeks when the widow was informed that the entire house was to be taken over by the commander in chief. Major John Tyson, the unlucky officer who was charged with delivering the news, reported that the flinty widow "sat some time in sullen silence her passion . . . too big for utterance." Tyson told the widow not only that her home was to be taken but that "additional buildings were to be erected" on her property. She "made no reply." Finally, after more "sullen silence," the widow announced that she and "General Washington . . . could not both live in the House." That may well have been a relief to Tyson since he had no intention of allowing her to stay in any case. The disheartened widow left for nearby New Paltz, where she spent the remainder of the war with her relatives. The Pickerings left quietly.[16]

Once the widow and the Pickerings were out of the way, teams of carpenters arrived. For weeks, even during the coldest days, they worked furiously to convert a farmhouse into a proper headquarters for the commander in chief. The wharf had to be repaired first so that vessels could offload supplies. Once building materials arrived, stables and barracks went up to accommodate the soldiers and servants accompanying the general. The interior of the house was altered. A kitchen was constructed on the south side sufficient to prepare meals, some of them elegant and formal, for the general, his staff, and visiting dignitaries. Breakfast was ordinarily served at nine, dinner at two, tea at seven, and "family supper" at nine.[17]

As the work went ahead, not everyone was pleased with the drain on resources. From West Point Heath complained that "we have scarcely any Hands here, they being employed at Newburgh, in erecting Stables, etc for his Excellency." Despite the full press Colonel Hughes had a different view, lamenting to Heath, "I am afraid the Commander in Chief will be at Newburgh before I can possibly be ready for him."[18]

On April 1, 1782, the Washingtons arrived accompanied by aides, servants, and nearly two hundred soldiers of his Life Guard, under the command of Caleb Gibbs. The soldiers and their mounts found temporary space in nearby barns as well as in the newly erected barracks and stables. Inside the house, in addition to the general and his wife, about a dozen people took up residence. These included Washington's slave Billy Lee and assorted servants. Also present, although never at the same time, were four aides who served the commander as secretaries, speechwriters, messengers, and confidants. These men were part of the "official family."[19]

Closest to Washington was David Humphreys, a Connecticut-born graduate of Yale, a former schoolmaster, and a skilled writer. After the war he returned with Washington to Mount Vernon to help him organize his papers and write a biography. Richard Varick of New York had been Benedict Arnold's aide. Although cleared of any involvement in Arnold's treason, Varick stood tainted until Washington appointed him a personal aide. Jonathan Trumbull Jr. came from a powerful Connecticut clan, his father being governor of the state. Benjamin Walker, born in England, had the distinction of being the only foreign officer in the "family."

For their bedroom the general and his wife took a small room in the northeast corner of the first floor. It had only one window, overlooking the river, and no fireplace. Heavy beamed ceilings and dark wooden floors made the Hasbroucks' home a far cry from the lively sunlit rooms characteristic of Mount Vernon or the Georgian townhouses of Philadelphia. The jambless fireplaces, wide gaping stone apertures fronted by huge hearths, were foreboding.[20] On the other hand, as Colonel Hughes noticed with some relief, these oversized chimneys drew well.[21]

Away from the Washingtons' small private space the house was abuzz with activity as aides bustled about. Unbeknownst to most of the staff at Hasbrouck House even as they were moving in, a secret operation was under way that could change the course of the war. Washington was anticipating important news.

In September 1781 Prince William Henry, the seventeen-year-old son of King George III, had arrived at New York City serving as a midshipman aboard Admiral Digby's flagship *Prince George*. The prince's arrival created a hubbub in the city. Never before had a royal visited the colonies. Crowds gathered as the young prince came ashore, gawkers craning their necks to catch a glimpse of the heir to the throne. To the dismay of the city's elite, the young prince kept a low profile; he spent most of his time aboard ship tending to his naval duties or in his shoreside quarters in Hanover Square.[22] His presence was the stuff of endless gossip, which quickly reached beyond British lines.[23] Among those who paid special attention to the prince's arrival was Colonel Matthias Ogden, one of Washington's chief spies. His agents reported that when not aboard ship the prince shared quarters with Commodore Edmund Affleck. The place, according to Ogden's spies, was only lightly guarded. Seeing an opportunity for a grand coup, Ogden proposed kidnapping the prince. With a prince in hand, Washington would have a powerful lever for prisoner exchange. The commander in chief embraced the scheme and encouraged Ogden to go forward. "The spirit of enterprise so conspicuous in your plan for . . . bringing off the Prince William Henry and Admiral Digby, merits applause; and you have my Authority to make the attempt." He cautioned Ogden "against offering insults or indignity to the persons of the Prince and Admiral." As soon as he had them, Ogden was "to delay no time in conveying them to Congress."[24]

General Clinton also had an intelligence network, directed by Captain George Beckwith.[25] Beckwith's spies brought word back of Ogden's plot. Clinton then doubled the guard at his own quarters "at eight o'clock every night" and did the same for the prince and the admiral. Ogden abandoned his plan.[26] A few weeks later the prince sailed for the West Indies.[27]

Far less diverting than plotting a royal kidnapping was the public brawl that broke out that spring between two of Washington's most senior generals, William Heath and Alexander McDougall.

New Yorkers knew the rough-hewn McDougall from the heady days of protest leading up to the Revolution. The son of "Milkman John" who carried pails of milk about the city, he was a leader of the "Sons of Liberty."[28] McDougall's fiery temper and incendiary writings landed him in jail when he publicly assailed the legislature for supporting British troops. His imprisonment elevated him to the status of patriot martyr.[29]

At the start of the war McDougall commanded the First New York Regiment. By 1777 he was a major general. Like so many of his peers, McDougall had an outsized ego. When the state legislature elected him to the Continental Congress he demanded that he retain his rank as major general and collect both salaries. Congress, always suspicious of military aggrandizement, refused to recognize his rank and insisted on addressing him as Mister. In a slap back McDougall wore his uniform during sessions. The final straw came when Congress, in March 1781, offered him a post as secretary of the Marine Department.[30] Once again he demanded two salaries. Congress declined, and McDougall resigned in a huff, returning to his command in the Hudson Highlands a bitter man with little use for politicians.

Heath, the self-important general, and McDougall, the fiery radical, detested each other, but as long as Washington was in the Highlands the two generals suppressed their mutual disdain. The commander in chief's presence also masked the chain of command since it gave McDougall the false impression that he and Heath were on a par in their relationship to Washington. McDougall was at West Point, and Heath kept to his post at Fishkill on the opposite side of the river and a dozen miles to the south. Washington's departure for Yorktown in the summer of 1781 left a void in the command structure, into which Heath rushed to establish his legitimate, albeit unrecognized, authority over McDougall.

Angry letters flew in both directions. In late November 1781, when Heath dispatched a staff officer to deliver orders to McDougall, the dour soldier shot back that the next time he sent orders so "unmilitary and absurd" he would put the messenger under "arrest."[31] The sniping escalated until finally, after McDougall made a particularly vicious attack on his character, Heath issued an order for his arrest, charging him among other things with "conduct unmilitary and unbecoming an officer."[32] Quickly both men wrote to Washington, McDougall exploding that Heath had treated him "like a Bastard."[33]

It was not the first time that Washington had to quell an internecine war among his officers, but this one was especially difficult. He told Heath that he was "extremely sorry" that this had come about, but he was prepared to order a general court-martial of McDougall. Washington could not have begun to imagine the headache to follow. McDougall, perhaps harkening back to his days of bedeviling royal authority as a Son of Liberty, used every tactic possible to delay and prolong the proceedings. He objected to the officers appointed by Washington. The place set for the trial, he said, was inconvenient. He constantly asked for additional information, all the while doing everything he could to rally support for himself, publicize the affair, and humiliate Heath, even threatening to retaliate by pressing official charges against him. McDougall was, Benjamin Lincoln confided to Nathanael Greene, "very severe in his remarks on General Heath."[34] Fortunately, McDougall backed away from pressing charges, not because he felt his accusations were ill founded, but because "an altercation between officers . . . might have an ill aspect in the eyes of our allies."[35]

The dispute dragged on for six months as verbal salvos echoed up and down the Hudson Valley. Gossip and rumors about the generals enlivened the dull days of camp life. Enlisted men found entertainment in the battle of the brass, while in the officers' mess and at Hasbrouck House the reaction was embarrassment. Congress, on the other hand, was neither entertained nor embarrassed, viewing the squabble as further evidence of a decline in patriotic spirit and collapsing discipline in the army.

When McDougall's trial finally finished in August 1782, the court found him guilty of only one of the seven charges: "Pulling down two buildings and moving them to West Point without the knowledge of the commanding general."[36] Punishment was a simple reprimand from the commander in chief, which Washington issued "with extreme reluctance."

In Washington's estimation the whole sorry affair had brought "ill consequences" and damaged the reputation of the entire army.[37]

The affair of Heath and McDougall was a visible sign of Washington's greatest challenge: anger and despair in the army. At the end of prior winter encampments the army had been stirred to action by the promise of a new campaign, but in the spring of 1782 no campaign was expected. There still lingered a faint hope that the French fleet would return and an attack might be launched against New York or Charleston. Others speculated that a march to Canada was being planned, but none of this was real. The French were not coming back, and no one had an appetite for a second invasion of Canada. At the same time the British in New York City held tight, showing no inclination either to provoke Washington or to abandon the city. In this uncertainty Washington awaited the arrival of Sir Guy Carleton. He was particularly anxious to address Sir Guy on two issues of pressing importance: prisoners of war and the "murder" of Captain Joshua Huddy.[38]

Prisoners of war were a heavy burden to both the Americans and the British. After Yorktown the Americans held at least twelve thousand prisoners while the British guarded barely five hundred.[39] Given the numbers, the Americans bore the greater brunt of responsibility and expense. They did not always acquit themselves well.[40]

Since the king spurned recognition of any legitimate American government, formal communication was difficult. Under the usual eighteenth-century "rules of war" the prisoners' home country was duty bound to provide support for soldiers held by the enemy. When Congress reneged on the arrangements Gates had made at Saratoga in 1777 to allow Burgoyne's troops to return home, Clinton was furious. In retaliation for Congress's actions he declined to provide supplies or cash for troops he alleged were being held in violation of the Saratoga agreement, leaving Congress with several thousand enemy mouths to feed and bodies to clothe. A number of meetings had been held between American and British representatives, but until the king would agree to pay Congress the £200,000 that it estimated the British owed, it would not discuss any release or exchange of prisoners.[41] In the meantime Washington ordered that the British prisoners be moved to Lancaster, Pennsylvania.[42] In December 1781 Benjamin Shield visited the Lancaster prison and reported to Secretary at War Benjamin Lincoln that the prisoners were "a set of poor miserable wretches without the common necessaries pinning thro neglect and want."[43] Partial relief for the imprisoned German mercenaries arrived when informal arrangements were made to "lease" German prisoners to local farmers. Once released to work, many of these prisoners disappeared into the German-speaking countryside.[44]

On the other hand, Washington admitted that he had "no reason to complain of the treatment of the Continental land prisoners in New York."[45] The same, however, could not be said for American seamen held in the city. Many were confined in crowded filthy prison ships moored in Wallabout Bay. Poor ventilation, rotten food, and festering disease took an incredible toll. Each morning the watch opened the sealed hatches and called down below, "Rebels turn out your dead."[46] Although there was little that Washington could do about such inhumane treatment, the one action he might have taken—an exchange of prisoners—he refused to undertake.

A murder and hanging exploded the issue of prisoners of war. The crisis began on the evening of March 28, 1782, when a gang of New York loyalists led by Philip White set out from New York City to raid the New Jersey coast.[47] They landed at Sandy Hook and then made their way farther down the coast to Long Branch, where a band of local patriot vigilantes, the "Monmouth Retaliators," surprised them and captured White. The "Retaliators" set their prisoner on a horse and headed toward the town of Freehold about fifteen miles inland. A few miles down the road White leaped off the horse and dashed for nearby woods. One of the American guards fired and hit him in the back, but White showed no sign of stopping. As he crawled toward the wood line a horseman drew his saber and rode at him, calling furiously, "Give up, you shall have good quarters yet." Ignoring the order, White continued toward the trees. The horseman closed and slashed him to death. When news of White's savage death—he was, after all, wounded and unarmed— reached New York City, loyalists screamed for revenge. White's murder, they argued, was only the most recent atrocity committed by the Monmouth Retaliators, whom they accused of murdering a number of the king's loyal subjects. Retaliation was long overdue. They pressed Clinton to release to them a rebel prisoner for execution.

When he reacted coolly to their demand, with Governor Franklin's encouragement they began to plot their own revenge.[48] The plan's architect was Captain Richard Lippincott, a member of the Associated Loyalists and the late Philip White's brother-in-law.

Like Franklin, Lippincott was a New Jersey loyalist who early in the war had been imprisoned and driven from his home. He fled to New York and became an officer in a loyalist regiment. On the morning of April 9, less than two weeks after White's death, Lippincott with several other loyalist soldiers presented himself to the provost's guard at the prison where a number of Americans were being held. He was accompanied by Walter Challoner, the commissary of prisoners. Challoner ordered the jailers to turn over three Americans to Lippincott, one of them Captain Joshua Huddy, a leader of the Monmouth Regulators, who was notorious for his boast that he hanged the loyalist Stephen Edwards: "[I] tied the knot, and greased the rope."[49]

Under what authority Challoner and Lippincott were operating remains shrouded, although at several points Governor Franklin's name was invoked. In any case Lippincott removed the three prisoners to the guard ship *Britannia*.[50] Eventually two of the prisoners were released, but not Huddy. After three days confined aboard *Britannia*, on April 12 Lippincott brought Huddy to Navesink Hills "on the Jersey shore near the Hook." Lippincott stood Huddy on a barrel, placed a rope around his neck, and pinned a sign to his chest proclaiming UP GOES HUDDY FOR PHILIP WHITE, and then shook his hand. As Huddy proclaimed his innocence, a "Negro" executioner kicked the barrel away.[51]

During the American Revolution burnings, lootings, and even murder, particularly where irregular forces were involved, were not rare. Huddy's brutal death, especially spectacular and public, brought a flood of demands for retaliation. Pressed to act, Washington ordered a council of senior officers at West Point to convene on April 19. Washington was not present, but through General Heath, who presided, he placed three questions before the council: "Shall there be retaliation for the murder of Captain Huddy?" "On whom shall it be inflicted?" "And how shall the victim be designated?"[52] By secret ballot the officers voted unanimously to take retaliation and that "it should be inflicted on an officer of equal rank, viz a Captain; not under Convention or capitulation, but one that had surrendered at discretion; and that in designating such a one, it should be done by lot."[53]

Hanging a British captain gave Washington pause, and so he wrote to Clinton, "To save the innocent, I demand the guilty." Lippincott, Washington demanded, must be "turned over."[54] If not, retaliation would follow.

Despite Washington's rhetoric, "I shall hold myself justifiable in the Eyes of God and man," and Clinton's claim that he was "greatly surprised and shocked" at the behavior of the Associated Loyalists, neither side could claim much virtue in this matter.[55] Philip White, an escaping prisoner, had been wounded and then cut down by a saber-wielding American trooper. Without the slightest nod to a legal proceeding, Joshua Huddy had been executed in an act of vengeance. To Clinton, whose main preoccupation by this time was salvaging his reputation, the behavior of the loyalist banditti was another potential blot on his command. He described the Associated Loyalists as an "obnoxious Institution" and their behavior as an "audacious breach of humanity, and an insult to the dignity of British arms."[56] What they had done was "reprehensible." Clinton was convinced that the loyalists, under Franklin's direction, were involved in a plot "to involve the navy and army . . . in the guilt, for the purpose of exciting the war of indiscriminate retaliation which they appear to have long thirsted after."[57]

Clinton held Franklin responsible. At the very moment when he was trying to negotiate a prisoner exchange and avoid confrontation with Washington, by this barbarous act the governor and his friends had up ended his plans. They had committed a heinous crime, for which Clinton was convinced his enemies in America and England would hold him accountable. Clinton could barely wait to hand the mess over to Carleton.[58]

On April 26 Clinton brought the matter before a council of officers. Following their advice, he ordered Lippincott arrested and held for a general court-martial. Franklin protested vigorously, arguing that Lippincott was a civilian over whom the military had no authority.[59] Clinton rejected Franklin's claim. Refusing Washington's demand that Lippincott be turned over to him, Clinton ordered a court-martial. On May 1, 1782, a court of sixteen officers, with General James Robertson presiding, convened to hear the case.

.   .   .

Washington reacted quickly. He ordered Brigadier General Moses Hazen, commanding the enemy prisoner camp at Lancaster, to select "by Lot" a British officer to be sent immediately to Philadelphia.[60] In the instruction Washington specifically noted that the officer chosen had to be an "unconditional Prisoner," that is, an officer taken on the field of battle who surrendered without conditions. Since all of the prisoners at Lancaster had been taken "conditionally" through a negotiated surrender, how Hazen was to find such an officer was unclear.[61] He could not, and two weeks later Washington ordered Hazen to disregard the written pledges that had been made at Saratoga and Yorktown and select a "Captain" for retaliation.

Washington's reasoning is difficult to fathom. Ordinarily he had been inclined to leave matters related to local partisan warfare in the hands of civil authorities. "Irregulars" were often not under his control, and he made this point during negotiations with Cornwallis. Loyalists serving under British arms had to answer to civil authorities.[62]

With Washington's order in hand Hazen, who, ironically, early in the war had himself been a prisoner of the British, arrived at Lancaster. He had an unhappy task. On the morning of May 27 he assembled all the camp's captains and announced to them that they were to choose by lot from their number a captain to be hanged if General Clinton did not turn over Lippincott.[63] Moses Hazen was a professional soldier, and so were the British officers who stood in line at Lancaster to draw lots. Neither Hazen nor the captains had been party to the unlawful events in New Jersey, and both condemned them. Neither was comfortable with what was about to take place. Solemnly the British officers drew straws. The "unfortunate Lot" fell on "Captain Charles Asgill, of the Guards, a young Gentleman of Seventeen years of age . . . the only son of Sir Charles Asgill, Baronet; Heir to an extensive Fortune, [and] an honourable title."[64] Hazen reported to Washington that the British officers were "enraged" at Sir Henry Clinton for not bringing the loyalists to heel, and for leaving the officers "to suffer for the Sins of the Guilty." It was, wrote Hazen, "a disagreeable Situation."[65] Hazen and Asgill left for Philadelphia accompanied by Asgill's friend Captain Ludlow, who carried a letter from Major James Gordon, the ranking British officer at Lancaster, to Secretary Lincoln. Gordon minced no words. He pointed out to Lincoln that Lippincott and his men, who called themselves "Refugees," were no better than "Banditti." They were not part of His Majesty's regular forces. That they had lynched poor Huddy was regrettable, but that such a violent and illegal act should lead to another unconscionable act, "an ignominious death" for Asgill, was equally outrageous. The young captain was innocent of any offense, and furthermore, wrote the major, he was protected by article 14 of the Yorktown capitulation that specifically forbade any "reprisals" against surrendered officers and soldiers.[66] The secretary at war did nothing, leaving the matter to Washington and the Congress.

Almost as soon as he had given the order to take a hostage, Washington regretted his actions. He realized, too late, that what he had done was morally questionable and undoubtedly illegal. He sought desperately to find an "unconditional prisoner." If such a person had been found, at least he would have cleared the legal hurdles, but he had no luck.[67] He turned to the members of Congress for support, which they gave by a unanimous vote endorsing his actions.[68] Nonetheless, he continued to agonize. "I most devoutly Wish his [Asgill's] Life may be saved," but "Duty calls me to make this Decisive Determination," he wrote to Brigadier General Elias Dayton."[69]

Not everyone on the American side agreed with Washington. Alexander Hamilton, who had served closely with the general and knew him well, thought that the whole business of retaliation was "repugnant, wanton and unnecessary."[70] Hamilton knew that Washington's pride made it difficult for him to back away. He urged Henry Knox, Washington's closest confidant, to help him find an honorable exit. Might Knox, he wrote, engage some "obscure agents" to settle the crisis? "It is said the Commander in Chief has pledged himself for it and cannot recede. Inconsistency in this case would be better than consistency. But pretexts may be found and will be readily admitted in favor of humanity."[71] Knox too was troubled, but he made no reply to Hamilton. Second-guessing the commander in chief was dangerous business.

For once, General Clinton fell into some luck. Two days after Lippincott's court-martial convened, Sir Guy Carleton arrived. Clinton was relieved of duty. The matter rested with Sir Guy and the American Congress.

CHAPTER FIVE

After a brisk twenty-five-day passage, on Sunday morning May 5 *Ceres* hove off to Sandy Hook to await the pilot. As soon as they spotted the ship, lookouts at the Hook hoisted signals relayed to the city announcing Carleton's arrival. At last General Henry Clinton's long American ordeal was coming to a close. In the afternoon *Ceres* dropped anchor off the Battery. While the guns of Fort George rendered their traditional salute, a small boat came alongside the quay and made fast. Carleton, followed by his secretary and the commissary general, ascended the stairs to be greeted by Clinton, Robertson, and Admiral Digby.[1] With the general and admiral were several other officers, including the Hessian commander General Wilhelm von Knyphausen. Governor Franklin was there as well, and so too was Andrew Elliott, lieutenant governor of New York. As loyalist leaders, Franklin and Elliott hoped that the new commander might prove more sympathetic to their cause than Clinton. The welcoming ceremony was brief. Carleton reviewed the honor guard and then retired to quarters.

As he rode up Manhattan Carleton was taken aback by what he saw. The city was a sad scene of devastation. Six years before, on the evening of September 21, 1776, at a moment when American and British forces were still fighting on the island, a mysterious fire had broken out near the Fighting Cocks Tavern on Whitehall Street, a place known for its after-curfew tippling. Driven by a fresh breeze, the flames had whipped up the west side past the Paulus Hook ferry. Before being extinguished, the flames had consumed nearly five hundred buildings, about one quarter of the city. Since then virtually nothing had been rebuilt or repaired. Indeed, in the aftermath of the devastation even more had been lost as soldiers and refugees went on a rampage vandalizing and looting damaged and abandoned property. Maintaining order amid the rubble of war was a challenge for British authorities.[2]

On the evening of May 5 Clinton hosted a dinner for his newly arrived guests.[3] Despite the usual boastful toasts, conversation was subdued. Neither the new nor the departing commanders were in a festive mood. From Carleton Clinton wanted news of home, particularly about the Shelburne ministry and the prospects for peace. He may also have wanted to pry from his guests any hints of slander that might have been circulating about him in court circles, in order to prepare himself for attacks upon his character and conduct.

Carleton, on the other hand, probed his dinner companion about the situation in the American colonies. Nothing he heard from the distracted and distraught Clinton could have given him cause for optimism. The general told him that he had issued orders to redeploy troops from Charleston to the West Indies and had published a General Order suspending hostilities against the Americans.[4] The enemy, he was quick to add, had yet to respond. Congress, as everyone knew, was close to bankrupt, but the Continental army, despite some agitation, showed no sign of collapse. Washington was at Newburgh, and the French land forces were still in Virginia but preparing, so his spies informed him, to march to Boston to embark for the West Indies. To the north, the British commander Frederick Haldimand reported that thus far he had had little success stirring up the Vermonters to join the king's forces, and he continued to fear the Americans might attack from the south, going up Lake Champlain.[5]

Five days later, a second gathering of notables assembled at Roubelet's Tavern on Cortland Street.[6] They had come to bid farewell to General Clinton. One distinguished royal official, however, was conspicuously absent: the chief justice of the province, William Smith. Relations between the justice and the general were cool, having eroded over "the torpor that had clung to Sir Henry."[7] The general had increasingly distanced himself from the loyalists and seemed to think of little but going home to defend his reputation. Despite his disappointment, Smith did see the pathos in the scene. He noted in his diary that Clinton had long served in America. He had arrived at Boston in May 1775 with Generals Howe and Burgoyne and later watched both those unfortunate commanders return home in defeat and shame. Now it was Clinton's turn. "I pity him in his disgrace," wrote Smith.[8]

Pleased to see Clinton depart, Smith welcomed Carleton. Politically, the chief justice was a moderate. In the tumultuous years leading up to the Revolution he had been a friend to the Whigs and spoken in opposition to the unpopular acts of Parliament. He preached against parliamentary taxation of the colonies. John Adams celebrated Smith's outspoken opposition to the Stamp Act. When rhetoric turned to violent protest and then to revolution, Smith, like many Americans, could not abjure his loyalty to the king. Initially, however, he sought refuge in silence, remaining behind doors at his country estate outside the city while hoping that the tumult would pass him by. For more than two years, 1776–78, Smith kept to his retirement and looked to his friends, including his former law clerk George Clinton, now governor of New York, for protection. Unfortunately for Smith, as tempers rose, not even his past popularity and continuing friendships could shield him from suspicion. In July 1778 the New York commissioners for conspiracies, suspecting his Tory sympathies, summoned him to appear before them. He needed no further warning. Understanding his predicament, Smith declared for the Crown and asked permission to move to New York City.[9] Thanks to the influence of friends, with unwonted grace the rebel authorities allowed him to leave unmolested, even permitting him to take along "his household furniture, his library, at least one of his servants, and several horses."[10] General Clinton welcomed Smith into the British camp. He soon became a leading spokesperson for loyalist interests and in 1780 was appointed chief justice of the province, a position of great prominence, but of little actual importance since the city was under military rule and civilian courts were suspended.[11]

Smith quickly got Carleton's ear. Before the war the chief justice had advocated for colonial union with a lord lieutenant at the head, on the model of English rule in Ireland. Under such a structure Smith hoped Americans might exercise some autonomy but still remain tucked under the wings of king and Parliament. Smith was desperate to prevent the creation of an independent American republic which would threaten loyalist lives and property. To thwart the rebels, he had gone so far as to suggest to Germain in March 1781 the partitioning of America with France and Spain. European despotism was preferable to rule by American rascals.[12] Smith pressed his views with the new commander, even hinting that Sir Guy might make a fitting lord lieutenant.[13]

General Robertson proffered his own advice. Like Smith and the loyalists, he believed that some sort of victory was still possible. He was confident that the British forces could continue to hold Charleston and that the troops in New York would "defeat any [force] Washington [could] collect." Robertson's most pressing concern, however, was not the strength of the enemy but the condition of his own troops. He had earlier warned that "an army confined to a defensive in posts is not only useless but ruinous, an army without the hope of getting back America should not stay in it."[14]

Carleton listened but held his opinions close. Smith's flattering comments and Robertson's faith in the army notwithstanding, Carleton had come to America on behalf of the king not to wage war but to negotiate peace. To win back the "minds and affections of His Majesty's American subjects," Shelburne instructed Carleton "to provide for withdrawing the garrison, artillery, provisions, stores of all kinds . . . from New York . . . Charleston and Savannah." The king, Shelburne informed Carleton, was convinced that "such open and generous conduct [will] captivate their hearts and remove every suspicion of insincerity." Before Carleton sailed for America Shelburne had in person assured the general that this was his prime mission. Carleton understood that the minister had tasked him as his chief negotiator to end the war in America. He would reunite the empire.[15]

Once in New York, Carleton wasted no time reaching out to his enemy. Two days after his arrival he sent a conciliatory message to Washington announcing his arrival and his mission of peace. He assured Washington that the "Government and People of England" have a "pacific disposition" toward America, and he hoped that such feelings were reciprocal. In a slight shift of tone Carleton also assured Washington, "If War must prevail I shall endeavour to render its Miseries as light to the People of this Continent as the circumstances of such a condition will probably permit." Striking next on an oblique angle, Carleton alluded to the fact that there might be some unnamed people on his side who had escaped from "effectual controul which have begot Acts of Retaliation." They must stand together, he suggested to Washington, "to Preserve the name of Englishmen from Reproach." He never mentioned Asgill or Lippincott by name. Carleton concluded by asking Washington to grant permission to Morgann to pass through the lines in order to carry important dispatches to Congress.[16]

Carleton's four-hundred-word letter, replete with beguiling adjectives, prompted a much shorter and far less fawning response from Washington. In regard "to a late Transaction, to which I presume your Excellency alludes" (that is, Lippincott and Huddy), "I have already expressed my Resolution . . . from which I shall not recede." The fact that after seven years of war Sir Guy could embrace Washington as a fellow "Englishman" and suggest that he ought to help redeem the reputation of Englishmen was insulting. Washington no longer considered himself a "Briton." The American commander in chief shot back that it was the enemy's conduct that "stained the reputation of Britons," a comment undoubtedly connected to the Huddy execution.[17] Washington concluded on a sharp note. He would not grant a pass to Morgann. Whether such an emissary should be received at all, he noted curtly, was a matter for Congress to decide. Convinced that Sir Guy offered nothing that previous failed peace commissioners had not laid on the table, Washington suspected that the ministry had dispatched Carleton and Digby as a delaying tactic. Washington's terse reply was followed a few days later by a second notice informing Carleton that Congress had directed him "to refuse the request of Sir Guy Carleton, of a passport for the passage of Mr. Morgan [*sic*] to Philadelphia."[18]

Time was not on Carleton's side. He knew that antiwar sentiment was on the rise in Parliament, and that while a majority of members, and most certainly the king, were thus far unwilling to swap independence for peace, their strength was ebbing. The king had given him wide discretion to deal with the Americans, expecting quick progress. As he had just learned from Washington and the Congress, however, the Americans were not receptive to his soft words.[19] Quickly, he had to find ways to open communication. For the moment the most serious obstacle standing in his way was the ongoing matter of Richard Lippincott. Until he stepped off the boat at the Battery, Carleton had no knowledge of the nasty affair. Washington's cold response to him and Congress's rejection of an emissary, however, left no doubt that this was a festering wound and a jagged obstacle to any communication with the American commander in chief or the Congress.

Huddy's hanging appalled Carleton. Such conduct ran counter to his notions of the proper conduct of war, and while both sides shouldered shame for this "common Dishonor," he was consoled by the fact that neither he nor Washington had condoned such vicious violence.[20] Partisan irregulars, operating on the fringes of command, bore the guilt and infamy for these acts. Chief among them on the British side were the Associated Loyalists led by William Franklin.

Carleton, like Clinton, found Franklin and his company a tiresome burden. While Carleton sympathized with their loss of property and status, their rising crescendo of complaints and demands, inversely related to the fortunes of British arms, was nettlesome. Clinton passed on his sour opinions to Carleton and undoubtedly warned the new commander about the difficulty of keeping his loyalist charges in check.

Shortly after being briefed on the Lippincott affair, Carleton summoned Franklin and Chief Justice Smith to headquarters. He viewed Franklin as a rogue who had defied authority and gone beyond the bounds of decency. Franklin, disillusioned, disheartened, and feeling abandoned by his country, viewed Carleton as just another careerist general who, like all the others—Gage, Howe, Burgoyne, and Cornwallis—would spend time in America, fail in his mission, and then return home to excuse his conduct and win promotion. Franklin described his first conversation with Carleton as "unpleasant." It never got any better.[21] Carleton and Franklin held a hearty dislike for each other.

Carleton tried to distance himself from Franklin, Lippincott, and the "obnoxious" loyalists. According to his secretary, these men committed "evils" in the name of an "improper institution." They valued "plunder over pay."[22] Carleton's first move was to suspend the military court proceedings against Lippincott ordered by Clinton. He then toyed with the idea of simply surrendering Lippincott to the Americans. He quickly drew back from that edge and moved on to explore with Smith the possibility of placing Lippincott in the dock of a civilian court. That, he learned, might not be easy.

Since the British occupation of New York in 1776 the city, and those parts of the province under British control, had been locked down under military authority. Although there had been some pressure to restore at least a semblance of civil government, if for no other purpose than to demonstrate the Crown's commitment to elected authority, nothing had come of it.[23] Civil government could only be reestablished when the commander in chief, acting as peace commissioner, declared the province at peace. Until almost the day of his departure Clinton stood opposed, asserting that the reestablishment of civilian government was window dressing, and its only outcome would be to interfere with his duties as commander in chief.[24]

Window dressing or not, Carleton was favorably inclined toward restoring civil authority. Restoration, he believed, would placate the loyalists and at the same time be a gesture toward the Americans, testifying to his aim at reconciliation. It would also open a door through which he might send Lippincott to a civilian court. The general was quickly disappointed. Smith advised that if Carleton wished to form a civilian government, he must first call for an assembly. Carleton was perplexed and told Smith that calling elections for a provincial assembly, which would represent only a tiny portion of the province, "would make them all look ridiculous."[25] Smith further agitated the general when he informed him that even if civilian courts were convened, they would have no jurisdiction over the Lippincott case since the crime took place in New Jersey.

Carleton lost patience with Smith, Franklin, and the Associated Loyalists. With no recourse left to him, and with some suspecting that the general was moving from plan to plan trying to "get rid of Lippincott's affair by Procrastination," he ordered the court-martial to reconvene.[26] He also made up his mind to be rid of the Board of Associated Loyalists. Within a few weeks he suspended the board, a move that neatly coincided with

Franklin's departure for England. Carleton was pleased. He had rid himself of an obnoxious institution and, as Franklin's biographer describes his subject, "a mongering extremist."[27]

On Monday morning June 17 General Robertson, sitting as president, opened the court. He was joined by fourteen other officers, seven of them from loyalist units. Stephen Payne, deputy judge advocate, acted as prosecutor. Lippincott spoke in his own defense. The charge was murder. The central issues were whether Lippincott had acted under orders, and if so, whether those orders were given properly.[28]

Lippincott opened his defense by asking that the proceedings be stopped since as a civilian the military court had no jurisdiction over him. Robertson rejected the request.[29] For the next three days the court heard testimony. The prosecution summoned more than a dozen witnesses, including several loyalist refugees. No one present at the hanging disputed the fact that Lippincott was present and in charge. Beyond that, however, the evidence was murky. Lippincott had not actually kicked the barrel out from under Huddy. That was left to a "Negro" loyalist. The prosecutor asked whether at the time of execution Lippincott had produced any authority for the act. No, said a witness, but "Captain Lippincott and another person had a paper between them; but that paper was not publicly read."[30] Lippincott never produced the "paper." All agreed the board had given Huddy to Lippincott, and that Governor Franklin approved the action. Whether Franklin and the others realized what Lippincott intended was not provable. For his part, Lippincott argued that they knew and approved of the execution.

For two days the court deliberated in private. On Saturday morning they delivered their verdict.

> The court having considered the evidence for and against the prisoner, Capt. Richard Lippincott, together with what he had to offer in his defence; and it appearing that (although Joshua Huddy was executed without proper authority) what the prisoner did in the matter was not the effect of malice or ill-will, but proceeded from a conviction that it was his duty to obey the orders of the board of directors of associated loyalists, and his not doubting their having full authority to give such orders, the court are of opinion that he,

the prisoner, Captain Richard Lippincott, is not guilty of the murder laid to his charge, and do therefore acquit him.[31]

To Washington's annoyance, it took Carleton more than two weeks to send him notice of the verdict, by which time the American commander already knew the results of the trial. Adding to the irritation, Carleton failed to send the trial minutes, explaining that they were "long." He promised that he would "order them to be copied" and send them as soon as possible.[32] Carleton's letter arrived at Newburgh just as Washington was preparing to depart for an official visit to Philadelphia. Irritated at Carleton for not sending the minutes, since he knew Congress would certainly query him on the status of the trial, he left orders with Heath that should the minutes arrive, he was to send them immediately.

Washington distrusted Carleton. On the surface, according to the American commander, the general was trying to "lull our people into a state of security," but in reality he continued to "seize all our vessels" and suffocate "our Seamen . . . in Prison ships." While to the north, General Haldimand under Carleton's direction "(with his Savage Allies) [was] scalping and burning the frontiers."[33]

Washington's ire toward Carleton rose even higher when he returned to Newburgh on July 27 to find a letter from the British commander announcing that after five weeks of delay, the minutes and other documents were ready to be delivered. Ever conscious of his own position and the dignity of the American army, Washington found Carleton's letter insulting. The British commander requested a "passport" for Chief Justice William Smith and "his Servant or Servants to attend your Excellency with the Minutes of the Court Martial." Carleton explained that he was sending Smith, a civilian, "to offer such further explanations," which, he had no doubt, would give Washington "the fullest Satisfaction."[34]

That Carleton was sending Smith, a civilian bureaucrat (and a prominent loyalist), was an affront to Washington. In reply he told Carleton, "The Assurance which your Excellency has given me of the fullest satisfaction in this Matter is as pleasing as it is interesting." He minced no words. The Huddy matter was "Murder," which he implied needed little explanation. As for who would deliver the court-martial documents, he informed Carleton that he was dispatching "Major General Heath, second in Command, with two Aides-De-Camp" to meet "an Officer of equal Rank at your Excellency's Appointment."[35] He made no mention of Smith. He then ordered Heath to the rendezvous with explicit instructions to receive the documents and "explanation *in Writing*." Should Heath "find that the design of Sir Guy Carleton," was "to procrastinate this business, to envelop it in as much intricacy and difficulty as possible . . . , thereby attempting to avert our purposes of Retaliation," the major general was to "assure him . . . , if not explicitly, at least by strong inclination," that he would miss "his Aim." It was, wrote Washington, entirely in Carleton's hands to determine "whether the guilty person, or an innocent Officer, shall be made the subject of Retaliation."[36]

Carleton sniped back to Washington that if he would not permit Justice Smith to pass through the lines, there was no need to give "an Officer of so high Rank as General Heath the trouble of receiving and conveying a mere Packet of Papers." Nor could Carleton "see any motive whatever [to] require it." He added, "Unless I hear further on the subject of the passports I shall send these papers in the ordinary conveyances," meaning that they would not leave his headquarters for several days.[37] Washington would simply have to wait for the mail. The commander in chief ordered Heath to remain in camp.[38]

Normally, important messages moved between New York City and Newburgh in a day or two. It took two weeks for Carleton's package to travel the distance. The cover letter expressed Carleton's regret at the hanging of Huddy, which he described as "an act of great barbarity." Although Lippincott had been acquitted, the British commander promised "to make further inquisition and to collect evidence for the prosecution of such other persons as may appear to have been criminal in this transaction." Carleton had behaved properly in every way. Although Lippincott was a rogue and a scoundrel, there was enough evidence to suggest that he had acted on authority which he at least considered legitimate. A military court composed of "men of rank and character" had found him innocent. There must be an end to this senseless round of retaliation which "lead to evils and misfortunes of the blackest and most pernicious sort." The matter, Carleton wrote to Washington, is now in "your own hands."[39]

No soldier ever wished to be admired and respected as a proper officer more than George Washington. From the moment he took rank as a young officer in the Virginia militia through the years of the Revolution, he was deeply aware of the importance of proper military conduct. Captain Charles Asgill had committed no crime, nor had he been charged or tried in any court. He was an innocent man. His death could only be for the sake of vengeance, and as Washington wrote to Congress on August 19, it would be an improper act that an "impartial and unprejudiced World" would judge as "unfavorable and perhaps unjustifiable."[40]

It had always been Washington's practice as commander in chief to keep Congress fully informed of his conduct, at the same time carefully carving out and preserving his own authority as a military commander. Thus far with Lippincott he had followed this policy. Congress knew and approved what he was doing, but he took full charge. As an officer in the field, Washington was accustomed to managing an army and dispensing orders. For seven years, with a few exceptions, he had been able to keep Congress at bay and away from meddling with the army. The arrangement was reciprocal—he left politics to the Congress. This messy business spilled over into both worlds. It was a military/political problem wrapped in moral ambiguity. Admitting that the matter was above his grade, Washington wrote to the president of Congress asking for that body's determination as the issue was "a great national concern, upon which an individual ought not to decide."[41] Carleton had put Asgill's fate into Washington's hands, so now he passed it to Congress. Washington's letter, along with the packet from Carleton, arrived in Philadelphia on August 25 and was assigned to a committee of five, and there it sat in silence. Others, however, were not silent, particularly Captain Asgill's mother, Lady Theresa.

With the young captain's father, Sir Charles Asgill, sidelined by "an apoplectic fit," Lady Asgill took up her son's cause.[42] She left no stone unturned, and with her family connections she waged a vigorous letter-writing campaign, including correspondence with the French foreign minister, the Comte de Vergennes. "My son (an only son) and dear as he is brave, amiable as deserving to be so, only nineteen, a prisoner under Articles of Capitulation of York-Town, is now confined in America an object of retaliation!"[43] She pleaded with Vergennes to intercede. "I will

pray that Heaven may grant you may never want the comfort it is in
your power to bestow on [my son]."[44] She also played her own English
connections and wrote to Lord Cornwallis, asking that he intercede.[45]

Lady Asgill's aristocrat-to-aristocrat line of communication worked.
Vergennes shared her plea with the king and queen and then wrote to
Washington not as a "minister of the king" but as a "tender father" urging "clemency."[46] Passing the buck again, Washington forwarded the
two letters—Lady Asgill to Vergennes and Vergennes to him—to Congress "without any observation." Not everyone in Congress was inclined to clemency, but the letters did have an impact. They were, in the
words of Elias Boudinot, "enough to move the Heart of a Savage."[47] By
a unanimous vote Congress freed Captain Charles Asgill "as a Compliment to the King of France."[48] Washington conveyed the news to Asgill
while doing what he could to preserve his own honor in the sad business. He assured Asgill:

> In whatever light my agency in this unpleasing affair may be viewed,
> I was never influenced thro the whole of it by sanguinary motives;
> but by what I conceived a sense of my duty, which loudly called
> upon me to take measures however disagreeable, to prevent a rep-
> etition of those enormities which have been the subject of discus-
> sion. And that this important end is likely to be answered without
> the effusion of the Blood of an innocent person is not a greater relief
> to you than it is to [me].[49]

Guy Carleton's hopes of being the agent of America's reconciliation
with Great Britain were fading fast. The ugly business of Huddy and
Lippincott fashioned a world of such bitter and deep-seated animosity
between loyalists and rebels that reconciliation between the two seemed
impossible. Washington himself had shown little inclination to accommodation. Carleton admitted to Shelburne in June that he had "not found
the least disposition in the rulers of the provinces to come into pacific
measures."[50]

In his official correspondence to Shelburne, Carleton was discreet
and restrained. His secretary, Maurice Morgann, whose long friendship

with the minister put him in a special relationship with the earl, was far less circumspect. He echoed Carleton's pessimism but in a more colorful manner. The loyalists, he reported, were deeply divided among themselves and prone to exaggerate their strength. Some, Morgann wrote, were "privately negotiating" their own deals with the enemy. Morale in the British army was low, and the officers were without "hope."[51] As for the rebels, Morgann observed, "The Fancy of Independence has indeed struck so Deep into the Minds of the Americans that they must be suffered to run their course, for by arms alone I am sufficiently persuaded they cannot be subdued."[52] But there was hope, for he predicted the "Fancy of Independence" would lead the thirteen provinces to a bad end. The "federal union" of thirteen provinces, based foolishly on "verbal maxims of general liberty and brotherly love," would collapse in "despotism and mutual rage."[53] An accomplished man of letters, Morgann could not resist conjuring up examples from English history to prove his point and offer comfort to Shelburne in what otherwise might seem a hopeless enterprise.

The secretary spoke of Washington's "domination." The American commander, according to Morgann, had "lately reformed his officers and new modeled the Army, with a view of retaining only those officers as seem best disposed to coalesce with the French."[54] Washington was Cromwell. History was repeating itself. A revolution overthrows a monarchy, devolves into republican chaos, and from the ashes rises a despot. "This was," Morgann wrote Shelburne, "the case in England at the period above referred to [that is, the Commonwealth period]. The republicans *tried all things* [underlined in original] before they returned to that which was right."[55] Morgann was convinced that while American independence was inevitable, it was not permanent. Once their "republican experiment failed," as he was convinced it would, they would seek "reunion." Unfortunately, the secretary could not provide a timeline, but for the moment he urged the minister to do all that he could to woo the Americans away from their French allies with soft words and proffers of friendship.

If Morgann was right about the inevitability of independence, Carleton's hope of teasing the provinces back into the empire was lost. Whether the secretary shared his views with the commander in chief is uncertain; nonetheless, from all that he saw about him, Carleton could not have held much confidence that he could prevail with his plan of reconciliation.

Shortly after Shelburne took office in March 1782, Benjamin Franklin wrote a congenial letter to the minister expressing hope that his ascension to power might produce the following result: "a general Peace, which I am persuaded your Lordship, with all good men, desires, which I wish to see before I die [and] to which I shall with infinite Pleasure contribute every thing in my Power."[56] Shelburne took advantage of this friendly gesture and dispatched the affable and wise Richard Oswald to meet with Franklin. At seventy-nine, Oswald had been around long enough to remember fondly the halcyon days of peace in the empire and a prosperous American trade. He had been a contractor in America during the French and Indian War and remained in the colonies for some years after managing to acquire a considerable fortune and a circle of international acquaintances, including Franklin, Adam Smith, the Comte de Vergennes, and Shelburne. Known to Shelburne as a man sympathetic to the Americans, Oswald would, the minister believed, enjoy easy access to his old friend Franklin. He also hoped that Oswald might pry the Americans away from their French allies.[57]

Franklin had been in Paris since December 1776. His initial charge was to negotiate assistance from the French and a treaty of alliance, both of which he managed to accomplish. In June 1781 Congress appointed him one of the commissioners to negotiate a peace, to be joined by John Jay, Henry Laurens, Thomas Jefferson, and John Adams. At the time of the appointment French influence in Congress, orchestrated by the French minister Luzerne, was riding high, and so Congress instructed the commissioners to act only with the "knowledge and concurrence" of their French allies.[58]

At the moment Oswald arrived, Franklin was the only commissioner in Paris. Jefferson never left America. Laurens was captured at sea by the British and imprisoned in the Tower of London. Jay was at his post in Madrid, and Adams was busily engaged at The Hague negotiating a loan from the Dutch.[59]

It took but a few moments for the two septuagenarians to rekindle their old acquaintance. They reminisced over the world they had known before the war. Oswald assured Franklin that Britain desired peace. So too did the Americans, Franklin replied, but only with independence and a general peace that included their French allies. Nothing was settled or agreed, but talks, albeit informal and secret, had begun.[60]

Oswald's stay in Paris was brief. He hurried back to London and reported to Shelburne his encouraging conversation with Franklin. Still, the question of independence and British suspicion of France remained to trouble the ministry. Oswald shuttled back across the Channel to Paris, returning to London two weeks later with the same message: American independence had to be recognized. However, according to Oswald, Franklin had added in private that if the British "allowed the independence of America the treaty she had made with France for gaining it ended."[61] Here was the opening Shelburne had hoped for, the chance to split America from France. He told Oswald, in words he would repeat to Carleton in a letter on June 5, that in these circumstances "His Majesty has been induced to give a striking proof of his royal magnanimity and disinterested wish for the restoration of peace by commanding his ministers to direct that *the independency of America should be proposed by him in the first instance instead of making it a condition of a general treaty.*"[62] Shelburne had crossed the Rubicon and carried a reluctant king with him.

Carleton received the June 5 letter sometime during the last week of July. As usual, the general was cautious and circumspect, but there can be little doubt that he felt betrayed by the politicians in London. He had come to America not, as he said, "to be employ'd as a mere Inspector of embarkations" but to negotiate reconciliation with the provinces.[63] His work, he had believed, was central to the preservation of the empire. Shelburne's letter threw him to the margin.

For a day or two Carleton held the news from London, sharing it only with Digby, Morgann, and a few staff. Aside from his own disappointment and embarrassment, Carleton was deeply concerned about the loyalists. Despite all the angst and irritation that they had caused him, he knew how much they had lost and sacrificed. Now it appeared that it had been for nothing. He knew, better than his superiors in London, that these "Good Americans" who had sought the protection of British arms would find no peace or security in an independent America. As the hanging of Joshua Huddy had shown, the ravages of war had left deep wounds that could not be healed easily. Whatever might be decided in Paris or London, on the local level retaliation trumped reconciliation.

Carleton invited William Smith to dine with him on the evening of August 1. Before dinner the general took the justice aside. Smith later recorded in his diary that Sir Guy seemed unusually pensive. "Great trusts," he remarked to the justice, "were honourable but difficult." Smith was unclear whether he was referring to the trust he had placed in Shelburne or the trust that Smith and other loyalists had given to the king or whether both had been compromised. The elliptical conversation took another twist when Smith, in response to Carleton's comment about trust, told the general that "the Path to Glory had always difficulties." Carleton nodded. Those words had special meaning for him.[64] They reminded him of a day nearly twenty-five years before when he had stood in battle with his friend James Wolfe, one of England's greatest heroes.

Wolfe hagiography knew few bounds. Artists, poets, and writers portrayed the fallen general not only as a courageous soldier but in good eighteenth-century fashion as a man of letters as well. Wolfe shared a love of literature, particularly the poetry of Thomas Gray, then one of England's most revered and popular poets. According to the rising story, Wolfe's favorite poem was Grays's "Elegy Written in a Country Churchyard." On the evening before the battle Wolfe read Gray's poem to his officers. He paused over the lines:

> The boast of heraldry, the pomp of power,
> And all that beauty, all that wealth e'er gave,
> Awaits like the' inevitable hour:
> The paths of glory lead but to the grave.

After reading those lines Wolfe reportedly looked up and whispered, "I would rather be the author of that poem than take Quebec."[65] Carleton knew this moment.

Justice Smith was aware of the legends surrounding Wolfe's death and of Carleton's relationship with the general. Smith had chosen his words carefully, reminding the general that his hero Wolfe had been a brave soldier who went to a desperate undertaking with a brave heart and a clear mind. Carleton understood, but confessed to Smith, "[My task] may exceed my abilities and require assistance." To that, the justice replied, "Great men always wanted Instruments for the Greatest could not be great in executing every Thing themselves."[66] On that note the two joined the dinner party during which the general uttered "scarcely a syllable."[67] The next day Carleton summoned the loyalist leaders to headquarters, where Morgann announced the news to them. There was, according to an eye witness, Royal Marine captain William Feilding, "melancholy in the Face of every Spectator, and the whole dispersed very much displeased."[68]

Whatever the machinations in London and Paris, about which the loyalists knew virtually nothing, what Smith and his fellow refugees understood clearly from Morgann's announcement was that American independence was inevitable. They were overwhelmed. For more than seven years they had heard pledges of support from their king, and now he had abandoned them. Washington's spies reported that the loyalists were in "fits of despair—they [were] rendering their facings from their uniforms, plucking out their cockades and uttering execrations."[69] What faith could they place in any facile promise of compensation?

Carleton was less surprised at the government's apparent capitulation, but he was disappointed at the pusillanimity of his political superiors. His "path of glory" had come to a dead end. Two weeks after announcing the news from London, Carleton, no longer believing that he could render "any considerable service," asked to be relieved of his command.[70]

The news deepened the rift between Carleton and the loyalists. As the relationship cooled, the general became prickly. When a delegation of loyalist refugees, desperate for food, petitioned the general for eight thousand rations, he reportedly denied their request, telling them that if they wanted rations, they should ship themselves "in the Fleet or enter into the Army."[71]

Little did the general know that even as he wrote for permission to come home, the ministry was in upheaval. On July 1, after only fourteen weeks in office, Rockingham died. Shelburne took the reins, while Fox resigned. Finally at the helm, Shelburne held a steady course toward independence and peace. At this critical moment, changing commanders in America would only roil the waters. On Shelburne's orders Thomas Townshend, the new minister in charge of colonial affairs, informed Carleton, "His Majesty thinks proper for the present to defer accepting your resignation."[72]

WITH THREE THOUSAND MILES of ocean and weeks of travel separating him from the ministry in London, Carleton often felt neglected by his superiors. Ironically, although Washington was barely 150 miles away, and only a few days' travel from Congress, he too felt deprived of information and overlooked by politicians in Philadelphia. From Hasbrouck House Washington pleaded to Secretary at War Benjamin Lincoln to send him news: "You are the Fountain of Intelligence." Unfortunately, the flow from Lincoln's fountain was a trickle. Despite his elevated title, the amiable Lincoln was, as Congress intended, not much more than a clerk. Lincoln himself acknowledged his status. When he sat for an official portrait as secretary, he requested the artist Charles Willson Peale paint him in the uniform of major general rather than a civilian bureaucrat. In every way but title Washington was both commander in chief and secretary at war. William Clagdon, a close associate of General Horatio Gates (neither man a friend to Washington), remarked, "In some countries the Secretary at War commands the Commander in Chief, in this infant republic the Commander in Chief commands the Secretary at War."[1]

As if living in the shadow of Washington was not enough, Lincoln also had to contend with the energetic and savvy superintendent of finance, Robert Morris, whose authority over money—what little could be found—was nearly absolute. Lincoln struggled mightily to assert himself in this competitive and tangled bureaucratic web. When Washington left for Newburgh Lincoln hoped to assume a portion of the commander in chief's mantle, giving him greater influence at the Monday night gatherings and in Congress. But Morris beat him to it and rushed to fill the political gap left by the commander in chief's absence.[2] In Washington's presence Morris had always been careful to frame his opinions in ways designed to avoid unpleasant confrontations with the revered leader. Once the general departed, however, and as the financial situation of the Congress imploded, the superintendent was far more forthcoming in his views. When asked by the hectoring quartermaster general, Timothy Pickering, to approve additional army supply contracts, Morris refused, telling him "it is better that the Campaign should stop than that I should Authorize engagements which cannot afterwards be fulfilled."[3] When Pickering reported Morris's comment to Washington, the commander in chief cautioned the financier that while he understood "the Necessity of economizing the public Monies," he feared that in the case of the army Congress would "spin the thread of oeconomy till it breaks."[4] The army had already borne more than its proper share of congressional parsimony, and Washington urged that it not to be called upon to suffer more misery.

Washington had heard the Cassandras wail before. The toll of nearly eight years of war bore heavily on him. He had been home only twice in that time. He was a commander who had lost more battles than he had won; witnessed thousands of soldiers die; endured long weary marches; suffered through brutal winter encampments, all the while laboring under the direction of a weak and nattering Congress struggling to finance a war, gain international recognition, and hold a teetering thirteen-state coalition together. Worried, but not discouraged, at least in his public persona, Washington pressed ahead. He did not trust the British with their "delusive offers of Peace." He warned that the enemy was trying to lull America into a "stupor." In his view the ministry was toying with Congress and using the post-Yorktown interlude to regroup and consolidate its forces.[5] News from the Caribbean of Admiral Sir George

Rodney's crushing victory over the French at the Battle of the Saintes reinforced the fear that the British might try a comeback.

For the British, the entry of France into the Revolution in 1778, followed by Spain in 1779, turned their colonial rebellion into a world war against old imperial adversaries.[6] Once in the fray, France seized the opportunity to descend on the rich sugar islands in the British West Indies. Jamaica was the juiciest plum of all. In pursuit of this prize on the morning of April 8, 1782, Admiral de Grasse, having returned to the islands after Yorktown, departed his base at Martinique with a battle squadron of thirty-five ships of the line convoying a large fleet of transports for an assault on Jamaica. De Grasse planned to rendezvous off Hispaniola with a Spanish fleet bringing additional ships and soldiers. Anticipating the French movement, the British commander, Admiral Rodney, positioned his fleet at nearby St. Lucia ready to intercept. When warned by his scouting frigates that de Grasse was on the move, Rodney got under way with thirty-six ships of the line. That evening the two fleets came within sight of each other in a narrow passage known as the Saintes between Guadeloupe and Dominica. At dawn on the ninth, the battle commenced. It was a running fight that lasted nearly four days and resulted in a decisive victory for Rodney, including the capture of Admiral de Grasse. Although he was criticized for not pursuing the scattered French fleet, Rodney's triumph gave the Royal Navy unchallenged superiority in the West Indies.[7]

Rodney's victory, reported to him in early May, worried Washington on several fronts. He was still harboring hope of an attack on New York City. Such a move depended upon naval support, which only the French could provide. The news from the islands sank any expectation of that happening. Second, with the Royal Navy now in control of the West Indies and Jamaica secured, Washington feared that the enemy might feel sufficiently confident to redeploy forces to North America. He distrusted Shelburne, writing his friend James McHenry that "no Man has ever heard him" agree to independence, while to George Clinton, governor of New York, he confided that the British "want to amuse us in America, whilst they attend to other parts of their Empire; which being secured, they will have time and means to revert to this Continent again, with hopes of Success."[8] Washington was concerned that the British would use Rodney's triumph as propaganda to play "an insidious game" to discredit the French and undermine American resolve. Only "vigorous preparations" to meet them would "make them think of peace."[9]

Should the enemy "revert to this Continent," Washington had no doubt that New York City would be their first stop. From that secure post they might strike almost anywhere they pleased. The American commander's first consideration was always to confine the enemy to the city. Even as he focused on New York, however, rumblings from Vermont caught his attention.

Tucked between New York and New Hampshire, Vermont (also known as the New Hampshire Grants) was tempting fare for both states, which for decades had been quarreling over ownership. In the mid-eighteenth century New Hampshire's royal governor, Benning Wentworth, pushed the claims of his colony far beyond the natural border of the Connecticut River, across the Green Mountains to the fertile valleys abutting Lake Champlain.[10] His nephew and successor as governor, John Wentworth, continued his uncle's policies, causing even more consternation in New York, where the colony's government roundly denounced New Hampshire's claims and moved to assert its own control over the disputed lands. Both Wentworths ignored New York's objection and went ahead offering hundreds of land grants and creating 128 New Hampshire townships. Land titles were a tangled mess while political authority over the disputed land was left in hot contention.

The collapse of royal authority in 1775 opened the door for disgruntled Vermonters to claim an independent status free from the Crown, New York, and New Hampshire. Among the leaders of the "separatists" was Ethan Allen, who led a vigilante band calling themselves the Green Mountain Boys, a group of "stout fellows" who carried "a firelock with ball or buckshot answerable, and a good tomahawk."[11] When he first met Ethan Allen Washington thought him "too ambitious."[12] Later, after the rambunctious Allen had led an ill-fated attack on Canada, and had been taken prisoner, Washington complimented him for "his fortitude and firmness."[13] While Allen was a prisoner Vermont declared independence and wrote a constitution (the first in North America to abolish slavery) and elected Thomas Chittenden its chief magistrate.[14] Over the vocal protests of New York and New Hampshire, the new republic quickly petitioned

Congress for admission as a state. But the delegates from New York and New Hampshire roared their objections to admitting Vermont into the confederation. Congress danced about the issue, and by the time Washington retired to Newburgh in the spring of 1782 Vermont's status was still in dispute. In the meantime, Vermonters, on the lookout for a better deal, began negotiations with General Haldimand in Canada.[15] In a porous world, however, those negotiations were hardly secret. Haldimand reported to General Clinton, "[I have read] the substance of all that has passed in my negotiations with Vermont" in a Fishkill, New York, newspaper.[16] Notwithstanding his "negotiations," Haldimand placed little faith in the flirtatious Vermonters. He reinforced the Crown Point garrison on Lake Champlain to keep an eye on them.[17]

Washington had even more reason to distrust Vermonters. Not only were they playing both sides in a "political Game"; they were also harboring hundreds of deserters from the Continental army.[18] The "Grants," as he referred to the region, was "an asylum to all deserters" who had been lured there by promises of protection and land.[19] In a sober tone he wrote to Chittenden, being careful not to address him as "Governor." He warned him that by their double-dealing Vermont was fast losing "Friends," and that his correspondence with the "enemy" was a "bad tendency." In a somewhat soft but pointed tone Washington assured Chittenden that while "coercion" on the part of Congress against Vermont might be "disagreeable," he did not rule it out.[20] In private, however, he admitted that invading Vermont was highly risky if for no other reason than that the men there would be fighting with "Halters about their Necks."[21]

Chittenden and his allies got the message and stood off from the British, but they continued to press their extravagant border claims against New York. Such behavior kept Vermont out of the American republic until its admission as the fourteenth state in 1791. However, without support from Vermont Haldimand could never hope to mount an invasion, so Washington's northern flank was secure.

By late spring 1782 Washington's Hudson River encampments numbered 8,500 soldiers fit for service.[22] The bulk of the army bivouacked on the west side of the river, with outlying posts to the south at West Point and King's Ferry (Stony Point) and on the opposite bank at Verplanck's Point, where a ferry crossed the Hudson. Washington's chief challenge was maintaining discipline and morale. In this he had little help from the states, for the replacements they sent were often recruited at local taverns in the haze of booze and the promise of bounties. The commander in chief was "astonished," he told Heath, when he saw the recruits from Massachusetts, who were "so very improper for service." They were a "horrid imposition on the public." The officer who signed them up ought to be "arrested," wrote Washington.[23]

In the same week in early May when the new recruits from Massachusetts marched into camp, worse news arrived from a Connecticut regiment under the command of Colonel Heman Swift. On the morning of the fourth Swift discovered that men in his regiment were plotting a mutiny. Under the guise of gathering to play ball, the conspirators planned to rally their fellow soldiers and then march to the arsenal at nearby Fishkill, seize the cannon, and descend on the Connecticut legislature in Hartford to demand their pay. Summoning loyal troops to assist him, Swift arrested the ringleaders, Sergeants Jarold Bunce, Ambrose Gaylord, and Wyman Parker. Washington ordered the conspirators held for court-martial. On May 12 the court acquitted Bunce and Gaylord. Parker was found guilty and hanged the next day.[24]

Quick and harsh justice was a hallmark of eighteenth-century military establishments, and the Continental army was no exception. On June 30, 1775, barely two weeks after creating the army, Congress approved Articles of War, a set of rules and procedures for administering military justice. Although modeled on British regulations, under which Washington himself had served in the French and Indian War, the American version was decidedly less harsh. Indeed, in Washington's judgment the Articles of 1775 were too lenient. In the face of high rates of desertion and a blatant disregard for discipline, Washington urged Congress to revise the Articles. In September 1776 Congress enacted a new and harsher set of regulations that, among other things, raised the limit on flogging from thirty-nine lashes to one hundred.[25]

The revised Articles described both procedures and punishments. Critical distinctions were made between officers and enlisted men.

Minor offenses were dealt with on the regimental level, while more serious charges passed up to higher command. When charged with an offense, officers might be arrested but not generally confined. Enlisted men were confined. Trials themselves rarely lasted more than a single day. The most common punishment for an officer convicted of a less than capital crime was dismissal from the service. Enlisted men were more likely to be flogged, one hundred lashes not being unusual. Dr. James Thacher, a surgeon in the Sixteenth Massachusetts Regiment, and an eyewitness to many floggings, described the scene.

> In aggravated cases, and with old offenders, the culprit is sentenced to receive one hundred lashes, or more. It is always the duty of the drummers and fifers to inflict the chastisement, and the drum major must attend and see that the duty is faithfully performed. The culprit, being securely tied to a tree, or post, receives on his naked back the number of lashes assigned him, by a whip formed of several small knotted cords, which sometimes cut through the skin at every stroke. However strange it may appear, a soldier will often receive the severest stripes without uttering a groan, or once shrinking from the lash, even while the blood flows freely from his lacerated wounds. They have adopted a method they say mitigates the anguish in some measure; it is by putting between the teeth a leaden bullet, on which they chew, while under the lash, till it is made quite flat and jagged.[26]

General courts-martial, charged with hearing the most serious crimes and empowered to impose the death penalty, could only be convened "by order of the Commander in Chief, The Commanding Genl., in any of the States, or the Secretary at War in the place where Congress may reside."[27] Convening authorities also had the authority to review decisions by inferior courts-martial.[28] In the administration of military justice Washington had the same, but no more, authority as other convening authorities. He did not review decisions beyond his immediate command. In the South, for example, General Greene exercised as much authority over his troops as did Washington in the North. On a day-to-day basis line officers confronted with the pressing need to coerce their men to submission generally had little sympathy for enlisted men who defied authority. Hence, when sitting in judgment they were likely to adhere to a strict interpretation of the Articles and mete out punishment according to the letter of the law.

By far the most common crime in Washington's military world was desertion. In the Continental army it was never difficult to walk away. An expansive frontier and a population unwilling to turn in deserters made it relatively easy for soldiers to disappear. During the course of the war 20 to 25 percent of the American army took their own leave.[29] Simple desertion merited flogging and return to service. Desertion with fraudulent reenlistment—deserting one unit and enlisting in another to obtain a bounty—was also a flogging offense. Desertion to the enemy was punishable by hanging. Going over to the enemy and mutiny were considered among the most heinous crimes and were punished by death. Other lesser crimes included theft, violation of regulations, and assault, all generally subject to flogging, confinement, fine, or discharge.[30]

Washington paid close attention to the courts meeting under his authority.[31] He was a strict disciplinarian but also a realist who understood that, unlike the British and German automatons that served King George III, American soldiers were civilians only temporarily in uniform. Washington's soldiers held notions of liberty, rights, and status that often interfered with good military discipline. As commander he faced the fact that nearly one in four of his soldiers deserted every year and that in seven years of war his army had been rocked by no fewer than fifty mutinies, including the one most recently discovered by Colonel Swift.[32] Had he adhered rigidly to the Articles, the hangmen and firing squads would have enjoyed little rest. Terror had no place in Washington's repertoire of command techniques. "Soldiers cannot simply be ordered to die—they must first be persuaded." The object of discipline was to "persuade."[33]

Wednesday May 22, 1782, was a busy day at Hasbrouck House, and no one was busier than Washington's aide Colonel Jonathan Trumbull.[34] One of Trumbull's tasks, which he shared with the other aides, was to draft letters for the commander in chief's signature. Since arriving at

Newburgh Washington had dispatched an average of three to four letters each day. On May 22 the number jumped to ten. Trumbull drafted eight. Among the letters was one to the secretary of foreign affairs expressing alarm at the news of Rodney's victory and the "derangement" it was likely to cause, and another warning Governor John Mathews of South Carolina that British overtures were "Delusory."[35] Half of the letters went to subordinate officers, including Nathanael Greene and William Heath. Also sent was a General Order approving the sentence of hanging to be meted out to Shem Kentfield for deserting to the enemy.[36]

Headquarters was buzzing on May 22, but not solely because of the volume of work. One of the letters drafted by Trumbull that day was to Colonel Lewis Nicola.[37] It was among the most important letters Washington ever signed.

Colonel Lewis Nicola was a distinguished American officer. Grandson of Huguenot refugees, Nicola was born in Dublin, Ireland, in 1717. His family purchased a commission for him in the British army at the somewhat advanced age of twenty-three. After marrying, over the next twenty years Nicola served in a variety of military posts mainly in Ireland. In the mid-1760s, faced with the reality of peace, and a reduction in the army, Nicola retired from the king's service. He and his family left Ireland sometime in 1766 for Philadelphia.

Blessed with a bit of money, good health, and a modicum of education, Nicola enjoyed success as a storekeeper and then branched out to establish a fee-based circulating library. Nicola moved in literate circles. In 1768 he was admitted as a member of Philadelphia's esteemed American Philosophical Society, a learned organization founded by Benjamin Franklin in 1743.[38] He also served a brief, albeit unsuccessful, stint as a magazine publisher.

When the Revolution broke out, he was one of the few ardent Whigs with professional military experience. The Pennsylvania Council appointed him town major of Philadelphia, a post akin to provost marshal. Having relaunched his military career, Nicola, urged on by his friends, took the opportunity to write and publish a long military manual aimed specifically at instructing the newly formed militia in Philadelphia.[39] He emphasized that his work was purely practical, omitting all exercises that were "only for Show and Parade."[40]

Although he was too old for frontline service, Nicola yearned to be close to the action. In March 1777 he wrote to Congress, proposing that it create an "Invalid Corps" of men who were no longer fit for combat but who would be competent for garrison and guard duty.[41] Three months later Congress agreed and created a corps of one thousand men "to be employed in garrisons, and for guards in cities and other places, where magazines or arsenals, or hospitals are placed." Reflecting Nicola's interest in training officers, Congress, after appointing him to command the Invalid Corps, charged the corps "to serve as a military school for young gentlemen" where they might learn "geometry, arithmetic, vulgar and decimal fractions, and the extraction of roots." Officers were "obliged to contribute one day's pay per month . . . for the purpose of purchasing a regimental library."[42]

By the spring of 1782 four invalid companies had been formed. One unit was in Philadelphia, another in Boston, while the remaining two were with Nicola guarding Continental stores at the Fishkill supply depot across from West Point. Each morning as he mustered his men for roll call, Nicola faced visible and stark reminders of the true cost of the Revolution. He looked at soldiers carrying the scars of battle. He felt deeply about his men. On May 21, 1782, he wrote to Washington explaining their sad condition. "Captain Woolpaper [?] [is] entirely disqualified from age." "Captain Williams paralectic [sic], he has lost the use of one side and his speech is much impaired." "Captain Cooper has had his thigh cut [off] so high he has not been able to walk out of the barracks."[43] These men had been faithful to a republic that Nicola believed had abandoned them. Congress was deaf to their pleas for compensation, and the country at large had forgotten them. Having described their sacrifice and pitiful condition, the next day Nicola wrote again to his commander with a message that could not be ignored.

Washington's concern for the welfare of his officers, and his "favourable reception" to Nicola's previous "representation," prompted this second communication; "[they] induced me," wrote Nicola, "to trouble you with a matter I conceive of importance."[44] Historians have often misrepresented and misunderstood Nicola's message. Many, when discussing this event, have referred to the Nicola "letter." That description is misleading, for in fact two separate documents were included, the short cover letter from Nicola, 125 words, followed by a seven-page, 2,000 word, detailed "memoir." Given its length and detail, Nicola must have labored some time over the text. Nicola began his memoir by briefly rehearsing the plight of the army, consisting mainly of the litany of promises made to them by Congress and then broken. Both the Congress's and the states' "schemes of oeconomy" seemed always aimed at the army. Such behavior in war augured ill for what might happen in peace when "our services are no longer needed." Anger and frustration among officers had given rise, Nicola said, to rumors that the officers would refuse to go home after peace unless Congress settled "all grievances . . . , engagements and promises." Nicola raised the specter of "blood and confusion."

An officer given to reflection, Nicola saw the unfortunate behavior of Congress and the states as a symptom of a far deeper problem. Republics did not work. "I am not that violent admirer of a republican form of government as numbers in this country are," he wrote. Nicola's answers to the nation's woes were twofold: a constitutional monarchy on the model of Great Britain but with a king more tightly controlled by a balanced government (he referenced Montesquieu) and a land-grant system to reward veterans that would create a "distinct state" settled by former soldiers who would present a formidable barrier and "advanced guard" to protect the frontier of the nation.

Nicola rejected both an absolute monarchy and a hereditary nobility. He even admitted that he was uncomfortable with the title of king, but he saw no alternative. Having laid out his ideas, he concluded by noting to Washington that "this war must have shown to all, but to military men in particular, the weakness of republicks, and the exertions the army has been able to make by being under a proper head." The last remark was a thinly disguised compliment to Washington's leadership. Nicola never suggested openly that the commander in chief should be king, but he left little doubt that Washington fit the job description. "Republican bigots will certainly consider my opinions as heterodox, meriting fire and [fagots]," but Washington need not worry for "I have . . . kept them within my breast."[45] Washington, however, did worry.

Washington's views of the feebleness of Congress differed little from Nicola's. Had Nicola thought otherwise, he would never have exposed his radical opinions to the most powerful man in America. The colonel's letter teetered at the edge of treason and certainly was in violation of section 2, article 1 of the Articles of War: "Whatsoever officer or soldier shall presume to use traitorous or disrespectful words against the authority of the United States in Congress assembled, or the legislature of any of the United States, . . . if a commissioned officer, he shall be cashiered."

Section 2 notwithstanding, a public sanction of Nicola, a highly respected officer, was out of the question. Discontent was rife in the enlisted ranks. Washington and his officers were the bulwarks of discipline. Should that wall crack, Washington feared that there would be no force sufficient to hold back desertion and mutiny. It was imperative that he move quickly to silence, chastise, and isolate Nicola. Within hours, with his aides Humphreys and Trumbull by his side, Washington composed a stinging rebuke to the colonel, a verbal flogging.[46]

He first told Nicola that he was astonished "that such ideas [existed] in the Army" as he had expressed. He did not, however, deny that they existed, but for the moment he would keep them in his own "bosom." Washington was urgent to separate himself from Nicola's views particularly in light of what the colonel had written in his letter about Washington's "favourable reception" to Nicola's previous "representation." "I am much at a loss to conceive what part of my conduct could have given encouragement to an address which to me seems big with the greatest mischief that can befall my Country." He finished by warning Nicola, "Banish these thoughts from your Mind, and never communicate, as from yourself or any one else, a sentiment of like nature."

In the copy of the letter kept at headquarters Washington wrote at the bottom of the page, "The foregoing is an exact Copy of a Letter which we Sealed and sent off to Colonel Nicola at the request of the writer of it." The note in Washington's hand was signed by Trumbull and Humphreys. This was his reputational insurance policy. Despite Nicola's assertion that he alone was author of the letter, there was no guarantee of the truth of that. For the sake of the army, the secret would be kept. For the sake of history, a record would be kept.

Washington's fierce rebuke tossed Nicola into full retreat. Sensing his own reputation was in jeopardy, the next day he sent Washington a fawning letter of apology. The day following he sent another and four

days later a third.[47] Washington never responded. The less said, he apparently believed, the better. Nicola continued in command of his regiment with no hint of dissatisfaction from his commander. Some years
later, in 1788, when the Reverend William Gordon was writing a history of the Revolution, he asked Washington for permission to publish
his response to Nicola. Washington replied that he "had quite forgot
the private transaction." Having been reminded of the event, however,
he refused Gordon's request: "No good but some harm might result
from the publication. The letter in my judgment had better remain in
concealment."[48]

Nicola was right that the army was in a melancholy and weary state.
From West Point Henry Knox reported to the secretary at war that the
officers were "much discontented," while farther down the chain of command a twenty-seven-year-old Massachusetts Lieutenant, Benjamin Gilbert, wrote home that his men were "calling for money." He feared they
might mutiny.[49] The ennui of camp life was sucking the energy out of the
army. Soldiers live to fight, and with an enemy apparently gone to ground,
American troops encamped along the Hudson, left with little else to do,
turned their minds toward lamentation and mischief. Washington needed
a distraction. Once again his French allies came to his side.

Louis Joseph Xavier François, the second child and the first son of
Louis XVI and his wife, Marie Antoinette, was born on October 22,
1781.[50] As heir to the throne of France, young Louis was immediately
titled Dauphin. To give proper recognition to this grand event, and to
please an ally, Congress invited the French minister, the Chevalier de la
Luzerne, to attend a public audience on Monday May 13. Escorted by a
troop of light horse, the minister's coach made its way to the statehouse,
where at the foot of the stairs two members of Congress waited to lead
him into a chamber packed with more than two hundred spectators, including members of Congress, secretaries of the executive departments,
military officers, as well as the president and council of the state of Pennsylvania. In a carefully orchestrated ballet that eschewed any notion of
"republican simplicity," members stood and bowed several times.[51] After
a minute or two of silence Luzerne rose and addressed the body in French,
presenting a letter from the king which Secretary Thomson read to the

body. After several more bows and formal acknowledgments, the minister took his leave and Congress adjourned for the day. The whole ceremony did not take more than thirty minutes.[52] That evening Congress "strained every nerve of Finance to give the Ambassador a dinner," followed by a grand display of fireworks.[53]

Washington too offered to celebrate the Dauphin's birth, recognizing a chance to plan a celebration on a scale worthy of a great ally and an event grand enough to divert the attention of his men to something other than their own condition. Early in May he summoned the chief engineer at West Point, the Chevalier de Villefranche, a French officer serving in the Corps of Engineers, to headquarters.[54] The "ingenious" Villefranche laid out a plan for a breathtaking event.

Washington positioned his entire command on both banks of the river so that they formed a circle surrounding West Point. Massachusetts regiments took positions on the west side and across the river between Nelson's Point and the Middle Redoubt. Connecticut troops marched to the Highlands behind Constitution Island. Other regiments assembled on the plain behind West Point. The focus of the ceremony was a huge arbor, six hundred feet long and thirty feet wide, erected in the middle of the plain. For more than a week one thousand soldiers, including all the "Carpenters and Joiners in the Army," worked under Villefranche's supervision to build the grand structure. It was, according to Dr. Thacher, built of "simple materials which the common trees in this vicinity afford." Impressed by "this superb structure," Thacher went on with his lyrical description. The roof "consists of boughs, or branches of trees curiously interwoven, and the same materials form the walls, leaving the ends entirely open. On the inside, every pillar was encircled with muskets and bayonets, bound round in a fanciful and handsome manner, and the whole interior was decorated with evergreens, with American and French military colors, and a variety of emblems and devices." Thacher fairly swooned that the arbor "in symmetry of proportion, neatness of workmanship, and elegance of arrangement, has seldom . . . been surpassed on any temporary occasion."[55]

Villefranche had set the stage. The commander in chief instructed "all the general, brigade and staff officers of the army to assemble." He also invited "officers's ladies with and in the neighborhood of the army" and "any other ladies of [the commander in chief's] acquaintance . . . Without the formality of a particular invitation."[56] For the enlisted men, Washington ordered "an extra gill of rum per man."

At two thirty on Friday afternoon the booming sound of cannon echoed down the valley. This was the signal for the officers and others to make their way to the plain. Five hundred people gathered under Villefranche's boughs. After the crowd quieted, the band from Colonel John Crane's Third Battalion of Continental Artillery struck up a martial tune as Washington, accompanied by his wife and an entourage of dignitaries, entered "through the line formed by" the men of the battalion.[57] After the feast, "the cloth being removed, the diners drank thirteen appropriate toasts, each one announced by the discharge of thirteen cannon and accompanied by music."[58] After dinner the guests relaxed as the Continental regiments, gathered along the river, fired volleys of cannon and musket salutes. Gradually sounds of the salutes died away, and fireworks lit up the sky as the guests returned to the shelter of the arbor now illuminated "by a vast number of lights" for an evening of dancing.[59] Washington was unusually cheerful. Known for his skill and fondness for dancing, the commander in chief took to the floor "with a dignified and graceful air, having Mrs. Knox for his partner."[60]

In the days following the grand party for the Dauphin, camp life along the Hudson returned to normal, with the men continuing to grumble about the lack of pay. This time the officers of the Massachusetts Line spoke up. Like the rest, they had not been paid. They decided to meet and prepare a petition to Congress, but in deference to the commander in chief they asked for his approval. General Heath was their emissary. He asked if Washington had any objection to the officers meeting at Colonel John Lamb's headquarters to draft a petition to Congress.[61] Washington replied that he had no objection. The men were only asking for "their just dues," but he was "very sorry there should be any occasion for such proceedings."[62] Washington had little hope that Congress would act.

By the summer of 1782 Washington, like everyone else in America including Congress and Carleton, waited for news from London as to whether peace would be proclaimed. At the same time, however, Washington still harbored a distant hope that the French might yet assist him in an attack on New York City or Charleston. In a somber mood at headquarters, Washington wrote to his Virginia friend Archibald Cary, "I pang for retirement."[63]

Unable to do so, Washington decided to travel north for a visit to Albany and his posts in that vicinity. He invited his friend Governor George Clinton to join him. On the same day when the officers of the Massachusetts Line were meeting at Colonel Lamb's, June 26, he and the governor left for Albany.[64] The trip, explained Washington, was "an opportunity of blending my public duty with my private satisfaction," and served, perhaps, as a means of distancing himself from the meeting at Colonel Lamb's.

Leaving Martha behind at Newburgh to enjoy the amiable company of her friend Mrs. Knox, Washington and Clinton set out for Albany. On the evening of the twenty-seventh the "suite" arrived to a grand reception. The *Pennsylvania Gazette* reported that Albany's mayor, Abraham Ten Broeck, presented the commander in chief with the "freedom of the city in a gold box."[65] Crowds gathered, and "at 6 o'clock, P.M. the bells of all the churches began to ring, and continued their joyful peals until sun set, when thirteen cannon, one for each state, were discharged from the fort and the city illuminated."[66] That night Washington was the honored guest at a sumptuous banquet.

Among those greeting Washington was his old friend General Philip Schuyler. Now retired from the military, Schuyler had given his daughter Elizabeth in marriage to Washington's former aide Alexander Hamilton. Schuyler, who owned more land in New York State than any other person, happily became Washington's tour guide. He took him north to see the Saratoga battle site. From there Schuyler accompanied Washington and Clinton on a trip west along the Mohawk River as far as Schenectady. Five miles outside the city a troop of sixty citizens greeted the general's party. As the barge neared, cannon boomed and bells rang while "one hundred warriors of the Oneidas and Tuscarora completely armed and painted for war" met him at the town gate.[67]

When he could take a minute and escape from the admiring throngs, Washington cast his keen eye on the land about him. He saw fertile valleys through which rivers flowed and rich lands farther west. As a planter and surveyor, he did not need anybody in his party to point out to him the promise of this vast territory, nor that the Mohawk, like his beloved Potomac, was a river that led west. All that was needed was to settle this "rising empire."[68]

Washington was back in Newburgh on July 2, in time to preside over festivities celebrating the sixth anniversary of independence. He ordered all the regiments to form "on each side of the river. The signal of thirteen cannon being given at West Point, the troops displayed and formed in a line, when a general feu de joie took place throughout the whole army."[69] One week later he bid farewell to his wife, who, having spent nine months in Newburgh, was returning to Mount Vernon.

During the commander in chief's absence army morale had not improved. Soon after he returned he opened a second startling letter from a senior officer, Major General James Mitchell Varnum of Rhode Island. Varnum had retired from the army in 1779 and returned to Rhode Island, where he was elected to serve in Congress. Rhode Island's political atmosphere was decidedly anti-Congress and in favor of states' rights. The smallest state had an extensive coastline and was thus most exposed to British attack.[70] Its economy, so heavily dependent upon maritime trade, had been devastated. Given their economic situation, as well as a long tradition of political independence dating back to Roger Williams, Rhode Islanders were wary of any central authority that attempted to exert control over them, particularly in matters of raising revenue. Rhode Island's independent streak had most recently put it in direct collision with the Congress when that body had approved a national impost fee to be levied for the benefit of Congress on imports into America. Rhode Island alone refused to vote in favor of the measure, and since the Articles of Confederation required unanimous approval, the issue was dead and Congress was still broke.[71]

Varnum's service in the army and in Congress had given him a perspective decidedly at odds with his constituents. Frustrated and angry that his fellow Rhode Islanders had so hobbled Congress, he placed the blame squarely on the Articles of Confederation, that "baseless fabric." He had lost faith that the citizens of Rhode Island, or for that matter all of America, were capable of governing themselves. He shared his feelings with Washington. "Avarice, Jealousy and Luxury controul their feelings," Varnum wrote of his fellow citizens. His solution went far beyond

Nicola's constitutional monarchy. The general wanted an "absolute monarchy or a military State." Sadly, he concluded, "we are too young to govern ourselves."[72]

Washington gave Varnum's letter short shrift and less emotion than he had directed at Nicola. He waited nearly three weeks to respond and then did so in a short three-paragraph letter that dealt for the most part with unrelated matters of mundane administration. He simply told Varnum, "I cannot consent to view our situation in that distrest [sic] light in which you seem to." Washington's soft answer was the response of a weary commander in chief.[73]

In this dreary atmosphere Washington had the spark of an idea. While officers in the Continental army had much to complain about, they could at least look forward to honors and recognition. Though not on the scale of European armies, on whom medals and titles rained down in torrents, American officers could receive recognition through official letters of commendation from the commander in chief, congressional resolutions of thanks, promotions, and on very special occasions fine swords, gold medals, and perhaps a horse. Enlisted soldiers, however, aside from an occasional promotion, could expect no special rewards for service or bravery. In an effort to help raise sinking morale, Washington sought to recognize the backbone of his army: the men in the ranks. In a General Order, August 7, 1782, he set a precedent. All "non commissioned officers and soldiers of the army who have served more than three years with bravery, fidelity and good conduct" were entitled to wear a chevron of "white cloth" on their left sleeve. Those in uniform six years might wear two chevrons. The commander in chief went one step farther, and for the first time in the history of the American army, he authorized a device to be worn on the "facings over the left breast" in recognition of "any singularly meritorious action" that demonstrated "unusual gallantry" and "extraordinary fidelity." This "Badge of Merit" was "the figure of a heart in purple cloth, or silk, edged with narrow lace or binding." Names of soldiers awarded the badge were to be enrolled in the "book of merit," and when on duty this badge permitted the wearer to pass guards and sentinels without challenge, a privilege previously accorded only to officers. With this badge, Washington announced, "the road to glory in a patriot army and a free country is thus open to all."[74]

As a morale booster, the badge of merit failed. It was left to regimental and brigade commanders to nominate candidates. They were at liberty to go back to the very beginning of the war. Virtually no commander took the initiative to recognize gallantry in the ranks. In the course of the entire Revolution only three badges were awarded and then only at the end of the war. All three went to volunteers from the Eighth and Fifth Connecticut regiments. One of those soldiers, Daniel Bissell of East Windsor, was recognized for his service as Washington's spy in New York City.[75] The badge of merit disappeared after the Revolution and was not fully revived until 1932, when President Herbert Hoover ordered "the Purple Heart established by General Washington at Newburgh August 7, 1782," reinstituted "out of respect to his memory and military achievements." This same order set eligibility to those wounded or killed in the line of service.[76]

As the summer ebbed away, Washington made preparations to receive his French allies. Following Yorktown, Rochambeau and his army had remained in Virginia to spend a pleasant winter encampment near Williamsburg. It was a season of parties and balls. By spring 1782, Virginia hospitality notwithstanding, there was no reason for the French to remain, and on June 28 Rochambeau gave orders, "which took everybody by surprise," to break camp and prepare to march. On his own, without any specific orders from Paris, he had decided to march north and join Washington.[77] By combining with Washington, Rochambeau could, he believed, threaten Carleton to the point where he dare not dispatch any part of the New York garrison to reinforce the West Indies.

The 439-mile march north took the French nearly three months, three times longer than they had needed to move in the opposite direction the year before.[78] The pace was leisurely as the officers and men of the regiments bathed in the celebrations given in their honor by nearly every town through which they passed. As the French made their way slowly north, Washington consolidated his troops at Verplanck's Point to await their arrival. Keen to impress his ally, Washington saw to it that the camp "presented the most beautyful and picturesque appearance; it extended along the plain, on the neck of land formed by the winding of the Hudson, and had a view of this river to the south."[79]

On the morning of September 17, the French army crossed the Hudson to Verplanck's Point and marched "4 miles" to their camp at "Peekskill . . . on top of an arid mountain surrounded by wilderness."[80] On the twentieth, the American commander reviewed the army of his ally. Two days later, Rochambeau inspected the American regiments. Impressed by the disciplined appearance of the Continentals, Rochambeau, according to Dr. Thacher, offered the ultimate eighteenth-century military compliment to Washington: "You have formed an alliance with the King of Prussia. These troops are Prussians!"[81]

Combined, the two armies numbered about twelve thousand men. To Carleton, their presence was only slightly threatening. He made some adjustments to his defensive lines, but he was certain that the enemy would not attack without sufficient naval support. In mid-August the arrival of a French squadron under the Marquis de Vaudreuil on the coast provided a moment of encouragement to the French and American forces, but it was brief. Vaudreuil's squadron of twelve ships of the line was too few to undertake an attack on New York.[82] They passed by the harbor entrance and sailed for Boston.

Through the early fall of 1782 the Franco-American forces held their position above the city. Aside from an occasional skirmish along the lines or raids by foraging parties the valley was quiet. The chief reminder of war was the twice daily echo of the morning and evening cannon fired by the British guard at Kingsbridge on the other side of the Harlem River. Quartermaster General Timothy Pickering summed up the feelings of most when he complained to a friend at home, "I am weary of this dreadful war but shall never live long enough to see the end of it."[83]

In spite of Washington's untiring attachment to attacking New York, Rochambeau had little interest in such a venture. He was more concerned with the disposition of his troops for the coming winter. Tying down an army in a winter encampment in New York would be an inexcusable waste of manpower, to say nothing of putting his ill-equipped army at risk to cold, snow, and ice. The warm climes of the Caribbean beckoned him as they did Vaudreuil, who after spending several weeks riding at anchor in Boston Harbor was preparing his squadron for a return south. Rochambeau ordered his army to sail with the marquis while he took passage directly for France.[84] On October 22 the French army broke camp and began the march east through Connecticut to Boston. Surrounded by the brilliant colors of a New England fall, the regiments moved at a leisurely pace, stopping frequently to the delight of gaping townspeople. It took six weeks to make Boston. Two more weeks were spent in port preparing the transports, but finally, on Christmas Eve 1782, the last French vessel cleared Boston Harbor.[85]

Washington's army too was on the move, albeit over a much shorter distance. The land about Verplanck's Point had too little forage, water, and timber to supply a winter encampment. A few weeks earlier Washington had sent Pickering north to scout a better location. Crossing over at Fishkill, the quartermaster found a suitable site at New Windsor, only a few miles from his headquarters at Hasbrouck House, where he reported that there was adequate water and sufficient timber for building huts.[86] Washington approved the location, but the glum prospect of another long cold season troubled him. He missed his wife and looked forward to her "annual visit," but he despaired "of seeing [his] home this Winter."[87] He worried too about the mood of the army. He warned Lincoln, "The patience and long sufferance of this Army are almost exhausted." In his years of service with the army he had never seen "so great a spirit of Discontent." He went on to say, "While in the field, I think it may be kept from breaking out into Acts of Outrage, but when we retire into Winter Quarters (unless the Storm is previously dissipated) I cannot be at ease, respecting the consequences."[88] What troubled him most was that "the spirit of discontent" infected the officers' mess as well as the enlisted men's tents. He had seen this firsthand in the letters of Nicola and Varnum, but he had heard it as well from others close to him, including Heath, Knox, and Pickering.[89] Nor was he comforted by the arrival of an officer forced upon him by Congress who now by right of seniority ranked second only to the commander in chief himself: General Horatio Gates.

Since relieving him after the fiasco at Camden, where he had suffered a humiliating defeat at the hands of Cornwallis, Congress had let Gates dangle in limbo for nearly two years. From his Virginia plantation, Traveler's Rest, the general railed at the injustices visited upon him and wrote rambling letters with vague references to "imperial thrones" and "old Rome" and the threats to "freedom." He decried those who were "illib-

eral enough" to "persecute with savage Barbarity the most faithful servants of the republic."[90] Some of his fellow officers, including Greene,
supported him, as did his friend Robert Morris, who thought Congress
had treated the general unfairly. Gates gave some consideration to coming up to Philadelphia while Washington was there to plead in person
for justice. His friends advised against that and suggested instead that it
would be more proper to await an invitation from Congress or Washington. He remained at home.[91] In early August 1782, assured that Congress
would welcome him, and after Washington had left the city, Gates went
to Philadelphia.[92] Shortly after arriving, he wrote the president of Congress asking for "Justice."[93] With the help of political friends, particularly New Englanders who harbored a coolness toward Washington,
Gates succeeded.[94] By a near unanimous vote, and without consulting
Washington, Congress ordered that Gates "return to his duty as the
Commander in Chief shall direct."[95] Pleased at his triumph and blaming
his two-year exile on "enemies of every kind," Gates wasted no time writing to Washington. He assured the commander in chief, "I shall hold myself constantly ready to Obey your Orders [and] earnestly request your
Excellency will be assured of my inviolable attachment and that no Time
or Circumstance shall ever shake that Resolution."[96]

Gates's letter annoyed Washington. He had heard rumors that the
general was in Philadelphia. He was certain that Gates was seeking a
new command, but neither the president of Congress nor the secretary
at war had bothered to inform him or seek his advice. Furthermore, he
had written Gates the previous March asking him his intentions. Gates
had never responded. To be informed by Gates himself without any official notification from either the Congress or the secretary violated protocol, to say nothing of the fact that Washington still harbored memories
of Gates's role in the "Conway Cabal," an alleged plot in the winter of
1777–78 aimed at removing him from command. Washington's response
to Gates was cold and to the point: "I have assigned to you a Command
in the Army under my immediate Direction . . . you will be pleased to
proceed to join the Army on the North River."[97] After spending a few
days at home with his wife, Elizabeth, who for some time had been seriously ill, Gates reported for duty on October 5. Washington gave him a
"gracious reception," posted him to command the right wing of the

army and to be, as his seniority dictated, second in command.[98] Despite his rank, Gates complained that he was "indifferently accommodated" in a damp and chilly tent.[99] Like Washington, he looked forward to moving into better quarters, where his wife might join him to keep him "from freezing."[100]

By the end of the month the bulk of the American army had crossed the river and marched to New Windsor.[101] Once the army had assembled, Washington issued a General Order for the construction of huts to be built with "regularity, convenience, and even some degree of elegance."[102] Pickering drew up specific plans; huts were to be twenty-seven feet by eighteen feet with a partition down the middle. Each company was to build two huts accommodating approximately sixty soldiers. Within days ax-wielding soldiers stripped the countryside of timber, gathered up stones, and, to the annoyance of local farmers, dismantled their rail fences. Seven hundred huts dotted the countryside, arranged by units and spaced in neat rows. General Friedrich Wilhelm Augustus ("Baron") von Steuben, a former Prussian officer, thought the army "more comfortable and better lodged" than at any time before in the war. Heath described the encampment as "regular and beautiful."[103] Notwithstanding the neat appearance of the camp, inside those drafty huts men were muttering. Discontent, according to Henry Knox, was reaching "alarming heights."[104]

WITHIN WEEKS OF HIS ARRIVAL in New York City in the spring of 1782, General Carleton knew that he had lost and was bitter. The ministers in London, Shelburne in particular, had deceived him. Instead of supporting him in negotiations, they had abandoned him and left America to the rebels. Always uncommonly reserved, the general confided in few people.[1] His closest associate, Maurice Morgann, wondered "what thoughts the commander in chief entertains. He is as determined as he is persistent, but his purposes are all his own."[2] Morgann also struggled to grasp what conditions had driven the men in London to their unfortunate decision to abandon America. "It is nobody's power here to judge of that totality of things by which great affairs ought to be governed. Our view here could be at most but speculative and the condition of the Empire may be too critically situated to allow the course of any speculations whatever."[3] Morgann was resigned to conclude that he and Carleton were simply cogs in the imperial machinery.

Although his superiors had knocked his diplomatic and political sticks out from under him, Carleton's military situation was quite secure.[4] His New York City garrison was twice the size of Washington's army, and he continued to hold naval superiority. Even though he had been ordered to withdraw from his posts, the Americans were not strong enough to drive him out by force. To the north he held Penobscot and controlled the area across the Gulf of Maine to Nova Scotia. Haldimand was under no threat in Canada.[5] At the same time, the Americans were growing weaker. Their French allies were marching east to Boston to board ships taking them away. Carleton's sources told him that the rebel army was dispirited, demoralized, and on the edge of mutiny.[6] Among the general population, Americans, sick of the war, were directing their ire at an impecunious and feeble Congress. All this was leading, according to some of the more optimistic intelligence reports, toward an increased desire on the part of disillusioned rebels to reconcile with the Crown.[7]

Much of Carleton's information came from his master spy Major George Beckwith, a cool and temperate man.[8] Beckwith had spent years in America, and a good deal of the king's purse, weaving a web of spies.[9] Using the alias G. B. Ring, earlier in the war Beckwith had initiated correspondence with Benedict Arnold to entice him to treason. The major had numerous informants in Philadelphia who kept him abreast of the business in Congress, particularly any news relating to the French. Carleton and his chief of intelligence poured over every scrap of information, looking for cracks in the Franco-American alliance that he might exploit.[10]

Beckwith's agents in the countryside reported signs of growing unrest. A New Hampshire source sent accounts of an uproar in the town of Walpole on the Connecticut River. When local authorities seized a farmer's herd of cattle for unpaid taxes and put them up for auction, five hundred angry townspeople packed the sale and forced the sheriff to sell at rock-bottom prices to bidders, who then returned the herd to the original owner. Afterward, according to Beckwith's informant, "the People . . . proceeded in a body to the Liberty Pole, cut it down, gave three Cheers [and] drank punch to King George the third."[11]

Fear of republicanism and the likelihood of a government falling into the hands of a mob made many fence-sitting patriots anxious about their future. In Massachusetts, Connecticut, and Rhode Island, according to Beckwith's sources, contrite rebels were voting with their feet and fleeing to Vermont, where they hoped to come under the protection of Haldimand, who they were convinced was preparing to invade and be welcomed by Vermonters.

Beckwith's reports, along with the self-serving gossip rife among the loyalist community in New York, suggested that a stronger ministry in London could have given Carleton and Digby time to negotiate and to use their leverage to the Crown's advantage. As it was, however, the ministers were weak and eager to end the unpleasantness in America so that they could focus on their true enemy: the French. Whether Carleton and Digby might have been able to strike a deal with the Americans is unlikely; however, the loyalists were correct in regard to the French. France had become the prime focus. On the same day that Carleton dispatched his angry resignation to London, August 14, 1782, the ministry was sending him new orders. As soon as his replacement, Lieutenant General Charles Grey, arrived he was to leave New York and take command in the West Indies.[12]

Although the ministry had tied Carleton's hands in regard to dealing with rebels, it granted him great latitude in managing relations with the loyalists, particularly the several thousand who had taken refuge in New York City.

Estimates as to the total number of Americans who remained loyal to the Crown vary, but in terms of percentages, at least 20 percent of the population fell into that category.[13] The vast majority of them lived beyond the protection of the Crown, and so were left to suffer at the hands of their rebel neighbors unless they changed their allegiance or remained silent. Those with Carleton were an uneasy and powerless lot, entirely dependent upon him. In August Morgann reported to Shelburne that when the loyalists in New York learned of "Independency," "some passion followed," but according to him it "subsided upon views . . . of prudent respect to their future welfare." Still, the pot simmered, and as the summer closed, the secretary became increasingly concerned that the "stillness" in New York might simply be the "forerunner of a storm."[14] Benjamin Thompson, a prominent refugee from New England, agreed and warned his old friend Germain that the loyalists were in a mood "little short of rebellion."[15]

Shelburne instructed Carleton to make the best terms possible for the loyalists, but he provided few specific details. Some in London went so far as to hope that the rebels might offer direct compensation to their defeated foes or even welcome them back. If they could not return to their former homes, Shelburne instructed Carleton to treat the king's friends "with the tenderest and most honourable care giving them every assistance and prudent assurance of attention in whatever other parts of America in His Majesty's possession they chuse to settle."[16] Under no circumstances, however, could they be an obstacle to peace. As he explained during a speech in the House of Lords, "A part must be wounded that the whole of the Empire may not perish."[17] Since the independence of America, "the object of the war" had been conceded; all else, he told Carleton and Digby, was to "be considered rather as collateral and incidental than as principals to the present dispute."[18] The loyalists were "collateral" damage. Eventually, many of those who sacrificed for the king would gain compensation, but not from American pockets. Payment to them would be years in coming from the Crown and never arrived in amounts to compensate sufficiently those who had lost so much.

Carleton's most pressing challenge was withdrawing and redeploying thousands of troops accompanied by mountains of supplies, and growing numbers of loyalists, to various locations including the West Indies, England, and Canada. He had to coordinate the evacuations of Savannah, Charleston, New York, and Penobscot.[19] At no time is a military force more exposed than when it is leaving a position in the face of an enemy. Since there was no official truce, Carleton had reason to believe that given the chance, the Americans might strike.[20] Gradual withdrawal was an invitation to attack. Departure needed to be rapid. Every soldier and loyalist who left, and whatever they left with, would go by sea.

Supplying ships for evacuation was the responsibility of the Navy Board. A vital cog in the imperial machine, the board had charge of "the transport of troops, naval stores, military clothing, equipment, [and] provisions."[21] Technically under the direction of the Admiralty, the civilian members of the board had a habit of independence that often put them at odds with their uniformed superiors. Sir Charles Middleton, comptroller and head of the board, was a savvy "bureaucrat imperialist."[22]

In the early years of the war the board did a remarkable job transporting and supporting the king's armies in America. Hundreds of ships shuttled back and forth across the North Atlantic and along the American coast carrying men and material. Although the Continental navy and local privateers managed to harass the supply lines and capture some vessels, the North Atlantic weather was a tougher foe than anything the enemy might dispatch. Keeping up the Atlantic ferry wore out ships. At first the board managed to stay the odds put up by the enemy and nature, but the entrance of France and Spain into the war brought a global dimension to the board's work. Tasked to support the king's forces in Africa, India, and the West Indies as well as North America, the board stretched resources beyond its capabilities. Spanning distant waters brought great hazards. As Admiral Digby remarked when asked to send ships to the West Indies, "Whatever goes to the West Indies, seldom returns."[23]

Early in 1782, during the closing days of the North ministry, the Admiralty asked Middleton and the Navy Board what plan they might have to remove forces from America. The board responded that, according to its estimates, eighty-five thousand tons of shipping (approximately four hundred vessels) would be required to execute a full evacuation. Finding that amount of tonnage, the board proclaimed, was impossible. Its alternative was to gather forty to fifty thousand tons to evacuate New York first and then turn to the southern posts. But even that reduced scale of transport could only be achieved if virtually every bottom under the authority of the board could be gathered up and dispatched immediately to New York. The board's proposal arrived at an inauspicious moment, coming precisely when the North ministry was collapsing in March 1782. Nothing could be accomplished until a new government took the reins. Even then, however, preparations moved slowly, and when Carleton arrived in New York he was vexed to find only two dozen transports swinging at anchor. He wrote Shelburne that with the resources at hand it was "impossible" to evacuate America quickly.[24]

While Middleton scrambled to find tonnage, Carleton, faced with an obvious shortage of shipping, ignored the board's proposal and laid out his own scheme for leaving America. Being more vulnerable, the southern posts, not New York, would be evacuated first in the order of Savannah, Charleston, and, if necessary, St. Augustine. The latter, for the moment, was safely beyond American reach and not in immediate danger. New York City and Penobscot would come later. British regulars were to be sent to Canada and the West Indies while the German mercenaries, to get them off the payroll and save expense, he ordered returned to

Europe. Altogether, approximately thirty-five thousand troops needed transport along with their considerable supply train.[25]

Adding to this logistical nightmare were thousands of loyalists to be carried away. Estimates of their numbers grew to more than thirty thousand as each day more and more came across the lines into the city seeking sanctuary. The scale was unprecedented. Sir Guy Carleton had charge of the largest movement of ships and people in the history of the empire.[26]

Carleton dispatched orders to his subordinates in late June to prepare for embarkation. Not all were pleased. In a peremptory manner Georgia's royal governor, Sir James Wright, wrote Carleton, "I am afraid Sir, the situation of affairs here was not properly and sufficiently known to your Excellency or I trust such steps [evacuation] would not have been taken."[27] Carleton may have read Wright's letter with bitter irony, as it expressed the sentiments he wanted to write to his own superiors. Similar complaints came from Charleston, where the ever-whining Major General Alexander Leslie protested abandoning the city while begging on his own behalf, for reasons of health, to be relieved of command so that he might return to England.[28] In ranks closer to home at New York, muffled dissent echoed through the officers' mess. Captain William Feilding, a royal marine officer stationed in New York, expressed the feelings of his comrades. With the French defeat at the Saintes he thought the war was turning in favor of the British. "Independence" ought, he said, "never happen."[29]

Initially, Carleton viewed the refugees in a dim light. He had been instructed to negotiate with the Americans, but the loyalists stood in his way. The defiant and outrageous behavior of the Associated Loyalists and their leader, William Franklin, made negotiations with Washington impossible. Fortunately for the loyalists, events softened Carleton's attitude. Once he disbanded the Associated Loyalists, and Franklin sailed for England, he developed a more sympathetic understanding of their plight. He was also influenced through his friendship with the intelligent and thoughtful Chief Justice William Smith. Through him Carleton became acquainted with loyalists of similar character, who were, he concluded, worthy and deserving of his help.[30] To their great relief, the refugees discovered, according to the Tory historian Thomas Jones, that

Carleton was increasingly ready to listen to "all complaints, and was determined not to sacrifice the loyalists, nor leave the country, till every one of them who chose to go should be sent off."[31]

As "His Majesty's Commander in Chief in North America," Carleton had authority extending north to Canada and the province of Nova Scotia.[32] Encouraged by the government in London, Carleton launched a massive effort to transport and relocate loyalist refugees there.[33]

Ceded to Great Britain by the Treaty of Utrecht in 1713, Nova Scotia, then including present-day New Brunswick, had long enjoyed a close association with the other American colonies, particularly New England. Although fertile land was limited, confined mostly to areas abutting the Bay of Fundy, the province had abundant timber and its ports stood close to rich fishing grounds. Halifax on the Atlantic coast was one of the finest harbors in North America. Lightly populated, the province had vast areas of unsettled land belonging to the Crown.[34]

For some years Nova Scotia had been in political disarray. In 1776, alarmed by reports of unrest, the king summoned the province's governor, Francis Legge, home to answer serious accusations of misconduct. The Board of Trade cleared him of any specific charge but found him "wanting in that Gracious and Conciliating Deportment which the delicacy of the times and the tempers of men under agitation and alarm particularly demanded."[35] While Legge sat in political limbo in London, the province fell under the de facto rule of the Halifax elite, operating under a series of temporary naval lieutenant governors, "who took little interest in local matters."[36] The last of these naval governors, Andrew Snape Hamond, was on duty in the early fall of 1782 when Carleton dispatched orders instructing him to prepare to receive "upwards of 600 persons" who were about to embark for Nova Scotia. Carleton directed Hamond to assist them in choice of land and "help with building."[37] Two weeks later the first of hundreds of transports cleared Sandy Hook and laid a course for Halifax.[38]

Hamond's tenure as governor came to an abrupt end when, to his chagrin since he expected the post to be permanent, in July 1782 Shelburne appointed one of his London cronies, John Parr, to the governorship. Dismissal of the popular Hamond did not sit well with the

Haligonians, and Parr received a cool welcome. Almost immediately Parr had to cope with the onslaught of loyalist refugees, while also salving local resentment at the disruption caused by his appointment. Inevitably, not everything went smoothly. Lands promised to the new arrivals had not been properly surveyed, and methods of allotment were not clear. Adding to the distress was a lack of adequate food and shelter. Many refugees would have to endure a harsh winter outfitted with only the barest necessities, living off codfish, molasses, and hard biscuits.[39]

While managing the loyalist diaspora, Carleton continued to direct military and civilian evacuation from Savannah and Charleston. To avoid giving any cause for American interference, Carleton gave orders that those cities were to be left unmolested. Nothing, not even fortifications, was to be harmed.[40] Since Savannah was the smaller of the two cities, Carleton ordered that it be abandoned first. Transports arrived in late June. They took nearly two weeks to load, but finally, on July 11, 3,200 loyalists and 3,500 slaves embarked for New York. A few days later, on July 20, six ships with ten white families and more than 1,500 slaves left for Jamaica, and seven vessels sailed two days later with 580 loyalists and 748 slaves for St. Augustine. Last to depart were 2,000 troops bound for New York. Since there were not enough ships to accommodate everyone, 5,000 whites and slaves were left to trek south through stifling summer heat to the safety of St. Augustine, where Carleton had determined the garrison would, for the time being at least, remain in place.[41]

Charleston posed a greater challenge than Savannah. General Leslie was in a perilous position. Thousands of loyalists had sought refuge with him in the city. Most had brought their slaves with them, creating a huge number of mouths to feed. Cut off by the Americans from the countryside, and having no reliable supply by sea, Leslie proposed a truce to the American commander Nathanael Greene and asked permission to purchase supplies, assuring the general that this was only a temporary measure, and that as soon as possible he would withdraw. Greene dodged the issue and referred the request to Congress, suspecting that the British were likely to starve before that body took any action. Seeing no alternative, Leslie decided reluctantly to launch a series of foraging expeditions into enemy territory. Greene was ready, and on August 27 the two forces engaged at Combahee Ferry about forty miles southwest of Charleston. The fight was indecisive, the British withdrew, but with sufficient time to complete their mission. The most memorable result from this relatively insignificant engagement was the unfortunate death of Colonel John Laurens, the son of South Carolina's most notable patriot Henry Laurens.[42] Young Laurens was a gallant officer with an impressive combat record. He had also served briefly in Paris with the American delegation and for a time had been aide-de-camp to Washington, where he and another aide, Alexander Hamilton, had become close friends.[43] The usually stoic commander in chief was particularly touched upon learning of Laurens's death.[44] "The death of Colo Laurens I consider as a very heavy misfortune." He was "particularly dear."[45]

After considerable delay, on September 20 Carleton was finally able to dispatch the first convoy of transports to Charleston.[46] The ships left New York and ten days later dropped anchor off the town. The first to board were 1,400 loyalists, nearly 1,700 slaves, and 1,200 provincial troops bound for St. Augustine. A few days later another contingent left for Halifax. By late fall enough additional vessels had arrived for a full evacuation. Fearing an American attack on his rear guard, Leslie, in defiance of Carleton's orders, warned the American commander Anthony Wayne that should any attempt be made on his men, he would burn the town. Without consulting his superiors, Wayne agreed quickly to a de facto truce, later telling Greene that "the preservation of Charlestown [sic], and the lives and property of it's inhabitants being of much greater consequence, than striking or capturing a rear guard of a retiring enemy."[47] The last British troops were ferried to their waiting transports on December 14. A few days later the convoy cleared the harbor, leaving the city unharmed.[48] On Carleton's orders, most of the whites, nearly 4,000, accompanied by more than 5,000 slaves, went to St. Augustine, Jamaica, or St. Lucia. The bulk of the troops, including Germans eventually bound for Europe, sailed for New York.[49]

With the arrival of the southern evacuees the population of St. Augustine swelled to more than seventeen thousand, making it one of the largest cities in North America. In the final treaty (1783) St. Augustine, as part of East Florida, was given over to the Spanish, forcing those who had left Georgia and South Carolina to move once again, some to Nova Scotia, a few back to the United States, and the remainder to the sugar islands.[50]

British concern for loyalists did not extend to Native Americans who had also been faithful allies of the Crown. In the North the Iroquois had played a critical role assisting General Haldimand in the borderlands of upstate New York. Led by the indomitable Joseph Brant (Thayendanegea), whose elder sister "Molly" was mistress to Sir William Johnson, Iroquois warriors, principally from the Mohawk, Onondaga, Cayuga, and Seneca tribes, helped keep the area in upstate and central New York in violent turmoil. In retaliation, adopting a scorched-earth strategy, a powerful American force under General John Sullivan swept through Iroquois territory in the summer of 1779, burning more than forty villages and destroying thousands of bushels of corn, beans, and squash that the Iroquois needed to survive the coming winter. To escape the Americans, nearly five thousand Iroquois fled north to the safety of Fort Niagara.

Sullivan's expedition brought only a momentary respite to the northern frontier. As one of Sullivan's officers, Major Jeremiah Fogg, wrote, "The nests are destroyed, but the birds are still on the wing," and in the spring of 1780 Iroquois warriors swept south to take bloody revenge. For the rest of the war upstate New York remained unsettled.[51]

Having sacrificed so much in the cause of his king, Brant was stunned when he learned that peace was in the offing and that Indian attacks would cease. No one had consulted them. Haldimand reported that the Indians were "thunderstruck" at being abandoned. "Policy, as well as gratitude, demands of us an attention to the sufferings and future situation of these unhappy people, involved on our accounts in the miseries of war."[52] He feared that under the circumstances they could not be "entirely restrained."[53] Brigadier General Allan Maclean, the British commander at Fort Niagara, shared Haldimand's concern. Brant, he told Haldimand, must "be detained" for "he is much better informed and instructed than any other Indian" and so is "much more sensible of the miserable situation in which we have left this unfortunate people that I do believe he would do a great deal of mischief here at this time. I do from my soul pity these poor people."[54]

London responded by telling Haldimand that he ought to persuade the Iroquois to abandon their homelands in the United States and move to the north side of Lake Ontario, where they might find new hunting grounds and perhaps even take up farming.[55]

In the South the situation was equally pitiful, but more confused. At various times during the war the two dominant tribes, Cherokee and Creek, confronted both the British and the Americans.[56] Early in the war the British persuaded the Cherokee to attack American settlements in Georgia and the Carolinas. Warned in advance of the Cherokee attack, General Charles Lee, commander of Continental forces, gathered a joint body of militia from Georgia, the Carolinas, and Virginia to march against the Cherokee towns. With no British support available, the Cherokee (unlike the Iroquois, who could depend upon help from the British in nearby Canada) found themselves at a considerable disadvantage, and in May 1777 they sued for peace, surrendering a huge chunk of their ancestral lands to the Americans.

Other southern tribes took a lesson from the fate of the Cherokee and were cautious about confronting the rebels. The Creek, for example, the most powerful of the southern nations, initially adopted a policy of neutrality but with a pro-British tilt. In 1778, however, with the British capture of Savannah and a renewed focus by them on the South, the Creek abandoned neutrality and openly sided with the king's forces. The decision proved to be unwise, and as British fortunes declined in the South the Creek found themselves in a dire situation. The capture of Pensacola in West Florida, in May 1781, by a Spanish force led by Bernardo de Gálvez cut the Creek off from British supplies, forcing them to flee to the safety of St. Augustine, the last British post in the South.[57] In the spring of 1783, when they learned that Florida was to be returned to Spain and that the British were leaving, they begged unsuccessfully to join them. A dismayed Thomas Browne, the king's Indian agent, and the person who had been instrumental in recruiting the Creek, wrote to Carleton, "I don't believe it; an Englishman will never turn his back and betray his friends."[58]

Against considerable odds, by the end of 1782 Carleton and Digby had managed to concentrate the majority of their forces at New York. Each day more loyalists trudged across the lines to crowd the city. Often hungry and destitute, some refugees made annoying demands. When one group sought additional food rations, Carleton, whose own supplies were growing scarce, declared he had nothing more to give them.[59] His patience also ran short with the navy. When Digby suggested the general had not been sufficiently cooperative with him, Carleton gave a prickly response: "Are we not serving one master?"[60] Such exchanges were rare, however. Carleton's chief problem was keeping order in a city jammed with unhappy and frightened loyalists.

Street disorders had become more common. Carleton had depended upon loyalist militia to police the city, believing that his regular troops could be better used manning fortifications. He was also aware that deploying regulars amid a civilian population could be problematic, particularly in a situation where so many of his soldiers were German mercenaries. To his dismay, when loyalist officers learned of independence they "sent word to the General that they would do no more Duty in Town," forcing Carleton to weaken his defences and bring "to Town" his own soldiers "to relieve the guards and posts."[61]

Like Washington, Carleton sought ways to maintain morale and discipline among thousands of idle troops whose chief interest was in going home from an "unfortunate war."[62] Even Robertson, Carleton's most senior officer, was testy, lamenting to his friend Lord Jeffrey Amherst that keeping the army in New York was "not only useless but ruinous, an army without the hope of getting back America should not stay in it."[63] Drills and parades filled the time, as did constant digging to improve fortifications.

While Washington and Carleton struggled to cope with unhappy soldiers and disgruntled officers, politicians across the Atlantic in Paris were engaged in secret talks inching the belligerents toward a peace settlement.

Shelburne was living up to his reputation for duplicity. In his June 5 letter to Carleton and Digby, the one that had shattered the general's ambitions to play negotiator and sent the loyalists into panic, he had admitted in confidence to the general and the admiral that he was trying to divide the American states from one another and the whole from France. Inexplicably for a man so deeply schooled in politics and diplomacy, when Shelburne sent Richard Oswald back to Paris at the end of June he gave him a copy of this letter, inviting him to share its substance with the Americans. He mistakenly believed that it would assure the American commissioners of his sincerity and convince them of his government's willingness to grant independence. It backfired. Although the letter spoke of independence, it did not commit the king to unconditional independence, which was the American demand, and even worse it laid bare the ministry's plan to divide the states and colonies from one another and all from France.[64] As if this was not distressing enough, the wording in Oswald's official commission authorized him to negotiate not with the United States but with "certain colonies in North America."[65]

At the time of Oswald's return to Paris in July 1782, only two of the American commissioners were present, Franklin and John Jay. Adams was still at The Hague negotiating a loan with the Dutch, while the unfortunate Henry Laurens remained a prisoner in the Tower of London. Upon learning about the Carleton Digby letters and the wording of Oswald's commission, the astute Adams wrote, "[The British] are only amusing us."[66] Jay agreed. As usual, Franklin entertained a more generous interpretation. In an interview with Oswald Jay let loose on the king's emissary and left him reeling. He was particularly astonished by Jay's deep antipathy toward England. Jay had, reported Oswald, no "regard for England" and behaved "as if he had never heard of it in his life."[67]

The situation was ticklish. The peace commissioners were under the following instructions from Congress: "to make the most candid and confidential communications upon all subjects to the ministers of our generous ally, the king of France; to undertake nothing in the negotiations for peace or truce without their knowledge and concurrence; and ultimately to govern yourselves by their advice and opinion."[68] When shown Oswald's imperfect commission, the French recommended that the Americans ignore the technicalities and begin negotiations. Jay would not agree and persuaded his fellow commissioners to stand with him. They defied their congressional instructions and rejected French advice. Jay explained to his friend Gouverneur Morris, "Had I not violated the Instructions from Congress their dignity would have been in the dust."[69] Until Oswald's commission addressed the "United States," he wrote to Robert Livingston, there could be no official negotiation.[70]

Parallel to discussions with Oswald, Jay was also in conversation with the Spanish minister, the Conde de Floridablanca. While not an official ally of the United States, Spain in 1779, as a result of intense pressure from the French, entered the war against Great Britain. The two Bourbon monarchies had signed a secret treaty by which France agreed not to make peace until Spain recovered Gibraltar from Great Britain, information they did not share with the Americans.[71] From his cryptic conversations with the Spanish envoy, Jay sensed duplicity at work, which heightened his suspicions toward the Spanish and the French.

In a secret report to Shelburne the New York Tory minister John Vardill, one of Jay's classmates at King's College (soon to be Columbia University), described his former friend as "naturally controversial," "obstinate," and "indefatigable."[72] He was also, according to the editor of his papers, known for his "touchiness and vanity."[73] Jay's encounters with Oswald, the emissary of the devious Shelburne, with Floridablanca, representing a nation whose only interest in the war was the return of a "pile of stones," and with Vergennes, spokesman for a nation obsessed with a desire for revenge against the English, fed his natural suspicions. Jay quickly concluded that none of the European powers, friend or foe, had any interest in seeing a prosperous and independent America.

Franklin found Jay's testiness toward the French and Spanish to be disturbing, and he told him so, but the irascible Jay would not retreat. In a particularly blunt encounter he told Franklin that France could not be trusted; it had "no interest that we should become a great and formidable people." The old doctor shot back that America must be "mindful of the generosity of France." Jay's response was direct and simple: "We have no rational dependence except on God and ourselves."[74]

In private meetings with Oswald Jay pressed home the absolute requirement of a new commission that recognized explicitly and without conditions the independence of the United States. Oswald, convinced that peace with America was at hand but might, if not seized, slip away, urged Shelburne to concede independence and prepare a new commission. The war in America was lost. Best, argued Oswald, to reconcile with the new nation and hopefully draw it to the bosom of the empire and away from the dreaded French. Ending the war in America would release the king's forces to pressure the Spanish and French elsewhere to bring them to the table as well. Oswald was not a solitary voice. Benjamin Vaughan, a close friend to the earl, and an acquaintance of Franklin's, was also in Paris. Vaughan was born in Jamaica, and his mother, Sarah Hallowell, hailed from a prominent New England family. Ostensibly a "private citizen," Vaughan was in fact another set of eyes and ears for Shelburne, to whom he often reported. Vaughan echoed Oswald. The choice he reported was "good sense" or "ruin."[75]

Oswald's sage advice, corroborated independently by Vaughan, pushed Shelburne toward conciliation. As an astute politician, however, he feared getting too far in front of his party. He also needed to be attentive to an obstinate king. Public opinion, too, had to be weighed, as national pride was at stake. At considerable risk Shelburne took the tiller and edged the nation toward peace. At an August 29 meeting Shelburne in a clever maneuver persuaded his cabinet colleagues to agree that if necessary, American independence should be recognized "unconditionally before the treaty." Three weeks later, at a hastily called cabinet meeting on September 19, Shelburne took the next step and told his colleagues that it was now necessary to alter Oswald's commission to please the Americans."[76] A week later Oswald had his new commission in hand, and negotiations began.

With unwonted speed the talks moved ahead, and by October 8 a provisional draft treaty, drawn by Jay and approved by Franklin, was agreed upon. Contrary to Congress's instructions, at no time during this intense period did Jay or Franklin consult with the French. The provisional treaty, however, did begin with the caveat that the treaty was not "to be concluded until his Britannic Majesty shall have agreed to the terms of peace between France and Britain."[77] The other provisions, in addition to recognizing independence, were extraordinarily generous. Great Britain granted the new nation fishing rights in Canadian waters and set boundaries in the North beginning at the St. John River over to the St. Lawrence and thence west at forty-five degrees to Lake Nipissing. On the western edge the line ran south along the Mississippi to thirty-one degrees and then east to the St. Marys River in East Florida. Most remarkable of all, Britain offered trade privileges to its former colonies, a provision undoubtedly urged by Oswald, who envisioned drawing the new nation into a close economic relationship if not dependency. The treaty made no mention of compensation for the loyalists; nor did any provision appear about the need to honor prewar debts owed by Americans to British merchants.[78] Oswald signed the agreement and returned to England to submit the treaty to His Majesty's consideration.

Oswald's largesse threw Shelburne and the cabinet aback. The ministers grumbled that their commissioner had abandoned the loyalists, forgiven huge American debts to British merchants, and surrendered vast territories for no good reason. Oswald had given everything and gotten virtually nothing in return. Oswald was dispatched back to Paris, and to "assist" him he was accompanied by Henry Strachey, a seasoned bureaucrat and one of ministry's principal undersecretaries. According to Shelburne, he was a "proper and confidential person" upon whom the ministry could rely.[79]

Shelburne was caught in a tight tangle. He was anxious to conclude a peace but not on the terms presented. Time was pressing in both Paris and London. Delay in Paris would annoy the Americans and provide an incentive for prolonging the war. At home he faced a vexing political problem. Parliament had been absent from the city since early July—a boon to a ministry pursuing controversial policies. Unfortunately, it was due to reconvene in early December. Shelburne had barely two months to complete a peace before that meddling body returned with "so many opinions and Passions supported by party and different mercantile interests that no negotiation can advance."[80]

The peace commissioners—John Adams, Franklin, Jay, and the two Englishmen, Strachey and Oswald—began deliberations on October 29 and worked day and night to reach agreement. Tories, debts, and the fisheries formed the core of disagreement, but even these were not sufficient to derail the talks. In a draft approved on November 4 compensation to loyalists went unaddressed, while in the matter of prewar debts Congress would recommend to the states that they open their courts to litigation where British creditors might seek compensation. Thanks to Adams, Americans retained the right of the fishery. In return, the commissioners consented to a new, less favorable, northern boundary that would run down the St. Lawrence and through the middle of the Great Lakes rather than along the forty-fifth parallel, thus giving up a good

deal of territory in what is today the province of Ontario. Still absent at
the table were the French.

As they prepared to dispatch the November draft to London, Strachey
and Oswald were uneasy. From the ministry's perspective their work left
much to be desired, particularly the points concerning debts and recompense to loyalists. Oswald answered his critics by saying that under the
circumstances it was simply the best that could be expected.[81]

On November 11, 1782, the cabinet reviewed the draft. Once again
they discussed demanding compensation for loyalists. Whatever sympathy there might have been in the cabinet rooms for these unfortunates,
the reality was that there was great risk in pushing the Americans on the
issue. In most states loyalist property had been confiscated and the former owners driven away. As one angry American Whig put it, these
"ancient idolaters" had to be purged.[82] Jay and Franklin were no less
fierce in their denunciation. The Tories were "savages" against whom
"every American must set his face and steel his heart."[83] No one stood to
speak on behalf of the loyalists lest the whole deal be defeated. It was
obvious that notwithstanding the justness of their claims, the loyalists
were to be thrown aside for the sake of peace. In the final language all
that could be extracted from the Americans was that Congress would
"earnestly recommend it to the Legislatures of the respective states to
provide for Restitution" to the loyalists. In regard to debts, the statement
read, "Creditors on either Side shall meet with no lawful Impediment to
the Recovery of full Value . . . of all bona fide Debts."[84] No mention was
made of trade. On Saturday November 30 the parties gathered at Oswald's suite in the Grand Hotel Muscovite. As the representative of the
"more venerable state," Oswald signed first, followed in alphabetical order
by Adams, Franklin, Jay, and Laurens.[85]

In a curious twist William Temple Franklin, the twenty-two-year-old
grandson of Benjamin Franklin and the illegitimate son of Governor
William Franklin, was also present. Unlike his father, young Franklin
had joined the American cause and was employed by his grandfather as
secretary to the American commission. Having finished the business,
the Americans were anxious to dispatch the treaty to Philadelphia, but
before they could do so they needed to inform their French allies of the

signing and explain to them why they had ignored Congress's instructions and excluded them from the negotiation. They chose Benjamin Franklin for the mission.

Paris was crawling with spies. From his own informants Vergennes was aware of the communications between the British and Americans across the Channel. Nonetheless, a few hours after the signing, when Franklin came to inform him of what had happened, he feigned surprise at the news. He asked that the Americans delay sending the treaty to Congress since its arrival and publication "might make the people in America think a peace was consummated."[86] France and England had yet to make peace. Vergennes's request went unanswered, and the commissioners made their own plan.

An American packet, the *George Washington* commanded by Captain Joshua Barney, had just arrived from Philadelphia. Barney's arrival was a godsend to the commissioners. Benjamin Franklin, without consulting Vergennes, ordered Barney to take the treaty and prepare to return to Philadelphia as quickly as possible. To ensure safe passage, Franklin requested an official passport from the British. King George III consented and signed an elaborate document commanding that all "permit and suffer the Vessel called the *Washington* commanded by Mr. Barney belonging to the United States of North America, to sail from either of the ports of France to any Port or Place in North America."[87] Before Barney left, Franklin had the temerity to approach Vergennes to ask if the minister might want to take advantage of Barney's safe-conduct voyage to send cash to Congress. Even this calloused minister of the king was a bit nonplussed at such audacity. Given that the Americans had thus far kept the French in the dark, Franklin's request put Vergennes "at a loss" to explain their conduct.[88] Never starved for words, Franklin responded that it would be a shame if this "great work" would be "ruined" by neglecting "a point of bienseance." If the French did not give assistance, Franklin warned, "the whole edifice sinks to the ground immediately."[89]

While miffed at the Americans for their duplicitous behavior, Vergennes was impressed with what they had accomplished. The peace terms were even good for France, for it had succeeded in its goal of separating the colonies from Britain and thereby embarrassing and weakening its ancient enemy. If not completely victorious, the French were at least satisfied that the war was coming to an end.

Spain, however, had not been accounted for. Vergennes had dragged the Spanish into the war by promising to help them recapture Gibraltar. After besieging the British for more than two years, in September 1782 the allies made a "Grand Assault" on the fortress. The British commander, Sir George Eliot, threw back the attack, virtually destroying the entire attacking force. The repulse lifted the siege and made it clear to all that the British would hold the "Rock," making it impossible for the French to fulfill their promise to return it to their Spanish ally. Despite the failure to take Gibraltar, the Spanish were adamant and pushed France to hold to the agreement, but it was of no use. With their naval superiority the British held an iron grip on Gibraltar, and they had no intention of surrendering it. Ever duplicitous, Vergennes was not even sure he wanted Spain to regain that prize, for as long as England was on the Iberian Peninsula Spain would be ill advised to stray from its French alliance. To placate the Spanish, Vergennes negotiated the return to them of the island of Minorca, which England had taken by the 1763 Treaty of Paris, and secured agreement with the British that Spain would take possession of both West and East Florida. The latter concession provided a welcome southern barrier to the new United States, while putting Spain in control of the entire coast of the Gulf of Mexico. In separate agreements in January 1783, Grenada, the Bahamas, and Montserrat—Caribbean islands captured by the French and Spanish—were returned to Great Britain. France's net gain was the Caribbean island of Tobago and Senegal in West Africa. The Dutch, who had joined the war in 1780, regained possessions lost in the East Indies, but in recompense had to grant trading privileges to the English in that part of the world.[90]

While Barney made ready to sail and Vergennes prepared to meet with the Spanish in London, an extraordinary scene took place. On the morning of December 5 members of Lords and Commons gathered to commence the third session of the Fifteenth Parliament.[91] As usual, the opening ceremonies included the king's address. Long before His Majesty arrived, members and guests crowded into the chamber. Among them was Elkanah Watson, a young American merchant from Plymouth,

Massachusetts. Watson sat with his friend John Singleton Copley, an American artist. The two men, according to Watson, had seats "exactly in front . . . elbow to elbow with the celebrated Admiral Lord Howe." Outside "it was a dark and foggy day," and inside Watson felt the "gloom." Among the saddest he spotted were "some dejected American royalists."[92]

Watson and the others waited nearly two hours until "a tremendous roar of artillery" announced the arrival of the king. "He entered by a small door on the left of the throne, and immediately seated himself upon the Chair of State . . . Apparently agitated, he drew from his pocket the scroll containing his speech." Watson was close enough so that he could hear "every tone of his voice" and see the "expression of his countenance." After a few perfunctory remarks King George III, who was "celebrated for reading his speeches, in a distinct, free, and impressive manner . . . hesitated [and] choked" as he told the House that he had declared the colonies "Free and Independent States."[93] When Watson heard those words, "every artery beat high, and swelled with [his] proud American blood." With evident joy he proclaimed, "The great drama was now closed."[94]

Watson was premature. Not only was there still much to tidy up in Europe—France and Great Britain had not signed a treaty, and there was the question of Dutch and Spanish interests—but in America Congress knew virtually nothing of what had been transpiring in Paris. Its commissioners had kept that body in the dark.

CHAPTER EIGHT

WHILE NEGOTIATIONS WERE PROGRESSING slowly in Paris, in New York Carleton was trying his best to open relations with Washington. On August 2, the day after he delivered the disheartening news to Justice Smith that the king was consenting to American independence, Carleton wrote to Washington with the same information, expecting that the American commander would recognize this concession as evidence of "the pacific disposition of the Parliament and People of England towards the Thirteen Provinces." He was also pleased to tell him that the king had ordered the release of the American diplomat Henry Laurens, who for more than a year had been confined in the Tower of London. Laurens had been set free on parole in the hope that Congress would reciprocate by releasing General Cornwallis from his parole.[1] As much as the loyalists believed that the news from London announced the end of the world, Carleton was convinced that in contrast the rebels would be jubilant. He had misjudged his adversary.

Having endured seven years of war "and the wide-spread desolation, resulting from the stubbornness of this very King," American patriots were not in a forgiving mood.[2] In a terse three-sentence letter from Newburgh on the same day, Washington acknowledged receipt of Carleton's letter and told the general that he was forwarding it to Congress and would await the members' "Instructions."[3] True to his word, he conveyed the letter "to the Eye of Congress" and asked that he be furnished with "Directions."[4] The post rider delivered the package on the evening of Thursday August 8 toward the end of a long and exhausting week in Congress.

Philadelphia was hot. Inside the stuffy halls of the Pennsylvania statehouse (Independence Hall) tempers had grown warm. Congress had spent the day in a fierce and unpleasant debate. The session had opened well enough. Members were still congratulating themselves on the good news from The Hague. Although they had not received any official communications, unofficial accounts had drifted in reporting that their undiplomatic diplomat John Adams had persuaded the Dutch burghers to recognize the United States, raising hopes that as a consequence of recognition Dutch bankers might offer a substantial loan.[5] Coming at a moment when the Congress was, as usual, nearly broke, this news was a tonic to all. It was especially pleasing to an anti-Gallican clique who saw in Dutch support an opportunity to wean the Congress off dependence on French gold.

Even in the euphoria surrounding the Franco-American alliance, there had always been persistent skeptics who welcomed French aid but not the entanglements that went with it. The notion of hitching America's wagon to a French team produced queasy feelings. Critics of the alliance complained "that their great cause had become intricately entangled in the affairs of Europe." The war for independence had become, as far as Europe was concerned, a skirmish in an interminable "struggle for supremacy between two great powers."[6] The loudest voice in this chorus of dissent belonged to a Virginian, the unreconstructed revolutionary Arthur Lee.

"Ambitious, impetuous, witty, talkative and fond of scheming and intriguing," Arthur Lee had at one time or another offended nearly everyone.[7] Born into one of the "First Families of Virginia," he left the Old Dominion to seek education in England, which included attending Eton College and earning a degree in medicine from Edinburgh. From Edinburgh he went to London to study law at Middle Temple. He found law a congenial vehicle in which to advance his political ambitions. In the tumultuous years leading up to the Revolution, Lee gained a reputation as an outspoken radical and a strong supporter of colonial rights.[8] Signing himself Junius Americanus, he authored pamphlets asserting colonial rights against the royal prerogative and parliamentary authority. His writings brought him to the attention of the Massachusetts House of Representatives and its Speaker, Samuel Adams, who noted, "[Lee] has served the American Cause in a manner which I have long wished some able pen would have undertaken."[9]

In the fall of 1770, following the death of its longtime London agent, the elderly Dennys de Berdt, the Massachusetts House sought a replacement.[10] Although they had never met Arthur Lee, Adams, James Otis, and other Whig leaders had read his essays and shared his radical views. They lobbied for his appointment as agent for the colony. A more cautious faction argued for the ever popular, and less radical, Benjamin Franklin as a better choice. Franklin won the contest but not before Adams engineered an agreement that Lee might be Franklin's substitute should he be incapacitated or absent. In effect they were coagents. Neither appointee was pleased with the other.[11]

In the fall of 1776 Congress sent Lee to Paris to join Benjamin Franklin and Silas Deane as commissioners charged with securing French aid.[12] Lee's appointment led to the infamous scandals that had resulted in Deane's recall in 1778 and Lee's in 1780. The affair had left deep divisions in Congress.[13]

In 1781 the Virginia House of delegates elected Lee to Congress. His mere presence, let alone his actions, rekindled the flames of controversy. Not surprisingly, Lee was particularly agitated toward the French and often vented against their influence on Congress. The news from The Hague gave him occasion to rise again to inveigh against the French. What especially stuck in his craw were the instructions of June 15, 1781, which had ordered the American commissioners to place themselves entirely in the hands of the French government.[14] On Thursday morning August 8, Lee spoke of the "honor and safety of these states." To preserve this "honor," Lee moved "that the instructions given on the 15th June 1781 to the ministers plenipotentiary for negotiating a peace be reconsidered."[15]

Lee's motion flared a heated and long debate. His fellow Virginian James Madison sought a compromise. After first admitting that the instructions of June 15 were "a sacrifice of national dignity" and then justifying them as a necessary "sacrifice of dignity to policy," Madison "parried" the issue and offered a typical legislative compromise: form a committee. And so it was done.[16]

On Friday morning in the wake of Thursday's raucous debate, Washington's dispatch came to the floor. Although rumors of peace had been floating about, the news from Washington was the first official confirmation of progress. Embarrassment may well have been the first feeling in the chamber. The members were chagrined that such vital news came via General Carleton. Their own commissioners had been silent for nearly six months, yet obviously they had not been inactive. They simply had neglected to inform Congress.[17]

Aside from chagrin, the members of Congress had little to say except that "having received no advices from their ministers abroad of what was passing in Europe," they thought it wise "to refer the letter to a Committee that they might consider and report what was proper to be done." Arthur Lee, John Rutledge of South Carolina, and John Witherspoon of New Jersey took the assignment.[18]

Over the weekend the committee prepared their report. They dismissed Carleton's communication as a "mere matter of information." Since they had "received no information on this subject from their commissioners negotiating a peace, no public measure can or ought to be taken." The only course was to carry "on the War with vigor."[19] Secretary at War Benjamin Lincoln warned General Knox, "We must not relax in the present state of things and thereby lay ourselves open to a stroke."[20] Others saw the overture as little more than an offer of "Irish" independence.[21]

Some members, not wanting to appear completely intransigent, sought to smooth Congress's sharp edge of rejection by offering a measure to release General Cornwallis from his parole. The motion brought down a howl of protest. The most virulent objections came from the South Carolinian Edward Rutledge, John's younger brother. His state had suffered mightily under the rampages of Cornwallis's army. According to Charles Thomson, Rutledge "inveighed against" the motion "with so much warmth and indignation that it was rejected with a loud and general *no* from every part of the house."[22]

Not everyone in Congress welcomed the prospect of peace. Gouverneur Morris, for example, the influential assistant superintendent of finance and a former member from New York, was blunt on the point. He told his friend Matthew Ridley that it was "not much for the Interest of America that [peace] should be made at present."[23] Morris feared that any prospect of an imminent end to the war would freeze the Congress into a state of inaction. It was only the discipline of war and the threat of an enemy that kept Congress, indeed the entire nation, focused and together. Morris's views were shared by a small but powerful cadre of politicians and military officers whom historians have dubbed "nationalists." Although hardly consistent or cohesive, these members shared a belief in the need for a more powerful central government. In their opinion the revolutionary spirit had worn thin. "Benevolence, disinterestedness, virtue"—the fuels that had stoked the "Spirit of '76" had been driven to ground by selfishness, parochialism, and greed.[24] Powerful centrifugal forces tore at the weak fabric of union. Men like Gouverneur Morris, his boss Robert, along with Alexander Hamilton, James Madison, and others, urged a more national view.

Within the Congress there was a general division between nationalists (conservatives), who favored a strong central government, and their opponents, who rested their faith on local and state governments. The various state constitutions and the Articles of Confederation embodied the views of those attached to local government.[25] While these two worldviews persisted—radicals and conservatives—only rarely did they come to the floor of Congress.[26] For the most part Congress was kaleidoscopic. Members came and went with an alarming frequency. States often did not have enough members present to vote. (The Articles required two members present for a state to vote.) Regional alliances did exist (South, Middle, North), but these were unstable and at no time did any one region have sufficient strength to control events. This was particularly true since the Articles required an extraordinary majority of nine votes on any major issue and a unanimous vote to amend the Articles. These stiff requirements guaranteed stalemate.[27] Instead of any broad alignment Congress grouped in "clusters," appearing as "aggregates of individuals who generally thought alike and sometimes acted together, but who also felt free to 'defect' from their ostensible allies on particular (and often critical) issues."[28] In the summer of 1782, as Congress confronted the threat of peace, the want of money, and a restless army, nationalists and radicals divided openly into opposing forces.[29]

In its search for a secure and regular income, on February 3, 1781, Congress approved the imposition of a national impost of 5 percent on goods entering the United States. In terms of revenue, it was relatively modest, estimated to raise slightly more than $500,000. Symbolically, however, it was of enormous import since it would give to the central government, for the first time, an independent source of revenue.[30] Congressional approval, however, was only the first step. To become law, the impost needed the unanimous approval of all thirteen state legislatures. Radicals, who saw the impost as an invasion of states' rights, fought the measure tooth and nail, particularly in New England and most especially in Rhode Island. Nonetheless, by the summer of 1782 all states but Rhode Island had given their approval. The measure hung in limbo with the nationalists, led by Robert Morris, pressing hard for approval, certain that peace would erode political will. Good news from Paris would create bad news in Philadelphia. They feared the confederation would collapse.

The fate of the impost was inextricably linked to another issue upon which the Congress split. As the impost and peace remained suspended in uncertainty, disturbing rumors arrived from Newburgh. The long-suffering officers of the Continental army, men to whom Congress had made multiple unfulfilled promises, were grumbling. It was hardly the first time that the officers had murmured among themselves, but now there was urgency to their protests. Like the nationalists who fretted that peace would undermine the confederation, they realized that an end to the war would lessen their influence with Congress. A body that had ignored them in war would surely abandon them in peace.

Pay was the issue. When the Revolution was new, the "Rage Militaire" swept America. Enthusiastic young men, "Sunshine Patriots" certain of victory, and convinced it would be a short war, rushed to enlist in the ranks of the American cause. More substantial citizens, the stuff of which officers were made, were equally enthused. Seeing glory and honor in the struggle for independence, they too were carried along by the rushing stream of patriotism.[31] This was a citizens' army that disdained the European model of a well-drilled, well-dressed professional body distinct from the people it served. Righteousness, virtue, and élan would triumph over the manual of arms. Such bright and shining dreams faded quickly. Romantic notions that moral superiority would win battles shattered as Washington's army took a drubbing in New York, made a brief comeback in Trenton and Princeton, but then suffered defeat around Philadelphia and marched to a special Gethsemane at Valley Forge. Despite defeat in the field, however, popular support for independence grew, but not necessarily the desire to fight or pay for it. Sensing abandonment by the people at home, an increasing number of soldiers opted to leave the army. Many went home legally as their enlistments expired. Thousands deserted. Finding new recruits was difficult. Volunteering went out of fashion.

Reluctantly, Congress came to the conclusion, as did the commander in chief, that only a professional army could win the war. Money and benefits, particularly cash bounties, not emotional appeals, became the inducements to serve, and so Congress and the states, sometimes in competition, rushed to offer promises of pay, bounties, and land to those who would enlist or stay in service. In making these commitments, they were erecting a preposterous structure on a pitiful foundation. Congress and the states had saddled themselves with commitments they could not possibly honor and upon which they soon waffled.

Broken promises ate away at morale. In the enlisted ranks soldiers protested with sullen behavior or simply deserted. In more extreme situations men stayed in camp and mutinied. Over the course of the Revolution on at least fifty occasions armed soldiers refused to obey lawful orders and threatened their officers. The scale of these mutinies ranged from a few disaffected individuals to the rising of entire regiments.[32] Such miscreant behavior in the Continental army, combined with its increasing "professionalism," did great harm to its public image and made it appear more and more like the oft-despised European armies rather than a virtuous American militia. The gap between civilian and military was growing.

Officers too felt disaffection. By British standards, the only comparison that mattered, American officers were poorly compensated. In order to maintain a proper professional style through uniforms, horses, and equipment, they often had to dig into their own meager resources. Frustrated, they voted with their feet in opting to resign. According to General Nathanael Greene, "near a thousand officers resigned" during the winter at Valley Forge.[33] By spring 1778 Washington was reporting two or three officers per day were asking leave to return home.[34] Both those who stayed and those who left were increasingly angry and blunt about their treatment. Blaming Congress for the ills they endured, they pictured themselves as martyrs who alone were holding true to revolutionary principles. General Gates's views were not unusual when he told Robert Morris that Congress was filled with "Tyranny and Ambition." If there was any hope, according to the general it would be found in "Our Military men" who have "Honour, Wisdom, and Attachment to one another."[35]

Valley Forge was the nadir. "Our Troops are naked" and "worn out with fatigue," wrote Greene, describing those dark winter days.[36] Food was scarce. Morning, noon, and night, mess was the same—fire cake, a foul concoction of dough cooked on a hot stone. General James Mitchell Varnum warned that "the situation is such that in all human probability the Army must soon dissolve," while the commander in chief described the dire situation as a "fatal crisis."[37] With the rank and file starving and officers departing at an alarming rate, Washington decided on radical measures. He ordered Greene to forage the countryside, taking all "Cattle and Sheep fit for slaughter." Greene carried out his orders with a vengeance, reporting to Washington, "[The] Inhabitants cry out and beset me from all quarters, but like Pharoh I harden my heart." He ordered his men to "forage the Country very bare."[38] Supplies arrived, and for his efforts Greene was appointed quartermaster general.

While Greene fed the men, Baron von Steuben drilled them into soldiers. Under von Steuben's strict regimen troops of the Continental army mastered the art of maneuver and fire well enough to fit them to stand against British regulars.[39]

But this new model army would have been of little use if it were not led by the very men on the brink of abandoning the cause, experienced officers. Keeping this skilled cadre in service became a vital goal. In late

November 1777 a delegation of disgruntled army officers, led by Colonel Theodorick Bland of Virginia, presented a series of astonishing recommendations to the commander in chief.⁴⁰

The officers first called for the abolition of all state forces and the formation of a single "grand army" of sixty thousand soldiers under the command of a "captain general." Subordinate general officers were to be nominated by the captain general and commissioned by Congress. To recognize the elevated status of high-ranking officers, "some order of knighthood and adequate pensions" were proposed. In the matter of pay, officers were thought to be entitled to half pay for life when retired and given the opportunity to sell their commissions. "An Army being modell'd and the officers thus selected, there would be little doubt that order, and regularity and discipline would take place, and that Slovenly dress, straggling, filth and their Concomitants, Sloth, desertion, and disease would be banished. [in] the camps of the American army."⁴¹

Not wanting to offend his officers, but understanding that their proposals were completely out of touch with sentiments in Congress, Washington offered a brief measured response, noting simply that the general's recommendations were not practical.⁴²

Although not intended for the eyes of Congress, the officers' memo found its way to the chamber, where it was greeted with disbelief and sarcasm. James Lovell of Massachusetts described it as the work of "the agitating genius of the Men of Leisure," while the usual dour secretary of the Congress, Charles Thomson, fell to sarcasm and with a "roguish sneer" declared that with the adoption of Bland's proposals "Order and Regularity and Discipline will immediately take place. Every soldier will be clean and neatly dressed, his head combed and powdered . . . ; nay what is more, they will be well fed and their meat will be boiled instead of fried or broiled."⁴³

While members pummeled such unreasonable proposals, they could not dodge the very real problem of stopping the hemorrhaging of officers. On November 28 they dispatched Robert Morris, Elbridge Gerry, and Joseph Jones to headquarters for a private confidential consultation with General Washington. They met with him over several days in early December. On the tenth, before heading back to Congress, Morris shared the committee's thoughts with the general.⁴⁴ He told him that the committee was prepared to present to Congress a series of proposals aimed at making "a Commission a desirable object to the Officer," including half pay, pensions for widows, and the right of officers to sell their commissions. Washington was skeptical. Because of its "enormous expense," and the "disgust" it would "give to the people at large," he told Morris that he doubted Congress would approve. Morris and the committee differed and assured him that they had every "reason to suppose" the measure would be "established."[45] Deferring to their political judgment, Washington came around and gave the measure his public support with the exception of selling commissions—on that point he was silent.[46] With the commander in chief's endorsement Morris and his two colleagues returned to Philadelphia to present their recommendations to Congress, confident of approval.

"[It is a] design to put our military officers upon the footing of European," wrote James Lovell, a Massachusetts delegate, to his friend Samuel Adams. "This was in the beginning a *patriotic* war." Lovell railed at the idea that officers should be singled out for such an untoward reward, while ordinary soldiers, militiamen, and their widows got no recompense. Lovell reached a high pitch denouncing the plan as nothing less than a conspiracy brought on by "Extortioners" to reward a class of "haughty, idle, imperious" officers, sparing them the necessity to work at honest "labor." He promised Adams that there would be no "half pay majority in Congress."[47]

Lovell understood his colleagues better than Morris. Congress declined to support the committee and instead sent a second committee to visit with Washington. On March 26 Congress took up their report, which was little more than a rehash of the previous committee's work.[48] After considerable debate the report was recommitted to the committee. For the next two months in committee, in Congress, and "out of doors" debate raged. It was, according to the Connecticut delegates, the "most disagreeable question that hath ever been agitated in Congress."[49] To push their program, the pro-pension forces offered a concession: half pay would be for seven years rather than life. With this compromise in hand on May 15, 1778, Congress enacted the measure.[50]

Although they supported the compromise, nationalists, particularly Gouverneur Morris, remained unhappy. He lay in wait for a year; then on May 24, 1779, he rose and made a motion to provide half pay for life. The chair ruled the motion out of order.[51] The indefatigable Morris pressed ahead. Later in the summer, while serving on a committee to review "allowance for the officers of the army," he slipped into its report a resolution for half pay for life. This proposal got to the floor for debate, but on August 17, 1779, Congress voted to postpone consideration, at the same time recommending that the states grant their own pensions to officers and widows.[52] Here the matter rested for several weeks until December 1, when a committee report written by Philip Schuyler recommended half pay for life. It went down to quick defeat.[53]

Half pay for life stayed in remission until the following October, when again it resurfaced unexpectedly. On October 3, 1780, in a surge of economy Congress decided to reorganize the army by eliminating sixteen regiments and incorporating the rank and file into already existing regiments "by the first day of January next."[54] Fewer regiments meant fewer officers. As of January 1, 1781, hundreds of veteran officers were to be "deranged." To mollify the distressed officers, Congress resolved that the officers separated from the service "from the time the reform of the army takes place [January 1, 1781], be entitled to half pay for seven years."[55]

While the members of Congress thought that their actions were necessary and generous, the commander in chief suggested otherwise. When the president of Congress, Samuel Huntington, asked his opinion on the reduction and compensation, Washington was blunt. At a moment when officers were held by "the feeblest ties" and were "mouldering away by dayly resignations" Congress was doing too little. Even among those who stayed, he warned, this action would plant "durable seeds of discontent."[56] This "brings me," he wrote, "to that which I have so frequently recommended as the most economical, the most politic and the most effectual that could be devised. A half pay for Life."[57]

This time Congress's rapidly shifting political winds blew in favor of Washington. There had been an almost complete turnover in the House since the last discussion of lifetime half pay.[58] In the meantime, as Congress's reputation soured, the nationalist coalition grew stronger while Washington's personal reputation rode strong.[59] The commander in chief was persuasive and persistent. On October 21, in a reversal of several previous votes, Congress approved 9 to 3 (Massachusetts, Connecticut, and New Jersey voted no; Delaware was not present) "that the officers who shall continue in the service to the end of the war, shall also be entitled to half pay during life."[60]

On January 1, 1781, the bills came due. Officers "deranged" by the October reform began to petition Congress for their promised pay. Whether the members of Congress passed the measure in October without thinking of January, or whether they simply crossed their fingers hoping money would show up in January, is uncertain. Indisputable, however, is the fact that Congress remained impoverished. When a contingent of officers from a Pennsylvania regiment sought their pensions, Congress responded that even though it had "the best opinion of their personal merits," it was not "practicable to pay any but those in actual service at this time and even those but partially."[61] Officers continued to press their demands without success. By the summer of 1782 the temper of demands had reached the point that Congress forwarded the petitions to the office of Robert Morris, who was quick to observe that the "dishonorable Neglect" of the states had left the Continental coffers empty.[62] The issue came to a crisis over dinner at Morris's home on July 3, 1782.

Morris had invited Secretary at War Benjamin Lincoln, the Philadelphia merchant Pelatiah Webster, and Captain William Judd, a deranged officer of a Connecticut regiment. Conversation focused on a petition submitted recently to Congress by Judd and Webster on behalf of the Connecticut officers seeking their promised pay. This was hardly the first time that Morris had listened to such pleas, but Webster's voice added a new urgency.[63]

A member of the class of 1746 at Yale College, Webster spent the early years of his career preaching in western Massachusetts. Finding the ministry not to be his calling and drawn by the promise and opportunity of America's largest city, Webster moved to Philadelphia, where by the eve of the Revolution he had acquired a tidy fortune. A strong supporter of the Revolution, Webster was also a fierce "hard money" man.[64] In a series of pamphlets published in Philadelphia between 1779 and 1783 he laid out a detailed plan for financial solvency that included retiring all paper money, an end to foreign loans, and a course of "general and heavy taxes" that would "give demand to our currency, animate the industry of our people and banish idleness, speculation and a thousand visionary projects."[65] Ironically, nothing could have been more visionary than Webster's schemes. While professing respect for the states, he was an ardent nationalist and a true republican who with evangelical rhetoric preached a sermon of self-denial, simplicity, and a central government supported by heavy taxes. He abhorred borrowing from abroad. "What we can raise among ourselves is all that we can pay and we cannot attempt expenditures beyond this without bankruptcy."[66] Nor was he optimistic about an early peace since he was certain that the "war may last many years," for Britain and France would fight to the very last. All the more reason, he argued forcefully, to establish a strong government and sound financial system for "a man who has a long race before him is mad if he exhausts all his strength in the first mile."[67] To float on its own bottom, the Congress needed regular and substantial national revenue.

Webster's answer was a tax on domestic spirits, whiskey and rum, and imported luxury goods including wine, sugar, tea, and coffee. Such a tax offered the dual benefit of raising money while encouraging public virtue inasmuch as it "would admit a check on consumption." It would also, according to Webster, only hit the "richer kind of people." But even these taxes, he recognized, would not be sufficient to fill the public coffers, and so "a small duty of perhaps five per cent on all other imported goods" might be necessary.[68] Without a strong competent central government with independent revenue, "our public union with all its blessings" would "dissolve and waste away into its original atoms."[69]

Morris was well aware of Webster's views and in agreement with them. Webster was equally impressed with Morris, once opining that "a good financier is as rare as a phoenix."[70] Undoubtedly the dinner conversation involved a philosophical discussion about public finance, but the main point of the evening was more practical: justice for officers of the Connecticut Line and other deranged Continental officers. The merits of the petition were clear. The question was not the justice of the claim, but rather where the money to satisfy it might be found. According to Morris, "after much Conversation it was agreed that the Secy at War should include the half pay of all deranged Officers in his Estimate of Expence for 1783 and that they should petition for some fund to be provided for paying the same."[71]

Two weeks later, on July 17, Webster and Judd laid a petition before

Congress, which referred it to the superintendent of finance, who then passed it to the secretary at war. Embedded in the petition was an explosive question. Was the expense of half pay to be born by the Congress or by the states?[72] In all of its previous promises to pay pensions Congress had been careful to step back from identifying any specific source of payment. Now the question was squarely before that body. Raising this fundamental issue was part of the plan crafted at dinner. By putting the officers' claims squarely in the lap of Congress, the nationalists sought to add the burden of half pay to the public debt, which would need to be funded by national taxes along lines suggested by Webster and supported by Morris. The nationalists were playing to the army as their ally.

On July 25, 1782, Lincoln returned with his report. For the moment he dodged the question of who would pay, but he made it clear that there was a solemn promise to pay. "I beg leave to observe that by the resolves of Congress of the 3rd and 21st [sic] of October, 1780 [the Connecticut regiment] was reduced, by which many officers were deranged, to whom Congress promised half pay for life."

Lincoln enclosed a list of Connecticut officers and gave his apologies that he did not have a complete list for the other regiments as well, but "returns from the different Lines have not been made to the War Office."[73] When (and if) they did arrive, there were likely to be hundreds more officers petitioning for pay. Congress sent Lincoln's report to a three-member committee (Ezekiel Cornell, Thomas McKean, and Joseph Montgomery). They reported back on the thirtieth "that it is not expedient at this time to grant the prayer of the memorialists."[74] On that note the next day Jesse Root of Connecticut moved that

> whereas Congress by their resolution of Oct. 20, 1780 did in consideration of the merit and sufferings of the officers of the army, grant to those who should continue in service to the end of the war or be deranged in pursuance of a resolve of the ———— day ———— of half pay for life:
>
> And whereas application is made by some of those officers for an adjustment of their half pay and Congress having no funds provided for discharging the same;
>
> Resolved, That it be recommended to the several States to carry

into effect the resolution of Congress of the ———— day of October 1780 granting half pay for life in regard to the officers in the
lines of their respective States; and every State which shall settle
with the officers belonging to their respective lines in regard to
their half pay aforesaid and cause the U. States to be exonerated
there from shall be discharged from contributing any thing towards the half pay of officers in the line of any other state.

If accepted, Root's motion would have undermined all that Morris and
his nationalist allies had worked to create. Clearly, were Congress to
direct officers to the states for pay, their loyalties would follow. Morris's
plan required the officer corps, the only viable national institution, to be
tied to Congress. Dispersing half pay to local interests would fray the
threads of union. There had to be a national army, a national debt, and
national revenue.

Root's motion set off a fierce debate. James Madison of Virginia, a consistent supporter of the impost tax, spoke most eloquently in support of
national interests, arguing that "all charges of war are by the Confederation to be paid out of one treasury."[75] Others objected on principle,
making the point "that no Country ever gave half pay for Life, which did
not maintain a standing Army."[76] Such a measure would allow half pay
officers to "strut about the streets" supported in their idleness by the
labor of honest citizens.[77] Better, they argued, to leave the matter to the
"Wisdom and Justice" of the states. Abraham Clark of New Jersey went
so far as to claim that Congress and states were not bound by the October
1780 act since it had been passed prior to ratification of the Articles of
Confederation on March 1, 1781.[78]

Such "sophistical" arguments skirted the central argument.[79] In a
long letter to his friend John Lowell the Massachusetts delegate Samuel
Osgood pinned the argument. "Whenever this is made a serious Question in Congress it will be warmly opposed; because some of the States
are exceedingly in Favor of half pay and will do all they can to make the
discharging of it a national Matter, from a Supposition, that it will have
a Tendency to cement the Union."[80]

As the summer afternoon wore on, the debate became more intense
and rancorous. Confident that they had enough votes to remand the issue

to the states for settlement, the antipension forces moved the question. Facing certain defeat, supporters of congressional assumption, led by James Duane of New York, asked leave to postpone, arguing that the subject was of "too much importance to be decided in this hasty way." Objections rose, but most members were happy to push the issue as far away as possible. Jesse Root, the delegate who had unleashed this debate, differed. Before the chair could call for a vote he rose to warn his colleagues, "The army in the field are watching." If soldiers interpreted a postponement as their being "neglected or trifled with they will either quit the service immediately, or refuse to lay down their arms when the war is over."[81] Root's caution went unheeded. Congress voted to delay consideration of half pay until "the first Wednesday in January next."[82]

Congress's pusillanimity disturbed Washington deeply. In early October he wrote to the secretary at war that his officers were being "turned into the World . . . without one farthing of money to carry them home." They had "spent the flower of their days [and many of them their patrimonies] in establishing the freedom and Independence of their Country," and now because of congressional inaction they faced nothing but "gloomy prospects." The commander in chief recited a litany of wrongs done to these men. His army was on the edge of mutiny. "The patience and long sufferance of this Army are almost exhausted, and . . . there never was so great a spirit of Discontent as at this instant . . . I cannot be at ease, respecting the consequences. It is high time for peace."[83]

Lincoln's reply gave no solace. In looking to Congress for justice, the secretary advised Washington that he would only find "Chagrin and disappointment."[84] Robert Morris, with whom Lincoln had apparently shared Washington's letter, offered a view that Washington must have found even more distressing. Contrary to what the general thought, it was not, Morris opined, "high time for peace." War was more "likely than Peace to produce funds for the public debt." It was war, not peace, that would give an "increase of authority to congress, and vigor to the administration as well of the union."[85] Lincoln decided that circumstances warranted a personal visit to camp.

LINCOLN MET WASHINGTON at Verplanck's Point on October 20, arriving at a most inconvenient time. Washington was bidding farewell to the French, who were on their march from Yorktown to Boston to embark for the West Indies.[1] At the same time, the commander in chief was busily organizing the American army for the move to its winter encampment across the river at New Windsor. Thankfully, the secretary's "short visit" lasted only four days, but long enough for Washington to arrange for "the whole American army" to turn out and salute him.[2] In response to the honor Lincoln expressed his "fullest approbation." That compliment did not echo back, for the soldiers on the parade ground felt something far short of "approbation" toward him and the politicians in Philadelphia. Indeed, despite his public praise, the secretary left camp shaken by the "heavy and universal complaint" Washington and his senior commanders had heaped upon him.[3]

Back in Philadelphia Lincoln reported the army's dire situation to Congress. While he did not quote Washington directly, it is clear that the two men were in agreement: officers had to be paid and soon; and since Congress had no money, it ought to look to the states, at least for the present, for compensation. Nationalists, including James Madison, were wary of turning soldiers toward dependence upon the states, which they feared would lessen the power of Congress. Nonetheless, even he had to admit "that some pay must be found for the army [but] Where it is to be found God knows."[4]

That Lincoln and Washington had caved in to the officers at the expense of strengthening the Union was unfathomable to Robert Morris. Over dinner the financier told Lincoln that the proposal would have "a bad influence as it regards our union."[5] Notwithstanding nationalist resistance, Lincoln assured the commander in chief that the proposal seems to be "generally approved," and on November 22 Congress ordered Morris to prepare a report by which "the several states [might] satisfy the Officers and Men of their respective Lines for the sums due to them for pay."[6]

When Morris seemed to be taking an extraordinary amount of time with this task, two members, Alexander Hamilton and Samuel Osgood, paid an unannounced visit to his home to inquire about progress. Morris was unexpectedly absent. According to his diary, he had gone to visit an unnamed "friend," "dangerously ill," and so was not available for consultation. A few days later he delivered his report and minced words.[7] "Balances" due to officers must "be certified in the usual Form . . . and the Principal and Interest thereof be payable in like Manner with other public Debts of the United States."[8] "Usual Form" was Morris's way of saying that it would take a long time.

Congress too was less than eager to plow ahead, and the report sat for a week before being assigned to a committee composed of Hamilton (who was increasingly involved in this matter), John Taylor Gilman, and Thomas FitzSimons. The committee may have met, but it never made a formal report. In any case it did not matter. While Congress dithered, a storm was rising behind Snake Hill, a granite eminence on the east side of the New Windsor winter encampment where a number of regiments, including several from Massachusetts, were "hutted."

In September officers of the Massachusetts Line had petitioned the House and Senate of the commonwealth for half pay, only to have their appeal rejected largely because of a very critical letter aimed at them. Written by Samuel Osgood, a Massachusetts delegate in Congress, the letter was addressed to his friend John Lowell. "Our officers are very numerous and many of them have not performed" was the crux of these disparaging remarks.[9] To Osgood's embarrassment, Lowell made the letter public, creating a furor that doomed the petition. News of the petition's failure caused "much chagrin," according to the usually discreet Henry Knox. He warned Lincoln, "Something must be done to relieve the recent distress which is intolerable."[10] Another Massachusetts officer was less restrained. Daniel Salisbury exploded that the "Almighty will never forgive nor forget our General Court. Damn their souls."[11]

Pushed from pillar to post by the Congress and their own state, the Massachusetts officers vowed to take action. Theirs would not be the polite approach made by the Connecticut Line—a quiet dinner with powerful politicians and a respectful petition for redress. On November 16 officers from the Massachusetts regiments gathered. Knox and Washington knew of the meeting, but neither attended. Although from Massachusetts, Knox was a staff officer and thus not part of the regimental chain of command. As for Washington, he was, conveniently enough, away from camp on a visit to Kingston, New York.[12]

The officers met at the headquarters of the Third Massachusetts Regiment. Colonel John Greaton, commander of the regiment, presided.[13] They elected a committee of seven men—Henry Knox; Colonels Rufus Putnam, John Crane, John Brooks, and Greaton; Lieutenant Colonel Hugh Maxwell; and Dr. James Thacher—to collect "in writing" from the officers of the line "a list of the several grievances of which they complain, and at the same time convey . . . their sentiments on the most probable measures to be adopted for ensuring a happy issue to their recent undertaking."[14]

Spurred by frustration and anger at what they had endured at the hands of elected officials, the committee, under Knox's direction, wasted no time. Within hours clerks in every regimental headquarters were busily copying down lists of "grievances." The men of the First Regiment set the tone, demanding that a "spirited address [be sent] to Congress hoping that the issue may be favorable to our wishes if otherwise we shall be obliged to take some other mode of procedure."[15] The soldiers of the Tenth Regiment expected nothing less than a "categorical answer" to their grievances while those of the Fifth Regiment set a deadline of January 1 for a response.[16]

The fountain of discontent spewing from the Massachusetts regiments spilled over into other camps. Rather than letting Massachusetts stand alone, officers from the entire army at New Windsor, including New York, New Jersey, and New Hampshire regiments as well as a Maryland detachment, signed on to the protest. The streams flowed together. A general committee of officers assembled at West Point on November 24 and elected a subcommittee led by Knox to write a memorial. One week later the full committee reconvened at the quartermaster general's headquarters to approve the work. As usual, Washington remained distant. Knox, however, was at the very center and kept his commander informed. The general committee approved the memorial and circulated it to all the regiments.[17] After a full week the memorial had made the rounds, and on December 7 it was approved and ready to be signed. The address began in the name "of the officers of the army of the United States." Unlike any other military petition to Congress, this plea came neither from a particular group of men nor from a single state. This was an address from the "army of the United States."[18]

The memorial began by acknowledging Congress as the "supreme power." The officers had neatly sharpened a double-edged sword. At one and the same time they played to the vanity of that body while also putting the members on notice that inasmuch as they were in charge, they had the authority to deal with the issue at hand. They would have no reason, other than through their own fecklessness, to hand the matter off to the states.

"We have struggled," the officers wrote, "year after year" for redress, hoping "that each year would be the last." Every time "we have been disappointed." By now the accumulation of the years of "embarrassment" weighed so heavily that they were "unable to go further." Taking a swipe at greedy merchants, profiteers, and politicians who had done well in the war, they noted that all they had were promises unfulfilled; "shadows have been offered to us while the substance has been gleaned by others." They hammered this point deeper, decrying the fact that "citizens murmur at the greatness of their taxes, and are astonished that no part reaches the army. The numerous demands, which are between the first collectors and the soldiers swallow up the whole." Because many citizens did not understand or were deceived, the army had become in

their eyes an "odious" institution with an insatiable demand for resources. This was demonstrably untrue and unfair. Nevertheless, "our
friends are wearied out and disgusted with our incessant applications."
"Our distresses are now brought to a point. We have borne all that men
can bear . . . The uneasiness of the soldiers, for want of pay, is great and
dangerous; any further experiments on their patience may have fatal effects." The army had been too long "sufferers by hunger and nakedness."

Having laid down powerful markers, the officers stepped back to offer
a compromise. To seek "harmony," they wrote, "we are willing to com-
mute the half-pay pledged, for full pay for a certain number of years, or
for a sum in gross, as shall be agreed to by the committee sent with this
address."

While some might have labeled such blunt language as impertinent,
perhaps mutinous, the officers claimed that they had no choice for "it
would be criminal   to conceal the general dissatisfaction which pre-
vails, and is gaining ground in the army, from the pressures of evils and
injuries, which, in the course of seven long years, have made their conditions, in many instances, wretched." They concluded, Congress must
convince "the army and the world that the independence of America
shall not be placed on the ruin of any particular class of her citizens."[19]

To carry the memorial to Congress, the committee elected three senior
officers: Major General Alexander McDougall, Colonel John Brooks,
and Colonel Matthias Ogden. The delegation was neatly balanced. Mc-
Dougall, irascible and dour, came with impeccable patriotic credentials
and a capacity to be outspoken, as he had demonstrated during his recent encounter with Heath. He had also served in the Congress and so
had political insight as well. Brooks, a physician from Reading, Massachusetts, and a veteran of Lexington and Concord, commanded the Seventh Massachusetts Regiment. Ogden, commanding officer of the First
New Jersey, had been the organizer of the failed plot to kidnap Prince
William Henry.[20]

On December 7 the committee gave the officers their instructions.
They were to present the army's demands "in that ready manner that is
expressive of the characters of the officers," in other words, straight and
direct. Knowing Congress's tendency to dance and delay, the men were

further instructed to "continue with Congress until you obtain their full determination on our address."[21] They were to deliver the memorial and stay to lobby.

As if to underscore the pathos of the officers' condition at Newburgh, the delegation delayed its departure to give McDougall time to take up a collection among his brother officers to finance the journey. While McDougall and his fellow officers were passing the hat and packing for Philadelphia, the commander in chief was discreetly preparing Congress for their address. Rather than writing directly to the president of Congress, who might then be required to make the letter public, he instead shared his view of events at camp in a private communication to his old friend, and Virginia delegate, Joseph Jones.[22] Knowing how critical it was that his letter arrive in advance of the delegation, he took the unusual step of sending his aide Lieutenant Colonel Tench Tilghman to deliver it in person. In addition to trusting Tilghman with the letter to Jones, Washington gave the colonel verbal instructions to meet with Robert Morris and brief the financier on the army's desperate situation.[23]

Washington painted a bleak picture. "This Address," he told Jones, "tho' unpleasing is just now unavoidable." "The temper of the army" has become so "soured," lamented the commander in chief, that contrary to his deepest desires, and the wishes of his wife and family, he had decided to remain at Newburgh for the winter. "The disaffection of the Army [has] arisen to alarming height." There are "combinations among the Officers." In his absence he feared the army might collapse, and so he would remain with his men. Although he gave his usual acknowledgment to the authority of Congress—"What the Honble Body can, or will do in the matter, does not belong to me to determine"—he also suggested that it consider "soothing measures." With ominous words he reminded Jones that when disaffected soldiers had rebelled in the past, the officers "at the hazard of their lives" had stood firm and "quelled very dangerous mutinies." Given all that these men had suffered, he could not vouch that such would be the case again.[24]

Knox added his voice. He wrote Lincoln, "The expectations of the Army from the drummer to the highest officer are so keen for some pay that I shudder at the idea of them not receiving it." There would be, he wrote, "convulsions."[25]

George Washington

Lieutenant Colonel David Humphreys

Jonathan Trumbull

Benjamin Franklin

Superintendent of Finance Robert Morris

Gouverneur Morris

General Sir Henry Clinton

William Franklin

Sir Guy Carleton

Chief Justice William Smith

Major General Henry Knox

Secretary at War Benjamin Lincoln

General Horatio Gates

Major General William Heath

Major General Alexander McDougall

Frederick, Lord North

King George III

Lord George Germain

Independence Hall, Philadelphia

George Washington's camp at Newburgh, Hasbrouck House

Head Quarters at Newburgh. 15th
March 1783

Gentlemen

By an anonimous summons, an
attempt has been made to convene you toge:
ther — how inconsistent with the Rules of propri:
ety! — how unmilitary! — and how subversive of all
Order and discipline! — let the good sense of the
Army decide! —

In the moment of this summons,
another anonimous production was sent into cir:
culation; addressed more to the feelings & passions,
than to the reason & judgment of the Army — The Au:
thor of the peice, is entituled to much credit for
the goodness of his pen: — and I could wish, he
had as much credit for the rectitude of his Heart —
for, as men see thro' different Optics, and are in:
duced by the reflecting faculties of the Mind, to
use different means, to attain the same End; the
Author of the Address, should have had more Chari:
ty, than to mark for suspicion, the man who should
recommend moderation & longer forbearance —
or, in other Words, who should not think as he thinks,
and act as he advises. — But he had another plan
in view, in which Candor & Liberality of sentiment,
Regard to Justice, & love of Country, have no part —
And he was right, to insinuate the darkest suspicion,
to effect the blackest designs —

That the

December 1782 was a month of despair in Philadelphia. It had been a tempestuous time. Rhode Island's delegate David Howell had been pilloried by his fellow members for breaking confidence and sharing privileged information with his constituents. The language was bitter and personal, laying bare the deep divisions in the Congress over the very nature of the union. The debate centered on Rhode Island's sole opposition to the impost. In a style Madison described as "extremely offensive," Howell defended his state and justified his own actions as a legitimate expression of free speech.[26] Members let loose attacks on one another that deepened old wounds and opened new ones.[27] According to the outspoken Connecticut delegate Eliphalet Dyer, Philadelphia had become a place "of Dissipation, unbounded Avarice, a City of Gambles," and Congress, tormented by "Divided Councils, Exhausted Finances," lay paralyzed. As for the army, he despaired that there was "no plan, System or practical method" to grant relief.[28] Alexander Hamilton, sunk in pessimism, wrote to his friend John Laurance, "God grant the union may last but it is too frail now to be relied on, and we ought to be prepared for the worst."[29]

Hampered by "bad and cold weather," McDougall and the colonels took a week to reach Philadelphia, arriving just before Christmas. The trip had been especially hard on the general, whose health was failing. Upon arrival in the city, McDougall found comfortable quarters at the popular Indian Queen Tavern on Fourth Street just south of Market and only two blocks from Independence Hall.[30]

Judging it "expedient," the officers decided "to converse with the delegates of the different States" privately before they delivered their memorial in public, making the rounds over several days.[31] On the evening of December 31 the officers made their most important visit, not to a member of Congress, but to Robert Morris. In his usual laconic style and with classic understatement, the financier described the meeting in his diary as a moment when "we had some Conversation respecting the want of Pay for the army."[32] Having lobbied nearly everyone, the following Monday, January 6, the officers were ready to present their memorial to Congress.

As soon as the officers laid their memorial on the table, Congress, according to Madison, "as a mark of the important light in which the memorial was viewed," assigned it to a "Grand Committee" made up of representatives from all the states present.[33] The memorial was "important" to the members in different ways according to their own political agendas. A significant number in the chamber viewed the memorial as yet another attempt by the nationalists to use the army as a lever, to move their political agenda and strengthen the central government at the expense of the states by granting Congress the compulsory power to collect revenue. The opposition was ready. The first sign of trouble for the nationalists came when the Grand Committee elected a chair: Oliver Wolcott of Connecticut. Five years earlier when the states had voted to grant officers half pay for seven years, Wolcott and James Lovell of Massachusetts were the only delegates to vote no. Since then, nothing had altered Wolcott's position on military pensions.[34]

Wolcott's election was only the first warning sign. Even before the committee convened, some members let loose with their opinions, most of them hostile. Samuel Osgood insisted that the committee ought not to "hold out any longer vain and delusory promises to the Army."[35] Robert Morris joined the verbal fray, warning the committee that "it was impossible to make any advance of pay in the present State of the finances to the army and imprudent to give any assurances with respect to future pay until certain funds [that is, impost] should be previously established."[36] The situation was, in his words, "alarming" and could only be calmed by recognizing the army's just claims and funding them through a national revenue. Madison shared Morris's views, citing the crisis as "proof of our poverty and imbecility."[37]

In a bit of cruel irony it was in the interests of both sides, nationalists and antinationalists, to reject the officers' memorial. Hamilton summed up the nationalist strategy to his friend Governor George Clinton. Rejection, he argued, "may be turned to good account [for] every day proves more and more the insufficiency of the confederation. The proselytes to this opinion [that is, a stronger central government] are increasing fast."[38]

Late Friday afternoon, January 10, the Grand Committee gathered. Although not a member of the committee, Morris arrived by special invitation. Also present were Colonels Ogden and Brooks. McDougall, the officers explained, having suffered greatly from the hard journey, was ill and confined to his quarters at the Indian Queen Tavern. They asked if the committee might adjourn to the tavern to accommodate the general. That sparked a discussion about the dignity of Congress. The committeemen agreed that it would be "derogatory" to the image of Congress for them to wait upon the general; instead they voted to adjourn until the following Monday, giving as their reason the lack of sufficient members in attendance due to "the extreme badness of the weather."[39]

Over the weekend the weather improved, but not the mood of Congress. On Monday morning the chamber took up, yet again, the tedious matter of national finance. This time the debate circled around the question of implementing article 8 of the Articles of Confederation: "All charges of war, and all other expenses that shall be incurred for the common defence or general welfare, and allowed by the United States in Congress assembled, shall be defrayed out of a common treasury, which shall be supplied by the several states, in proportion to the value of all land within each state."

As usual, a cacophony of voices filled the chamber. Not having been present at the creation of the confederation, Madison felt at liberty to describe article 8 as "chimerical" and impossible to execute.[40] The problems were "too vast" and "insuperable" to find solution.[41] Indeed, there was no practical way to determine "the value of all land within each state." For nearly the entire day members wrangled until finally, unable to craft a solution on the floor, they consigned the question to another "Grand Committee." That evening the army's Grand Committee met with the recovering McDougall accompanied by Colonels Ogden and Brooks.[42]

Wolcott called the meeting to order and recognized McDougall, who, after a few pleasant remarks, turned quickly to the matter at hand. He distilled the memorial into three principal points: "an immediate advance of pay, adequate provision for the residue, and half pay."[43] The outspoken "old revolutionary," according to Madison, described the woeful condition of the army "in very highly coloured expressions." If nothing were done, he told the committee, "serious consequences" would follow. The "seeming approach of peace" was a worry to the army for they feared that in a rush to end the war Congress would abandon them. Brooks and Ogden added to the glumness of the moment by relating their own tales of misery, describing the poverty in which the army struggled. Ogden went so far as to tell the committee that he would not "return to the army if he was to be the messenger of disappointment." After detailing all their grievances and sufferings, they concluded by reminding the members that they were in fact willing to compromise. They would swap the promised half pay for a commutation to any equivalent. Pressed by the committee to speculate what might happen should Congress not act, the word *mutiny* came back. The "temper of the army was such that they did [not] reason or deliberate coolly on the consequences" of their acts. "The army," warned McDougall, "were verging to that state which we are told will make a wise man mad."[44] In previous mutinies officers had stood firm and put down uprisings. This time, warned McDougall, leaders of the army, particularly "those of inferior grades," might waver or stand aside.

Having delivered their memorial, made their pleas, and answered questions, the officers took their leave. Committee members remained behind and after some discussion elected a subcommittee of Hamilton, Rutledge, and Madison, instructing the trio to prepare a report, in concert with the superintendent of finance, on the officers' memorial.[45]

Late in the afternoon of January 15 Hamilton, Rutledge, and Madison met with Robert Morris. The town was abuzz. Earlier in the day Congress had received official news from General Nathanael Greene that the British had evacuated Charleston. The fact that the war might truly be coming to a close was sinking in. That reality made Robert Morris uneasy. He knew that "the present Union of America is from Necessity. It is a Vessel whose Parts are kept together by exterior Compression. When that is entirely Removed, trivial Causes may burst it asunder."[46] With the news of Charleston and the perils of peace on his mind, Morris welcomed the subcommittee to his home, where they had "a long conference . . . on the business of the Army."[47] Prepared to hear once again a lecture from the financier about the want of money for the army and his inability to pay the officers and men, the delegation was stunned when Morris promised to provide a month's pay for the army at Newburgh. When they asked how he could make such a promise, Morris revealed to them that early in December he had dispatched in secret an American frigate to Havana to convoy home more than seventy thousand in gold coin, part of the loan secured by Adams from the Dutch.[48]

While he undoubtedly saw the justice in his act, Morris also had political goals which he did not share with his visitors. Should the army
disgrace itself in mutiny or disappear into the countryside, Morris and
his nationalist allies would lose their most powerful ally. The "Army
[must] be kept together," Morris observed.[49] By offering the men of the
regiments a taste of what they might eventually receive, should Congress have a national revenue, Morris was trying to buy time and cultivate their support.

It was an extraordinary gamble. Two days later, January 17, Morris
invited McDougall, Ogden, and Brooks to his home for a private meeting.[50] In an oblique reference to the Havana gold he told them that he
"had taken Measures to obtain a Sum of Money for the Purpose of . . .
[the army's] Pay [but] those measures are not yet ripe."[51] If all went well,
troops and noncommissioned officers would soon receive one month's
pay, and from his own private resources he pledged a month's pay for
officers.[52] He admitted that it was not all that they might justly expect,
but he asked them to be patient and "give time for wise Measures." One
week later, at a moment when the members of Congress were absorbed
in selecting "a list of proper books for the use of Congress," their attention
was diverted by report of a letter from the superintendent of finance. He
was resigning.[53]

According to those who knew him best, Morris was in a state of emotional "despondence." He had reached a point of physical and financial
exhaustion. He had come to a point, he wrote, where he could do nothing to see "justice done to the public creditors," the army properly paid,
or "public finances placed on an honorable establishment."[54] The news
shook Congress. Nathaniel Gorham lamented that the departure produced "a vacancy which no one knew how to fill and which no fit man
would venture to accept."[55] James Wilson of New Jersey moved that
Congress not accept the resignation and instead urge Morris to stay.
Even Morris's friends thought that was too much. For its own sake Congress could not "condescend to solicit Mr. M even if there were a chance
of its being successful." It was "improper." Still not sure of what to do,
and fearful that news of the resignation would roil the nation's already
fragile financial markets, the members could think of no alternative but
to keep the news secret.[56]

Morris's tenacious enemy and a perpetual opponent to "permanent taxes," Arthur Lee saw sinister hands at play. "Every engine is at work here to obtain permanent taxes," he warned.[57] In Morris's resignation Lee and his allies saw a grand plot aimed at deepening the financial crisis to the point where Congress, driven by fear of what the army might do and by sheer desperation, would see no choice but to adopt the nationalist agenda. In this poisoned atmosphere Hamilton presented his committee's report on the officers' memorial.[58]

The committee laid several recommendations on the table. All of them in one form or another had passed through the chamber before, and they all required new money. Debate followed, airing the usual tired arguments from both sides over the power of Congress to raise revenue and the propriety of pensions. On one critical point, however, the members agreed. Thanks to what they had heard from McDougall, Ogden, and Brooks, the delegates knew that the army at New Windsor was seething with anger, and unless soothing measures were taken, mutiny, mass desertion, or both were likely to happen. They also knew that Morris had some cash from Havana, and so they directed him "to make such payment and in such manner as he shall think proper."[59]

Morris had no intention of paying the soldiers in one lump sum. No one had any illusions about what cash-starved soldiers, bored by the endless routine of winter encampment, would do with coin. Sutlers stood ready to pour home-distilled whiskey in any amount, and local brothels were prepared to swing open their doors.[60] Discipline would collapse. Instead Morris presented a plan to dole out cash to enlisted men and noncommissioned officers at only fifty cents per week. At that rate of cash flow, he estimated he had enough money on hand to last thirteen weeks, betting that was enough time for other sources of money such as a French loan to arrive.[61] Whatever small satisfaction the enlisted ranks might draw from Morris's decision, the officers gained almost nothing. Instead of specie he offered them sixty-day "Morris notes" drawn on his own account.[62] In the matter of half pay Congress remained undecided.

After six weeks of endless meetings with members of Congress, McDougall, Ogden, and Brooks had failed in their mission. The sop of specie to enlisted men might ease tension in the ranks, but that would last only as long as the money, and those who had sent them, the officers of the army, aside from the personal notes drawn on the financier, got virtually nothing. Congress remained deadlocked over half pay. "Some of our friends," reported the officers, suggested that they ought to turn to the states, recognizing those with a nationalist bent opposed that route since it would weaken Congress.[63]

Colonel Brooks volunteered to carry the bad news back to Knox. Mc-Dougall, preferring the comforts of Philadelphia to a winter on the Hudson, opted to remain in Philadelphia to continue, he said, lobbying for the army. Ogden, true to his pledge, announced that he would not return to camp as a "messenger of disappointment." He went home to New Jersey.[64]

Brooks left Philadelphia on February 9. Before he departed, a small group of men including Ogden and McDougall, as well as members of Congress, among them Hamilton, joined by the ever-active bureaucrat Gouverneur Morris, and by Robert Morris, discussed the urgent situation. They were convinced that the only force that could move Congress, and the nation, was the threat that the army might either collapse or mutiny. They needed to seed a storm over New Windsor that would sweep down onto Philadelphia. To do this, they laid a plan to cajole Washington, Knox, Gates, and the officer corps to their side.[65]

Next to Washington, Henry Knox was one of the most respected and important senior officers in the army, the only person who might influence "His Excellency."[66] The first tactic was for Brooks, on behalf of the officers, to deliver to Knox, as chair of the committee that had sent them to Philadelphia, their lengthy report, which they asked that he share with other officers. Written principally by Ogden and McDougall, it laid out in detail the tale of the weeks of frustration spent with the Congress. Even so long a report was inadequate to express all that they had endured at the hands of a dithering, divided body, and so preferring not to put everything "in the compass of a letter," they instructed Colonel Brooks "to give particular detail."[67] In addition to the public report, Brooks carried a personal letter from Gouverneur Morris to Knox—one not to be made public.[68]

Morris's confidential letter aimed at undermining Knox's notion, which he had expressed previously, that the officers might depend upon the states for half pay. Setting aside the usual rhetorical formalities,

Morris began the letter "My Dear Knox." He continued, "It has given me much Pain to see the Army looking wildly for a Redress of Grievances to their particular States." The states were faithless, and any law that they might enact for the officers' benefit "they [would] repeal as soon as they [found] it expedient." He went on to warn of the dangers of peace and disbandment. "During the war they find [the army] useful, and after a Peace they will wish to get rid of you and then they will see you starve rather than pay a six Penny Tax." Morris told his "dear friend" that the army's only hope was to connect itself "with the public Creditors of every Kind both foreign and domestic" to force Congress to enact measures to create "general permanent Funds." With dramatic flourish he concluded, "The Army may now influence the Legislatures and if you will permit me a Metaphor from your own Profession After you have carried the Post the public Creditors will garrison it for you."[69]

With rumors of peace wafting in the air, there was no time to lose, and Brooks rode quickly. He arrived at Knox's headquarters on February 13 with both the report and the private letter. He likely spent the evening filling in the general with "particulars" and then the next day continued his journey to Washington's headquarters.

To what degree Brooks shared all the "particulars" with Washington is uncertain. Thus far the commander in chief had stayed out of the fray. Until Washington's position was better known, it was best to be cautious. What Brooks did tell him, however, was that a train of heavily guarded wagons was "on the road to camp, laden with money for the army." The commander in chief immediately dispatched "a Captain and fifty Men" to secure the "Treasure."[70]

CHAPTER TEN

CONGRESS'S DEBATES AND MANEUVERINGS through the cold winter months of December and January left the army at New Windsor wondering sadly about its future. Not far away the mood at Hasbrouck House was equally glum. Out of an "official family" of at least a half dozen senior officers who ordinarily attended Washington, only two remained: Colonel David Humphreys and Lieutenant Colonel Benjamin Walker. The others, including Colonels Jonathan Trumbull and Tench Tilghman along with Lieutenant Colonel David Cobb, had taken winter furloughs to be home with their families. When a junior officer, Major Hodijah Baylies, unwisely asked for a leave, Washington could barely restrain himself. "Nothwithstanding some Officers of the Army have supposed, there was nothing, or at least very little to be done in Winter Quarters, yet for my own part, I must confess I have never found it so, but on the contrary have frequently had as much business to be done by myself and Aids [sic] in that Season as in any part of the Campaign."[1]

Not only had members of his "family" departed for more comfortable environs, but so too had his generals. Of "nine Generals assigned to the command of the Troops in this Cantonment," he reported, "seven are either actually gone or have made application to be absent."[2] Of the senior

commanders, only Generals Horatio Gates and Robert Howe had stayed
with Washington, albeit reluctantly since neither of them were pleased
at the prospect of a winter on the Hudson. Howe had already asked for
leave to return to Boston, to which Washington had responded, "You
will not leave camp."[3] And Gates was pacing about his headquarters, the
former home of John Ellison located near the cantonment five miles from
Hasbrouck House, waiting for word from his wife back in Virginia from
whom he had been "without a Letter" since late October.[4] Having left
her when she was ill, he had good reason to fear the worst.[5]

Adding to the depressing mood was the sour presence of the quartermaster general and critic at large Colonel Timothy Pickering. He had
lingered (too long, thought Washington) in Philadelphia with his wife
and seemed determined to remain longer until on Christmas Day Washington ordered him, given the "bad state of Affairs" in his department,
"to proceed without loss of time to join the Army."[6] Pickering did what
he was told but with little grace. His letters to his wife and others were
replete with cynicism and venom. Pickering was more prickly than usual.
He was still smarting from a recent unfortunate encounter he had with
the local sheriff. As quartermaster general he had given out promissory
notes drawn on Congress, but over his signature, to merchants in payment for supplies. Not surprisingly, the notes were overdue. One evening as he was escorting Mrs. Washington and a friend to their carriage
after a convivial dinner, he was confronted suddenly by the sheriff, who
served him with a suit from local merchants naming him the debtor and
demanding payment. Pickering was furious and rightfully blamed Congress for his humiliation.[7]

Even the usually upbeat Knox was in a low mood. The war had worn
him out. His wife, Lucy, had suffered as well. Like Martha Washington,
she had stayed with her husband for a great part of the war, including
moments of personal tragedy. They were together in the summer of 1779
at artillery headquarters in Pluckemin, New Jersey, when their infant
daughter, Julia, died. On December 10, 1781, they rejoiced at the birth
of a son, Marcus Camillus Knox, and invited Washington to be the god-
father. In spring 1782, when the commander in chief moved his headquarters to Newburgh, Knox took command at West Point, where he
brought his wife and infant son. Tragedy followed the family north. "I

have the unhappiness my dear General," wrote Knox to Washington on September 8, "to inform you of the departure of my precious infant, your Godson." While grieving his departed son, Knox was deeply anxious over Lucy's well-being. Remembering what Washington and his wife had endured in their own family—Martha had lost all her children—he shared with him his hope that by leaning on "reason and religion" Lucy would survive "this repeated shock to her tender affections."[8] Washington shared his friend's sorrow over the loss of his son and held out hope for Lucy that "the lenient hand of time will no doubt be necessary to soothe the keener feelings of a fond and tender mother."[9]

Agitated generals, absent officers, and unpaid soldiers cast a gloomy atmosphere. Washington was increasingly alone. Seven years of war had taken a heavy toll on the weary commander. Martha was with him, as were the Knoxes, but his closest comrades from former days with whom he had shared victories and defeats were absent: Greene was in the Carolinas tidying up after the British evacuation, von Steuben was in Philadelphia, and Lafayette was home in France. "I am," Washington wrote, "fast locked by frost and snow." Surrounded by "rugged and dreary mountains," he prayed that this winter would be his last in the field.[10]

Adding to Washington's melancholy was ill news from home. Only twice during the entire war had he been home—brief visits before and after Yorktown. He had left his beloved Mount Vernon in the hands of his cousin Lund. Washington had hired him before the war to manage the plantation during his occasional absences. Since the plantation was his "*only means*" to support his family, he told Lund, he was anxious about its condition. He was pressing Lund, who incredibly had not made a full report in over four years, to send forward "the long promised account." When it arrived in late January, to Washington's dismay it turned out to be "irregular." That sent him into a verbal rage. He suspected Lund of mismanagement and demanded that he send to him immediately "accounts of [his] receipts and expenditures."[11] Anticipating an end to the ordeal of war, he told Lund, "I want to know before I come home (as I shall come home with empty pockets whenever Peace shall take place) how Affairs stand with me, and what my dependence is."[12]

Mount Vernon was not Washington's only personal challenge. His younger brother Samuel, married five times, had died in 1781, leaving a widow and seven children. Through Samuel's "sheer indolence and inattention to business," his estate was mired in confusion and debt. "In God's name," wrote Washington to his younger brother John Augustine, "how did my Brother Sam'l contrive to get himself so enormously in debt?" Washington sought quickly to distance himself from Samuel's misery. "Curiosity only prompts the inquiry." Although he had often helped his brother, he had, he told John Augustine, "never received a farthing" back from Samuel.[13] However, Washington could not so easily separate himself from his mother's problems.

To say that George Washington had a difficult relationship with his mother is an understatement. When he had last stopped to visit at her Fredericksburg home, shortly after Yorktown, she was away. Although he had not seen her in several years, he did hear from her on occasion. Most often she wrote to complain about money. Such was the case when a letter from her arrived at Hasbrouck House early in the winter of 1782–83.[14]

According to Mary Ball, the "Knavery of the Overseer" whom Washington had appointed to keep charge of the Fredericksburg property had left her penniless. The overseer had taken "the whole profit" and left her nothing. She expected her son to find a new overseer and in the meantime send her money. Deep into his own financial problems, Washington was pained at the personal and financial cost of having to bail out his mother again. He had bought her the comfortable home in which she now lived in Fredericksburg, she had slaves to attend to her, and her daughter Betty Fielding Lewis lived within walking distance. Nonetheless, he felt a son's responsibility and perhaps a bit of guilt since he had hired this apparent scoundrel. To John Augustine, who lived near Fredericksburg, he lamented his woeful situation: "[While] I am suffering in every other way (and hardly able to keep my own Estate from Sale)," it is unreasonable "to be saddled with the expense of hers."[15] Would his brother handle the matter?

Washington and his brother had a tartar on their hands.[16] Reports had reached Washington that "upon all occasions, and in all Companies," his mother was "complaining of the hardness of the times, of her wants and distresses." All this "by strong innuendo" she laid at the feet of her children. In fact, Washington told his brother, "she can have no *real* wants that may not be supplied. [Her] *imaginary* wants are indefinite and often-times insatiable, because they are boundless and always changing." As keen as she was to inflict personal pain on her illustrious son, her actions also threatened political harm. She shared her complaints with every visitor who came by. On one occasion when she was working in her garden, Lafayette stopped to visit. She unloaded all her woes on him. So pitiful did she appear that Washington learned the Virginia Assembly was preparing to grant her a pension. Washington exploded at the thought of the public humiliation that would bring upon him as both the negligent son and the commander in chief. At a moment when Congress was refusing to grant pensions to his officers, his mother might end up with a public annuity! This needed to stop, and so he instructed John Augustine: "Represent to her in delicate terms the impropriety of her complaints and acceptance of favors even where they are voluntarily offered, from any but relations. It will not do to touch upon this subject in a letter to her, and therefore I have avoided it."[17]

For the sake of his wife and family, his estate, and his health, Washington did indeed "pant for retirement."[18] In the midst of his personal travails came the sad news that Major General William Alexander, "Lord Stirling," had died suddenly at his headquarters in Albany. Stirling had been with Washington since the New York campaign and was in command of the northern army.[19] Washington's mood sunk even deeper when a few weeks after Stirling's death he learned that an attack he had approved against the British post at Oswego on Lake Ontario had failed miserably.[20]

Physical stress was beginning to show in the commander in chief. A man who in his younger years had been eager to trek the wilderness in harsh conditions, spend evenings around a fire, and sleep in the open under the stars had grown weary of long marches and endless encampments. Poor teeth and sore gums plagued him, causing Pickering to confide to his wife that the "General is unwell with a badly swollen face."[21] His eyes, under the constant strain of reading and writing endless reports, had weakened. His vision improved somewhat with new glasses, prepared by the Philadelphia instrument maker David Rittenhouse. "The spectacles suit my Eyes extremely well," he told Rittenhouse, but he was having a problem adjusting to their use for reading. He found it difficult to find "the proper focus." He was certain, however, that with time he would "get more accustomed to the use of them" and be able to see "objects very distinctly."[22]

Discipline was essential, but the ennui of camp life had made it brittle. Washington described the wanton behavior of his soldiers as "scandalous beyond description and a disgrace to any army." He had in November rebuked his officers for allowing their men "to ramble about the country" stealing from neighboring farmers and causing other mischief wherever they roamed. This "must and shall be corrected."[23] A flurry of courts-martial followed Washington's stern order. Men were flogged, confined, and otherwise publicly humiliated, but punishment treated only the symptoms and did little to root out the causes: anger and idleness.

Initially, "hutting" had kept the troops busy, but by mid-December that job had been finished. Washington looked for other tasks to occupy his men. Always available were the daily routines of any army: policing the camp, digging latrines, chopping firewood, tending equipment, standing guard. When weather permitted, regiments drilled. Washington ordered frequent inspections and reviews. He stood and watched as his soldiers marched by and performed a variety of intricate battlefield maneuvers. When pleased, he would give glowing praise in a General Order. When necessary, he was also keen to lambast the troops for being out of step or improperly attired.[24] Officers bore the brunt of his sharp criticism.

Anxious to relieve the boredom and engage the men in a new project, Washington embraced an idea brought to him by Chaplain Israel Evans. A Princeton graduate, the thirty-six-year-old Evans was one of the longest-serving chaplains in the Continental army. He enlisted in 1775 as chaplain to the First New York Regiment, which marched on General Richard Montgomery's ill-fated invasion of Canada. After surviving that debacle, in the summer of 1779 Evans served with General John Sullivan in his expedition against the Iroquois. Soon after he returned to the main army Congress consolidated the New York regiments, leaving the chaplain without a permanent billet. He was with Washington at Yorktown and followed the commander in chief to Newburgh, where he took the post as chaplain to the New Hampshire brigade. Washington knew and respected Evans and was eager to hear his suggestion.[25]

Evans proposed a public works project to engage the army. He pointed
out to the commander in chief that the Newburgh encampment lacked a
visible center. While neatly arranged, the huts of the encampment were
spread out over a wide area. General Gates and his staff were at Ellison
House, about a mile from the encampment. The commander himself was
a more distant five miles up the road at Hasbrouck House, while the various administrative departments, including Quartermaster, Adjutant, and
Paymaster, were scattered about New Windsor and Newburgh. Each
headquarters and office produced daily stacks of paper, which had to be
bundled up and shifted from location to location. Evans proposed to
eliminate the burden by constructing a large public building that could
serve as a central headquarters. It could also, the chaplain remarked, be
used as a place of worship and for social gatherings.

Washington embraced the idea and on Christmas Day 1782 ordered
that the "General and Field officers . . . who are desirous of promoting
so useful a scheme will be pleased to meet at Major-General Gates' quarters tomorrow at ten o'clock."[26] Present at the meeting was Major Stephen Rochefontaine, formerly an engineer in the French army, who had
served in the Continental army since the spring of 1778. He was with
Washington at Morristown and had drawn notice from the commander
in chief for his splendid work at the siege of Yorktown. Promoted to
major, he was the ranking engineering officer at Newburgh.[27] Gates appointed him, along with Colonel Benjamin Tupper, to prepare plans and
estimates for the construction of a public building.[28] It took them less
than a week to draw plans and prepare estimates for an ambitious and
expensive project.[29]

Rochefontaine rode about the area searching for a site fit for the most
important building in the cantonment. He found the best spot on a high
ridge near the center of the cantonment overlooking the huts. Like an
ancient temple to the gods, the building would stand high above the popu-
lace and so was quickly dubbed "the Temple of Virtue," a likely reference
to the ancient Roman Temple of Honor and Virtue.[30]

It took six weeks, working on the windy summit of a naked hill in the
bitter cold, to complete the project. Every regiment in the cantonment
had an assignment. Axmen scoured the snowy woods, felling timber to
bring back on sleds drawn by snorting oxen. Other work parties pried

loose stones from frozen ground to lay as a foundation for the building. From the blacksmiths' shops hammers could be heard pounding on anvils shaping thousands of nails. On one part of the site men with ax, adze, and saw shaped rough timber for framing, while others nearby split thousands of shingles for the roof and exterior walls. Carpenters recruited from the regiments fashioned dozens of benches, chairs, and tables to furnish the interior. Every day Tupper, Rochefontaine, and Chaplain Evans walked about to supervise and encourage the men. Their words, accompanied by extra rations of whiskey, lifted spirits. So too did exhortations from General Gates, who made it clear to his officers that he did not expect to "meet a single dissenting voice or an unwilling hand."[31] When some regiments were "dilatory" in delivering up men and material, Gates reprimanded them and warned his officers that he would "not require another hint on the subject."[32] More "hints" were required. Two days later Gates faced a work stoppage when the Second Massachusetts failed to deliver its quota of men. Gates described the behavior as "ungracious," drawing a quick apology and promise that the men were on the march.[33]

Not all went as planned. With so many officers absent on furlough, supervision was lax. Some soldiers saw a chance to make some extra cash. Thanks to the nearly insatiable demand for timber for both building the "Temple" and heating the huts, the local forests had been clear-cut of trees. Wood was scarce and pricey. The quartermaster officers in charge of tallying incoming timber for the public building noticed that a number of foraging parties were returning to camp with short loads. On investigating, they discovered a dramatic difference between the volume of timber cut and the size of the loads showing up in camp. Men were selling the army wood to the locals. When Quartermaster General Pickering discovered the scam he reported it to Washington, who immediately ordered that a stop be put to the theft.[34]

On January 29 Washington stepped up the pressure on Rochefontaine and Tupper to complete the building by announcing that "the 6th of February, being the anniversary of the alliance with France, a *feu de joie*, will be fired on that day in celebration of this auspicious event."[35] In advance of the firing, Washington ordered the troops to form on the parade ground for his inspection. Following the review and the salute,

"the General will be happy to see, not only all the officers of the cantonment, but all the gentlemen of the army and other gentlemen and ladies
who can attend with convenience at the new Public Building where a
cold collation will be provided."[36]

Washington's announcement left Tupper and Rochefontaine less than
a week to finish the job. Upon hearing the deadline, all Tupper could
manage was a halfhearted "poor me."[37] Luckily, a thaw arrived toward
the end of January, providing a few favorable days for some soldiers to
finish shingling the roof while others bustled inside framing windows
and putting the final touches on the floor, walls, and ceiling.[38] With little
time to spare, Tupper breathed easier as he supervised soldiers tidying up
the construction site.

Considering the barely six weeks provided for construction, the crude
materials available, and the often unhelpful weather, Tupper and his soldier crews had accomplished a great deal.[39] It was an impressive building
measuring 110 feet by 30 feet. The main entrance stood on the west side
facing the cantonment. Standing above the entrance was a modest flag-
staff, while crowning the roof was a long gable. Large sash windows cut
into the walls, twelve panes each, admitted light into the interior. The
walls and ceiling were plastered, giving an additional touch of elegance
to the chamber. At each end of the room were two offices to be used, reported General Heath, "for the sitting of Boards of Officers, Courts
Martial, etc, and separate offices and storerooms for the Quarter-Master
and Commissary departments."[40] In the center of the Temple the carpenters installed a small raised platform or pulpit from which chaplains
might preach.

By the late afternoon of February 6 all was in readiness. Guards
opened the doors, and hundreds of people crowded into the Temple. The
commander in chief and his wife were there to greet the guests. The hubbub in the hall quieted as Chaplain Evans moved to the platform. Having
conceived the idea of the place, Evans had the honor of delivering the
inaugural sermon.

Not everyone was pleased. Quartermaster General Timothy Pickering
thought the whole enterprise unrepublican and unnecessary. He found
it particularly ironic that the building had been nicknamed "Temple of
Virtue" when so "little" of that quality was present in camp. Nor was he

impressed by Evans's address, which "fell vastly short" of his expectations."[41] Notwithstanding Pickering's comments, most thought the celebration was a great success. The exhausted Tupper asked for a furlough the next day. Despite the shortage of officers in camp, Washington could hardly refuse the request. Tupper left for his home in Chesterfield, Massachusetts, to enjoy a few weeks of much deserved rest.[42]

Unsettling rumors continued to waft about that peace was imminent and Congress planned to disband the army without pay. Officers waited expectantly for the report of their delegation to Congress. One week after the opening of the Temple, on February 13, Brooks arrived at West Point from Philadelphia with the long-anticipated report. He also brought his "particulars."

Brooks confirmed to Knox all that he had feared: Congress had essentially abandoned the army. The next morning he rode the last few miles to Hasbrouck House, leaving Knox to read in private Gouverneur Morris's letter. He was shaken by its contents.[43]

On the same day that Brooks arrived at West Point, in Philadelphia another piece of the nationalist plan was falling into place. Just as Gouverneur Morris had been chosen to write to Knox because of their close relationship, Alexander Hamilton won the task of lobbying Washington. The general and Hamilton had a long, albeit sometimes rocky, relationship. Born in modest circumstances on the island of Nevis in the West Indies, in 1772 at the age of fifteen Hamilton arrived in New York City and enrolled in King's College. Revolution soon trumped education. In 1776 Hamilton took a commission as a captain in the Provincial Company of New York Artillery. He distinguished himself in the ill-fated New York campaign, gaining the attention of General Nathanael Greene, who recommended him to Washington. Washington was taken with this "quick, proud, bony-faced young man, with cold blue eyes and a smiling mouth."[44] The commander in chief was also impressed with Hamilton's writing craft—a skill he needed. On March 1, 1777, while encamped at Morristown, he appointed the young man (barely twenty) his aide-de-camp and promoted him to lieutenant colonel.

For nearly four years, through some of the most trying moments of the Revolution, Hamilton was at Washington's side. In December 1780

Hamilton improved his fortunes by marrying Elizabeth Schuyler, daughter of Washington's friend Philip Schuyler, the richest man in New York. Hamilton was increasingly unhappy living the dreary life of a staff officer. He yearned for a field command. He got his wish as the result of an unfortunate encounter with his commanding officer in February 1781. At headquarters Hamilton was scurrying down a stairway anxious to deliver a message to his fellow aide-de-camp Tench Tilghman. As Washington passed him going up the stairs, he told Hamilton to come immediately with him. Instead of doing an about-face, the proper response, Hamilton excused himself and told his commander that he would join him as soon as he had delivered his message to Tilghman. Not one to be treated so cavalierly by a junior officer, Washington was annoyed into an angry exchange.

> Colonel Hamilton, you have kept me waiting at the head of the stairs these ten minutes. I must tell you, sir, you treat me with dis respect.
> I am not conscious of it, sir; but since you have thought it neces sary to tell me so, we part.
> Very well, sir if it is your choice.[45]

They parted unhappily, but on July 31, 1781, Hamilton got his wish for a field command and took charge of a battalion in Moses Hazen's brigade of Lafayette's Light Infantry Division, then preparing to march to Yorktown. Hamilton played a key role in the siege. On the night of October 14 he led his battalion on a bayonet charge to seize Redoubt Number 10, a vital British position. The captures of Number 10 and nearby Redoubt Number 9 on the same night by the French were the last battles of the siege. Their fall made the British position completely untenable. Hamilton's courageous behavior impressed Washington and helped to rekindle their friendship. Hamilton left the service in the days following Yorktown, returning to New York to be elected to Congress, where he took a leading role in the nationalist cause. To Hamilton fell the task of sounding out Washington as to his sentiments about using the army to pressure Congress.

While no surviving evidence exists directly linking Morris's and

Hamilton's letters, given their timing and purpose, and the fact that for months the two men had been working closely together, along with several other nationalist-minded members of Congress, to advance their political agenda, they clearly collaborated. Hamilton began his letter to Washington with soft words: "Flattering myself that your knowledge of me will induce you to receive the observations I make as dictated by a regard to the public good, I take the liberty to suggest to you my ideas on some matters of delicacy and importance." The state of finances and the army were "critical." "There has scarcely been a period of the revolution which called for more wisdom and decision in Congress." Congress, however, was "not governed by reason [or] foresight, but by circumstances." The circumstance Hamilton feared most was peace. "If peace should take place," Congress would have "no necessity for [the army.]" Once the soldiers "lay down their arms, they part with the means of obtaining justice." The army, he urged, could not lay down its arms. "The claims of the army urged with moderation, but with firmness may operate on those weak minds [Congress] which are influenced by their apprehensions more than by their judgments." In making these observations, Hamilton realized that the army was a dangerous tool to be used against Congress. "The difficulty will be to keep a *complaining* and *suffering army* within the bounds of moderation." "This Your Excellency's influence must effect." Washington was "not to discountenance their [the army's] endeavors" but "to take the direction of them." The commander in chief was to "guide the torrent." Hamilton concluded his suggestive letter by striking a personal blow at his former commander. He hinted that his soldiers had lost faith in him. Rumors were circulating in the army, according to Hamilton, that the general, out of a concern for "delicacy," had not been "espousing its interests with sufficient warmth." He assured Washington, "The falsehood of this opinion no one can be better acquainted with than myself, but it is not the less mischievous for being false." In the present crisis these suspicions would "impair that influence, which you may exert with advantage, should any commotions unhappily ensue." Then, as if to suggest that Washington might need counsel from someone more in tune with the soldiers, Hamilton added a postscript to his letter, further evidence that he knew the contents of

Morris's letter to Knox. "General Knox has the confidence of the army and is a man of sense. I think he may safely be made use of."[46]

Neither Washington nor Knox responded immediately to their Philadelphia correspondents. It took Knox a week to conjure a reply. Washington took more than twice that time. Given Hamilton's closing remark about Knox, to say nothing of the close relationship between Knox and the commander in chief, it is likely that the two generals conferred. Perhaps they even shared letters. In any case they almost certainly took counsel with Colonel Brooks, who had the "particulars."[47]

Precisely what Brooks might have advised Knox and Washington is not clear. Having sent him as their emissary, the nationalists must have expected that he would urge the two generals to support their efforts and use the army to pressure Congress directly. If this was Brooks's mission, it failed. Brooks may have been unpersuasive, or more likely, perhaps he never did embrace the nationalist agenda and simply nodded agreement at the Philadelphia meetings, waiting to return to Newburgh and inform Washington of the plot afoot. Once beyond the noxious political fumes of Philadelphia, Brooks could have seen clearly the horror that would unfold should the army enter politics.

Shortly after meeting with Knox and Washington, Brooks reported to the committee of officers who had dispatched him, McDougall, and Ogden. According to Timothy Pickering, who was present, all the colonel offered to the group was a "broken recitation of matters already mentioned in the letter with no mention of consequences," a sanitized version of the situation in Philadelphia so as not to excite the officers to untoward action. Pickering later alleged that before Brooks met with the officers he had "closeted" with Washington and Knox and had committed "treachery" by revealing to the generals all that had gone on in Philadelphia.[48] John Armstrong, an aide to General Gates, agreed, calling Brooks a "Villain."[49]

After meeting with Brooks, and perhaps consulting with Washington, Knox made his reply to Gouverneur Morris.[50] It was a short and cool letter. The general made no attempt to respond directly to Morris's condemnation of Congress or his call to action. Instead he referred to the politicians in Philadelphia as "good patriots" who, while gone astray, were yet redeemable and who could be "taught" by "proper authority." He then turned the tables on Morris. Since "the present constitution is so defective," he asked, "why do not you great men call the people together, and tell them so." With remarkable prescience he went on to urge that the "great men" call the states to a convention to draft a better constitution. This undoubtedly is what he meant by "proper authority."

Carrying affairs to a new extreme, on February 12 McDougall, writing to Knox under the pseudonym "Brutus," went so far as to touch on the possibility of an army mutiny and violence.[51] Knox was thunderstruck. Lest there be any misunderstanding about where he stood, on the same day that he responded to Morris, Knox let loose a thunderous volley against any suggestion that the army should sully itself by meddling in politics. "I consider the reputation of the American Army as one of the most immaculate things on earth," and "I hope to God [it] will never be directed than against the Enemies of the liberties of America."[52]

Rebuffed by Knox, the nationalists were running out of time. Congress would not be moved on either the impost or half pay.[53] News from London added to their anxiety. The king had announced to Parliament that he had agreed to the independence of the American colonies. Peace was coming.[54]

While hints of mutiny and violence were being recklessly tossed about, such actions were never likely nor intended. What the nationalists in Congress wanted was for the army, led hopefully by Washington and Knox, to take a stand and refuse to disband until paid. That, they believed, would provoke a crisis sufficient to push Congress to act. Having failed in that part of the plan, they worked to ferment fear within Congress, hoping that they might frighten enough members to tip the political scale in their favor. They even tried undermining Washington's reputation. The commander in chief, according to Madison, had "become extremely unpopular amongst almost all ranks," to the point that he might not be able to control the army.[55] In a coded message Madison reported to Edmund Randolph, governor of Virginia, that Washington's influence was "rapidly decreasing in the army insomuch that it is even in contemplation to substitute some less scrupulous guardian of their interests."[56] To further punctuate the crisis, Robert Morris asked permission to make public his intention to resign.[57]

Thus far Washington had remained silent. He had not yet responded to Hamilton. Some interpreted his silence as a kind of consent to action. Hamilton did not share that view. Knox, he suspected, spoke for the commander in chief; indeed, it is likely that Washington may even have seen and approved the letter. Writing from Philadelphia, Baron von Steuben summed up the situation by stating that without Washington or Knox "we are lost."[58] Not everyone, however, was ready to give up. If neither Washington nor Knox would step forward, there remained Horatio Gates, whose turbulent past with Washington and ambition made him an ideal candidate to undermine the commander in chief. He was also the senior officer in command of the army at New Windsor.[59]

S TOKED BY THE DISAPPOINTING REPORT of the committee to Congress and Colonel Brooks's "particulars," the mood of the officers encamped along the Hudson had turned ever more sour. Most were convinced that Congress had turned its back on them and that the politicians in Philadelphia stood ready to heave them over the side at the first whiff of peace. The generals had even more reason for concern. The private letters from Gouverneur Morris and Hamilton, although kept close, worked unhappily on the minds of the two men who mattered most, Washington and Knox. They now knew for certain that there were men in Congress who sought to use the army for political gain. Washington had faith that he could count on the ever loyal Knox to do his best to soothe discontent at West Point. He was not so certain about General Gates.

Gates had read the committee's report and heard most of Brooks's "particulars," but he also had his own informants in Philadelphia, among them Richard Peters. A member of a wealthy Philadelphia family with close ties to Pennsylvania's Proprietary party, Peters abandoned his Tory friends and went over to the Whigs when the Revolution erupted. Recognizing his political and administrative skills, on June 13, 1776, Congress elected him secretary to the Board of War, a position he held for five years. From this perch he looked in the direction of the army, where he came to know every important officer, at the same time keeping a close gaze on Congress and the Pennsylvania Assembly. He and his fellow Philadelphian Gouverneur Morris were much alike: astute politicians, skilled bureaucrats, and avid nationalists. When he left his post as secretary Peters did not abandon politics. On November 12, 1782, the Pennsylvania Assembly elected him a delegate to Congress.[1] Having experienced firsthand the dire consequences of a feeble Congress, Peters drew close to the nationalist faction, sometimes sharing his views over dinner and port in the company of the brace of the Morrises, Hamilton, Madison, and others. Madison in particular gave special weight to Peters's judgment regarding the mood of the army.[2]

Shortly after Brooks's return to camp Gates wrote Peters: "The political pot in Philadelphia Boils so furiously," he had been informed, "that I suppose as a stranger rides through their town They cry scaldings as they do on Ship board when the tea kettle is logging fore and aft." The "Boiling" kettle, thought Gates, might produce a useful brew. "What a Blessed prospect we Republicans have before us." He closed with a cryptic comment, "The Financier has the prayers of the Army."[3]

Gates wrote from his headquarters at Ellison House east of the main cantonment. Although attractive, the building was not large. Gates took over the house late in 1782 with the unusual understanding that the family could remain. Soon he invited his wife, Elizabeth, to join him, telling her he had "a warm Stone House."[4] That would have been its only recommendation, however, as Ellison House was small and cramped. Gates described it as a "kennel."[5] The general had the only private chamber; the rest of the small rooms not occupied by the family were filled by numerous staff and aides whose constant comings and goings gave a sense of frenzy to the place. As if to remind these men, whose chief task was battling paperwork, of the real cost of the war, in the room below the general "a young officer of the cavalry," suffering the consequences of a "shocking wound," lay "dying by inches." Small wonder that within a few weeks of his invitation to Elizabeth to join him, Gates told her not to come to camp.[6]

Gates's controversial career in the Revolution had earned him a legion of enemies, but whatever his critics' opinion of him, his young aides at Ellison House, particularly Majors John Armstrong and William Barber and Captain Christopher Richmond, found the general likable, patriotic, and a goodhearted commander. Because of his wispy gray hair, a pronounced stoop, and spectacles hanging at the tip of his nose, they called him affectionately "Granny."[7]

Armstrong came from a well-connected Pennsylvania family. His father, John, had served in the French and Indian War and was remembered famously as the commander of the militia force that destroyed the Delaware village at Kittanning. Later in the same war he, along with Colonel George Washington of Virginia, marched with General John Forbes against Fort Duquesne. The two officers rekindled their friendship at the opening of the Revolution. Congress commissioned Armstrong brigadier general, and Pennsylvania promoted him to major general in the state militia. He served until 1778, when poor health forced him to retire from the field.

With his father's encouragement at the outbreak of the Revolution, John Armstrong Jr., barely eighteen years old, headed for New York seeking a commission. One of his father's comrades from the days of Kittanning, General Hugh Mercer, obliged the ambitious young man and took him on as his brigade major and aide. When Mercer fell at the Battle of Princeton in January 1777, Armstrong lost his patron, but again his father interceded. The senior Armstrong not only had served with Washington and Mercer but also had marched during the war with a young British officer, Horatio Gates. Armed with a letter of introduction from his father, Armstrong found a new patron. Only a few weeks prior to taking command of the northern army in August 1777, Gates appointed him major and aide-de-camp, beginning a friendship that, despite the difference in ages, lasted a lifetime.[8]

The thirty-nine-year-old English-born Captain Christopher Richmond entered the service as a lieutenant and paymaster in the Second Maryland Regiment. In April 1780 Washington ordered the regiment to the Carolinas as reinforcement for the southern army under the command of Gates. After Gates's ignominious defeat at Camden in August 1780 and his subsequent replacement by Nathanael Greene, Richmond accompanied the deposed general to his Virginia home. In the fall of 1782 both men, under orders from Washington, "join[ed] the Army on the North River."[9]

Unlike Armstrong and Richmond, Major William Barber was not a member of Gates's official family. He was, nonetheless, close to those at Ellison House. Like his two colleagues, he had spent the entire war as a staff officer. Appointed an ensign in the Second New Jersey Regiment, he became aide-de-camp to its commander, Brigadier General William Maxwell. After Maxwell left the service in 1777, Barber took a post with another New Jersey general, William Alexander, Lord Stirling. Early in 1781, when the British invaded Virginia, he went south to join Lafayette's light infantry as division inspector. Grazed by a cannonball at Yorktown, he took some weeks to recover from his injuries. In January 1782 Inspector General von Steuben appointed Barber assistant inspector of the northern army to serve under the northern army's Inspector Colonel Walter Stewart.[10]

Nicknamed "the boy colonel," Stewart was reputed to be the "handsomest officer in the Continental army." He was a well-connected Ulsterman and a prominent Philadelphian.[11] As inspector of the army, Stewart was supposed to stay with Washington and the army. Much to the commander in chief's annoyance, however, like Quartermaster General Pickering, the colonel seemed unable to pry himself loose from Philadelphia. Stewart pled illness as his excuse for remaining in the city and away from his post, but his recent marriage to the beautiful eighteen-year-old Deborah McClenachan and the arrival of an infant son gave Washington cause to suspect his motives. The commander in chief lumped the young colonel in with a growing list of officers who were doing all that they could to avoid the rigors of a winter camp. He also knew Stewart to be an intriguer and a close friend of both Robert Morris and Horatio Gates.[12]

While Stewart dallied in Philadelphia, his assistant Barber took charge of the inspector's duties at Newburgh. These powers included maintaining all rosters, regulating "the details of the formation and march of all the guards, detachments, etc," and although he did not ordinarily distribute orders—that was the function of the adjutant general—as inspector he could examine everything. Barber's position gave him extraordinary independence to collect and communicate information.[13]

While we can only speculate about conversations among officers in the crowded quarters at Ellison House during the bleak winter of 1782–83, there can be little doubt that anger and frustration flowed freely. Aside from Gates, all the others were "young men of the Revolution."[14] Most had been in the army from the very beginning of the struggle. They had experienced the humiliation of defeat at New York, depravation at Valley Forge, victory at Yorktown, as well as exhausting marches and endless days of sheer boredom punctuated by the terror of combat. There was no emotion that they had not felt. The ebb and flow of the war had carried them to all parts of America. No longer did they simply know villages and farms of Pennsylvania, New Jersey, or New York. They had been to the other colonies, now states, where citizens were finding it increasingly comfortable to call themselves "Americans." They sensed that the Revolution, at least the military aspect of it, was nearly over and hence their usefulness. When they should have been celebrating and wearing garlands of victory, their overriding sentiment was not jubilation but a gnawing sense of abandonment by Congress and country.

Having finally recovered from his "illness," Stewart arrived in camp on March 8. He stopped first at Hasbrouck House to pay his respects to the commander in chief. Still annoyed at his long absence, which had added to their own administrative burden, the general and his aides gave him a chilly reception. After the usual formalities Stewart rode to Ellison House.

Gates and his staff were eager to hear Stewart's latest news from Philadelphia. His long sojourn in the city had coincided with the intense and fruitless debates in Congress over army pay. Because he was inspector of the northern army, Stewart's opinion counted, and it was likely sought. His military rank and social standing gave him easy access to the principal players in government, including Robert Morris. There is little reason to think that these men in Philadelphia did not share with the inspector their own opinions on the crisis to the point of divulging confidential information. They would have done so with comfort because they knew Stewart was on their side.[15]

In discussing Stewart's arrival and his role, Gates described him as "a kind of agent from our friends in congress and in the administration."[16] In all likelihood Stewart brought with him the same entreaty that these "friends" had made to Knox, which he had rejected: if the army would carry "the Post the public creditors will garrison it for you."[17] The nationalists' only hope was an army "in being," a force remaining in place on the Hudson that could hover and by its presence "intimidate" the states and force Congress into action. Peters told Gates in early March that Congress was on the edge of approving half pay: "We want only one state to get it through."[18] For this to happen, however, the army had to remain intact, refuse any orders to retire, and not allow itself to be dispersed by Congress. Washington and Knox had already made their position clear: they would not defy Congress. Gates was the nationalists' last best hope.

A few miles up the road at Hasbrouck House Washington understood that disaffection was rife in the ranks. Repeatedly he had pleaded with the members of Congress to address the needs of the army and warned them numerous times of the dire consequences of inaction. In December he had written to his friend Joseph Jones, a Virginia delegate, warning of "dangerous mutinies" and the "soured" temper of the army, hoping that Jones might influence Congress.[19]

Jones did not respond for ten weeks. He blamed illness for the delay. That may have been only partly true. In a long detailed letter Jones described a sympathetic Congress that few in the body, or outside, would have recognized. Congress would provide "ample justice," he said. It had nothing but the "purest intentions." The impost would "be finally adopted." The policies under discussion would prove "efficacious."

However, Jones put the onus on the army and its commander. "Reports are freely circulated here that there are dangerous combinations in the Army, and within a few days past it has been said, they are about to declare they will not disband until their demands are complied with." Jones went on to write, "I trust these reports are not well founded" and admonished Washington to remember "that when once all confidence between the civil and military authority is lost, by intemperate conduct or an assumption of improper power, especially by the military body, the Rubicon is passed and to retreat will be very difficult, from the fears and jealousies that will unavoidably subsist between the two Bodies." Jones repeated Hamilton's hurtful message: "I have lately heard there are those who are abandoned enough to use their arts to lessen your popularity in the Army." The last hope to stem these "dangerous combinations" would be "the exertions of every worthy officer." None, of course, were more "worthy" than the commander in chief himself. "Whether to temporize, or oppose with steady unremitting firmness, what is supposed to be in agitation of dangerous tendency, or that may be agitated, must be left to your own sense of propriety, and better judgment."[20]

The length, detail, importance, and the long time taken to write suggest that Jones was expressing sentiments shared by others. This was not simply a message from a single delegate but from several. It has a hint of input from moderate nationalists such as Hamilton and Madison. Hamilton in particular was inclined to warn Washington of the schemers around him, particularly Gates, for whom he had a deep personal and professional dislike.[21] Jones's letter was intended to forewarn Washington of the evil consequences of inaction. "Propriety" and "better judgment" called for action. Jones's message and Colonel Stewart arrived in camp within a few days of each other.[22]

Thanks to his friends in Congress, particularly Hamilton and Jones, as well as faithful officers such as Knox and Brooks, Washington knew that he stood on "the brink of a precipice."[23] It was Gates he suspected—that "old leven is again, beginning to work, under a mask of the most perfect dissimulation, and apparent cordiality."[24] To what degree "old leven" was "working" remains unclear.[25] What is indisputable is that Gates's headquarters was a center of "activity," and that Stewart's arrival heightened tension.

On Sunday March 9 Major Armstrong, most likely with the assistance of others at Ellison House, drafted an "Address" to the officers.[26] Although there is no direct evidence, it stretches credulity to believe that General Gates was not aware of what was going on. Ellison House was small, and there was little privacy. His bedroom/office was on the second floor. The room in which Armstrong was busily writing was only a few feet away at the bottom of the stairs.[27] Armstrong finished his work in time for Barber and others to make sufficient copies for distribution to officers of the regiments. They may well have worked through the night. In the morning the assistant adjutant general, Captain John Carlisle, arrived at Ellison House to pick up the routine daily orders and carry them up to the public building for distribution. He also took with him a call for "a meeting of the general and field officers . . . on Tuesday next at 11 o'clock. A commissioned officer from each company is expected, and a delegate from the medical staff."[28] Accompanying the "Call" was the "Address," which when read shattered the ordinarily calm atmosphere of the adjutant's office. Standing by to receive the usual assortment of standard orders, the regimental adjutants were ill prepared for the drama unfolding. Taking the "Call" and the "Address," they rushed back to their camps.

Identifying himself only as "a fellow soldier, whose interest and affections bind him strongly to you," Armstrong addressed "the Officers of the Army." His tone was personal and emotional. "Like many of you," "[I have] seen the insolence of wealth" and "felt the cold hand of poverty." We suffered willingly because we "believed in the justice of [our] country" and expected that "the sunshine of peace" would bring "better fortune," and that "gratitude would blaze forth upon" us.

At this point in the Address Armstrong shifted his pitch from pious righteousness to deep anger. Congress and the country had "trample[d] upon your rights" and "distain[ed] your cries and insult[ed] your distresses." The "meek language of entreating memorials" had proven worthless. The hyperbolic Armstrong ratcheted up the rhetoric. "Change the milk-and-water style of your last memorial; assume a bolder tone— . . . and suspect the man who would advise to more moderation and longer forbearance." He warned against laying down "those very swords, the instruments and companions of your glory," for without them you will be "forgotten" and be left to "grow old in poverty, wretchedness and contempt." It was time "to draw up your last remonstrance" to Congress and warn the men in Philadelphia that should the soldiers once again be ignored, "the army has its alternative." The flamboyant Armstrong declared that the soldiers might elect to abandon the cause, gather up their families, and follow their "illustrious leader" west "to some unsettled country," leaving behind an ungrateful nation to defend itself. Armstrong's reference to the "leader" was vague; he never provided a name.

While adjutants raced down the hill toward camp with copies of the Address, a post rider spurred his horse to Hasbrouck House. For nearly eight years, despite momentary and isolated collapses of authority,

Washington had managed to keep the army whole and obedient both to him and ultimately to civilian authority. Armstrong's Address threatened disorder and destruction. It would lead the army into "the abyss of misery." Washington declared his "disapprobation" and canceled the meeting.[29] He knew, however, that canceling the meeting would not stem the anger in camp; indeed, it might even play into the hands of those who accused the general, in Hamilton's haunting words, of lacking "sufficient warmth" for his men. Having parried the thrust, the general counterattacked. With the assistance of his secretary, Jonathan Trumbull, he prepared a General Order responding to the Address.[30]

Not certain of the extent of support for the "fellow soldier," Washington was careful to avoid any precipitous action that might unleash forces he could not control. He aimed to offer an alternative and to buy time so that his officers might "more calmly and seriously . . . adopt more rational measures."[31] He needed first to be certain that the officers in line command were loyal. Staff officers, such as those at Ellison House, might plot and scheme, but they could do nothing without support of the troops and the officers who commanded them directly.[32] With advice from Trumbull and others at headquarters, including perhaps Knox and Brooks, the general prepared a General Order and laid his plan.[33]

In contrast to the dramatic language of Armstrong's Address, Washington's General Order was brief, focused, and subdued.[34] Had he wished, the commander in chief might well have condemned the Address as sedition and mutiny and used his powers to seize and punish the villainous authors. It would not have been a stretch to find in section 2, articles 1 and 3 of the Articles of War sufficient cause to arrest the author(s).[35] Nor would he have had difficulty finding the culprits.[36] Such action, however, might have led to violent resistance.

Early on Tuesday morning, March 11, the day called for the meeting, adjutants scurried from the public building back to their regiments with a General Order from the commander in chief. The commander in chief began by noting that by calling a meeting without his consent, "fellow soldier" had challenged his authority; so to eliminate any doubt about command, he canceled the meeting, declaring it to be "irregular" and "disorderly."[37] He assured his soldiers that he was not alarmed by the proceedings for he was confident that under any circumstances the "good sense of the officers would induce them to pay very little attention" to the Address.

Sinking the meeting was the first part of the plan. The men at Hasbrouck House were acutely aware that by scuttling the "irregular" meeting they had done nothing to alleviate anxiety in camp. The next step was to call another general meeting, but this one by the authority of the commander in chief and under his control. Washington ordered "that the staff of the army will assemble at 12 o'clock on Saturday next, at the new building, to hear the report of the committee of the army to Congress."[38] The purpose of the meeting was to "devise what further measures ought to be adopted as most rational and best calculated to attain the just and important object in view." Washington had kept aloof from any such public meetings and announced that the "senior officer in rank, present, will be pleased to preside and report the result of the deliberation to the Commander in Chief."[39] The "senior officer in rank, present" would be Gates.

The next day, March 12, Washington sent three letters to Philadelphia: a relatively short one to the president of Congress giving sparse detail of the affairs of the eleventh and two longer letters, one to Joseph Jones and the other to Hamilton, giving much information and frank opinion. In their previous correspondence both Jones and Hamilton had sought to lay a fair portion of fault for the army's discontent on the officers themselves and their commander in particular. Although annoyed at their critical intimations, Washington had not bothered previously to respond in his own defense. The crisis now brewing, however, made it imperative for the sake of his own reputation that he answer them and throw the blame back where he thought it belonged—with Congress.

In a tone verging on anger Washington dismissed Jones's suggestion that "dangerous combinations [had been] forming in the army." Before this moment, he told Jones, there was not a "syllable of . . . agitation in Camp." The pernicious rumors now infecting camp were "planned, digested and matured in Philadelphia" by people "playing a double game." These "vile Artifices" were carried north by Colonel Stewart, who with the aid of others "managed with great Art" to see to it that they were "industriously circulated" through the ranks.[40] "Let me entreat you therefore my good Sir, to push this matter [that is, pay] to an issue." Should

Congress fail in its duty, it must be "answerable for all the ineffable horrors which may be occasioned thereby."[41]

Washington's quick move to grab the initiative set the officers at Ellison House aback, but only temporarily. Armstrong went to work on a counterstroke, and through the afternoon of the eleventh and into the evening he composed a second "Address." It was ready by morning and dispatched for distribution.[42]

Armstrong thundered forth in a rhetorical style so florid and convoluted that it must have left readers bewildered. He tried to turn Washington on his head. "The weak may mistake" the "general order of yesterday" as an indication that the commander in chief disapproves of the meeting. That, Armstrong wrote, would be a wrong. "Till now the Commander in Chief has regarded the steps you have taken for redress, with good wishes alone." Washington, according to Armstrong, had now broken his silence. His call to meet had "passed the seal of office, and taken all the solemnity of an order." Washington's blessing "[would] give system to your proceedings, and stability to your resolves."[43]

Armstrong had set a clever trap. Washington had called and sanctified a meeting over which he declined to preside. With Gates in the chair, and the room packed with angry officers, an absent commander in chief would have no control over the outcome, and the "rational" and "best-calculated" measures Washington hoped for would likely fall victim to a madding crowd while being presented in a manner that bore his approval.

Over the next three days Washington and his staff maintained a business-as-usual demeanor, at the same time altering plans.[44] Permitting Gates, Armstrong, and company to control the meeting would lead to disaster, perhaps even a mutiny of the army itself. Only Washington in person could keep this raging river within its banks. Bucking precedent, he decided to attend the meeting but with no advance notice. The drama of an unannounced arrival would gain attention and force those who had been murmuring against the general behind his back to publicly acknowledge his authority.

On Saturday morning March 15 toward noon officers trudged up the hill to the public building. When General Gates appeared from an anteroom at the side, all eyes turned to him. He took his place and called the meeting to order. Officers took seats on the benches.[45] The sound of several horses approaching broke the silence. The rattling noise of armed men dismounting was unmistakable. Within moments a tall figure dressed in blue stood in the doorway. The officers were astonished. Never before in this war had the commander in chief come in person to address his officers. Even in the darkest and most perilous moments of the Revolution Washington had preferred back channels, third parties, or written communications. That he would come in person testified to the serious crisis at hand.[46]

As he moved through the room men stood, ranks parted to permit him to pass. A surprised Gates acknowledged his superior and moved to the side, offering the commander in chief the place of honor.

According to Major Samuel Shaw, who stood nearby, "Every eye was fixed upon the illustrious man, and attention to their beloved general held the assembly mute."[47] Washington began by apologizing for being there, which was, he said, "by no means his intention when he published the order which directed them to assemble."[48] So important was this moment, he told his audience, that he "had committed his thoughts to writing." Wrapping himself in humility and deference, he asked "the indulgence of his brother officers" to grant him "liberty" to read from his text. With that he took out a sheaf of papers and began.[49]

His speech was delivered in the grand tradition of battle orations and bore a striking resemblance to Henry V's St. Crispin's Day speech. Like the king, Washington stood before an army that had been in the field for a long time. The soldiers were demoralized, tired, and wanted to go home. His task was to remind them of their duty, their time together, and the history that would record their service. Twice before during the war, both times in writing, Washington had reminded his officers of their duty and destiny by calling forth the image of King Henry's "band of brothers." Perhaps fearing that it might sound trite on this occasion, he avoided using that phrase while delivering the same emotional message.[50]

Ordinarily the general's style was cool, deliberate, and restrained. This speech was personal. The anonymous writer had questioned his support of the army. To those who would challenge his loyalty, he declared, "I have been a faithful friend to the army." "I was among the first who embarked in the cause of our common country." "I have been the constant companion and witness of your distresses." "I have ever considered my own military reputation as inseparably connected with that of the army; as my heart has ever expanded with joy, when I have heard its praises." Washington entreated his men to permit him to make their case to Congress; "I have not a doubt," he assured them, that "justice" would be granted there.

Washington ended with a clarion call. By standing firm in defense of the country's liberties, he told his officers, "you will, by the dignity of your conduct, afford occasion for posterity to say, when speaking of this glorious example you have exhibited to mankind—'had this day been wanting, the world had never seen the last stage of perfection to which human nature is capable of attaining.'"

Finished, Washington put his text aside. The room was silent. The officers seemed unmoved. Washington feared that his message had failed. He looked out at his audience, paused, and took from his coat the letter he had recently received from Joseph Jones. He began to read portions of it to reassure the officers that Congress had their cause in mind. He struggled through the first sentences, hesitating over words. Standing nearby, Major Shaw watched as the commander in chief paused, "took out his spectacles," the ones David Rittenhouse had sent only a few weeks before, and to which he was still becoming accustomed. "He begged the indulgence of his audience while he put them on, observing that he had grown gray in their service, and now found himself growing blind." It was an emotional moment, Shaw wrote, that "forced its way to the heart, and you might see sensibility moisten every eye."[51] Washington "stood single and alone. There was no saying where the passions of an army, which were not a little inflamed, might lead; he appeared, not at the head of his troops, but as it were in opposition to them; and for a dreadful moment the interests of the army and its General seemed to be in competition." But then "he spoke,—every doubt was dispelled and the tide of patriotism rolled again in its wonted course." Hamilton's "torrent" was stemmed. "The whole assembly," according to Philip Schuyler, "were [sic] in tears."[52]

Washington left as abruptly as he had appeared. As he galloped away his supporters moved quickly. From the floor Brigadier General Rufus Putnam, commander of the Massachusetts Brigade, moved that a committee be elected immediately to draft resolutions that the commander in chief might forward to Congress.[53] Brigadier General Edward Hand rose to second the motion. Having lost control of the meeting, Gates and his aides must have gasped when in the next moment the assembly elected Knox, Brooks, and Captain Howard to prepare a draft.[54] A thirty-minute meeting in a side room chaired by Knox produced six resolutions, all adopted unanimously.[55] The officers declared that the army would never "sully the reputation and glory which they have acquired, at the price of their blood and eight years of faithful service." They went on to pledge their "unshaken confidence in the justice of Congress and their country" and asked Washington to present their case. With language unmistakable in its intent and target, the officers "reject[ed] with distain, the infamous propositions contained in a late anonymous address to the officers of the army; and resent[ed], with indignation, the secret attempt of some unknown persons to collect the officers together, in a manner totally subversive of all discipline and good order." They concluded by offering thanks to the committee (McDougall, Brooks, and Ogden) who had presented their case to Congress and asked that McDougall continue his efforts on their behalf. At the last moment of this drama all eyes focused on Gates as he "took the chair." He knew his place and his role. With "order, moderation and decency" he adjourned the meeting.[56]

Timothy Pickering, an eyewitness to the event and a friend to the folks at Ellison House, summed up the feelings of those who had hoped for more "manly" measures. The meeting, he wrote to his wife, was yet again "another instance of the fecklessness of popular assemblies." Washington's performance had "shown how easily a fluent orator with plausibility only to support him may govern . . . as he will." Once the commander had spoken, it was impossible to stand against the tide. Pickering admitted that when the resolutions came to the floor he even voted aye, explaining that had he done otherwise, he should "stand alone." No one other than Washington dared stand alone. Strangest of all, he observed, there were men in the room who had participated in and approved of the "Anonymous Addresses" who voted in favor of a resolution declaring their own work "Infamous."[57]

After the meeting Knox, accompanied by General Philip Schuyler, rode back to West Point in his carriage. The two men sat in absolute silence.⁵⁸ The next day was a quiet one at Hasbrouck House. Trumbull prepared only one dispatch for the commander's approval, a short notice to the president of Congress assuring him that all had gone well at the previous day's meeting and that as soon as possible full details would be forwarded. Ironically, the first task for Gates's staff was to prepare copies of the resolutions for dispatch to Congress.⁵⁹

While Washington was taciturn and reserved in his reactions to the meeting, Knox was far less restrained. Eager to spread the good news as quickly as possible, and to ease concern in Philadelphia, on Sunday he sent two long reports to that city. To his friend McDougall, the army's chief lobbyist, he wrote that the "ferment which was passed in the minds of the officers" had been relieved, but this was not the time to slack off, and he urged the general not to let up his "solicitations" on behalf of the officers. To Secretary at War Benjamin Lincoln, Knox reported that "the occasion though intended for opposite purposes has been one of the happiest circumstances of the war and will set the military character of America in a high point of view." He described the "masterly performance of Washington" and insisted that the secretary publish the speech "immediately." The members of Congress had to be pushed, for if they "ha[d] the most latent spark of gratitude the generous proceedings of the army must call it forth."⁶⁰

WHILE THE DRAMA at Newburgh was unfolding, Captain Joshua Barney's ship *Washington* dropped anchor at Philadelphia on March 12 with copies of the preliminary treaty negotiated in Paris. "The Public dispatches received by the vessel," reported the *Pennsylvania Packet*, "although they do not announce a peace to be concluded yet the negotiations were still going on every thing was settled between America and Great Britain."[1] Reports of Barney's arrival spread quickly, and within a few hours members of Congress were writing home to announce (albeit prematurely) the good news that the war was over.[2] The fears of the nationalists that in the comfort of peace the states would be lulled away into division and insouciance were now ignited.

Hardly had the news from Paris settled in when Washington's letters of March 12 to Jones, Hamilton, and the president of Congress arrived, alerting them to events at Newburgh. Pricked by the events at camp and facing the near certainty of peace and dissolution of the army, Congress asked Morris what steps had been taken to settle accounts for back pay. The question was rhetorical. The members knew that virtually nothing had been done. The next day Morris ordered the paymaster general, John Pierce, to collect all the necessary information to prepare for settlement. Given the chaotic condition of the records, Pierce faced a Sisyphean task.

On March 22 Congress received a packet from Washington containing a full report on the proceedings of March 15 as well as two supporting documents. The first was a representation made by the commander in chief to the committee of Congress more than four years earlier, on January 29, 1778, urging half pay for officers and warning of the consequences should Congress ignore the officers. The second enclosure was an extract from Washington's letter to the president of Congress dated October 11, 1780, expressing his concern about the manner in which Congress continued to treat officers of the army.[3] Washington sent these undoubtedly to give proof that contrary to what some might allege, he had not been lax in warning Congress of the dangers of discontent in the army. In an emotionally charged accompanying letter Washington described how he would feel if Congress did not answer the pleas of his officers and forced them "to grow old in poverty wretchedness and contempt": "Then shall I have learned what ingratitude is, then shall I have realized a tale, which will embitter every moment of my future life."[4]

On the same day that Washington's packet arrived, Congress voted "five years full pay . . . instead of the half pay promised for life" for "officers as are now in service, and shall continue therein to the end of the war." This was the very compromise suggested months earlier by McDougall and was fully acceptable to the officers. Events at Newburgh, Washington's most recent pleas, and the news of peace had combined to turn the tide.[5] With the war essentially over for financial and political reasons, disbanding the army became a top priority. Given their threats not to stand down unless they received pensions and pay, the officers stood as a potential obstacle to demobilization. By promising five years' pay Congress hoped to be able to disperse the army, divide its ranks, and break its political leverage. The promise of pay was both cynical and astute. Since Congress was nearly bankrupt and had little hope of raising new revenue, its commitment to pay was hollow. For their part, officers were aware of the empty treasury, but to go home with at least a promise of pay was better than refusing discharge and remaining in camp.[6] As for the enlisted men, invalids were promised a pension of five dollars per month, while ordinary soldiers were entitled only to their pay and a "gratuity" of eighty dollars at the end of their enlistment. Washington justified this treatment of the rank and file by arguing that in addition to what Congress provided, they had been amply rewarded by their states with enlistment bounties and land grants.[7]

The next day, March 23, Lafayette arrived to confirm the news in person of a "general peace." Over the next three weeks Congress recalled American warships at sea, suspended enlistments in the army, opened communications with Carleton and Digby, proclaimed a cease-fire, and finally, on April 15, approved the preliminary treaty of peace.[8]

From Newburgh Washington followed events closely. He still saw no evidence that the British were preparing to leave New York, and he remained deeply skeptical of the enemy's intentions. Having no official instructions from Congress, he summoned his senior officers. His greatest fear, he told them, was that when the soldiers who had enlisted for the duration of the war, the "war men," making up nearly two thirds of his entire force, heard the news of peace, they would demand discharge. But was the war over? Cessation of hostilities did not mean peace. General Heath caught the spirit of the men and warned that "the men inlisted to serve during the war are expecting their Discharge and probably cannot be held many days longer."[9] In New York Carleton's spies reported to him that the "dissolution of the American Army is hourly expected."[10] Left with no word from Philadelphia, Washington pondered with his officers how to prevent "the dissolution [sic] of the army."[11]

Perhaps, he suggested, the news from Paris ought not to be "communicated immediately," but his officers saw the folly in that approach. The soldiers were as well informed on current events as their commander. Keeping the news under wraps was "impracticable as well as impolitic" and could only result in "dangerous consequences."[12] Taking their advice, on April 18 Washington issued a General Order.[13]

> The Commander in Chief orders the cessation of hostilities between the United States of America and the King of Great Britain to be publicly proclaimed tomorrow at 12 o'clock at the Newbuilding, and that the Proclamation which will be communicated herewith, be read tomorrow evening at the head of every regiment and corps of the army. After which the Chaplains with the several

Brigades will render thanks to almighty God for all his mercies, particularly for his over ruling the wrath of man to his own glory, and causing the rage of war to cease among nations.

Having announced the great moment, Washington continued in his order to remind the army that this was an announcement of a "prohibition of hostilities and not the annunciation of a general peace." The war was not over, and the army was not discharged.

At noon the next day, April 19, the eighth anniversary of the battles at Lexington and Concord, officers crowded into the public building to hear the proclamation of peace.[14] Three loud "Huzzas" went up, after which "public thanks" was offered by the Baptist preacher Chaplain John Gano, followed by the singing of the anthem "Independence" by Boston's patriotic composer William Billings "accompanied with the band."

The States O Lord with Songs of
Praise Shall in their Strength rejoice And
Blest with Salvation raise to Heav'n their cheerful voice
To the King they shall sing Halleluiah
Thy Goodness and thy tender care have all our fears destroyed.
And the Continent shall sing: God is our rightful King.
God is our gracious King
May his Blessings descend, World without end,
On ev'ry part of the Continent.
May Harmony and Peace begin and never cease
And may the Strength increase of the Continent.
May American Wilds be fill'd with his Smiles
And may the Natives bow to our royal King.
May Rome, France and Spain and all the World proclaim
The Glory and the Fame of our Royal King.
Loud, Loudly sing that God is the King:
May His reign be Glorious, America victorious
And may the earth acknowledge God is the King.[15]

As the cheers faded and the band fell silent, soldiers made their way back to their huts, some shouting "discharge, discharge."[16] Even if it meant leaving without pay, Washington's soldiers were anxious to return home.[17] Discontent bubbled up. Washington warned that he could not "hold them much longer." The men were angry and sullen. They refused orders and insulted officers. He increased the "guards to prevt rioting." He wrote Hamilton on April 22 that discharging "the *War men* as soon as possible" was an absolute necessity."[18] Having not yet ratified a definitive treaty, Congress mulled over the issue until May 26, when it resolved that the commander in chief might at his discretion "furlough" the "war men." Since men on furlough might be recalled, these soldiers were technically still in service, though in the minds of men on their way home the difference would be purely semantic.[19]

Official dispatches regarding peace did not reach Carleton until April 6. Two days later he proclaimed a cessation of hostilities.[20] Within days a surge of loyalists flowed into New York City. "Since the proclaiming of the Cessation of Arms," according to New York's loyalist chief justice William Smith, "upwards of 2000 people have flocked hither."[21] He also observed, "The dissolution of the American Army is hourly expected" as a result of the news.[22]

Carleton did what he could to care for the refugees. He felt a deep responsibility for those who had lost everything only to end up ill treated by both friend and foe. He was not, however, inclined to such feelings toward others who sought entry into his city, including grasping predators prowling about seeking to buy goods at cheap prices from people likely to be forced to abandon many of their possessions as they fled America. Common criminals, "malignant villains," flocked into New York as well. Unwelcome on either side, they saw in the confusion of the city an opportunity to prey on frightened refugees.[23]

Even more distressing to the general were pestering "voyeurs," people who asked permission to visit the city with no other purpose than to gloat over forlorn loyalists. When a French officer, the Chevalier de Lavalette, sought a pass into the city for apparently just this reason, Carleton refused him: "People in grief shun the inspection of strangers such as have contributed to their misfortunes," wrote Carleton. "This city can afford no entertainment to you."[24]

Carleton's difficult situation was not made easier by the Americans. On the same day that he issued his proclamation ending hostilities, he ordered American prisoners released. Despite widespread accusations of British cruelty toward Americans in captivity, men held under Carleton's care had been well treated. When Luzerne, the French minister in Philadelphia, suggested otherwise, Carleton took quick umbrage and shot back that since he had come to America "no man ha[d] died in any prison under [his] command."[25] The issue of prisoners was weighing on the general's mind. Although he had released prisoners in British jails, the Americans were slow in reciprocating.[26] Carleton suspected that Washington was preparing a spring campaign against him, and was reluctant to release soldiers who would only reinforce his enemy. Carleton was also annoyed by the fact that when dealing with the Americans he often found it difficult to discover who was actually in charge, and with whom he should deal. Washington, wont to plead deference to civilian authority, often passed him off to the Congress, and that body in turn was inclined frequently to defer to state authorities. Such, for example, was the case with arrangements for the final evacuation of New York City.

Few in America were more pleased at the news of peace than New York's governor, George Clinton. Elected first governor of the newly formed state in 1777, he and Washington had long been close associates. As soon as Clinton had news of Carleton's proclamation he rushed to Washington's Newburgh headquarters from the state's temporary capital at Kingston. After seven years of occupation he was anxious to see the removal of the British from New York City. Washington agreed, but in his usual style the commander in chief deferred to his friend the civilian governor to open correspondence with Carleton. Given the importance of the moment, no ordinary messenger would do, so Clinton summoned the state attorney general, Egbert Benson, and pressed into his hands instructions to "wait on his Excellency Sir Guy Carleton . . . to make a Convention for the speedy obtaining possession of the Southern District of this State and for gaining Possession of any Port or Place occupied by the British Troops."[27] Accompanied by Captain John Stapleton, the deputy adjutant general of the British army in North America, Benson crossed the lines in northern Manhattan at Kingsbridge on Friday April 11, where he took quarters in a local tavern while Stapleton rode on to British headquarters. In the morning Stapleton reappeared, announcing to Benson that "Sir Guy Carleton was ready to receive" him immediately.[28]

As soon as the attorney general arrived at headquarters trouble began to surface. Puffed up by the whiff of victory, Benson cast aside the customary niceties of indirection and oblique conversation that generally accompanied such moments. He drove right to the point, telling Sir Guy that he saw no need of explaining why he was there; "the Instructions," which Captain Stapleton had delivered to him the day before, "were sufficiently explicit as to the object of my errand," a convention to provide for the evacuation of the city "as soon as Possible."[29]

Carleton deflected Benson with "much Conversation . . . very foreign . . . to the business" of his mission, reported Benson. Impatient with the general's verbal chaff, Benson told him that he would take "no farther part in the Conversation than a due Regard to Decorum and Civility" obliged him. No doubt Benson's "Decorum and Civility" did not meet Carleton's aristocratic standards of behavior. When the general got down to business he ended the meeting by passing the baton, telling Benson that "the Terms of the Convention ought to originate with" Governor Clinton.[30]

The next day Benson returned to resume negotiations. This time the general skipped the preliminaries and launched into a criticism of the states for passing harsh laws respecting the treatment of loyalists and their property that "imped[ed] the great Work of Peace." Benson, taken aback at the general's sudden change in tone, asked if this meant that he was "revoking his Offer of the day before to enter into a Convention." Carleton insisted that he was still committed to a "Convention," but he was "desirous [that] Matters might not be precipitated but left to mature of themselves." "Here," the American reported, "the conference ended."[31]

Carleton's evasive manner sparked suspicions about British intentions. Benson's own misgivings grew. Despite Carleton's repeated protestations that he lacked sufficient transports to move his troops and the refugees, Benson counted "upwards of 200 transports" swinging lazily on their anchors in the harbor and offering no indication of making ready for sea. Indeed, Benson observed that rather than preparing to leave, men were "still daily detached to work on the Fortifications." He concluded,

"I have the fullest Persuasion that Sir Guy Carleton is not seriously disposed to enter into a Convention, and that he only intends to save appearances to negotiate and by that means to effect a Delay."[32]

Although Benson did not speculate on Carleton's motives for delay, others were less reticent. Robert R. Livingston, the American secretary of foreign affairs, confided to Lafayette, who was then in Paris, that "some among us" believe that Carleton will not complete the "evacuation of New York . . . till the Tories are satisfied."[33] That, Livingston assured Lafayette, would "never be." John Morin Scott, New York's secretary of state, agreed, warning, "It is most certain We are not at peace with Great Britain."[34]

Benson and Livingston misjudged Carleton. Carleton had no desire to linger in New York nor to pry concessions out of the Americans. He was simply following orders. "His Majesty's pleasure [is] that you proceed in the several arrangements necessary for withdrawing the troops, provisions, stores, and British artillery from all the posts under your command to which the seventh article of the provisional articles of peace . . . hath reference."[35] Without transport, however, Carleton could give no assurances on a schedule for evacuation.

Unaware of Carleton's constraints, Washington decided that the best way to proceed was to arrange a face-to-face meeting. He dispatched Colonel David Humphreys to invite General Carleton to meet with him on "the earliest Day that your Excellency can name." As a precaution to prevent Carleton from using the occasion to drive a wedge between Washington and Clinton, the American commander added that "the Governor of this State, being particularly interested in Any Arrangement which respects the Restitution of the Post of N. York, will attend me, on this Occasion."[36]

Washington's invitation put Carleton in a dilemma. If he refused the invitation, he risked antagonizing the Americans and inviting retaliation. He was still waiting, for example, for the return of his prisoners. On the other hand, since he was still operating with limited instructions, if he accepted the invitation, the meeting was likely to be a repeat of the Benson exchange. Nonetheless, he could not refuse the meeting, and on April 24 the commander in chief of His Majesty's forces in North America answered "His Excellency General Washington," proposing how he planned to come up the Hudson: "in a frigate as near Tappan as may be where I understand you mean to lodge. If I hear nothing from you to occasion an alteration I intend being up on the 5th of May." Accompanying him, Carleton informed Washington, would be Lieutenant Governor Andrew Elliott and Chief Justice William Smith. The chief justice came reluctantly. He had warned Carleton that the Americans were only proposing the meeting so that they might "fish out secrets." He also had a more personal reason. In the years before the Revolution George Clinton had been his law clerk. "It would not be grateful to me to treat with a Man who was once my Clerk and now assuming the station of a superior . . . might [bring us] to altercate."[37]

Not particularly anxious to confer with either Washington or Clinton, Carleton attempted to postpone the meeting, noting to Washington that he expected to be replaced shortly and that it might be appropriate to delay the meeting until his replacement's arrival. "I am to apprize your Excellency that I have for some time expected Sir Charles Grey, who has been appointed to this command, and I have reason to think he has been detained only to bring out the final arrangement." Under the circumstances, Carleton suggested that they "defer" the meeting until Grey landed.[38]

News of Grey's appointment raised hackles at American headquarters. Few British officers were more obnoxious to the commander in chief. Grey had served before in America, earning a reputation rivaling in infamy that of Banastre "No Quarter" Tarleton and Cornwallis. Tagged "No Flint Grey," he had been responsible for the "Paoli Massacre" on September 21, 1777. According to the American side of the story, Grey led a night attack against General Anthony Wayne's division near the town of Paoli just outside Philadelphia. In order to maintain security and prevent any muskets from discharging that might give warning of the attack, he ordered his soldiers to remove their flints. Shortly after midnight Grey's men swept down onto the unsuspecting American camp. Within minutes Wayne's men were retreating in all directions. Most of the American casualties were victims of the bayonet. Survivors claimed that the British executed some of the wounded while leaving others to die. American propagandists had a field day and dubbed the incident the "Paoli Massacre" with "No Flint Grey" as the chief villain. Nor did Grey's behavior improve after Paoli. In 1778 he sacked and burned the port towns of New Bedford and New London and terrorized Martha's Vineyard. He capped off the year with a ferocious and bloody attack on a detachment of Continental dragoons commanded by Colonel George Baylor at Tappan, New York—the "Tappan Massacre."[39] The prospect of sitting across the table from Grey simply stiffened Washington's resolve to meet Carleton as soon as possible.

Washington left Newburgh by barge on Saturday morning May 3 for his rendezvous with Carleton. As host, Washington selected the De Wint House at Tappan, a spot halfway between Newburgh and New York City. He knew the house well, having signed Major John Andre's death warrant there in September 1780 following Benedict Arnold's treachery.

As Washington's party made its leisurely passage south on the Hudson, Carleton's barge pulled into the stream on Sunday the fourth, carrying the general and his staff to the frigate *Perseverance*.[40] Chief Justice Smith and Lieutenant Governor Elliott accompanied him on the smaller twenty-eight-gun *Greyhound*.[41] Forced to claw against the current and a shifting tide, Carleton did not reach Tappan until late morning on May 5.[42] To explain his delay and give warning of his approach, Carleton sent his intelligence officer Major George Beckwith ahead in a "whaleboat" with a flag of truce.[43] Beckwith met with the Americans and returned to *Perseverance* bearing an invitation from Washington for the general to dine with him the next day.

On Tuesday morning May 6 side boys mustered on deck to salute Carleton as he departed the frigate to head ashore. With rhythmic discipline the crew of the captain's barge rowed the general and his entourage toward shore. Carleton and Smith stepped from the barge, to be welcomed by Washington and his three aides, Colonels Trumbull, Cobb, and Humphreys.[44] Formalities concluded quickly. Washington and Carleton climbed into a "Chariot" and sped away toward De Wint House. "Horses were offered to the rest." Chief Justice Smith and Lieutenant Governor Elliott elected to walk.[45]

The rooms at De Wint's came alive with color and conversation as redcoats, bluecoats, and elegantly attired civilians milled about. According to Smith, "an hour was spent in Congratulations and seperate [*sic*] chat."[46] But then, at a signal, "the two generals took a room." "We all seated, Washington opened the business."[47]

Present were the two commanders and their staffs, Governor Clinton, New York secretary of state John Morin Scott, Attorney General Egbert Benson, Elliott, and Smith.[48] Addressing Carleton, Washington told the general he had three items on his agenda which he wished to discuss.

1. The preservation of property from being carried off, and especially the Negroes
2. The Settlement of the Time for Evacuation of Newyork [*sic*]
3. The extending the government of the state of Newyork [*sic*] as far as might be convenient before the intire [*sic*] Evacuation took place.[49]

According to Smith, the American commander spoke "with great Slowness" and in "a low Tone of voice."[50] It was his position that the preliminary treaty, although yet to be finalized and ratified, was in fact a treaty and its provisions were binding, particularly article 7.

His Britannic Majesty shall, with all convenient speed, and without causing any destruction or carrying away any negroes or other property of the American inhabitants, withdraw all his armies, garrisons and fleets from the said United States, and from every post, place and harbor within the same.

On the matter of evacuation Carleton told Washington that he would move "with all possible Expedition, but it must of Necessity take Time." What he did not reveal, however, was that since he still had no definitive orders from London, "Time" remained undefined. He then acknowledged that he had already dispatched six thousand "Souls" to Nova Scotia and that among them were a number of "Negroes." Although Washington almost certainly knew from his spies that this was the case, he "affected to be startled" by this information and exclaimed, "Already imbarked!" He then pointedly reminded Carleton of the unambiguous wording of article 7. By shipping away "Negroes," Washington charged that Carleton had violated the "treaty."

The issue of shipping away Negroes was not new. When evacuating Savannah the previous July, the British, by their own count, had taken more than three thousand slaves—men, women, and children. Although most were probably the property of fleeing loyalists, a significant number were escaped slaves who had sought refuge and freedom behind British lines. A similar scenario played out at Charleston in December when British transports carried away more than five thousand slaves.[51]

Carleton rejected Washington's charge. "No Interpretation could be put upon the Articles inconsistent with prior Engagements binding the National Honor which must be kept with all Colours." To prove his point, Carleton reminded the Americans that in November 1776 Lord Dunmore, royal governor of Virginia, had issued a proclamation declaring all "Negroes . . . free that are able and willing to bear Arms. They joining His MAJESTY'S Troops." What Dunmore did in 1776, Sir Henry Clinton repeated three years later when he issued his own proclamation declaring that no one could claim any "Right" over any "NEGROE" who was once "the Property of a Rebel" and who took "Refuge with any Part of this Army." General Clinton had gone on to offer those who escaped "full Security to follow within these Lines, any Occupation which he shall think proper."[52] Carleton would not budge. "Delivering up the Negroes to their former Masters would be delivering them up some possible to Execution, and others to severe punishments." Such action would be "dishonorable."[53] He would not betray those who had sought the protection of the king. In partial mitigation he did announce that three weeks earlier he had issued orders establishing a military commission to ensure that any property (including slaves) being shipped out of the port was legitimate and legal.[54] This commission, he assured Washington, was keeping a careful list of all Negroes so that after all matters had been settled adjustments might be made "by Commissioners to be hereafter appointed by the two nations."[55]

Washington was unsatisfied and was also invested personally in this dispute. As a Virginia planter and major slave owner, he had a significant financial stake at risk. Although he could not give an exact number, he was convinced that several of his slaves had in fact escaped to New York.[56] Carleton's pledge to keep a register of Negroes sent away was meaningless, Washington argued. Escaped slaves were most likely to give false names, and so tracking ownership would be near impossible. Furthermore, he pointed out, information contained in the register would be useless in ascertaining the worth of a slave since the value of the bondsman was in his "Industry and Sobriety."[57] Having made his public stance, in private Washington confessed "that the Slaves which have absconded from their Masters will never be restored.[58]

On the other main issue, removing troops, Carleton continued to be evasive but a bit more agreeable. He assured Clinton that at his request and within a few days he would withdraw to the south side of the Harlem River, but retreating from Long Island would have to wait as "he saw too many Difficulties."[59] What troubled him most was the "evil" that would arise should his troops leave before Clinton's forces took effective control. In such a vacuum "animosities" might be let loose, resulting in "disorder."[60] In sum he feared the havoc an uncontrolled patriot mob might wreck on any of the king's sympathizers unfortunate enough to be left behind.

The tone of the discussion intensified. John Morin Scott in particular took a sharp stance, insisting that the British evacuate quickly. Carleton continued to evade any firm commitment, but he did agree to allow Washington to send a three-man American commission to observe the evacuation. Since the commissioners would have no power other than simply to observe, the concession was virtually meaningless.[61] Sensing that nothing more might be accomplished, "Washington pulled out his Watch, and observing that it was near Dinner Time offered wine and bitters."

Following the preprandial libations the guests "walked out" to enjoy a "plentiful Repast under a Tent."[62] To prepare and serve the "Repast," Samuel Fraunces had come up from New York City. "Black Sam" Fraunces was the city's best-known tavern keeper.[63] Reputedly a Whig, Fraunces had deftly navigated the shoal waters of politics during the long British occupation well enough that the king's authorities allowed him to keep his business open and were wont to patronize it themselves. Good food and drink outranked politics. The dinner party sat at table until early evening, when Carleton and his men took their leave and ferried back to *Perseverance* and *Greyhound*.

Having bid farewell to his guests, Washington retired to consult Governor Clinton. The meeting, "diffuse and desulory [*sic*]," had yielded virtually nothing.[64] Undeterred, the governor and general decided to press the British in writing. Since Carleton had invited them to dine the next day aboard *Perseverance*, they prepared formal letters setting out an agenda for the meeting. Clinton asked for clarification about Carleton's schedule for evacuation, with particular notice of Long Island, and whether the general would permit vessels to travel up the Hudson to Albany. Washington repeated his concerns about the "large number of Negroes [which] had been carried away."[65]

As the barge carrying Washington and Clinton came alongside the next day, *Perseverance* fired a seventeen-gun salute acknowledging Washington as commander in chief, the same rank held by Carleton.[66] This was the first time the British had offered a public salute to their enemy.[67] The parties retired to the captain's cabin to dine and continue discussions, but Carleton was missing. He was confined to his bed "under a very severe Fit of the fever and Ague."[68] There would be no immediate answer to the American letters.[69] Carleton managed to rise from his sickbed long enough to say good-bye to his guests.[70] The next day *Perseverance* returned downriver to New York.

Whether Carleton read the letters immediately or passed them to his clerk for later action is uncertain, but he cannot have been surprised by their contents. Washington requested a written timetable for evacuation and an end to the "carrying away [of] any *Negroes or other property* of the American inhabitants."[71] Clinton's shorter letter reiterated the request for a timetable for evacuation as well as permission for American vessels to enter New York Harbor.[72]

Three days later, as agreed upon at Tappan, American commissioners Egbert Benson, Lieutenant Colonel William Smith, a member of Washington's staff, and Daniel Parker, a New York merchant and army contractor with whom Washington had worked, arrived in the city to "superintend all Embarkations."[73] There was, however, little for them to observe. Departures from the city were few as Carleton waited for Grey to arrive and relieve him of the tiresome business.

On June 2 the packet from Falmouth arrived, bringing the news of "a new ministry. The Shelburnes are all out."[74] The wheels of British politics had once again ground against Sir Guy Carleton. His patron Shelburne had resigned, and the king had called for a new coalition government to be led by Lord North and Charles James Fox. A change in government, however, even with North at the head, did not mean a change in course. Peace was still the goal, and the new government would continue to support the Preliminary Articles of Peace. Under these circumstances North determined a change in leadership in America would be unwise and requested that Carleton remain in New York.[75] Carleton, ambitious for honors, and fully aware that his future rested in the king's hands, had little choice but to agree. To keep matters calm in New York, Carleton assured his American friends "that not a soldier should stir till he had taken care of the Loyalists."[76] Admiral Digby wrote Secretary at War Thomas Townshend, "Nobody you could send here can do as much for the King's service or for the poor inhabitants as Sir Guy Carleton."[77]

Martha had come north to be with her husband and was at Hasbrouck House to welcome him back on the evening of May 9. As he settled back into the routine of life at headquarters he realized that his chief duty had shifted from keeping an army together to disbanding it in a peaceful and orderly fashion. He had already begun the process of demobilization by furloughing soldiers. That pleased the men bound for home but left those in camp angry and uncertain. Only with great "difficulty," Washington informed Lafayette, were the remaining men "kept under due Subordination."[78] Knox was not so fortunate. From West Point came disturbing news from Knox that soldiers had turned "highly mutinous." They were behaving in ways "totally repugnant to discipline . . . huzzaing and yelling indecent expressions."[79]

When he heard about the soldiers' behavior Major John Armstrong was nearly gleeful at Washington's distress. Having watched his schemes swept away by Washington's deft moves at Newburgh, Armstrong had resigned from the army in a huff and returned to Philadelphia to be appointed secretary of the Pennsylvania Council. To Gates, by then retired to Virginia, he wrote, "The soldiers are loud and insolent, the officers broken dissatisfied and despondent."[80] His friend Christopher Richmond, still on duty at Newburgh, went so far as to suggest that the officers, "pimping fellows" he called them, who had failed to support "stronger measures" in March had "let slip the best opportunity which could have represented itself to obtain that justice their services certainly merited."[81]

Desperate to be rid of troublemakers as quickly as possible, Washington told Knox, "If there are any Non Commissioned officers or Soldiers whose mutinous dispositions appear to arise from their anxiety to be discharged from the Army you have my full permission to give them Furloughs."[82] Knox was only too happy to comply. While the American army melted away, at the public building the paymaster's staff poured through piles of paper. Despite the fact that all they had to give the furloughed soldiers were "vague promises," the clerks recorded carefully what was owed so that those "promises" might someday be fulfilled. In the same building Quartermaster Pickering and his staff were busy sorting through a blizzard of confused accounts. Recognizing that the end was near, local farmers hastened to press overdue bills for "firewood, forage and carting" as well as numerous claims for damage done by soldiers who had cut down fences, destroyed property, taken away livestock, and stolen personal property.[83]

Washington took time to attend to personal matters. For most of his adult life he had suffered from severe dental problems. Constantly seeking the best advice, in 1772 he consulted with the English dentist John Baker, who instructed him on the use of a toothbrush. It was good advice but came too late for preventive care. The only effective treatment was extraction, and Washington suffered many. Eight years of army food had aggravated his condition. While at Tappan he mentioned his problem to Fraunces, who told him about a French dentist he knew in New York, Jean Pierre le Mayeur. He had come to New York three years earlier to attend to Sir Henry Clinton and other high-ranking British officers.[84] While appreciating his dental skills, his British patients suspected Mayeur's politics. One evening while dining with officers, Mayeur defended his homeland "with a degree of warmth displeasing" to his companions, who turned on him with a "cold Civility [and] permitted him to remain ever after unattended to except for the Eye of Suspicion."[85] Fearing for his personal safety, two months before the Tappan meeting he had written to Washington asking for permission to come across the lines.[86] At that moment Mayeur was just one of dozens of people seeking refuge. Deluged with such requests, and since Mayeur was French, Washington referred him to the "Minister of France at Phila." Fraunces's recommendation put a different light on matters. Washington wrote immediately to Lieutenant Colonel William Smith in New York City to give him a special mission to find Mayeur. It was to be done discreetly, "not to be made a parade of."[87] Thanks to Fraunces's connections, Smith found the dentist and within a few days a pass was issued and Mayeur was in Newburgh attending to Washington. Alas, Mayeur was not able to provide a permanent fix for Washington's dental difficulties, but he did, nonetheless, afford the general some respite from pain.[88]

The New York commissioners undertook other personal business for the general. Shortly after the announcement of peace Carleton opened the port of New York to trade. Goods flooding in dropped prices dramatically. James Madison reported that in both New York and Philadelphia "all foreign commodities have fallen." These were "the sweets of peace . . . to be amply enjoyed."[89] Washington wasted no time taking advantage. Looking ahead to their return home, he and Martha went on a veritable shopping spree. He sent Smith to scour the shops in New York for "Tin Plates" and "Dishes" as well as books for his library at Mount Vernon, including biographies of "Charles the 12th of Sweden, Louis XV of France and a History of the Reign of Czar Peter, the Great." Although lacking much formal education, the commander in chief was an avid reader and told Smith, "If there is a good Booksellers Shop in the City I would thank you for sending me a Catalogue," so "that I may choose such as I want."[90] He also purchased four pipes (nearly five hundred gallons) of the "very choicest (old) Madeira Wine, a box of Citron and two baskets of figs," all to be sent to Virginia. For his table he ordered a "dozn large Table Cloths" and "3 dozn Napkins." For Martha he ordered "three yards of black silk." Nor did he forget his slaves. For them he ordered "1000 Ells [approximately 3,000 feet] of German Oznabgs" and "200 blankets." Some of these blankets, he hoped, might be bought from the "King's stores" as Carleton might be anxious to have cash rather than the trouble of packing and transporting them. The surest sign that Washington was planning retirement were his instructions for Daniel Parker to buy "six strong hair Trunks well clasped and with good Locks" into which he could pack his papers for their journey to Mount Vernon. The trunks were to be purchased on the "Public acct."[91]

On the afternoon of May 13, whether from ill health, the press of making preparations to go home, his usual reluctance to stand before a group of officers, or simple modesty, Washington decided not to attend a meeting being held across the river from Hasbrouck House at Mount Gulian, the headquarters of General von Steuben. For some time a proposal had been floating among the officers of the army to form a fraternal order. One concept, proposed by a group of officers, envisioned an " 'Order of Freedom' to be instituted on 4 July 1783." According to this proposal, the French Crusader king St. Louis would be the patron of the Order of Freedom, with the president of Congress as chief, Washington as grand master, Benjamin Franklin as chancellor, and John Witherspoon as prelate.[92] Too fanciful and European for American tastes, the order never materialized. In its place, at the urgings of von Steuben and particularly Knox, an Americanized republican version took shape based upon the legendary Lucius Quinctius Cincinnatus, a Roman general called to defend the republic in the fifth century B.C., who upon the end of the war put down his sword and returned to his farm. Continental officers, most notably Washington, saw themselves in the model of Cincinnatus. With Knox presiding, the Mount Gulian meeting approved a constitution for the Society of the Cincinnati centered on three "Immutable Principles."

An incessant attention to preserve inviolate those exalted rights and liberties of human nature, for which they have fought and bled, and without which the high rank of a rational being is a curse instead of a blessing.

An unalterable determination to promote and cherish, between the respective States, that union and national honor so essentially necessary to their happiness, and the future dignity of the American empire.

To render permanent the cordial affection subsisting among the officers, this spirit will dictate brotherly kindness in all things, and particularly extend to the most substantial acts of beneficence, according to the ability of the Society, towards those officers and their families, who unfortunately may be under the necessity of receiving it.[93]

Whatever the motivation of the officers present—patriotism, adventure, or self-advancement—the men gathered at Mount Gulian had begun their service as Virginians, New Yorkers, southerners, and northerners. The hard experience of war had changed them. They had marched about the continent and served with, commanded, and been commanded by men from all states.[94] They emerged from this common experience with a vision of America less parochial and more national. The society, fraternal and voluntary, was a means to bond and remember shared wartime experiences.

The society was also controversial, for while the ostensible purposes were charitable and patriotic, there was a shadowy political agenda as well. Having "fought and bled" and then been ignored, these officers were banding together to continue pressuring Congress, and particularly the states, to honor their promises. Some at the meeting still resented Washington's actions in undermining their efforts with his "Newburgh Address." The Society of the Cincinnati was their next best hope.[95] Although the members modeled the society on other charitable organizations that helped support members and their families, it employed in its constitution a provision sure to raise concern in a nation deeply suspicious of the military.[96] Membership in the society was hereditary, the eldest son inheriting the right of membership. That plus the elaborate medal worn by members, smacking of European heraldry, struck a sour chord among many members of Congress. Samuel Osgood of Massachusetts assured John Adams, who shared his distrust of the society, that he was confident that "this Country will not consent to a Race of Hereditary Patricians."[97] In a fiery twenty-two-page pamphlet, *Considerations on the Society of the Cincinnati*, Aedanus Burke, a South Carolina delegate, railed against it, claiming its members were Caesars and Cromwells in the making. Taking a swipe at von Steuben, Burke charged that such a feudal society might be fit for the "petty princes of Germany," but it had no place in America and ought to be "extirpated." Opposition softened somewhat when, to no one's surprise, the members elected Washington to be their first president. Nonetheless, the society continued to stand as a blatant affront to those who cherished "republican principles."[98]

O N JUNE 2 Washington ordered "colonels and commanders of corps [to] immediately make return of the number of men who will be entitled to furloughs." Paymasters were to attend to the "settlement of accounts." The "Quartermaster will supply a sufficient number of printed furloughs," and generals were to make "arrangements for marching the troops of their respective States to their homes." And should anyone doubt that the war was over, the commander in chief was "pleased to grant a full and free pardon to all non-commissioned officers and privates now in confinement, and they are to be liberated accordingly."[1]

Within a few days of Washington's order, according to Lieutenant Benjamin Gilbert, "the Maryland, Jersy [sic], and New York Lines [quit] the field, and those of Massachusetts and the other States" were packing their kits.[2] Washington ordered units left in camp to consolidate into six regiments, five infantry and one artillery. Less than eighteen hundred soldiers were "fit for duty." Since the April 19 announcement of the cessation of hostilities, four fifths of Washington's army, some eight thousand men, had left.[3] When "the definitive treaty arrives," Gilbert predicted, "there will be a final desolation [sic] of our Army." Quartermaster Pickering noted to his wife, "The army are beginning to separate" under "circumstances truly distressing," while to his friend Samuel Hodgdon he wrote, "The Army is disgusted."[4]

The sight of so many unhappy, despairing soldiers marching from camp moved Washington to do something he had rarely done since becoming commander in chief: he meddled in politics. He knew that he would soon lay down his sword, but he also knew that Citizen Washington would have far less influence than "His Excellency." While he still had power, he decided to write a "Circular Letter to the States."[5] More than seven thousand words, it was his longest public message of the war, and although he addressed it to the state governors, he intended it for all Americans.

"I am now preparing to resign," he began, and "return to that domestic retirement . . . which I left with the greatest reluctance." At this moment in his life he saw a great future for America. "The citizens of America," he noted with pride, are in a "most enviable condition, as the sole lords and proprietors of a vast tract of continent, comprehending all the various soils and climates of the world, and abounding with all the necessaries and conveniences of life, are now by the late satisfactory pacification, acknowledged to be possessed of absolute freedom and independency." It was, however, a dangerous time. "The eyes of the whole World are turned upon [us]" for "it is yet to be decided, whether the revolution must ultimately be considered as a blessing or a curse; not to the present age alone, for with our fate will the destiny of unborn millions be involved."

At this "ill fated moment" the confederation was on the edge of "ruin." In such a fragile and divided condition the new nation was at risk of becoming "the sport of European politics." "In these grave circumstances," Washington wrote, "silence in me would be a crime." He confessed that some would accuse him of "stepping out of the proper line of [his] duty" and "ascribe [his actions] to arrogance or ostentation." But he was motivated not by such base motives as his enemies might suggest but by "the rectitude of [his] own heart."

First and foremost, he urged "an indissoluble Union of the States under one Federal Head." Only by a strong central government to which the states must yield authority could the nation preserve itself against domestic discord and foreign threats. Without a "supreme power to regulate and govern," he warned, "every thing [sic] must very rapidly tend to anarchy and confusion." He repeated his plea for "compleat [sic] and ample Justice" for the army. The promise of half pay and commutation was a "solemn" act that was "absolutely binding upon the United States." Although he did not endorse it directly, readers could not mistake the fact that Washington was urging approval of the unpopular impost. He finished "I now bid adieu . . . at the same time I bid a last farewell to the cares of office, and all the employments of public life."

Although widely reprinted and read, Washington's address had little impact.[6] It had all been said before and ignored before. In Virginia his address actually provoked ire. According to Edmund Randolph, some of his fellow Virginians thought Washington had stepped across the "proper line of duty" with this "unsolicited obtrusion."[7] David Howell of Rhode Island, who sympathized with Washington's plight, nonetheless lamented that in his judgment the general had been duped by "coxcombs" who "induced" him to use "his personal authority" to support "destructive" measures.[8]

It was a low moment for Washington. His public reputation was at stake. A rumor swept the capital, likely spread by Walter Stewart, that the commander in chief had "become so unpopular in his Army that no Officer will dine with him." The officers, according to Stewart, had rejected an invitation to "meet and have a general Dinner together . . . declaring they thought the present period more adapted to Sorrow than to mirth."[9]

"Our finances [are] low, Our resources small, Our affairs deranged," wrote Massachusetts delegate Stephen Higginson to Samuel Adams. But few seemed to care. Congress could not muster a quorum "above one day in a Week."[10] Recognizing the dire circumstances, the president of Congress, Elias Boudinot, dispatched an urgent message to the governors of Connecticut, New York, Maryland, and Georgia. Their states had failed to send delegates to Philadelphia. Boudinot admonished the governors that their irresponsible behavior made it impossible for Congress to act on any measures since the "business" of Congress requires the "assent of Nine States." Absence of their delegates was "extremely humiliating to us, as well as disadvantageous to the union." Unless they showed up, "the public business" would be "retarded" and "the most dangerous and destructive delays must unavoidably take place."[11] If the states neglected and ignored the body, the public at large disdained it. John Armstrong referred to Congress as full of "fools and rascals," while Ralph Izard of South Carolina noted that the states had so "totally annihilated" Congress's "strength and credit that no Enemy need be afraid of insulting us."[12]

Among those who had no fear of Congress were the men of the Pennsylvania Line bivouacked in Lancaster, eighty miles west of Philadelphia. The regiment's duties, to guard British prisoners, had ended with the release of the men in their charge. Not willing to bear the unnecessary expense of keeping the men in service, the Pennsylvania authorities, following the policy set down by both Congress and the commander in chief, ordered the men furloughed. Like every other furloughed soldier, the Pennsylvanians expected pay and got none. On the morning of June 16 a delegation of noncommissioned officers informed their commander, Colonel Richard Butler, that they were marching to Philadelphia to demand justice. Within minutes the sergeants at the head of eighty or more unhappy soldiers set off for the city.

Alarmed by the news that mutinous soldiers were heading their way, the members of Congress asked state authorities to call out the militia to protect them. John Dickinson, president of Pennsylvania's ruling body, the State Executive Council, refused the request, warning the members that the state militia "could not be relied on" and so he could not guarantee Congress's safety.[13] On that note the congressmen fled to Princeton, New Jersey, putting the Delaware River between them and the soldiers.[14] Armstrong sarcastically wrote to Gates, "The grand Sanhedrin of the Nation with all their solemnity and emptiness have removed to Princeton."[15] Even as they humiliated themselves with such a hasty and unceremonial departure, they ordered Washington, "[Send] some of your best troops, on whom you can depend; . . . towards the city" to preserve "the dignity of the Federal Government." Washington acted quickly and dispatched General Robert Howe with fifteen hundred "men of tried fidelity" (more than half of his remaining army) to face down the mutineers.[16]

Marching hard, Howe and his men arrived at Princeton on the evening of June 30. News that Continentals would soon be in Philadelphia sent the leaders of the mutiny into flight. As it collapsed, arrests were made, trials were held, sentences meted out, including orders for execution, but no one had the stomach for retribution. The soldiers had risen in a just cause. The convicted were pardoned. The real victim was Congress, which had been "insulted by the Soldiery, and unsupported by the citizens"; its image was tarnished yet again.[17] Even after the city was safe, and despite the fact that they all agreed with Charles Thomson that Princeton—a tiny village with barely "50 houses most of them low wooden buildings, several of them tumbling to pieces"—was "too small" for their accommodation, the members of Congress preferred to fuss and fume in a place they disliked than return to Philadelphia.[18]

With nearly half his army gone to Pennsylvania and with his wife just returned from a "jaunt" south, Washington decided to journey in the opposite direction.[19] "I have a great desire," he wrote to his friend Philip Schuyler, "to see the northern part of this State."[20] It would be "a Tour . . . as far as Tyconderoga and Crown Point, and perhaps as far up the Mohawk River as fort Schuyler."[21] Unlike his previous visit, this was not an inspection of posts, but pleasant travel with friends.

On the morning of July 18 the commander in chief's boat pulled away from the wharf at Hasbrouck House and made its way upstream. Joining Washington was Governor George Clinton and an Italian nobleman, Count Francesco dal Verme. The count, who had arrived recently in New York armed with a letter of introduction from Benjamin Franklin, was embarking on a grand tour of America.[22] After traveling to Philadelphia and making brief side trip to visit Congress at Princeton, the count headed up the Hudson, stopping at West Point to dine with von Steuben and Knox. The next day von Steuben rode with him to Newburgh to introduce him to Washington. The general took a liking to the count and invited him to join his party on their journey north.[23]

Cannons boomed a thirteen-gun salute as Washington's barge approached the shore at Albany. Abraham Ten Broeck, the mayor of the city, joined by scores of citizens stood at the river's edge to greet Washington. A grand concourse of people accompanied the general from the river landing along State Street as the victorious general made his way toward city hall and an elegant dinner where the city's most eminent citizens, including his good friend Philip Schuyler, offered congratulations and bountiful toasts. That evening Washington and dal Verme stayed with the Schuylers. The count, who had certainly seen his share of elegant homes, was impressed by Schuyler's large brick mansion. It was, he noted, a "magnificent" home "situated on a hill," surrounded by gardens and orchards, enjoying a "panoramic view" of the Hudson. It was the home of a "very rich man."[24]

For the next week Washington and his party toured the North. They visited Saratoga, the scene of General Horatio Gates's great victory. It was there they encountered a party of more than two hundred American prisoners on their way home from Canada. At Fort Edward they disembarked and trekked the short portage to Fort William Henry at the southern tip of Lake George, where the party, now grown to nearly forty people, boarded waiting boats. Having set off late in the day, they camped for the night along the lakeshore. In the morning they continued north, passing down the narrow lake between magnificent highlands. Once ashore at the head of the lake, they rode the short distance to Fort Ticonderoga. Not wishing to risk venturing too close to enemy lines (officially the war still continued), the party set out on Lake Champlain but proceeded only as far north as Crown Point.

On July 26 the travelers were back at the Schuylers' but only for an overnight stay. In the morning they headed west along the Mohawk River. Washington had a passion for the "West." Since his early days as a frontier surveyor trekking across the Alleghenies, he had been enthralled with the promise of western expansion. For more than two decades he had been speculating in western lands. On the other side of the mountains, he predicted, a "New Empire," an American empire, would rise.[25] Only the British, the Indians, and the mountains stood in the way.

As a Virginian living on the Potomac, Washington needed no instruction on the importance of "inland navigation."[26] Before the war he had been one of the principal supporters of a canal through the Dismal Swamp linking Virginia and North Carolina. He was also fascinated by the possibility of a waterway via the Potomac that could tie that river with the Ohio Valley.[27] Washington had a shrewd eye for real estate and was impressed by what he saw along the Mohawk. Dotted with farms and villages, the river snaked west, giving access to fertile lands. To be sure, there were rapids and other navigational obstacles, but as Clinton undoubtedly pointed out to him, for more than 150 years this route had been used by fur traders, Indians, and armies. With the war ending and settlers moving in, there was ample reason to build roads and canals to open these lands. Washington was certain that the Mohawk, like the Potomac, would link to the West.[28] In near rhapsody he wrote to his friend the Marquis de Chastellux that as he had gazed along the river he was "struck with the . . . goodness of Providence which has dealt her favors to us with so profuse a hand. Would to God we may have wisdom enough to improve them."[29] Not to let an opportunity pass, he made arrangements with Clinton to buy land along the Mohawk, eventually co-owning with his friend six thousand acres.[30]

Fort Stanwix (Rome, New York) at the southern end of the Wood Creek portage was as far west as the party journeyed. From there they turned south down to Lake Otsego at the headwaters of the Susquehanna River and then east back to Albany.[31] On August 5 Martha welcomed him home to Hasbrouck House. In nineteen days he had traveled more than 750 miles by horse and boat.[32] He had passed through vast and fertile land laced by rivers, awaiting only the arrival of farmers to till the soil and settle villages. And beyond what he had seen personally on his brief trip, Washington knew that an even greater expanse of land awaited those who would dare push farther west to plow and plant. The promise of what lay ahead for the young nation lifted his spirits. But he was troubled as to who would lead America to take up the challenge. At headquarters a letter awaited him that did not bode well. "I have it in command from Congress," wrote Elias Boudinot from Princeton, "that it is their pleasure that you should attend Congress at this place."[33]

Boudinot's summons annoyed Washington. The president did not explain why Congress needed to see him. Furthermore he was tired from his western trip, and his wife was ill. Given that the war was ending, he had anticipated only one more move: home to Virginia. Congress was asking him to disrupt his life and move to Princeton. Why, he asked his friend James McHenry, who was then sitting in Congress, should he suffer "the inconvenience of a removal for so small a distance, and a new establishment of a Household which must be formed in consequence of breaking up the menial part of my family here?"[34] For his own well-being, as well as for that of the army, the general believed his place was at headquarters.[35]

Boudinot and McHenry scrambled to assuage Washington and convince him that he was needed in Princeton. The members of Congress had been debating the need for a permanent military establishment. They were desperate "to get the Sunshine of the Generals name . . . to a peace establishment" which had encountered heavy opposition in the Congress from those who saw in the proposal a nationalist plot aimed at weakening the states.[36] To assure the commander in chief that Congress also cared for his well-being, McHenry told him that they were anxious to get him "out of a disagreeable situation, to one less disagreeable."[37] Boudinot promised him a fine home and furniture, and Congress offered a monument: "Resolved That an equestrian statue of General Washington, be erected at the place where the residence of Congress shall be established." For this purpose the impecunious Congress would spare no expense.

> That the statue be of bronze: The General to be represented in a Roman dress, holding a truncheon in his right hand in the other hand bearing a wreath of laurel, [and his head encircled with a laurel wreath]. The statue to be supported by a marble pedestal, on the four faces of which are to be represented, in basso relieve, the four principal events of the war, in which General Washington commanded in person, viz. The evacuation of Boston—the capture of the Hessians at Trenton—[the Battle of Princeton]—the action of Monmouth, and the surrender of York. On the upper part of the front of the pedestal, to be engraved as follows: The United States in Congress assembled ordered this statue to be erected in the year of the Lord 1783, in honor of George Washington, Esquire the illustrious Commander in Chief of their the [sic] Armies [of the United States of America], during the war which vindicated and secured their Liberty, Sovereignty and Independence.

Recognizing that no artist in America could execute the commission properly, Congress ordered the "Minister of the United States at the Court of Versailles" to find "the best artist in Paris [Europe]" to prepare this monument and that the Secretary also send "the best face and person of General Washington that can be procured, for the purpose of executing the above statue."[38]

Flattery worked. After allowing a few days for Martha to recover from her most recent bout of illness, on August 18 the Washingtons set off for Princeton. Accompanied by his aides Trumbull, Humphreys, and Walker, along with a small mounted guard and servants, they made their way south, stopping at Tappan, Hackensack, Acquackanonk Ferry, Elizabethtown, and Brunswick. The group arrived in Princeton on the twenty-third, to be welcomed by the townspeople and the "President and Faculty of the College" with a grand "display of colours and the firing of 13 cannon."[39] Tired from their journey, the Washingtons paused in Princeton only long enough to acknowledge their kind reception. The general and his wife, whose health had improved only slightly, were anxious to settle in the place Congress had secured for them.

Their new home, Rockingham, was in the nearby village of Rocky Hill, about four miles out of Princeton on the main road. It was the property of the widow Margaret Berrien.[40] The sight of the village conjured up pleasant memories. His last visit to the area was in January 1777, following his victories at Trenton and Princeton, when he had marched his army through the village to winter quarters at Morristown. Next to the elegant Vassall House in Cambridge, where they had lived during the siege of Boston, the Berrien mansion was the finest home they had enjoyed during the entire war. Rockingham was a "very healthy and finely situated farm." Set in 320 acres of "meadows and woodland," the house contained "upwards of twenty rooms of different kinds, including a kitchen very conveniently contrived" as well as "a large dining room, a tea room and a dressing room, with genteel furniture in each."[41] Outbuildings included "a good barn, and stables, coach house, granary and fowl house, all painted."[42] The scene brought memories of Mount Vernon.

Congress set Tuesday the twenty-sixth as the day for Washington to attend. Lest they be overwhelmed by the presence of the commander in chief, the members set forth a careful protocol aimed at preserving their dignity in the presence of so great a personality. Accordingly, at noon the doors swung open to the college library, where the members had gathered. All were seated, grouped as usual by state. They did not rise as the commander in chief entered. Washington took a place at the right hand of President Boudinot, who, according to Secretary Thomson, had "heightened his seat [with] a large folio to give him an elevation above the rest."[43]

The moment was brief. The president acknowledged Washington's role in the "success of a war" but then in a somewhat awkward comment noted, "Your Retreats have been marked with Circumstances not less honourable to your military Character than those which have distinguished your Victories."[44] Perhaps from his "elevated" position Boudinot was seeking to remind the audience that Washington had lost more battles in the Revolution than he had won.

The general replied by giving thanks to "the wisdom and unanimity of our national councils, the firmness of our citizens and the patience and bravery of our troops." He concluded his brief remarks by informing the members that as soon as either peace was formally declared or the British left New York, "I shall ask permission to retire to the peaceful shade of private life." His message was clear: once his job as commander in chief was completed, the general had no intention of lingering about to help Congress deal with postwar political issues. In less than fifteen minutes the entire event was over. Washington returned to Rockingham.

Waiting had become the principal activity for Congress and the general. Congress could barely make a quorum, and at Washington's headquarters, where once in the heady days of the war one hundred or more letters, orders, and dispatches passed across the desks of several busy aides, by mid-September the number was in single digits. Most of the correspondence had to do with affairs at West Point, where Knox was in command, and pension-hungry officers who were seeking confirmation of their wartime service.[45] At the request of Congress the general did prepare two reports, the first addressing "Indian Affairs" and the second "Observations on a Peace Establishment."[46]

Central to the new republic's relations with Indians was the question of land. On this matter Washington had no illusions. On one side were "Land Jobbers, Speculators and Monopolizers." By their "unrestrained conduct" conniving and cheating the Indians, these "avaricious Men" were an "embarrassment of Government" and bound to cause "a great deal of Bloodshed." Indians, however, were not blameless. Many of them had taken "up the Hatchet against us," Washington noted, "but as we prefer Peace to a state of Warfare, as we consider them as a deluded People," they had to be convinced "that their true Interest and safety must now depend upon *our* friendship. As the Country is large enough to contain us all and as we are disposed to be kind to them, and to partake of their Trade, we will draw from these considerations and from motives of comp[assion] draw a veil over what is past." Washington's solution: "a boundary line between them and us beyond which we will endeavor to restrain our People from Hunting or Settling."[47]

Washington's second brief report concerned the "Peace Establishment." In May he had delivered a lengthy and detailed analysis of his views on the nation's military requirement. Later, after Congress had virtually ignored all that he wrote, he described this effort as "a hasty production."[48] That was clearly not the case for he made very specific recommendations concerning the establishment of a regular army, organizing the militia, establishing arsenals, and even creating "Academies."[49] Given the persistent impecuniousness of Congress, Washington realized that there was little or no chance that anything he had recommended would be enacted. Being asked now to respond to changes in a plan that he doubted would ever be implemented seemed a meaningless exercise not worth a great deal of time, hence the short answer in which he simply reiterated what he had written previously.

Washington's focus was on going home, and for that he needed money. Like everyone else's, his accounts with Congress were hopelessly in arrears. He pleaded with Robert Morris to use his influence to secure reimbursement for the personal funds he had laid out eight years before at Boston. He needed the money, he told Morris, so that he and his wife, "hearing that Goods were under par in Philadelphia," might "purchase some Articles" for the "Estate."[50] Other Mount Vernon matters were on his mind as well, particularly the matter of the grand dining room.

Before he left for war Washington had begun the construction of a large room encompassing the entire north side of the mansion.[51] He hoped to have it reach up two full stories and decorated with some of the finest Adam-style wall painting, then the rage in England.

For this scale of entertaining the Washingtons would need appropriate ware. Through his agent Daniel Parker in New York City, he ordered several dozen "Plates, Butter boats, Dishes and Tureens," accompanied by six dozen "Wine and Beer glasses exactly like those which Mr. Fraunces brought to Orange Town."[52] Such elegant china and glass needed to be graced with the finest fare, and so Parker was also instructed to inquire after a German cook. Soon to be a farmer again, Washington sought to recruit a miller/cooper for his mill "Stone, large and commodious."[53]

In the midst of these domestic concerns Washington received a visitor. Anxious to send "the best face" of the general to Paris for the equestrian statue, Congress hired Joseph Wright to execute a painting of the general as well as to fashion a plaster cast of his face. Wright, a famous artist best known as an "eccentric modeler of wax heads," had studied at the Royal Academy under Benjamin West, and most recently had been in Paris, where he had finished several portraits of Franklin.[54] Wright was now armed with a letter from the secretary of Congress, Charles Thomson, describing the young man as "an Artist skilled in taking Busts," and asking that the general permit him "to try his talents."[55]

Washington agreed to sit, and over the next few weeks, while he languished at Rockingham, he gave the artist considerable access. Wright prepared both a painting and a bust. He executed the painting on a "small wooden panel, just the right size and durability to survive the packing and shipping to Paris. Washington later described the painting as "a better likeness of me, than any other painter has done."[56]

Having completed the portrait, Wright next turned to the bust.[57] Although he had posed several times for portraits, this was Washington's first experience being modeled in plaster; it was not pleasant. According to Washington, in an account recorded later by Elkanah Watson, Wright

> oiled my features over; and placing me flat on my back, upon a cot, proceeded to daub my face with the plaster. Whilst in this ludicrous attitude, Mrs. Washington entered the room; and seeing my face thus overspread with the plaster, involuntarily exclaimed. Her cry excited in me a disposition to smile, which gave my mouth a slight twist, or compression of the lips that is now observable in the bust which Wright afterward made.[58]

A few days after Wright began his work at Rockingham, the Washingtons had an occasion to plan a grand soiree to celebrate the Morrises' visit to Princeton. On September 6 a large number of guests (too many to fit in the house) gathered under a large "Marquis . . . tent taken from the British." Servants bustled about setting tables with fine china and silver cups. With the Morrises, the general and his lady held the places of honor, joined by the president of Congress on their left and the French minister Luzerne to the right. Scattered about at the other tables were "all the present members [of Congress], Chaplains and great officers."[59]

Among the guests was the irascible Rhode Islander David Howell, whose extreme states' rights position and general disdain for Congress made him one of the most unpopular people in the body. Despite his politics, however, Howell had a fondness for Washington that bordered on fawning admiration. "No honor short of those, which the Deity vindicates to himself, can be too great for Genl Washington."[60] Howell had first met Washington when as a young Rhode Island militia officer he marched with his regiment to the siege of Boston. He remembered the general from those days as "contracted, pensive," giving an air of "deep thought [and] much care." Soon to be freed of the terrible burden of war and command, "the Generals [sic] front was uncommonly open and pleasant." He moved among his guests with "a pleasant smile, sparkling vivacity of wit and humour." Howell went on to note that in a moment of conversation President Boudinot noted with concern that "*Mr. Morris had his hands full*, The General replied at the same Instant—*He wished he had his POCKETS full too*." A certain lightheartedness prevailed. When Richard Peters, a Pennsylvania congressman, noted that the fancy silver cups from which they were drinking were crafted by a silversmith who had turned Quaker, Washington rejoined that "*he wished he had been a Quaker preacher before he had made the cups*," suggesting that then they might have been simpler and cost him less.[61]

Aside from social events, little else enlivened the tedium of waiting for news from Paris. Months had passed since the American ministers had sent word. Their last communication from Franklin in mid-April had simply tried to assure Congress that while "the Definitive Treatys [sic] have met with great Delays," it was not for cause "but principally by the Distractions in the Court of England, where for six or seven Weeks there was properly no Ministry nor any Business effected."[62] In the meantime Congress idled in "fruitless debates."[63]

Nathanael Greene's triumphal arrival broke the boredom. He had left Charleston August 14 and made his way via Richmond, Fredericksburg, Alexandria, Annapolis, and Baltimore. On October 4 he entered Philadelphia to the sound of church bells ringing in his honor. Next to Washington he was America's most celebrated war hero—the conqueror of the South. With Washington's approval Congress voted that in recognition of Greene's "wisdom, fortitude and military skill," the commander in chief would present him with "two pieces of field ordnance taken from the British army at Cowpens, Augusta or Eutaw."[64] For six weeks Greene lingered in Philadelphia with visits to Princeton and Rocky Hill, spending most of his time trying to settle long overdue accounts.

On the same day that Greene arrived, Martha Washington left Rockingham for Philadelphia. Her health was not good. She and her husband thought it best that she return to Virginia before the onset of winter. After spending several days in Philadelphia with the Morrisses, she made her way to Mount Vernon, leaving her husband to endure, in his words, a "Bachelor's fare."[65]

A YEAR EARLIER Guy Carleton had boasted that he would not come to America "to be employ'd as a mere inspector of embarkations."[1] That, however, was exactly what he had become. Having had little to do with shaping the war, like a court-appointed receiver he had the unhappy duty of dismantling a bankrupt enterprise. "Had they called upon him earlier," remarked one disaffected loyalist, "he would have made Tories of all the Whigs."[2] Carleton was particularly resentful that while he struggled to sort out the perplexing details of evacuation, and was being congratulated by the king for his efforts, his bête noir Germain, the minister responsible in his eyes for losing the war, was enjoying life on his Sussex estate bathing in his newly conferred title: Viscount Sackville! Thinking he was entitled to equal recognition, Carleton asked that the king elevate him to the peerage. The king, he was told, at present "resists every application for British peerage."[3]

Carleton's chief problem was the rapidly rising flood of refugees. "Violence in some states, particularly New York," he reported to North, "has driven so many Loyalists to flight that transports are insufficient. But they cannot be left to the rage of these people."[4] A few days later Carleton warned again about the "violent associations" whose mission was to rein terror down upon many unfortunate Americans who were "not conscious of any other Crimes than that of residing within the British lines."[5] Whig propagandists heightened anxiety with fiery broadsides warning Tories about what was in store for them should they remain in America. "Flee while it is in your power," warned the anonymous writer Brutus, "for the day is at hand when to your confusion and dismay such of you as received this admonition will have nothing to deliver them from the just vengeance of the collected citizens."[6] Carleton appealed to both the president of Congress, Elias Boudinot, and Governor Clinton to place checks upon the vigilantes. They did nothing.[7]

By the end of July Governor John Parr of Nova Scotia reported that thirteen thousand refugees had landed in the province. In response Carleton told the governor to prepare for eight to ten thousand more. Among these were several thousand "Negroes." Much to the annoyance of the Americans, Carleton had remained faithful to his word.[8] Whatever their color, those who had been loyal to the king and now sought his protection would receive his care. By mid July Lieutenant Colonel Smith reported to Washington from New York that at least one thousand blacks had left for Nova Scotia and more were gathering for embarkation. Lest Washington once again insist on a protest, Smith wrote, "representations to Sir Guy Carleton upon these subjects I consider superfluous."[9] On the other hand, Smith noted, perhaps with quiet satisfaction, that a "great number of soldiers" whom Carleton was discharging in New York and planned to send to Nova Scotia had approached him to "be permitted to remain here. I have taken the Liberty," Smith told Washington," to give them encouragement."[10]

In August Alexander Hamilton, a retired army officer turned New York politician and lawyer, keen to enhance his law practice and certain that litigation would follow evacuation, visited the city seeking clients.[11] He took the occasion to visit with General Carleton, likely expressing to him his sympathies for the loyalist plight. When Hamilton tried to engage in conversation with him about the end of the war, the general, deeply suspicious of the American's intent, made no response. He simply, according to Hamilton, "shrug[ged] up his shoulders."[12]

As loyalists rushed to flee New York, and troops boarded transports for redeployment, the authorities who were left behind worked to keep order. With so many homes and buildings being abandoned, they feared arson and looting.[13] Street fights broke out, and ruffians made "it unsafe to walk the streets by night or be in a crowd by the day."[14] Carleton held firm. He maintained order and proceeded with the evacuation. To reassure his superiors in London that all was well, he dispatched his secretary, Morgann, home to report.[15]

As August ended, in Paris the final peace treaty was at hand. After innumerable delays, mostly the result of last-minute backroom diplomatic and political maneuverings, the definitive treaty was ready for signing.[16] On August 29, 1783, Vergennes informed Franklin that all matters had been resolved and "that nothing ought to prevent [the American commissioners'] signing at Paris on Wednesday next." France, Spain, and England had reached agreement.[17] At nine o clock in the morning on September 3, Benjamin Franklin, John Adams, and John Jay took a carriage to the lodgings of the British commissioner David Hartley at the Hotel d'York.[18] After a long traditional preamble—"It having pleased the Divine Providence to dispose the hearts of the most serene and most potent Prince George the Third, by the grace of God, king of Great Britain, . . . and of the United States of America, to forget all past misunderstandings . . ."—article 1 declared, "His Britannic Majesty acknowledges the said United States . . . to be free sovereign and independent states."[19] The remaining nine articles set geographic boundaries, granted fishing rights to American fishermen, made allowance for the collection of prewar debts, and provided for the release of all prisoners. Article 5 dealt with the loyalists. All that could be agreed was that "Congress shall earnestly recommend it to the legislatures of the respective states to provide for the restitution of all estates, rights and properties, which have been confiscated belonging to real British subjects." Practically speaking, the article was meaningless.

Within hours of the signing, couriers were rushing printed copies of the treaty to ships waiting at port. Captains set sail, racing their vessels to different destinations across the Atlantic in order to be the first to announce the glorious news. To deliver the official treaty, the one to be ratified by Congress, the American commissioners placed their trust in John Thaxter, John Adams's private secretary. Thaxter took passage on a fast British packet bound for New York.[20] Others arrived before Thaxter, and on November 1 newspapers in Boston, Newport, Providence,

and Philadelphia published the announcement of the final peace.[21] When
Thaxter finally arrived in Philadelphia, via New York, on November 22
it was anticlimatic. Congress had already given an "absolute discharge"
to all furloughed troops and discharged the few men left on active duty,
save a small body at Fort Pitt and the garrison guarding West Point.
With virtually no department left, Secretary at War Benjamin Lincoln
had resigned, and Washington had issued his "Farewell Orders to the
Armies of the United States."[22]

Washington's "Farewell Orders" was not inspiring. Unfortunately for
the commander in chief, his most able aide, David Humphreys, was on
leave.[23] His absence showed. The animated rhetoric that had mesmerized
the officers at Newburgh was gone, and in its place flowed heavy words
of caution and even foreboding. He spoke of the "hardships particularly
incident to our service" that came not from the enemy but from "ex-
tremes of nakedness and hunger," which by implication could only have
come from Congress. Although he repeated his support for a stronger
central government to fulfill its obligations to those who had served,
he clearly was not certain that this would happen. He counseled patience and forbearance to soldiers bound for home, and warned them
that they would likely meet "envious individuals who are unwilling to pay
the debt the public has contracted, or to yield the tribute due to merit."
He urged his men not to respond with "invective or . . . intemperate
conduct."[24]

His "Farewell Orders" was one of the last documents Washington
placed into the hands of his secretary, Lieutenant Colonel Richard Varick. Always concerned about his reputation, Washington was careful to
keep good records to be sure that his side of the story was safely preserved for posterity. In part Washington had always been driven by the
"spur of fame." He had a profound sense of history and his role in it.
However, keeping a documentary record in the midst of war was no
small task. In the eight years when he was in the field Washington moved
his headquarters, often under adverse conditions, nearly 170 times.[25]
Each move risked a loss of documents. Nonetheless, Washington was
determined to keep his papers with him. Aside from a brief period following his hasty retreat from New York City—when his parlous situation forced him to stuff the documents in "a large Box nailed up" and

ship them off to Congress "until [American] Affairs shall be so circum-
stanced as to admit of their return"—Washington kept close personal
control of his papers.[26] As the war progressed, the volume of paperwork
increased, as did the number of boxes to be carted about. Washington
assigned responsibility for the security and transport of these "papers
and other matters of great public Import" to his personal bodyguard.
By his order men of the guard had to be known for their "sobriety, honesty, and good behavior." Soldiery appearance was equally important.
Washington wished "them to be from five feet, eight Inches high, to five
feet, ten Inches; handsomely and well made, and as there is nothing in
his eyes more desirable, than Cleanliness in a Soldier," he insisted that
they be "neat and spruce."[27]

Security for the papers was one thing; access was another. As Washington watched the mound of paper grow, he realized that for his documents to have historic importance it was necessary to organize and, in
some cases, copy them. To manage the task, in the spring of 1781 he
turned to Richard Varick. Two years earlier Varick had had the misfortune of serving as an aide to Benedict Arnold when the plot to sell out
West Point was discovered. Although an investigation cleared him of
any complicity in Arnold's treachery, his reputation was tarnished. Convinced of Varick's loyalty, and needing someone to oversee the organization of his papers and supervise a "set of Writers," Washington
appointed him "Recording Secretary of headquarters."[28]

Beginning in the spring of 1781, at the end of each week Washington's aides gathered up documents, bound them carefully, and delivered
them over to Varick, who had set up shop at Dr. Peter Tappan's home in
Poughkeepsie.[29] For more than two years Varick and his staff cared for
this national treasure. In the fall of 1783 as he prepared to move his headquarters, for the last time, to West Point to await final word of British
evacuation, Washington gathered all his papers, and on November 9 he
ordered Lieutenant Bezaleel Howe, commander of his guard, to "take
charge of the Waggons [sic] which contain my Baggage; and with the
Escort, proceed with them to Virginia, and deliver them at my House ten
miles below Alexandria." Among the baggage were the "six strong hair
Trunks well clasped and with good locks" that Daniel Parker had purchased in New York.[30] "As you know," Washington admonished Howe,

the trunks "contain all my Papers, which are of immense value to me, I am sure it is unnecessary to request your particular attention to them."[31] Leaving nothing to chance, Washington provided Howe a detailed itinerary, including a stop in Philadelphia to pick up anything "Mrs Washington left" and to deliver "The Bundle which contains my Accts . . . to Mr. Morris." In his travels Howe was to be especially careful about crossing on ferries "if the Wind should be high." And under no circumstances could the "Waggons" ever "be without a Sentinel over them; always locked and the Keys in [Howe's] possession."[32]

While his baggage was going south, Washington headed north to West Point to await news from New York City, arriving at West Point on the evening of November 12. There to greet him were Knox, McDougall, and Pickering. The mood was somber. Before his arrival the three generals had been designated by their peers to present a reply to the "Farewell Orders." Without ceremony they presented it to Washington on the fifteenth. More lamentation than celebration, it did "not abound with panegyric."[33] "If [Washington's] attempt to secure to the Armies the just, the promised rewards of their long, severe and dangerous services have failed of success we believe it has arisen from causes not in your Excellency's power to control" but is the product of the "ultimate ingratitude of the people." Yet they assured their commander not even the "ingratitude" of the people they fought to make free could "shake the patriotism of those who had" suffered in the cause of the Revolution. "Posterity will do justice" was their hope as they called down the "blessings of liberty."[34]

Never pleased with being at Princeton, but adamantly opposed to returning to Philadelphia because of the ill treatment given them by state authorities, the members of Congress had been debating relocation for weeks. After a lengthy and rancorous discussion (mostly along sectional lines), on October 21 the members resolved that until a permanent capital were located "at or near the lower falls of Potomac or Georgetown," they would "alternately at equal periods, of not more than one year, and not less than six months" establish their residence at "Trenton and Annapolis." The first move would be to Annapolis.[35] On November 4, two days before Washington headed for West Point, Congress adjourned, setting three weeks hence, November 26, as the date for reconvening in Annapolis.[36]

Through informal communication with his agents in New York City, Washington knew that Carleton was hoping to complete his evacuation by the end of November. On November 13 Carleton's emissary, Major Beckwith, arrived at West Point to deliver the final plan. Carleton proposed to "relinquish the Posts he [held] on York Island from Kings Bridge to McGowens Pass inclusive, on the 21st Instant, Herricks and Hempstead with all to the Eastward on Long Island, on the same day, and if possible to give up the City with Brooklyn on the day following; and Paulus Hook, Denyers, and Staten Island as soon after as practicable."[37] Washington and Clinton met the next day to plan their triumphal entry into New York City.

Under the circumstances Washington as commander in chief of the victorious army might well have insisted on an entry worthy of a conquering hero with himself at the head of the parade. However, in defer ence to civilian authority, Washington suggested that he and Clinton ride side by side into the city. As commander in chief entering a city thought to be in disorder, Washington could also have insisted that New York be put under his direct command until civilian authority was established.[38] Once again, however, he deferred to civilian authority and acknowledged the authority of New York State and city authorities to take immediate charge.[39]

By the twenty-first fewer than two thousand British troops were left in the city.[40] Carleton had promised to have all his men out by Saturday November 22, but a last-minute complication regarding moving sick and wounded soldiers caused delay, and with the consent of Washington and Clinton, Tuesday the twenty-fifth was set for the final departure. While British soldiers boarded waiting transports, the king's lieutenant governor, Andrew Elliott, was sifting through the province's public records removing incriminating documents that he feared might embarrass people who had elected to remain behind. He was also careful to cart away the province's great seal lest this symbolic vestige of royal authority fall into rebel hands.[41]

Timothy Pickering, who was with Washington, reported on November 16 that "the light infantry, and the fifth and fourth Massachusetts regiments," nearly one thousand troops, marched from West Point "for the environs of Kingsbridge, to be prepared to take possession as the British relinquish the posts."[42] To honor Knox, Washington ordered two companies of artillery commanded by Major Sebastian Bauman to accompany the occupying force. In a gesture of triumph, and to embarrass the vanquished British, the artillery companies were to trail "four six pounders, all trophies engraved with the times and places of their capture from the enemy."[43] Washington, accompanied by his staff and Life Guard, left West Point on the eighteenth. The next day they crossed the Hudson River to meet Governor Clinton at Tarrytown. At dawn on the twenty-first as the Americans drew within sight, British sentries marched away crisply from their posts at Kingsbridge. Within minutes Knox's advance guard was across the Harlem River. For the first time since 1776 American forces were on Manhattan. As soon as Knox secured the area, Washington and Clinton crossed and rode to Day's Tavern in Harlem, where they waited for the final word from Carleton.[44]

As the British abandoned the city, order broke down. A Hessian lieutenant, Philip De Krafft, recorded in his journal that drunken sailors went on a violent spree setting fires and assaulting people in the streets, making it "quite a restless night."[45] Some impatient "avowed friends to the American cause" "hoist[ed] the American flag on their houses." The gesture was premature. According to newspaper reports, roving "British Hannibals" pronouncing "double-headed Dams" tore down "the obnoxious colors" while screaming epithets at the "rebel bitches."[46] Later that evening a "fracas" erupted in a local coffeehouse when a "British officer" insulted an American and the patrons turned on him. As bodies and furniture flew about the room, "the British Son of Bellona received the discipline of the horsewhip."[47]

On the afternoon of November 24, a messenger arrived from Carleton. "I propose to withdraw from this place to-morrow at noon, by which time I conclude your troops will be near the barrier."[48] To prevent any untoward incident, Carleton asked Washington to hold his troops in place until an officer was sent out to give information to his advanced guard.[49]

Knox's troops formed up at eight the next morning and marched to Bowery Lane, where they waited until one in the afternoon, when a

British officer informed them that the last redcoats were embarking for their transports. Knox led his soldiers past the barrier, swinging down Chatham Street to Queen (now Pearl) Street, west across Wall Street to Broadway halting at Cape's Tavern (Trinity Place and Broadway). After sending a small detachment to take possession of Fort George at the Battery, Knox hurried back uptown to the Bull's Head Tavern on the Bowery "about the Old Tea Water Pump," where Washington and Clinton were waiting to begin their historic ride.[50]

According to eyewitnesses, within minutes of Knox's arrival Washington, "straight as a dart and noble as he could be," mounted on a "spirited gray horse," gave the command to advance. Next to him rode Governor Clinton on "a splendid bay."[51] Behind them came the lieutenant governor, members of the council, General Knox, and "citizens on horseback, eight a-breast," and "citizens, on Foot, eight a-breast."[52] Slowly the procession made its way from the Bull's Head "through, Queen . . . Street, where it joined with Wall Street, thence to the Broadway, where the main body drew up in front of Cape's Tavern."[53] Along the route crowds pressed forward. Veterans who served in the American army proclaimed their service by sticking a sprig of laurel in their hats and wearing a "Union cockade, of black and white ribbon on the left breast."[54] Crowds "with happy faces . . . lined the streets" and shouted out "joyful acclamations" while "fairer forms drawn to the windows and balconies, by the beat of the American drums" watched the parade down Broadway to Cape's Tavern. It "was the triumphal march of conquerors."[55] The grand procession paused at the tavern and then continued toward the Battery and Fort George to raise the American flag.

As the "cavalcade" drew near the tip of the island they were "astonished and incensed" at what they saw. "The Royal ensign was still floating as usual over Fort George."[56] To make matters worse, the departing British, in a moment of pique, had cut the halyards, nailed the flag to the staff, and greased the flagpole. While Knox's artillerymen unlimbered their cannon and stood with matches lit ready to fire a thirteen-gun salute, Sergeant John Van Arsdale slapped on a pair of cleats, climbed to the top, and ripped the Union Jack away, replacing it with the American flag. American cannon boomed a salute as small boats packed with British soldiers pulled toward waiting transports. Manhattan was clear of the British but Governors and Staten islands were not; a few more days passed before the men on those islands boarded ship. Nonetheless, for all intents and purposes the British were gone.

On the evening of the twenty-fifth Governor Clinton hosted a sumptuous dinner at Fraunces Tavern.[57] When the meal was finished and the cloths were removed, "the feast of reason and flow of soul" began as jovial guests charged their glasses and in carefully prepared fashion drank thirteen toasts.[58]

> The United States of America
> His most Christian Majesty[59]
> The United Netherlands
> The King of Sweden[60]
> The American Army
> The Fleet and Armies of France which have served in America
> The Memory of those Heroes who have fallen for Freedom
> May our Country be grateful to her military Children
> May justice support what Congress has gained
> The Vindicators of the Rights of Mankind in every Quarter of the Globe
> May America be an Asylum to the Persecuted of the Earth.
> May a close Union of the States guard the Temple they have erected to Liberty.
> May the Remembrance of This Day be a Lesson to Princes.

Lieutenant Silas Morton of Massachusetts recorded that sporadic looting by American troops broke out. "Locks" were stolen from the college, and soldiers walked away with "partition boards and window sashes" from abandoned British barracks. "Lashings on the naked back" restored order quickly, and the city took easily to civilian control.[61]

Celebrations went apace. On November 28 "citizens lately returned from exile, gave an elegant entertainment, at Cape's Tavern, to his Excellency, the Governor, and the Council for governing the City."[62] On December 2 Governor Clinton hosted a grand soiree at Cape's for the French ambassador Luzerne. That evening, at the Bowling Green, the "Definitive Treaty of Peace" was celebrated by "an unprecedented exhibition of fireworks."[63] The display was announced by "a Dove descending with the Olive Branch, which communicates the fire to a Marron Battery." That was followed by "Rockets" arching into the night air. "Vertical Wheels" spun on stands erected in the field. "Tourbillons" spiraled up, while star shells illuminated the night. "Chinese fountains" flowed. For nearly an hour the crowd stood and sat in the chill night air admiring the incredible sight. The finale appeared as "Fame descending," followed by "a flight of 100 Rockets."[64]

Having enjoyed the adulation heaped upon him, Washington felt that he could not take his final leave until every last British soldier was away.[65] A few still remained on Staten Island and near Sandy Hook. Finally, on December 1 the long-awaited message came. "If wind and weather permit," wrote Carleton, "I hope we shall be able to embark the Remainder of His Majesty's troops . . . and take our final departure on the 4th Instant."[66]

With that news Washington made his own final preparations. He had one last military ceremony to attend. Few events in American history are as emotional, well remembered, and so poorly documented as "Washington's Farewell to His Officers." The only surviving firsthand account is one written nearly a half century after the event by Colonel Benjamin Tallmadge, a New York officer who served as Washington's chief of intelligence.[67] According to Tallmadge, Washington had made it known to his officers that he was leaving the city on December 4 and wished to see them that day at Fraunces Tavern. Shortly before noon the officers assembled in the tavern's Long Room. A few minutes after the clock struck twelve Washington, followed closely by his aides David Humphreys and Benjamin Walker, entered the room. "We had been assembled but a few moments."[68]

For more than eight years of war—through victory, defeat, neglect by Congress, and sniping criticism—Washington, always a fine actor, had crafted a personal image of the stolid commander. This moment was different. "His emotion [was] too strong to be concealed," and so too were the feelings of the men standing near. A number of field officers stood by, but only three of the seventy-four men Congress had appointed as generals to serve under Washington were present: Baron von Steuben, Alexander McDougall, and Henry Knox.[69] In "breathless silence" the officers looked upon their commander. He then turned toward them, "filled his glass with wine," and offered a toast: "With a heart full of love and gratitude, I now take leave of you. I most devoutly wish that your latter days may be as prosperous and happy as your former ones have been glorious and honorable." As the officers returned the salute Washington invited each one of them to "come and take [him] by the hand."

Appropriately enough, the first to approach was Henry Knox. Washington took his hand. Neither could speak, and then in a gesture that none in the room had ever before witnessed, the two "embraced each other in silence." Only the sound of boots shuffling on the floor and the slight noise of rattling dress swords could be heard as "every officer in the room marched up to, kissed, and parted with the General in Chief." Nearly a half century later Tallmadge was still filled with emotion as he remembered "such a scene of sorrow and weeping [he] had never before witnessed."

> Tears of deep sensibility filled every eye   and the heart seemed so full, that it was ready to burst from its wonted abode. Not a word was uttered to break the solemn silence that prevailed or to interrupt the tenderness of the interesting scene. The *simple thought* that we were then about to part from the man who had conducted us through a long and bloody war, and under whose conduct the glory and independence of our country had been achieved, and that we should see his face no more in this world, seemed to me utterly insupportable.

Although the moment was highly emotional, Washington soon turned and exited the tavern onto Queen Street, where a corps of infantry snapped to attention offering a final salute to their commander. Turning onto Water Street, he walked past cheering crowds a short distance to the ferry slip. Awaiting him at the landing was a barge to carry him across the Hudson to Paulus Hook. As the oarsmen pulled away, Washington gave a last wave to the crowd. At the same moment past Sandy Hook Carleton was bound home on the frigate *Ceres*, the same vessel that had brought him to New York eighteen months before.

Washington had one final official act to complete. Among the papers Washington had carried with him during the war, nothing was more precious than the commission as commander in chief of the army of the United States given to him by Congress June 19, 1775. This was the one document in his official papers that he had never entrusted to clerks or later to Richard Varick. In eight years he had never parted with it, but now the moment had come to return his commission.

From Paulus Hook Washington traveled for four days via New Brunswick and Trenton, through villages and towns, to Philadelphia. Everywhere people gathered to cheer and huzzah. About noon on the eighth he drew near the outskirts of Philadelphia to be welcomed by the president of the state, John Dickinson.[70] With him as well as a "number of citizens," including his old friend Robert Morris, he entered Philadelphia to the sound of booming cannon, bells tolling, and citizens lining the street shouting "repeated acclamations."[71] For nearly a week Washington remained as addresses and honors poured in. Receptions, parties, dinners, and balls were held in his honor. Finally the exhausted general left the city on the fifteenth, hurrying to Annapolis to return his commission and "get translated into a private Citizen," as he wrote to his friend James McHenry.[72]

Progress along the road to Annapolis was slow. Americans were excited to catch a glimpse of their national hero. Every community through which he passed begged the privilege of honoring him publicly. At Wilmington, Delaware, the townsmen feted him at a dinner and then invited him to step outside to watch a bonfire lit in his honor. More dinners and addresses followed in Baltimore.[73]

While its streets were not yet paved, Annapolis was a pleasant little town on the Severn River. Barely four years old, Maryland's impressive statehouse stood on a commanding rise at the north end of the town. It was spacious and elegantly finished. State authorities had graciously offered the Senate chamber to the Congress. The Rhode Island delegate David Howell counted Annapolis far more beautiful than Philadelphia. As to the manners of the people, he was less complimentary. The stiff New Englander noted that while he could find "a play house, a ballroom, [and] many good taverns," he had yet to discover a "place of public worship."[74] Nor was he pleased with the loose atmosphere of his lodgings. On his first Saturday evening when he came down to the common room expecting to read and converse with his fellow lodgers, he was taken aback when a "servant brought into the room [and] set on the Table two candles [and] two packs of Cards. Some of the company soon spread around the Table [and] went to playing for money," but Howell left the room. In a letter dripping with disapproval, he reported home to his friend William Greene "that in New England the Table would have been furnished with a bible [and] Psalm book instead of two packs of cards."[75] Howell's North Carolina colleague Hugh Williamson had a more enchanting view that perhaps spoke to the country's cultural divide. To him, the place and people of Annapolis were charming. He was particularly struck by the "lovely girls here, a younger man perhaps would call them angels."[76]

It was a good thing that Annapolis was charming and lively, for aside from the distractions of walking, gambling, drinking, dancing, and writing letters home, there was little in the line of official business to occupy the members' time. Although they had agreed when leaving Princeton to reconvene on November 26, not enough members took their seats on that day to make a quorum. In the opinion of Thomas Jefferson, one of the few delegates to arrive on schedule, the states and their representatives had become careless in their responsibilities.[77] Congress was in a downward spiral, its powers ebbing. Even the Rhode Islander William Ellery, one of Congress's longest-serving and most faithful members, saw minimal use for the body. "If the States were represented, and in earnest," he wrote to his colleague Benjamin Huntington, a Connecticut delegate whose state was among the no-shows, "I think we could dispatch all the business of importance in the course of three months, and adjourn leaving small matters to a Committee of the States."[78] For the moment, "the business of importance" was receiving the commander in chief.

As Washington neared Annapolis late in the afternoon of December 19, a distinguished delegation greeted him. As usual on these occasions it included the principal inhabitants of the place, plus a large concourse of ordinary citizens. Riding at the head of the reception committee was a familiar figure: General Horatio Gates. The general had come up from Virginia to settle some private accounts and took the opportunity to ride out to greet the commander in chief. It was the first time the two had met since Newburgh.[79] No record remains of any exchange between them.

To the distant sound of a thirteen-gun salute, the gentlemen escorted Washington to Annapolis's most splendid hostelry, Mann's Hotel, "where apartments had been prepared for his reception."[80] Washington retired to his "apartments" to prepare a letter to the president of Congress.

> Sir: I take the earliest opportunity to inform Congress of my arrival in this City, with the intention of asking leave to resign the Commission I have the honor of holding in their Service. It is essential for me to know their pleasure, and in what manner it will be most proper to offer my resignation, whether in writing, or at an Audience; I shall therefore request to be honored with the necessary information, that being apprised of the sentiments of Congress I may regulate my Conduct accordingly.[81]

That night when he came to dine with the president, Thomas Mifflin of Pennsylvania, Washington delivered his letter. The evening may not have been entirely pleasant. Mifflin was among those members of Congress who in 1778, as part of the "Conway Cabal," had sought to replace Washington with Gates. Washington knew of his actions and held a hearty dislike of the man.

The next day Congress convened to consider the general's request. Following a brief discussion, the members resolved "that his Excellency the Commander in Chief be admitted to a public audience, on Tuesday next, at twelve o'clock." However, in advance of the "public audience," the members agreed to give a "public entertainment" on Monday December 22. Moments before the vote a member, most likely William Ellery, whose passion for proper procedure was legendary, rose to ask the embarrassing question whether seven states, two short of a quorum for important business, were "competent to receive the resignation of a Commander in Chief." The president called for a vote. Ellery, the first to vote, answered no. As the roll call continued, every other member voted yes. Before the secretary made the official entry in the *Journals*, Ellery asked that his vote be changed to aye, making the decision unanimous.[82] And so seven states were sufficient to receive the resignation of the commander in chief. It was deemed "ordinary" rather than "important" business. No one, not even Washington, commented on the irony.[83]

Notwithstanding the question of a quorum, the members were conscious they were planning an event that had few precedents in history, wherein a victorious military commander was surrendering his authority to a civilian body. Congress elected three men "to make the necessary arrangements for the public audience of General Washington": Elbridge Gerry, James McHenry, and Thomas Jefferson. The committee split the assignment; McHenry and Gerry worked on protocol for the occasion, and Jefferson retired to his chambers to prepare the text of a response to the general's address, which he had been given in advance.[84] They had two days to prepare the stage for one of the most important moments in American history.

On Monday evening they suspended their work, prior to the ceremony, to join their fellow members and more than two hundred guests gathered for an elegant dinner at Mann's to honor Washington. James Tilton of Delaware described the feast as "the most extraordinary" he ever attended. According to Tilton, "cheerful voices [all men]," combined with the clanging of knives and forks, "made a din of a very extraordinary nature and most delightful influence." The wine was "in plenty," and glasses were hoisted for the traditional thirteen toasts, but "not a soul got drunk." The high point of evening came when the general stood to offer his toast: "Competent powers to congress for general purposes."[85] In reply, some in the room raised their glasses more quickly than others.

Once dinner was finished, guests left the hotel to make their way to the statehouse, where the governor was hosting a ball. Martha Washington did not attend; owing to her fragile health and the difficulty of winter travel, she had wisely decided to remain at home. In her absence Washington, known for his love of dancing and his grace on the floor, selected as his first partner the young, and reportedly beautiful, twenty-year-old Martha Rolle.[86] The Delaware delegate James Tilton noted admiringly that he "danced every set, that all the ladies might have the pleasure of dancing with him, or as it has since been handsomely expressed, *get a touch of him.*"[87]

Washington rose early on Tuesday to prepare for the momentous occasion ahead of him. He wrote to his friend von Steuben, "[This is] the last Letter I shall ever write while I continue in the service of my Country; the hour of my resignation is fixed at twelve this day; after which I shall become a private Citizen on the Banks of the Potomack."[88]

Shortly before noon Mifflin called the Congress to order. The chamber was filled, including the gallery. First to rise was Hugh Williamson of North Carolina. Looking about the chamber and seeing, yet again, no quorum, he moved, and Jefferson seconded, "that letters be immediately dispatched to the executives of New Hampshire, Connecticut, New York, New Jersey, South Carolina and Georgia, informing them, that the safety, honor and good faith of the United States require the immediate attendance of their delegates in Congress." After quickly approving Williamson's motion, Congress, "according to order," turned to the main business of the day.

Protocol was followed to the letter. At noon the doors to the Senate chamber opened, and a messenger announced the arrival of "His Excellency." Washington, dressed in the blue buff uniform of the Continental army, entered followed by Humphreys and Walker. The general was entering a chamber where a bare quorum (eighteen members, seven states) had assembled, presided over by Mifflin.[89] Members remained "seated and covered." Washington took a seat at the front of the chamber, to the side of the president, Walker and Humphreys stood near him. "The ladies occupied the gallery," while a "throng of men" mingled on the floor and "filled all the avenues."[90] Secretary Thomson called for silence. In the hushed room Mifflin turned to the General and announced, "Congress sir are prepared to receive your Communications."[91]

The commander in chief's friend, and Maryland delegate, James McHenry described the scene to his fiancée, Margaret Caldwell: Washington "rose [and] bowed to congress, who uncovered but did not bow." As usual in these public occasions, the general was succinct.[92] "Happy in the confirmation of our Independence and Sovereignty," Washington offered his resignation from a post which he admitted he had accepted eight years earlier "with diffidence." He asked the members to recognize those officers who had served with him "as worthy of favorable notice and patronage of Congress." As he spoke his hands "shook" and his "voice faultered [sic] and sunk." Emotion swept the audience. According to McHenry, "All wept, and there was hardly a member of Congress who did not drop tears."[93]

Washington concluded his brief remarks with a dramatic gesture worthy of the man who had led the Revolution. Turning toward Mifflin, he thrust his hand into his coat and announced, "I here offer my Commission." He "drew out from his bosom his commission and delivered it up to the president of Congress."[94] It was a "spectacle inexpressibly solemn and affecting."[95] President Mifflin took the document, paused, and then read "the reply that had been prepared . . . without any shew of feeling tho' with much dignity."[96]

When Mifflin finished, Washington "bowed again to Congress, they uncovered and the general retired." As soon as the former commander in chief left the chamber, Congress adjourned and invited Washington to return. He went about the room and "bid every member farewell."[97] The good-byes were brief. Washington was anxious to take advantage of what daylight was left to begin his journey home. Maryland's governor, William Paca, escorted Washington and his companions—Humphreys, Walker, and his slave Billy Lee—a few miles out of town to the South River Ferry. Once across, the group rode directly to Mount Vernon.[98]

It was winter, and darkness came early. Mount Vernon was too far to reach in one day. On Christmas Eve Washington finally arrived home. One can only imagine the scene of welcome as he rode by the fields, meadows, and orchards he loved so well, and through the wooden gates leading up to the mansion. Despite the chill, everyone must have been out to see him. Martha was there, as well as their youngest grandchildren, Nellie and Wash.[99]

If the breeze was right, he probably caught the holiday scent of baking pies and gingerbread. Martha greeted him believing in her heart "that from this moment [they] would grow old together, in solitude and tranquility."[100]

Although Christmas was always special at Mount Vernon, 1783 was especially poignant and joyful. As was the custom in plantation society, the holiday spanned several days during which the entire Mount Vernon community, including two hundred slaves and servants, laid their tools aside and joined in eating, drinking, game playing, and endless socializing. Washington was so pleased that he wrote Secretary Thomson that not even the "Snow and Ice" which had "fast locked" them in could dim the festivities.[101] In the main house the Washingtons enjoyed the holidays in the company of friends and relatives.

Undoubtedly, Martha brought out all the china, silver, and linens she had acquired from New York and Philadelphia, while her husband refilled glasses with fine wine. The table in the new room on the north side groaned with offerings from the kitchen. Certain to be presented was Christmas pie. Encased in a "good standing crust," this mountainous pie was stuffed with boned "turkey, a goose, a fowl, a partridge, and a pigeon." After being seasoned with mace, nutmegs, cloves, black pepper, and salt, and four pounds of butter, it was baked "in a very hot oven . . . at least four hours."[102]

Christian tradition extends the feast of the Nativity to the Epiphany, January 6, when the Magi arrived bearing gifts for the Christ child. The Washingtons had a very special reason to celebrate this Epiphany, January 6, 1784, for it was their twenty-fourth wedding anniversary. Food was again central to the festivities. For Twelfth Night it was a special "great cake," which included more than three dozen eggs, four pounds of butter, cream, four pounds of sugar, along with five pounds of flower and fruit. Two hours to bake and doused with "half a pint of wine [and] some frensh [sic] brandy," the concoction was ready to eat.[103] This was hardly the fare of the officers' mess upon which he had subsisted for so many years.

EPILOGUE

WHILE CITIZEN WASHINGTON ENJOYED the fruits of retirement, Congress, having lost its quorum after his departure, remained paralyzed in Annapolis. Thaxter had delivered the final treaty, but without a quorum (nine states) it sat on the secretary's desk. The body had dodged the issue of a quorum when it accepted Washington's resignation, but ratification could not be dealt with so easily.[1] It took more than a month, but finally on January 14 delegates from New Jersey and Connecticut arrived. Nine states, a bare quorum, were now present. Lest someone leave, die, or fall ill, no time was to be lost. The vote was taken quickly, and ratification was unanimous.[2] Fortunately, the members voted on the fourteenth, for three days later they lost their quorum.[3]

Washington took little notice of the news from Annapolis. It was anticlimactic. Despite the soothing metaphors by which he proclaimed his retirement from public life—sitting in "the shadow of this Vine and Fig tree"—he was agitated and deeply concerned about the future of the nation. The republic for which he, more than anyone else in America, had risked his life, fortune, and sacred honor to establish was now, he complained to his fellow Virginian Benjamin Harrison, in the hands of "a half-starved, limping Government, that appears to be always moving upon crutches, and tottering at every step."[4]

While Congress was "tottering" in Annapolis, Washington was confronting problems at Mount Vernon. His eight-year absence had taken a heavy toll. Rents had gone uncollected, what debts he could collect were being paid in nearly worthless paper currency, and cousin Lund's erratic bookkeeping made sorting through accounts a difficult task. Washington could, however, take some consolation from the fact that aside from the escape of eighteen slaves, his property, for the most part, had escaped the physical ravages of war.

Washington wasted no time in embracing the social life of a Virginia planter and attending to the improvement of his mansion. The "new room," he wrote his English friend Samuel Vaughan, was nearly completed. "The Doors, Windows and floors being done," he decided to finish the space in "stucco which is the present taste in England."[5] The grounds too captured his attention. He made plans to build a greenhouse and to pave his piazza with "stone, or some other kind of Floor, which will stand the weather."[6]

As workmen bustled about the grounds, Washington's immediate household was growing. He and Martha continued to care for their grandchildren Nelly and Wash. Lund, despite having disappointed his cousin, lived at Mount Vernon as well, and within a few months George's younger brother John Augustine and his wife, Nancy, moved in. Seven at dinner was the minimum at table, but the number was often greater. The plantation tradition of hospitality and genteel behavior demanded that Washington welcome all who came to his door, causing him to complain that his home had become "a well resorted tavern, as scarcely any strangers who are going from north to south, or from south to north, do not spend a day or two at it."[7] Among those who arrived and stayed the longest was the Reverend William Gordon.

Minister at the Third Church in Roxbury, Massachusetts, and "astute in recognizing the significance of his times," Gordon was writing a history of the American Revolution.[8] Washington of course was the central character in his story. In October 1782 Gordon wrote to Washington asking permission to examine his papers. Although Washington agreed that it was "impracticable for the best Historiographer living, to write a full and correct history of the present Revolution, who has not free access to the Archives of Congress, those of Individual States, the papers of the Commander in Chief, and Commanding officers of separate departments," he could not, he explained, "while the war continues," give over to Gordon materials "sacred in [his] hands."[9]

Undeterred, Gordon persisted in his efforts and continued to press Washington.[10] In May 1784 he received an encouraging answer from Washington. Replying to Gordon's most recent request to examine his papers, Washington told him a visit to Mount Vernon could be arranged, but only on the condition that Congress must first open its archives to him. "I have always thought that it would be respectful to the Sovereign power of these United States (i.e. Congress) to *follow*, rather than to take the lead of them in disclosures of this kind." Under that condition, Washington told Gordon, "[I will] lay before you with cheerfulness, my *public* papers for your information."[11]

Armed with Washington's letter, Gordon, the diligent scholar, petitioned Congress for "access to the documents and records in the archives of Congress." With little discussion the members ordered the secretary "to lay before Dr. Gordon, any papers or files which he may be desired," except diplomatic correspondence and "any acts or records which hitherto have been considered as confidential or secret." As for Washington's papers, "having the fullest confidence in the prudence of the late Commander in Chief," Congress had no objection "to his laying before Dr. Gordon, any of his papers which he shall think, at this period, may be submitted to the eye of the public."[12] With the resolution in hand Gordon arrived at Mount Vernon on June 2. Indefatigable, for more than two weeks Gordon, "rising at daylight and continuing far into the evening," poured through more than thirty volumes of letters and documents.[13]

While Gordon sought to capture the history of the Revolution through the experience of Washington, other visitors came to immortalize him in portrait and sculpture. In April 1785 Robert Edge Pine, an English portraitist, arrived carrying letters of introduction, including one from Robert Morris who described him as "an Historical and portrait painter of some eminence. He is drawing some interesting parts of our History and your Portrait is indispensably necessary to his Werks."[14] Although

painted several times before, Washington seemingly never tired of pos-
ing for an artist. "No dray moves more readily to the Thrill, than I do to
the Painters Chair."[15] Pine stayed long enough to paint not only Washington but his wife as well, along with Frances Bassett Washington (George
Augustine's wife) and the four Custis grandchildren, Martha, Eleanor,
Elizabeth, and George.[16]

Barely two weeks after Pine left to return to Annapolis, the Washingtons welcomed the internationally renowned Catherine Macaulay
Graham. One of the most prolific woman writers of the eighteenth century and an ardent Whig who had spoken for the American cause, she
had arrived in America to tour the eastern states and had decided to
make a special trip to Virginia to meet Washington.[17] He admired her as
well, particularly her eight-volume *History of England from the Accession
of James I to That of the Brunswick Line*.[18] Recounting her ten-day stay at
Mount Vernon, Washington told Knox, "A visit from a Lady so celebrated in the Literary world could not but be very flattering to me."[19]

Washington's international reputation drew another famous visitor in
the summer of 1785: Jean-Antoine Houdon. Houdon carried letters of
introduction from Lafayette, Jefferson, and Washington's former aide
David Humphreys; the latter describing him "as one of the ablest statu-
aries in Europe." Houdon and his entourage, including three assistants
and an interpreter, arrived by boat from Alexandria near midnight on
October 2, awakening the household and causing a stir. As usual in
Washington's "well resorted tavern," nearly every room was taken, and
so it took a while for the servants to prepare accommodations. For two
weeks Houdon and his assistants took careful measurements of their
subject and prepared plaster models. In his letter introducing Houdon,
Jefferson had cautioned that while the sculptor's work at Mount Vernon
might not occupy more than two weeks, the final execution was likely
to take years. He was right. Houdon left Mount Vernon on October 17.
The completed life-size marble statue was not unveiled in Richmond
until 1796.

Washington's visitors brought news from all parts of the nation and
abroad, and so too did the mails. Washington was in correspondence
with a wide variety of people. Although much of his attention was focused
on Mount Vernon and his other properties, increasingly the deteriorat-

ing political situation in America drew his notice. Through conversation with visitors and letters from dozens of politicians and former officers, Washington grew increasing pessimistic about the fate of the republic. In February 1785, he wrote Knox that he feared that England's continuing unfriendly attitude will "give us a good deal of trouble"; "and yet, it does not appear to me, that we have wisdom, or national policy enough to avert the evils which are impending—How should we, when contracted ideas, local pursuits, and absurd jealously are continually leading us from those great and fundamental principles which are characteristic of wise and powerful Nations; and without which we are no more than a rope of Sand, and shall be easily broken."[20]

Since Congress lacked authority to address the issues facing the confederation, some states decided to act on their own. Virginia and Maryland were in dispute over issues of navigation on Chesapeake Bay. To solve the issue, both states appointed commissioners to meet at Mount Vernon in March 1785. Washington hosted the gathering.[21] The meeting went so well that the Virginia assembly sent out an invitation for all of the states to meet "to take into consideration the trade of the United States; to examine the relative situations and trade of the said States; to consider how far a uniform system in their commercial regulations may be necessary to their common interest and their permanent harmony; and to report to the several States, such an act relative to this great object as, when unanimously ratified by them, will enable the United States in Congress effectually to provide for the same."[22] They set the time for September in Annapolis.[23] Washington saw promise in the Annapolis meeting, telling Lafayette "much good is expected from this measure," and although he did not attend he followed events carefully.[24] Two days before the meeting convened, Washington wrote anxiously to his friend John Fitzgerald in Alexandria for news: "Have you heard from Annapolis since Monday? Have the Commercial Commissioners met? Have they proceeded to business? How long is it supposed their Session will last? And is it likely they will do anything effectual?"[25]

The "Session" lasted four days. Although several states had promised to send delegates, only New York, New Jersey, Pennsylvania, Delaware, and Virginia fulfilled their pledge. Nonetheless, the convention issued a report, signed by the chairman, John Dickinson of Pennsylvania, calling for another meeting of all the states to be held in Philadelphia "to render the constitution of the Federal Government adequate to the exigencies of the Union."[26] Dickinson returned to Philadelphia and on September 20 presented the report to Congress, where it sat for several days since the body was unable to summon a quorum. Further postponements and debates delayed action until February 21, when Congress resolved, "It is expedient that on the second Monday in May next a Convention of delegates who shall have been appointed by the several states be held at Philadelphia."[27]

Washington approved heartily of the Philadelphia meeting, even though he decided not to attend. Attendance at a "public theater," he wrote to Edmund Randolph, governor of Virginia, would "sweep me back into the tide of public affairs, when retirement and ease is so essentially necessary for, and is so much desired by me."[28] Resistance, however, was futile. Randolph, Madison, Knox, and a host of others urged him to lend his presence.[29] Finally, he agreed.[30]

By May 25 seven states were present, enough to convene the convention. Among the first order of business was the election of a president. Benjamin Franklin, home after his long stint in Paris, planned to attend in order to nominate Washington to the post. Ill health kept him away, and so in his place Robert Morris rose and nominated him. John Rutledge of South Carolina seconded the nomination, "expressing his confidence that the choice would be unanimous, and observing that the presence of Genl Washington forbade any observations on the occasion which might otherwise be proper."[31] The vote was unanimous.

Escorted by Rutledge and Morris, Washington took the chair "from which in a very emphatic manner he thanked the Convention for the honor they had conferred on him, reminded them of the novelty of the scene of business in which he was to act, lamented his want of (better qualifications), and claimed the indulgence of the House towards the involuntary errors which his inexperience might occasion."[32] Those words were among the very few words spoken publicly by him during the entire convention. Despite his silence, however, there was no doubt where he stood. He had come to Philadelphia to help create a strong federal union. Indeed shortly after the convention finished its work Gouverneur Morris told him, "I am convinced that had you not attended the Convention, and the same paper handed out to the World, it would have met with a colder Reception, with fewer and weaker Advocates, and with more and more strenuous opponents."[33] But, Morris argued, Washington's work was not done. The states still had to ratify, and the outcome was not certain. Washington must, pleaded Morris, "accept of the Presidency." If he did not, "it would prove fatal" to the constitution. The "thirteen Horses now about to be coupled together" will only "listen to your Voice."[34] Pierce Butler, a South Carolina delegate to the Philadelphia convention, went so far as to claim that the extensive powers granted to the president in the new constitution would not "have been so great had not many of the members cast their eyes towards General Washington as President; and shaped their Ideas of the Powers to be given to a President, by their opinions of his virtues."[35] For the third time in a dozen years—1775, commander in chief; 1787, president of the convention—the nation looked to Washington for leadership. In accordance with article 2 of the new constitution, elections were held, electors chosen, and on April 6, 1789, the House and Senate met in joint session as John Langdon, president pro tem of the Senate, declared "that he, in their presence, had opened and counted the votes of the electors," and "whereby it appears, that George Washington, Esq. was unanimously elected President."[36]

Congress dispatched its veteran secretary, Charles Thomson, to deliver the news to the president elect.[37] Arriving at Mount Vernon on April 14, he found Washington already apprised of his election and prepared to leave for New York City. (Congress had moved there from Annapolis in January 1785.)[38]

Two days later Washington bid farewell to his family and his beloved Mount Vernon, climbed into the carriage, and with Thomson and Humphreys accompanying him, he began his journey to New York City, confiding to his diary that he did so understanding that he was leaving behind his "private life and domestic felicity" but was buttressed with "a due sense of this last and greatest token of affection and confidence which [his] country could confer upon [him]."[39] Retirement would have to wait.

ACKNOWLEDGMENTS

For anyone interested in George Washington, the gravitational pull of
Mount Vernon is irresistible. The museum, education center, grounds,
and mansion are extraordinary, and so too is the staff. I am deeply grateful to Gay Hart Gaines, whose generous support of a fellowship in her
name allowed me to visit and lecture at Mount Vernon. While I was there
James Rees, Ann Bay, Nancy Hayward, Debbie Baker, and Joan Stahl
were most helpful. Indeed, without their encouragement I might never
have pursued this project.

As usual, the librarians at Snell Library, Northeastern University
were my partners in research. I am especially grateful to Yves Hya-
cinthe, who never failed to find the book I needed. Peter Drummey at
the Massachusetts Historical Society was, as is his wont, always helpful,
as was the society's curator, Anne Bentley. Mary Warnement at the
Boston Athenaeum (home to George Washington's library) answered
questions about Washington's reading habits. Elizabeth Frengel at the
library of the Society of the Cincinnati was of great help in identifying
Continental army officers. Ben Huggins at the Papers of George Washington responded to an important question about the Newburgh Address. Stefan Bielinski, community historian at the New York State
Museum, advised me on New York local history, while Susan Leath
provided information about the town of Bethlehem, New York. Mike
McGurty at the New Windsor Cantonment and Kathleen Mitchell at
nearby Hasbrouck House were kind enough to guide me through the

cantonment and Washington's headquarters. Suzanne Prabucki at Fraunces Tavern responded to several requests for information, as did Michelle Cox at Christ Church, Alexandria, Virginia, Colonel Jim Johnson, Hudson River Valley Institute, and William Betts, biographer of John Armstrong Sr. Kellie Laughman, my undergraduate research assistant, tracked down a number of newspaper references, and my friend Gary Boyd Roberts answered genealogical questions.

Among other institutions to which I am indebted, I include: the Boston Public Library; the American Antiquarian Society; Clements Library, University of Michigan; Library and Archives Canada; Library of Congress, Manuscript Division; New York Historical Society; New York Public Library; Clerk's Office, County of Orange, New York; Rhode Island Historical Society; British National Archives; and the Falmouth Library (Dorset, United Kingdom).

To my editor, George Gibson, I offer my heartiest thanks. His wisdom and patience never wanes. I must also recognize the splendid work of my copy editor, Vicki Haire. I am also in debt to my friend Martin Wain of Ottawa, Canada, whose hospitality allowed me to spend several days at the Library Archives Canada. My colleagues in the History Department at Northeastern, particularly my friend Ray Robinson, as well as my friends elsewhere on campus, were unwaveringly encouraging. Chief among my campus advisers was Linda Smith Rhoads, editor of the *New England Quarterly*. To this campus list I must add my students, whose interest and enthusiasm for history convince me every day that I have the best job in the world.

No scholar works alone. We rely on the work of others and wisely seek their advice. In this regard I was fortunate to have had the counsel of three eminent scholars: Edward Lengel, editor in chief of the Papers of George Washington, University of Virginia; Richard Kohn, professor of history and peace, war, and defense, University of North Carolina, Chapel Hill; and John E. Ferling, professor emeritus, University of West Georgia. I am also grateful to my friends Richard Miller and David McCullough, whose examples of scholarship and good writing should encourage us all.

Throughout my career my family has always been present to provide support. To my wife, Marilyn, and children, Alison and Nathaniel, I say once again, but never too often, thanks.

To the General, Field & other Officers Assembled at the New Building pursuant to the General Order of the 11th. Instant March.

Head Quarters Newburgh
15th. of March 1783.

GENTLEMEN,

By an anonymous summons, an attempt has been made to convene you together—how inconsistent with the rules of propriety!—how unmilitary!—and how subversive of all order and discipline—let the good sense of the Army decide.—

In the moment of this summons, another anonymous production was sent into circulation; addressed more to the feelings of passions, than to the reason & judgment of the Army.—The Author of the piece, is entitled to much credit for the goodness of his Pen:—and I could wish he had as much credit for the rectitude of his Heart—for, as men see thro' different Optics, and are induced by the reflecting faculties of the Mind, to use different means to attain the same end;—the Author of the Address, should have had more charity, than to mark for Suspicion, the Man who should recommend moderation and longer forbearance—or, in other words, who should not think as he thinks, and act as he advises.— But he had another plan in view, in which candor and liberality of Sentiment, regard to justice, and love of Country, have no part, and he was right, to insinuate the darkest suspicion, to effect the blackest designs.

That the Address is drawn with great Art, and is designed to answer the most insidious purposes.—That it is calculated to impress the Mind, with an idea of premeditated injustice in the Sovereign power of the United States, and rouse all those resentments which must unavoidably flow from such a belief.—That the secret Mover of this Scheme (whoever he may be) intended to take advantage of the passions, while they were warmed by the recollection of past distresses, without giving time for cool, deliberative thinking, & that composure of Mind which is so necessary to give dignity & stability to Measures, is rendered too obvious, by the mode of conducting the business to need other proof than a reference to the proceeding.—

Thus much, Gentlemen, I have thought it incumbent on me to observe to you, to shew upon what principles I opposed the irregular and hasty meeting which was proposed to have been held on Tuesday last:—and not because I wanted a disposition to give you every opportunity, consistent with your own honor, and the dignity of the Army, to make known your grievances.—If my conduct heretofore, has not evinced to you, that I have been a faithful friend to the Army, my declaration of it at this time wd. be equally unavailing & improper.—But as I was among the first who embarked in the cause of our common Country—As I have never left your side one moment, but when called from you, on public duty—As I have been the constant companion & witness of your Distresses, and not among the last to feel, & acknowledge your merits—As I have ever considered my own Military reputation as inseperably connected with that of the Army—As my Heart has ever expanded with Joy, when I have heard its praises—and my indignation has arisen, when the mouth of detraction has been opened against it—it can *scarcely be supposed,* at this late stage of the War, that I am indifferent to its interests.—

But—how are they to be promoted? The way is plain, says the anonymous Addresser—If War continues, remove into the unsettled Country—there establish yourselves, and leave an ungrateful Country to defend itself—But who are they to defend?—Our Wives, our Children, our Farms, and other property which we leave behind us.—or—in this state of hostile seperation [*sic*], are we to take the two first (the latter cannot be removed)—to perish in a Wilderness, with hunger cold & nakedness?—If Peace takes place, never sheath your Sword says he untill you have obtained full and ample Justice—This dreadful alternative, of either deserting our Country in the extremest hour of her distress, or turning our Arms against it, (which is the apparent object, unless Congress can be compelled into instant compliance) has something so shocking in it, that humanity revolts at the idea.—My God! What can this writer have in view, by recommending such measures?—Can he be a friend to the Army?—Can he be a friend to this Country?—Rather is he not an insidious Foe?—Some Emissary, perhaps, from New York,* plotting the ruin of both, by sowing the seeds of discord & seperation [sic] between the Civil & Military powers of the Continent?—And what compliment does he pay to our understandings, when he recommends measures in either alternative, impracticable in their Nature?

But here, Gentlemen, I will drop the curtain;—because it wd. be as imprudent in me to assign my reasons for this opinion, as it would be insulting to your conception, to suppose you stood in need of them.—A moments reflection will convince every dispassionate Mind of the physical impossibility of carrying either proposal into execution.—

There might, Gentlemen, be an impropriety in my taking notice, in this Address to you, of an anonymous production—but the manner in which that performance has been introduced to the Army—the effect it was intended to have, together with some other circumstances, will amply justify my observations on the tendency of that Writing.—With respect to the advice given by the Author—to suspect the man, who shall recommend moderate measures and longer forbearance—I spurn it—as every man, who regards that liberty, & reveres that Justice for which we contend, undoubtedly must—for if Men are to be precluded from offering their sentiments on a matter, which may involve the most serious and alarming consequences, that can invite the consideration of Mankind; reason is of no use to us—the freedom of Speech may be taken away—and, dumb & silent we may be led, like sheep, to the Slaughter.

I cannot, in Justice to my own belief, & what I have great reason to conceive is the intention of Congress, conclude this Address, without giving it as my decided opinion; that that Honble. Body, entertain exalted sentiments of the Services of the Army;—and, from a full conviction of its Merits & sufferings, will do it compleat Justice:—That their endeavers, to discover & establish funds for this purpose, have been

---

* That is, from the British in New York.

unwearied, and will not cease, till they have succeeded, I have not a doubt.—But, like all other large Bodies, where there is a variety of different Interests to reconcile, their deliberations are slow.—Why then should we distrust them?—and, in consequence of that distrust, adopt measures, which may cast a shade over that glory which, has been so justly acquired; and tarnish the reputation of an Army which is celebrated thro' all Europe, for its fortitude and Patriotism?—and for what is this done?—to bring the object we seek for nearer?—No!—most certainly, in my opinion, it will cast it at a greater distance.—

For myself (and I take no merit in giving the assurance, being induced to it from principles of gratitude, veracity & Justice)—a grateful sence of the confidence you have ever placed in me—a recollection of the chearful assistance, & prompt obedience I have experienced from you, under every vicisitude of Fortune,—and the sincere affection I feel for an Army, I have so long had the honor to Command, will oblige me to declare, in this public & solemn manner, that, in the attainment of compleat justice for all your toils & dangers, and in the gratification of every wish, so far as may be done consistently with the great duty I owe my Country, and those powers we are bound to respect, you may freely command my services to the utmost of my abilities.

While I give you these assurances, and pledge my self in the most unequivocal manner, to exert whatever ability I am possessed of, in your favor—let me entreat you, Gentlemen, on your part, not to take any measures, which, viewed in the calm light of reason, will lessen the dignity, & sully the glory you have hitherto maintained—let me request you to rely on the plighted faith of your Country, and place a full confidence in the purity of the intentions of Congress; that, previous to your dissolution as an Army they will cause all your Accts. to be fairly liquidated, as directed in their resolutions, which were published to you two days ago—and that they will adopt the most effectual measures in their power, to render ample justice to you, for your faithful and meritorious Services.—And let me conjure you, in the name of our common Country—as you value your own sacred honor—as you respect the rights of humanity; & as you regard the Military & National character of America, to express your utmost horror & detestation of the Man who wishes, under any specious pretences, to overturn the liberties of our Country, &

who wickedly attempts to open the flood Gates of Civil discord, & deluge our rising Empire in Blood.——

By thus determining——& thus acting, you will pursue the plain & direct road to the attainment of your wishes.——You will defeat the insidious designs of our Enemies, who are compelled to resort from open force to secret Artifice.——You will give one more distinguished proof of unexampled patriotism & patient virtue, rising superior to the pressure of the most complicated sufferings;——And you will, by the dignity of your Conduct, afford occasion for Posterity to say, when speaking of the glorious example you have exhibited to Mankind, "had this day been wanting, the World has never seen the last stage of perfection to which human nature is capable of attaining."

G: WASHINGTON

Address to Officers.

A Circular Letter to States on the Distress of the Army Head-Quarters, Newburgh, New York, June 18, 1783

SIR, The great object for which I had the honor to hold an appointment in the service of my country, being accomplished, I am now preparing to resign it into the hands of Congress, and return to that domestic re tirement, which, it is well known, I left with the greatest reluctance; a re-tirement for which I have never ceased to sigh through a long and painful absence, in which (remote from the noise and trouble of the world) I meditate to pass the remainder of life, in a state of undisturbed repose: But, before I carry this resolution into effect, I think it a duty incumbent on me to make this my last official communication, to congratulate you on the glorious events which Heaven has been pleased to produce in our fa-vour, to offer my sentiments respecting some important subjects, which appear to me to be intimately connected with the tranquility of the United States, to take my leave of your Excellency as a public character, and to give my final blessing to that country, in whose service I have spent the prime of my life; for whose sake I have consumed so many anxious days and watchful nights, and whose happiness, being extremely dear to me, will always constitute no inconsiderable part of my own.

Impressed with the liveliest sensibility on this pleasing occasion, I will claim the indulgence of dilating the more copiously on the subject of our mutual felicitation. When we consider the magnitude of the prize we contended for, the doubtful nature of the contest, and the favourable manner in which it has terminated, we shall find the greatest possi-ble reason for gratitude and rejoicing: This is a theme that will afford infinite delight to every benevolent and liberal mind, whether the event in contemplation be considered as the source of present enjoyment, or the parent of future happiness; and we shall have equal occasion to felicitate ourselves on the lot which Providence has assigned us, whether we view it in a natural, a political, or moral point of light.

The citizens of America, placed in the most enviable condition, as the sole lords and proprietors of a vast tract of continent, comprehending all the various soils and climates of the world, and abounding with all the necessaries and conveniences of life, are now, by the late satisfactory pacification, acknowledged to be possessed of absolute freedom and independency; they are from this period to be considered as the actors on a most conspicuous theatre, which seems to be peculiarly designated by Providence for the display of human greatness and felicity: Here they are not only surrounded with every thing that can contribute to the completion of private and domestic enjoyment, but Heaven has crowned all its other blessings by giving a surer opportunity for political happiness, than any other nation has ever been favored with. Nothing can illustrate these observations more forcibly than a recollection of the happy conjuncture of times and circumstances, under which our Republic assumed its rank among the Nations. The foundation of our empire was not laid in the gloomy age of ignorance and superstition, but at an epocha when the rights of mankind were better understood and more clearly defined, than at any former period: Researches of the human mind after social happiness have been carried to a great extent: The treasures of knowledge acquired by the labours of philosophers, sages and legislators, through a long succession of years, are laid open for use, and their collected wisdom may be happily applied in the establishment of our forms of government: The free cultivation of letters: The unbounded extension of commerce: The progressive refinement of manners: The growing liberality of sentiment, and, above all, the pure and benign light of Revelation, have had a meliorating influence on mankind, and encreased the blessings of society. At this auspicious period the United States came into existence as a Nation, and if their citizens should not be completely free and happy, the fault will be entirely their own.

Such is our situation, and such are our prospects; but notwithstanding the cup of blessing is thus reached out to us, notwithstanding happiness is ours, if we have a disposition to seize the occasion and make it our own; yet it appears to me, there is an option still left to the United States of America, whether they will be respectable and prosperous, or contemptible and miserable as a nation: This is the time of their political probation; this is the moment, when the eyes of the whole world are turned upon them, this is the moment to establish or ruin their national character forever; this is the favorable moment to give such a tone to the federal government, as will enable it to answer the ends of its institution; or this may be the ill-fated moment for relaxing the powers of the union, annihilating the cement of the confederation, and exposing us to become the sport of European politics, which may play one State against another, to prevent their growing importance, and to serve their own interested purposes. For, according to the system of policy the States shall adopt at this moment, they will stand or fall; and, by their conformation or lapse, it is yet to be decided, whether the revolution must ultimately be considered as a blessing or a curse; not to the present age alone, for with our fate will the destiny of unborn millions be involved.

With this conviction of the importance of the present crisis, silence in me would be a crime; I will therefore speak to your Excellency the language of freedom and of sincerity, without disguise. I am aware, however, those who differ from me in political sentiments may, perhaps, remark, I am stepping out of the proper line of my duty; and may possibly ascribe to arrogance or ostentation, what I know is alone the result of the purest intention; but the rectitude of my own heart, which disdains such unworthy motives; the part I have hitherto acted in life, the determination I have formed of not taking any share in public business hereafter; the ardent desire I feel and shall continue to manifest, of quietly enjoying in private life, after all the toils of war, the benefits of a wise and liberal government, will, I flatter myself, sooner or later, convince my countrymen that I could have no sinister views in delivering with so little reserve the opinions contained in this address.

There are four things which I humbly conceive are essential to the well-being, I may even venture to say, to the existence of the United States as an independent power.

1st. An indissoluble Union of the States under one Federal Head.

2dly. A sacred regard to Public justice.

3dly. The adoption of a proper Peace Establishment. And,

4thly. The prevalence of that pacific and friendly disposition among the people of the United States, which will induce them to forget their local prejudices and policies, to make those mutual concessions which are requisite to the general prosperity, and, in some instances, to sacrifice their individual advantages to the interest of the community.

These are the pillars on which the glorious fabric of our independency and national character must be supported. Liberty is the basis, and whoever should dare to sap the foundation or overturn the structure, under whatever specious pretexts he may attempt it, will merit the bitterest execrations, and the severest punishment, which can be inflicted by his injured country.

On the three first articles I will make a few observations; leaving the last to the good sense, and serious consideration of those immediately concerned.

Under the first head, although it may not be necessary or proper for me in this place to enter into a particular disquisition of the principles of the Union, and to take up the great question which has been frequently agitated, whether it be expedient and requisite for the States to delegate a larger proportion of power to Congress, or not; yet it will be a part of my duty, and that of every true patriot to assert, without reserve, and to insist upon the following positions. That unless the States will suffer Congress to exercise those prerogatives they are undoubtedly invested with by the constitution, every thing must very rapidly tend to anarchy and confusion. That it is indispensable to the happiness of the individual States, that there should be lodged, somewhere, a supreme power, to regulate and govern the general concerns of the confederated republic, without which the Union cannot be of long duration.

That there must be a faithful and pointed compliance on the part of every State with the late proposals and demands of Congress, or the most fatal consequences will ensue. That whatever measures have a tendency to dissolve the Union, or contribute to violate or lessen the sovereign authority, ought to be considered as hostile to the liberty and independency of America, and the authors of them treated accordingly. And lastly, that unless we can be enabled by the concurrence of the States to participate of the fruits of the revolution and enjoy the essential benefits of civil society, under a form of government so free, and uncorrupted, so happily guarded against the danger of oppression, as has been devised and adopted by the Articles of Confederation, it will be a subject of regret, that so much blood and treasure have been lavished for no purpose; that so many sufferings have been encountered without a compensation, and that so many sacrifices have been made in vain. Many other considerations might here be adduced to prove, that without an entire conformity to the spirit of the Union, we cannot exist as an independent power. It will be sufficient for my purpose to mention but one or two, which seem to me of the greatest importance. It is only in our united character, as an empire, that our independence is acknowledged, that our power can be regarded, or our credit supported among foreign nations. The treaties of the European powers, with the United States of America, will have no validity on a dissolution of the Union. We shall be left nearly in a state of nature, or we may find by our own unhappy experience, that there is a natural and necessary progression from the extreme of anarchy to the extreme of tyranny; and that arbitrary power is most easily established on the ruins of liberty abused to licentiousness.

As to the second article, which respects the performance of public justice, Congress have, in their late address to the United States, almost exhausted the subject; they have explained their ideas so fully, and have enforced the obligations the States are under to render complete justice to all the public creditors, with so much dignity and energy, that, in my opinion, no real friend to the honour and independency of America can hesitate a single moment respecting the propriety of complying with the just and honourable measures proposed; if their arguments do not produce conviction, I know of nothing that will have greater influence, especially when we recollect that the system referred to, being the result of the collected wisdom of the continent, must be esteemed, if not perfect, certainly the least objectionable of any that could be devised; and that, if it shall not be carried into immediate execution, a national bankruptcy, with all its deplorable consequences, will take place before any different plan can possibly be proposed or adopted; so pressing are the present circumstances, and such is the alternative now offered to the States.

The ability of the country to discharge the debts, which have been incurred in its defence, is not to be doubted: An inclination, I flatter

myself, will not be wanting; the path of our duty is plain before us: Honesty
will be found, on every experiment, to be the best and only true policy.
Let us then, as a nation, be just; let us fulfil the public contracts which
Congress had undoubtedly a right to make for the purpose of carrying on
the war, with the same good faith we suppose ourselves bound to perform
our private engagements. In the mean time let an attention to the cheerful
performance of their proper business, as individuals, and as members of
society, be earnestly inculcated on the citizens of America; then will they
strengthen the hands of government, and be happy under its protection.
Every one will reap the fruit of his labours: Every one will enjoy his own
acquisitions, without molestation and without danger.

In this state of absolute freedom and perfect security, who will grudge
to yield a very little of his property to support the common interests of
society, and ensure the protection of government? Who does not remember the frequent declarations at the commencement of the war, that
we should be completely satisfied, if at the expence of one half, we could
defend the remainder of our possessions? Where is the man to be found,
who wishes to remain indebted for the defence of his own person and
property to the exertions, the bravery and the blood of others, without
making one generous effort to repay the debt of honour and of gratitude? In what part of the Continent shall we find any man, or body of
men, who would not blush to stand up and propose measures purposely
calculated to rob the soldier of his stipend, and the public creditor of his
due? And were it possible, that such a flagrant instance of injustice
could ever happen, would it not excite the general indignation, and tend
to bring down, upon the authors of such measures, the aggravated vengeance of Heaven? If, after all, a spirit of disunion, or a temper of obstinacy and perverseness should manifest itself in any of the States; if such
an ungracious disposition should attempt to frustrate all the happy effects that might be expected to flow from the Union; if there should be a
refusal to comply with the requisitions for funds to discharge the annual
interest of the public debts, and if that refusal should revive again all
those jealousies and produce all those evils which are now happily removed: Congress, who have in all their transactions shewn a great degree of magnanimity and justice, will stand justified in the sight of God
and man! And that State alone, which puts itself in opposition to the

aggregate wisdom of the continent, and follows such mistaken and pernicious councils, will be responsible for all the consequences.

For my own part, conscious of having acted, while a servant of the
public, in the manner I conceived best suited to promote the real interests of my country; having, in consequence of my fixed belief, in some
measure, pledged myself to the army, that their country would finally
do them complete and ample justice; and not wishing to conceal any instance of my official conduct from the eyes of the world, I have thought
proper to transmit to your Excellency the enclosed collection of papers,
relative to the half-pay and commutation granted by Congress, to the
officers of the army; from these communications, my decided sentiment
will be clearly comprehended, together with the conclusive reasons
which induced me, at an early period, to recommend the adoption of this
measure in the most earnest and serious manner. As the proceedings of
Congress, the Army, and myself, are open to all, and contain in my opinion sufficient information to remove the prejudices and errors which may
have been 'entertained by any, I think it unnecessary to say any thing
more, than just to observe, that the resolutions of Congress, now alluded
to, are as undoubtedly and absolutely binding upon the United States, as
the most solemn acts of confederation or legislation.

As to the idea, which I am informed has in some instances prevailed,
that the half-pay and commutation are to be regarded merely in the odious
light of a pension, it ought to be exploded forever: That provision should be
viewed, as it really was, a reasonable compensation offered by Congress, at
a time when they had nothing else to give to the officers of the army, for
services then to be performed: It was the only means to prevent a total der-
eliction of the service: It was a part of their hire, I may be allowed to say, it
was the price of their blood, and of your independency; it is therefore more
than a common debt, it is a debt of honour; it can never be considered as a
pension, or gratuity, nor cancelled until it is fairly discharged.

With regard to the distinction between officers and soldiers, it is sufficient, that the uniform experience of every nation of the world, combined
with our own, proves the utility and propriety of the discrimination.
Rewards in proportion to the aids the public draws from them are
unquestionably due to all its servants. In some lines the soldiers have perhaps generally had as ample compensation for their services, by the

large bounties which have been paid to them, as their officers will receive in the proposed commutation; in others, if, besides the donation of land, the payment of arrearages of cloathing and wages (in which articles all the component parts of the army must be put upon the same footing) we take into the estimate, the bounties many of the soldiers have received, and the gratuity of one year's full pay, which is promised to all, possibly their situation (every circumstance being duly considered) will not be deemed less eligible than that of the officers. Should a further reward, however, be judged equitable, I will venture to assert, no man will enjoy greater satisfaction than myself in seeing an exemption from taxes for a limited time (which has been petitioned for in some instances) or any other adequate immunity or compensation granted to the brave defenders of their country's cause: But neither the adoption nor rejection of this proposition will, in any manner, affect, much less militate against, the act of Congress, by which they have offered five years full pay, in lieu of the half-pay for life, which had been before promised to the officers of the army.

Before I conclude the subject of public justice, I cannot omit to mention the obligations this country is under to that meritorious class of veterans, the non-commissioned officers and privates, who have been discharged for inability, in consequence of the resolution of Congress of the 23d of April, 1782, on an annual pension for life: Their peculiar sufferings, their singular merits and claims to that provision, need only to be known, to interest the feelings of humanity in their behalf: Nothing but a punctual payment of their annual allowance can rescue them from the most complicated misery; and nothing could be a more melancholy and distressing sight, than to behold those who have shed their blood, or lost their limbs, in the service of their country, without a shelter, without a friend, and without the means of obtaining any of the comforts or necessaries of life, compelled to beg their daily bread from door to door. Suffer me to recommend those of this description, belonging to your State, to the warmest patronage of your Excellency and your Legislature.

It is necessary to say but a few words on the third topic which was proposed, and which regards particularly the defence of the republic. As there can be little doubt but Congress will recommend a proper peace establishment for the United States, in which a due attention will be paid to the importance of placing the militia of the union upon a regular and respectable footing; if this should be the case, I would beg leave to urge the great advantage of it in the strongest terms.

The militia of this country must be considered as the palladium of our security, and the first effectual resort in case of hostility: It is essential, therefore, that the same system should pervade the whole; that the formation and discipline of the militia of the continent, should be absolutely uniform; and that the same species of arms, accoutrements, and military apparatus, should be introduced in every part of the United States: No one, who has not learned it from experience, can conceive the difficulty, expence and confusion, which result from a contrary system, or the vague arrangements which have hitherto prevailed.

If, in treating of political points, a greater latitude than usual has been taken in the course of this address, the importance of the crisis, and the magnitude of the objects in discussion, must be my apology: It is, however, neither my wish nor expectation, that the preceding observations should claim any regard, except so far as they shall appear to be dictated by a good intention; consonant to the immutable rules of justice, calculated to produce a liberal system of policy, and founded on whatever experience may have been acquired by a long and close attention to public business. Here I might speak with the more confidence, from my actual observations; and if it would not swell this letter (already too prolix) beyond the bounds I had prescribed myself, I could demonstrate to every mind, open to conviction, that in less time, and with much less expence than has been incurred, the war might have been brought to the same happy conclusion, if the resources of the continent could have been properly called forth: That the distresses and disappointments which have very often occurred, have, in too many instances, resulted more from a want of energy in the continental government, than a deficiency of means in the particular States: That the inefficacy of measures, arising from the want of an adequate authority in the supreme power, from a partial compliance with the requisitions of Congress in some of the States, and from a failure of punctuality in others, while they tended to damp the zeal of those which were more willing to exert themselves, served also to accumulate the expences of the war, and to frustrate the best concerted plans; and that the discouragement occasioned by the complicated difficulties and embarrassments, in which our affairs were by this means involved, would have long ago produced the dissolution of any army, less patient, less virtuous, and less persevering, than that which I have had the honor to command. But while I mention those things, which are notorious facts, as the defects of our federal constitution, particularly in the prosecution of a war, I beg it may be understood, that as I have ever taken a pleasure in gratefully acknowledging the assistance and support I have derived from every class of citizens; so shall I always be happy to do justice to the unparalleled exertions of the individual States, on many interesting occasions.

I have thus freely disclosed what I wished to make known before I surrendered up my public trust to those who committed it to me: The task is now accomplished; I now bid adieu to your Excellency, as the Chief Magistrate of your State; at the same time I bid a last farewell to the cares of office, and all the employments of public life.

It remains, then, to be my final and only request, that your Excellency will communicate these sentiments to your Legislature, at their next meeting; and that they may be considered as the legacy of one who has ardently wished, on all occasions, to be useful to his country, and who, even in the shade of retirement, will not fail to implore the divine benediction upon it.

I now make it my earnest prayer, that God would have you, and the State over which you preside, in his holy protection; that he would incline the hearts of the citizens to cultivate a spirit of subordination and obedience to government; to entertain a brotherly affection and love for one another, for their fellow-citizens of the United States at large, and particularly for their brethren who have served in the field; and finally, that he would most graciously be pleased to dispose us all to do justice, to love mercy, and to demean ourselves with that charity, humility and pacific temper of mind, which were the characteristics of the Divine Author of our blessed religion; without an humble imitation of whose example, in these things, we can never hope to be a happy nation.

I have the honor to be, with much esteem and respect, Sir, Your Excellency's most obedient, and most humble servant,

G. WASHINGTON.

NOTES

ABBREVIATIONS FOR FREQUENTLY CITED PEOPLE, TITLES, AND COLLECTIONS

BLP   Benjamin Lincoln Papers
BPL   Boston Public Library
CPNAC   Papers of Sir Guy Carleton
DAR   *Documents of the American Revolution*
DCB   *Dictionary of Canadian Biography*
FW   *The Writings of George Washington*
GW   George Washington
GWCS   *The Papers of George Washington, Confederation Series*
GWLC   George Washington Papers at the Library of Congress
HGP   Horatio Gates Papers
JCC   *Journals of the Continental Congress*
KP   Henry Knox Papers
LD   *Letters of Delegates to Congress, 1774–1789*
LMCC   *Letters of the Members of the Continental Congress*
MHS   Massachusetts Historical Society
NYPL   New York Public Library
PAH   *The Papers of Alexander Hamilton*
PJJ   *The Papers of John Jay*
PNG   *The Papers of Nathanael Greene*
PP   Pickering Family Papers
PPGC   *Public Papers of George Clinton*
PRM   *The Papers of Robert Morris*
RDC   *The Revolutionary Diplomatic Correspondence of the United States*
SPCL   Shelburne Papers, Clements Library

Introduction

1 GW to Governor Thomas Nelson, October 27, 1781, *FW*, 23:271.

2 Thomas Jefferson to GW, April 16, 1784, *GWCS* 1:289.

Chapter One

1 Christopher Ward, *The War of the Revolution* (New York: Macmillan, 1952), 2:655–64.

2 Ibid., 2:737–38.

3 Sydney Fisher, *The Struggle for American Independence* (Philadelphia: J. B. Lippincott, 1908), 2:337–38.

4 Richard M. Ketchum, *Victory at Yorktown* (New York: Henry Holt, 2004), pp. 135–159.

5 Washington was at his headquarters along the Hudson north of New York City while Rochambeau was in Rhode Island.

6 *Military Journal of Major of Ebenezer Denny*, October 18, 1781 (Philadelphia: J. B. Lippincott, 1859), p. 44.

7 Ketchum, *Yorktown*, p. 239.

8 Edward M. Riley, ed., "St. George Tucker's Journal of the Siege of Yorktown, 1781," *William and Mary Quarterly*, third series, 5 (July 1948), pp. 390–91.

9 GW to Cornwallis, in ibid., p. 391.

10 Edward M. Riley, "Yorktown During the Revolution, *Virginia Magazine of History and Biography*, 57, no. 3 (July 1949), p. 283.

11 "Articles of Capitulation," the Avalon Project Web site, accessed March 12, 2008. http://Avalon.law.yale.edu/18th_century/art_of_cap_1781.asp.

12 Ibid., article 8.

13 Dr. James Thacher, *Military Journal, During the American Revolutionary War, from 1775 to 1783* (Hartford: Silas Andrus and Son, 1854), pp. 288–89.

14 Ibid., p. 290.

15 Washington also likely motioned to Lincoln since he had been the general who had surrendered Charleston to the British in 1780.

16 Thacher, *Journal*, p. 291.

17 Donald Jackson, ed., and Dorothy Twohig, assoc. ed., *The Diaries of George Washington*, 6 vols. (Charlottesville: University Press of Virginia, 1978), 3:433–35; GW to de Grasse, October 28, 1781 (two letters) *FW*, 23:284–86; de Grasse to Lafayette, *Ville de Paris*, October 24, 1781. Stanley J. Idzerda, ed., *Lafayette in the Age of the American Revolution* (Ithaca: Cornell University Press, 1981), 4:427–28.

18 Ketchum, *Yorktown*, p. 284.

19 Lieutenant Colonel Banastre Tarleton, *A History of the Campaigns of 1780 and 1781 in the Southern Provinces of North America* (London: T. Cadell, 1787), p. 427.

20 GW to President of Congress, October 19, 1781, *FW*, 23:243; Washington to John Sullivan, quoted in *Memoir of Lieut Col. Tench Tilghman* (Albany: J. Munsell, 1876), p. 35.

21 *JCC* 21:1071.

22 GW, *Diary*, 3:437n.

23 GW to de Grasse, October 25, 1781, *FW*, 23:267–68.

24 General Orders, in ibid., 23:320–23. It is not certain that all twelve men were hanged. Last-minute reprieves were not uncommon, but the action was often unrecorded. James C. Neagles, *Summer Soldiers: A Survey and Index of Revolutionary War Courts Martial* (Salt Lake City: Ancestry, 1986), pp. 32–40.

25 GW to Governor Thomas Nelson, October 27, 1781, *FW*, 23:271.

26 John Parke Custis to Martha Washington, October 12, 1781, in Joseph E. Fields, comp., *"Worthy Partner": The Papers of Martha Washington* (Westport, CT: Greenwood Press, 1994), p. 188n; Washington, *Diary*, 3:437; Patricia Brady, *Martha Washington: An American Life* (New York: Viking, 2005), p. 139.

27 Elizabeth Parke, 1776–1832, Martha Parke, 1777–1854, Eleanor Parke, 1779–1852, and George Washington Parke, 1781–1857.

28 Bassett had married Martha's sister Anna Maria.

29 GW to President of Congress, November 6, 1781, *FW*, 23:338.

30 Mary Washington to Washington, March 13, 1782, quoted in Douglas Southall Freeman, *George Washington: A Biography* (New York Scribner's Sons, 1952), 5:409; James Thomas Flexner, *George Washington and the New Nation* (Boston: Little, Brown, 1969), 2:471–72. Benson Lossing, *Mary and Martha The Mother and Wife of George Washington* (New York: Harper and Brothers, 1886), pp. 62–63, gives an alternative account with a long description of the emotional reunion between Washington and his mother. This seems unlikely.

31 GW to Bartholemew Dandridge, November 19, 1781, *FW*, 23:353; Nelly remarried in 1783, to David Stuart. Her two youngest children, Eleanor (Nelly) and George Washington Parke (Wash), stayed at Mount Vernon.

32 *Pennsylvania Journal*, November 28, 1781.

33 Although Spain fought against Great Britain as an ally of France, it never officially allied with the United States. Richard B. Morris, *The Peacemakers: The Great Powers and American Independence* (New York: Harper and Row, 1965), pp. 13–16.

34 The house was large enough that the Washingtons occupied the front portion while Francisco Rendon, the Spanish agent in Philadelphia, lived in the rear. *PRM*, November 28, 1781, 3:296.

35 John Hill Morgan and Mantle Fielding, *The Life Portraits of Washington and Their Replicas* (Philadelphia: printed for the Subscribers, 1931), pp. 10–52. Peale painted at least sixty-seven images of Washington during the general's lifetime. Charles C. Sellers, *Charles Willson Peale* (New York: Charles Scribners Sons, 1969), pp. 189–92; Peale also made jewelry for Martha Washington. Charles Willson Peale to Martha Washington, January 16, 1781, in Fields, *"Worthy Partner,"* p. 185.

36 *Pennsylvania Packet*, December 4, 1781.

Chapter Two

 1 William S. Baker, *Itinerary of General Washington from June 15, 1775, to December 23, 1783* (Philadelphia: J. B. Lippincott, 1892), p. 147. Washington did pass through Philadelphia in early September 1781 on his way to Yorktown, but he did not attend a formal session of Congress. Ibid., pp. 236–37. memory.loc.gov/ammem/amlaw/lwjc.html

2 *JCC* 1:14. The First Continental Congress convened in the newly built Carpenters Hall. The members chose this site over the Pennsylvania statehouse (better known later as Independence Hall) in order to distance themselves from the Pennsylvania Assembly, which was a moderate body. Edmund C. Burnett, *The Continental Congress* (New York: W.W. Norton, 1941), pp. 30, 33.

3 Burnett, *Continental Congress*, p. 30

4 Ibid.

5 *JCC*, 2:91.

6 The president of the Continental Congress was elected by the body. He served almost exclusively as a presiding officer and had virtually no executive responsibility.

7 *JCC*, 21:1143.

8 William M. Fowler, *William Ellery: A Rhode Island Politico and Lord of Admiralty* (Metuchen, NJ: Scarecrow, 1972), p. 40.

9 Jack N. Rakove, *The Beginnings of National Politics: An Interpretative History of the Continental Congress.* (New York; Alfred A. Knopf, 1979), pp. 192–239; H. James Henderson, *Party Politics in the Continental Congress* (Lanham, MD: University Press of America, 1987), pp. 246–80; Calvin Jillson and Rick K. Wilson, *Congressional Dynamics: Structure, Coordination, and Choice in the First American Congress, 1774–1789* (Stanford: Stanford University Press, 1994), pp. 91–131.

10 Silas Deane, "To the Free and Virtuous Citizens of America," *Pennsylvania Packet*, December 5, 1778.

11 Adams to William Tudor, February 4, 1817, in *The Works of John Adams*, ed. Charles Francis Adams (Boston: Little, Brown, 1856), 10:241–42.

12 Rakove, *The Beginnings of National Politics*, pp. 275–84.

13 On Saturday November 3, 1781, the Second Continental Congress resolved "that the several matters now before Congress be referred over and recommended to the attention of the United Sates in Congress Assembled to meet at this place on Monday next" (*JCC*, 21:1099). When the members of Congress assembled on Monday, they elected John Hanson of Maryland as their first president. (ibid., 21:1100).

14 Burnett, *Continental Congress*, pp. 489–92.

15 *JCC*, 21:1144.

16 The Hudson River was often referred to as the North River.

17 GW to Frederick A. Muhlenberg, November 29, 1781, *FW*, 23:363–64; Baker, *Itinerary*, pp. 250–58.

18 Unfortunately, Washington apparently did not keep diaries during this period. Donald Jackson, ed., and Dorothy Twohig, assoc. ed., *The Diaries of George Washington* (Charlottesville: University Press of Virginia, 1976) 1:xli. His activities can be tracked in *FW*, vols. 23–24, as well as in Philadelphia newspapers.

19 *PRM*, December 3, 1781, 3:317; Edward Lawler Jr., "The President's House in Philadelphia," *Pennsylvania Magazine of History and Biography* (January 2002), pp. 5–6.

20 Quoted in Ellis P. Oberholtzer, *Robert Morris* (reprint, New York: Burt Franklin, 1968), pp. 20–21.

21 Quoted in Richard Brookhiser, *Gentleman Revolutionary: Gouverneur Morris, the Rake Who Wrote the Constitution* (New York; Free Press, 2003), p. 11. He actually injured his leg in a carriage accident (ibid., p. 10).

22 Max Mintz, "Gouverneur Morris: The Emergence of a Nationalist" (Ph.D. diss., New York University, 1957), p. 178.

23 Gouverneur Morris to Greene, December 24, 1781, *PRM*, 3:439–40.

24 Douglas Southall Freeman, *George Washington: A Biography* (New York: Charles Scribners' Sons, 1952), 5:385 opposite illustration of Lincoln.

25 *JCC*, 21:1087; David B. Mattern, *Benjamin Lincoln and the American Revolution* (Columbia: University of South Carolina Press, 1995), pp. 123–24.

26 Article 8 provided that the costs of the central government "shall be defrayed out of a common treasury, which shall be supplied by the several states, in proportion to the value of all land within each state, granted to or surveyed for any Person, as such land and the buildings and improvements thereon shall be estimated according to such mode as the united states in congress assembled, shall from time to time direct and appoint." Congress never agreed on a system to assess the states. Article 9 also raised a hurdle to action inasmuch as it required the vote of nine states to approve any important legislation.

27 Washington to Jonathan Trumbull, November 28, 1781, *FW*, 23:359.

28 Quoted in Frank E. Grizzard, "George Washington and the Society of the Cincinnati," the Papers of George Washington Web site, http://gwpapers.virginia.edu/articles/grizzard_2.html, accessed March 21, 2010.

29 Washington to Lafayette, November 15, 1781, *FW*, 23:340–42.

30 Richard Buel, *In Irons* (New Haven: Yale University Press, 1998), pp. 158–211; John J. McCusker and Russell R. Menard, *The Economy of British North America, 1607–1789* (Chapel Hill: University of North Carolina Press, 1991), pp. 358–70.

31 The finances of the Revolution are complex. E. James Ferguson, *The Power of the Purse: A History of American Public Finance, 1776–1790* (Chapel Hill: University of North Carolina Press, 1961), pp. 109–76.

32 Diary entry, January 5, 1782, *PRM*, 3:493.

33 Gouverneur Morris to John Jay, January 20, 1782, *PRM*, 4:81–83.

34 David McCullough, *John Adams* (New York: Simon and Schuster, 2001), pp. 242–73.

35 François Barbé-Marbois, *Our Revolutionary Forefathers: The Letters of François Barbé-Marbois*, trans. and ed. Eugene Parker Chase (New York: Books for Libraries, 1969), p. 15. Gregg L. Lint et al., eds., *Papers of John Adams* (Cambridge: Harvard University Press, 1989), 7:xx.

36 Barbé-Marbois. *Our Revolutionary Forefathers*, p. 113.

37 Richard B. Morris, *The Peacemakers: The Great Powers and American Independence* (New York: Harper and Row, 1965), pp. 191–217.

38 *JCC*, 20:606; William C. Stinchcombe, *The American Revolution and the French Alliance* (Syracuse: Syracuse University Press, 1969), pp.153–69.

39 Franklin to Robert Morris, November 5, 1781, *PRM*, 3:149.

40 Robert Morris to Chevalier de la Luzerne, November 3, 1781, in ibid., 3:132–34.

41 Chevalier de la Luzerne to Robert Morris, November 3, 1781, in ibid., 3:140–41.

42 Robert Morris to Chevalier de la Luzerne, November 6, 1781, in ibid., 3:156.

43 *JCC*, 21:1139.

44 What is the equivalent in "real money" is a question nearly impossible to answer. A rough calculation for current value would put the 28 million livres at approximately 3 billion dollars.

45 Robert Morris to Franklin, November 27, 1781, *PRM*, 3:274.

46 *JCC*, 22:68–70. For a detailed list of these loans, see Rafael Bayley, *The National Loans of the United States from July 4, 1776, to June 30, 1880* (Washington: Government Printing Office, 1882), pp. 5–19. It is virtually impossible to translate the value of these loans into modern terms. Suffice it to say that French support was absolutely vital. For an analysis of the value of money during this period, see John J. McCusker, *How Much Is That in Real Money?* (Worcester: American Antiquarian Society, 1992), *passim;* and McCusker, *Money and Exchange in Europe and America, 1600–1775* (Chapel Hill: University of North Carolina Press, 1978), pp. 3–25. For a contemporary summary of the public debt, see *JCC*, 24:286–90.

47 *JCC*, 11:502. May 15, 1778. Seven years was a compromise. The original proposal was half pay for life.

48 GW to Lincoln, May 28, 1782, *FW*, 24:296.

49 Robert Morris to Lincoln, January 11, 1782, *PRM*, 4:9.

50 Circular to the states, January 22, 1782, *FW*, 23:459.

51 Thomas Paine, *Common Sense* (New York: Peter Eckler, 1918), p. 37.

52 Thomas Paine, *The Crisis* (London: James Watson, 1835), p. 3.

53 Paine to Robert Morris, January 24, 1782, *PRM*, 4:111.

54 Diary entry, January 24, 1782, in ibid., 4:107–8.

55 Diary entry, January 26, 1782, in ibid., 4:115–16.

56 Ibid.

57 *PRM*, 4:201.

58 Diary entry, February 19, 1782, in ibid., 4:262. David Hawke, *Paine* (New York: Harper and Row, 1974), p. 123.

59 Although *The Crisis* of December 23, 1776, is the best known of this series, Paine actually published several issues under the same title.

60 *Crisis*, March 5, 1782.

61 For a general overview of Paine's mission, see "Memorandum," February 1782, *PRM*, 4:327–29.

62 General Orders, January 18, 1782, *FW*, 23:449–50.

63 *JCC*, 21:1120; *JCC*, 22:29.

64 Knox was denied a promotion three times. It was finally approved on March 22, 1782, with the promotion to date from November 15, 1781, the day he had been first recommended by Washington. *JCC*, 22:146; North Callahan, *Henry Knox* (New York: Rinehart, 1958), p. 194.

65 *JCC*, 21:1127.

66 GW to Cornell, February 13, 1782, *FW*, 23:497–98.

67 Ibid., p. 498. When Benjamin Lincoln was appointed secretary at war he insisted on
    keeping his rank as major general. Lincoln to son, November 25, 1781, BLP, reel 6,
    MHS.

68 *FW*, 11:212; Betsy Knight, "Prisoner Exchange and Parole in the American Revolu-
    tion," *William and Mary Quarterly*, third series, 48 (April 1991), p. 203.

69 For an overview of the condition of prisoners, see Larry Bowman, *Captive Americans:
    Prisoners During the American Revolution* (Athens: Ohio University Press, 1976), *passim*.

70 J. J. Boudinot, ed., *The Life, Public Services, Addresses and Letters of Elias Boudinot,
    LL.D. President of the Continental Congress* (Boston: Houghton Mifflin, 1896), 1:76.

71 Henry Clinton to Welbore Ellis, May 3, 1782. *DAR*, 19:290.

72 GW to President of Congress, December 27, 1781, *FW*, 23:408.

73 The British also held a considerable number of American seamen. Washington was
    consistently unwilling to exchange soldiers for seamen, believing that such an arrange-
    ment would "give the enemy a very considerable reinforcement." GW to President of
    Congress, February 18, 1782, *FW*, 24:5

74 Harry Ward, *George Washington's Enforcers: Policing the Continental Army* (Carbon-
    dale: Southern Illinois University Press, 2006), p. 25; James H. Edmonson, "Deser-
    tion in the American Army During the Revolutionary War" (Ph.D. diss., Louisiana
    State University, 1971), p. 242, comes up with a somewhat lower number.

75 GW to Lincoln, January 20, 1782, *FW*, 23:452–56.

76 Lincoln to GW, January 23, 1782, BLP, reel 6, MHS.

77 Diary entry, February 27, 1782, *PRM*, 4:315; Washington to Colonel Christian
    Febiger, January 12, 1782, *FW*, 23:442–44.

78 See, for example, Nathanael Greene to Robert Morris, *PRM*, 4:383.

79 GW to Congress, March 18, 1782, *FW*, 24:78.

80 *JCC*, 22:141.

81 Diary entry, March 22, 1782, *PRM*, 4:435; Even after Washington left Philadelphia,
    Morris continued to host his Monday evening meetings. Diary entry, April 22, 1782,
    in ibid., 5:33.

Chapter Three

1 *The American Campaigns of Rochambeau's Army. 1780, 1781, 1782, 1783*, trans. and
   ed. Howard C. Rice and Anne S. K. Brown (Princeton: Princeton University Press,
   1972), 2:62.

2 *Sherborne Mercury* (Dorset, United Kingdom), December 3, 1781.

3 North used title "first minister" rather than "prime minister."

4 Horace Walpole to Countess of Upper Ossory, November 23, 1775, *The Yale Edition of
   Horace Walpole's Correspondence*, ed. W. S. Lewis (New Haven: Yale University Press,
   1973), 32:276; Gerald Brown, *The American Secretary: The Colonial, Policy of Lord
   George Germain, 1775–1778* (Ann Arbor: University of Michigan Press, 1963), p. 40.

5 Until 1782 the secretary of state for the Northern Department was responsible
   for relations with the states of northern Europe. The Southern Department oversaw
   relations with southern Europe, the Muslim world, and the colonies.

6 This period in English history was a time of evolving roles and titles. The term *prime minister* was not yet fully in vogue, although in practice one of the ministers did take precedence over the others. Generally this was the first lord of the treasury. John P. Mackintosh, *The British Cabinet* (London: Stevens and Sons, 1968), pp. 64–68.

7 Quoted in John Brooke, *King George III* (New York: McGraw-Hill, 1972), p. 187; Stanley Weintraub, *Iron Tears* (New York: Free Press, 2005), pp. 304–5.

8 Quoted in Brooke, *King George III*, pp. 187–88.

9 Henry B. Wheatley, *The Historical and Posthumous Memoirs of Sir Nathaniel William Wraxall* (London: Bickers and Sons, 1884), 4:398.

10 Quoted in ibid., 4:401.

11 The text of the speech is in *Journals of the House of Lords*, Fifteenth Parliament of Great Britain, Second Session (November 27, 1781), pp. 365–66.

12 Ibid., p. 365.

13 *Journals of the House of Commons*, Fourteenth Parliament of Great Britain, Sixth Session (April 6, 1780), p. 763.

14 *Journals of the House of Commons*, Fifteenth Parliament of Great Britain, Second Session (November 27, 1781), pp. 8–9.

15 Ibid., p. 35.

16 *Journals of the House of Lords*, Fifteenth Parliament of Great Britain, Second Session (November 27, 1781), pp. 12, 18, 20.

17 *Journals of the House of Commons*, Fifteenth Parliament of Great Britain, Second Session (February 27, 1782), p. 310.

18 Ibid., p. 33.

19 Henry Seymour Conway to (?), December 20,1781, BPL, ms. 1152.

20 William Willcox, ed., *The American Rebellion: Sir Henry Clinton's Narrative of His Campaigns, 1775–1782* (New Haven: Yale University Press, 1954), pp. 332–50.

21 Duke of Newcastle to Clinton, January 2, 1782, in ibid., p. 458.

22 Philip Ranlet, *The New York Loyalists* (Knoxville: University of Tennessee Press, 1986), p. 170. For a loyalist view of their ill treatment by British authorities, see Thomas Jones, *History of New York During the Revolutionary War* (New York: New York Historical Society, 1879), 2:chap. 5.

23 Theodore O. Barck, *New York City During the War for Independence* (reprint, Port Washington, NY: I. J. Friedman, 1966), pp. 203–5.

24 Willcox, *The American Rebellion*, pp. 192–93n.

25 Jacob Judd, "Westchester County," in *The American Revolution Beyond New York City, 1763–1787*, ed. Joseph Tiedeman and Eugene R. Fingerhut (Albany: State University of New York Press, 2005), pp. 107–26.

26 Willcox, *The American Rebellion*, p. 238.

27 Article 10 of Capitulation.

28 Franklin to Germain, November 6, 1781, *DAR*, 19:208–9.

29 Reverend James Sayre to Germain, November 8, 1781, in ibid., 19:210.

30 Germain to Clinton, January 2, 1782, in ibid., 19:240; Clinton to Franklin, March 6, 1782 , CPNAC.

31 Quoted in I. N. Phelps Stokes, *The Iconography of Manhattan Island* (reprint, New York: Arno Press, 1967), 5:1140.

32 William Willcox, *Portrait of a General: Sir Henry Clinton in the War of Independence* (New York: Knopf, 1964), p. 462. The most important difference between Robertson and Clinton was their disagreement over the reestablishment of civilian government in New York. Robertson favored such a restoration, while Clinton opposed it. Robertson to Germain, March 22, 1782, *DAR*, 21:46–47.

33 Alan Valentine, *The British Establishment* (Norman: University of Oklahoma Press, 1970), 1:297.

34 Paul Reynolds, *Guy Carleton: A Biography* (New York: Morrow, 1980), p.1; G. P. Browne, "Guy Carleton," *DCB* online. http://www.biographi.ca/index-e.html.

35 Howard Peckham, *The Colonial Wars, 1689–1762* (Chicago: University of Chicago Press, 1964), pp. 222–25.

36 Reynolds, *Guy Carleton*, p.2.

37 Stephen Brumwell, *Paths of Glory: The Life and Death of General James Wolfe* (Montreal: McGill-Queens University Press, 2006), pp. 95, 142, 286; William M. Fowler, *Empires at War* (New York: Walker Books, 2005), p. 178.

38 Reynolds, *Guy Carleton*, p.152; "Carleton," *DCB* online.

39 Richard M. Ketchum, *Saratoga, Turning Point of America's Revolutionary War* (New York: Henry Holt, 1997), p. 425.

40 "Carleton," *DCB* online.

41 *Journal of the House of Commons, Fifteenth Parliament of Great Britain, Second Session* (February 22, 1782), p. 280, (February 27, 1782), p. 330.

42 "Carleton," *DCB* online.

43 Welbore Ellis to Carleton, March 26, 1782, CPNAC.

44 Quoted in Brooke, *King George* III, p. 222.

45 On May 2, 1782, Shelburne abolished the commissioners of trade and plantations. He took their portfolio as well. *DAR*, 19:3–4, 9.

46 Ibid., 19:3.

47 Lafayette to Hamilton, April 12, 1782, *PAH*, 3:71.

48 *Parker's General Advertiser*, May 30, 1782; Weintraub, *Iron Tears*, p. 320.

49 Quoted in "Carleton," *DCB* online.

50 Shelburne to Carleton, April 4, 1782, *DAR*, 21:53.

51 It is interesting to speculate what Washington's reaction might have been if he had seen Carleton's orders. The chance to attack and take another British army might have been too great a temptation to resist.

52 Shelburne to Carleton, April 4, 1781, CPNAC.

53 "Maurice Morgann," *DCB* online.

54 Ibid.

55 Ibid.

56 Commission to Brook Watson, March 17, 1782, DAR, 19:269.

57 Paul H. Smith, "Sir Guy Carleton Peace Negotiations and the Evacuation of New York," *Canadian Historical Review* 50 (1969), p. 247.

Chapter Four

1 William Heath, *Memoirs of Major General William Heath by Himself*, ed. William Abbatt (New York: William Abbatt, 1901), p. 1.

2 GW to Heath, March 3, 1777, *FW*, 7:232; Douglas Southall Freeman, *George Washington: A Biography* (New York: Charles Scribners Sons, 1951), 3:389, 4:216, 367, 384n.

3 Heath, *Memoir*, p. 299.

4 John Crane to Knox, December 19, 1781, KP, reel 8. The shortage of clothing was aggravated by the British capture of the French ship *Marquis de Lafayette* bound for Boston with a cargo of uniforms. Washington to Heath, February 28, 1782, *FW*, 24:25.

5 Lord Stirling to Washington, November 20, 1781, GWLC; Alan Valentine, *Lord Stirling* (New York: Oxford University Press, 1969), pp. 262–63.

6 John O. Dendy, "Frederick Haldimand and the Defence of Canada, 1778–1784." (Ph.D. diss., Duke University, 1972), p. 209.

7 Haldimand to Germain, November 18, 1781, *DAR*, 19:217; Dendy, "Frederick Haldimand," p. 222.

8 Jacob Judd, "Westchester County," in *The American Revolution Beyond New York City, 1763–1787*, ed. Joseph S. Tiedemann and Eugene R. Fingerhut (Albany: State University of New York Press, 2005), pp. 107–26.

9 Samuel Shaw to Knox, January 31, 1782, KP, reel 8.

10 Henry Jackson to Knox, February 28, 1782 in ibid. 8.

11 Greene to Morris, January 24, 1782, *PNG*, 10:254.

12 Heath, *Memoirs*, p. 306.

13 Web site http://gwpapers.virginia.edu/documents/revolution/itinerary/index.html.

14 Newburgh sits at the northern end of the Hudson Highlands, sixty miles north of New York City, at a place where the river is one mile wide. The village of New Windsor is immediately to the south. Washington's headquarters was in Newburgh, while the cantonment that his soldiers occupied in October 1782 was in New Windsor. Janet Dempsey, *Washington's Last Cantonment* (Monroe, NY: Library Research Associates, 1990), p. 1.

15 Walter C. Anthony, *Washington's Headquarters, Newburgh, New York: A History of Its Construction and Its Various Occupants* (Newburgh: Newburgh Historical Society, 1928), pp. 9, 18, 26, 34; Hamilton Fish, *George Washington in the Highlands* (Newburgh, NY: Newburgh News, 1932), p. 7; Anthony Waite, *Washington's Headquarters, the Hasbrouck House* (Albany: New York State Historic Trust, 1971), pp. 18–24. Pickering to his wife, December 2, 1781, PP reel 1.

16 Washington's first visit to the Highlands was in November 1776 when he visited with General William Heath. In July 1778 he made his first visit to West Point. From that point to the end of the war Washington spent more than half his time in the Hudson Highlands. He remained 505 days at Newburgh (April 1, 1782–August 19, 1783), which was a longer stay than at any of his other headquarters. Fish, *George Washington in the Highlands*, pp. 3–22.

17 Elizabeth Cometti, trans. and ed., *Seeing America and Its Great Men: The Journal and Letters of Count Francesco dal Verme*, 1783–84 (Charlottesville: University Press of Virginia, 1969), p.12.

18 Hughes to Heath, March 10, 1782 quoted in Dempsey, *Washington's Last Cantonment*, p. 28.

19 Emily Stone Whiteley, *Washington and His Aides de Camp* (New York: Macmillan, 1936), *passim*; during the course of the war thirty-two officers served as aides to the commander in chief. David Humphreys, *Life of General Washington*, ed. Rosemarie Zagarri (Athens: University of Georgia Press, 1991), pp. xvi, xvii.

20 A. J. Schenkman, *Washington's Headquarters at Newburgh* (Charleston: History Press, 2009), pp. 31–39.

21 Both Hasbrouck House and Mount Vernon enjoy spectacular river views.

22 Bernhard A. Uhlendorg, ed., *Revolution in America: Confidential Letters and Journals 1776–1784 of Adjutant General Major Baurmeister of the Hessian Forces* (New Brunswick, N.J.: Rutgers University Press, 1957), p. 467: Philip Ziegler, *King William IV* (New York: Harper and Row, 1973), p. 39.

23 Corey Ford, *A Peculiar Service* (Boston: Little, Brown, 1965), p. 296.

24 GW to Colonel Matthias Ogden, March 28, 1782, *FW*, 24:91.

25 Frank T. Reuter, "'Petty Spy' or Effective Diplomat: The Role of George Beckwith," *Journal of the Early Republic* 10 (Winter 1990), pp. 471–92.

26 Many years later Washington's March 28 letter came into the possession of Louis McLane, the United States Minister to the court of St. James (1829–31). McLane shared the letter with the king, the former Prince William Henry, who remarked, "I am obliged to General Washington for his humanity, but I'm damned glad I did not give him an opportunity of exercising it towards me." *FW*, 24:91n; I. N. Phelps Stokes, *The Iconography of Manhattan Island* (reprint, New York: Arno Press, 1967), 5:1145.

27 Diary of William Smith, April 13, 1782, NYPL.

28 Thomas Jones, *History of New York During the Revolutionary War* (New York: New York Historical Society, 1879), 1:24–25.

29 Pauline Maier, *The Old Revolutionaries: Political Lives in the Age of Samuel Adams* (New York: Knopf, 1980), pp. 69–72.

30 *JCC*, 19:332.

31 Roger J. Champagne, *Alexander McDougall and the American Revolution in New York* (Schenectady: New York State American Revolution Bicentennial Commission in conjunction with Union College Press, 1975), pp.174–75.

32 Ibid., p. 175.

33 Ibid., p. 177.

34 Lincoln to Nathanael Greene, August 16, 1782, BLP, reel 6A.

35 GW to Heath, August 25, 1782, GWLC.

36 James C. Neagles, *Summer Soldiers: A Survey and Index of Revolutionary War Courts Martial* (Salt Lake City: Ancestry, 1986), p. 53.

37 GW to McDougall, August 25, 1782, GWLC.

38 Katherine Mayo, *General Washington's Dilemma* (New York: Harcourt, Brace, 1938).

39 Henry Clinton to Welbore Ellis, May 3, 1782, *DAR*, 19:290.

40 In the eighteenth century prisoners of value were not calculated by a simple comparison of numbers. Each rank had an equivalent. In June 1782 the British headquarters in New York made the following calculation:

British	Value	American	Value
1 lieutenant general	1,044	1 brigadier general	200
1 brigadier general	200	8 colonels	800
2 colonels	200	13 lieutenant colonels	936
15 lieutenant colonels	1,080	12 majors	336
15 majors	420	88 captains	1,408
76 captains	1,216	66 lieutenants	396
117 lieutenants	702	20 ensigns	80
52 ensigns	208		
Total*	5,070		4,156

*Balance in favor of Americans: 914

Source: Comparative View of British and American officers Prisoners of War, New York, June 28, 1782, CPNAC.

41 Commissioners Dalymaple and Elliot to Henry Clinton, April 8, 1782, and Andrew Elliot to Henry Clinton, April 8, 1782, both CPNAC. Not mentioned, but understood, was the fact that most of the Americans held by the British were under short-term enlistment. Even if they should be released, it was likely that they would simply go home, whereas the British soldiers exchanged would return to the ranks.

42 GW to Henry Clinton, December 31, 1781, *FW*, 23:418; Albert G. Overton and J. W. W. Loose, "Prisoner of War Barracks in Lancaster Used During the Revolutionary War," *Journal of the Lancaster County Historical Society* 84 (1980), pp. 131–34. German prisoners were distributed at other locations in Pennsylvania, Maryland, and Virginia.

43 Benjamin Shield to Lincoln, December 10, 1781, BLP, reel 6.

44 For an overview of exchange and parole, see Betsy Knight, "Prisoner Exchange and Parole in the American Revolution," *William and Mary Quarterly*, third series, 48 (April 1991), pp. 201–22.

45 GW to President of Congress, December 27, 1781, *FW*, 23:408.

46 Arthur B. Tourtellot, "Rebels Turn Out Your Dead," *American Heritage Magazine* 21 (August 1970), p. 15.

47 In 1837 Martha Piatt, the only surviving daughter of Joshua Huddy, petitioned the United States Congress for payment in money and land in recognition of the services and tragic death of her father. As part of that petition, Piatt gathered a large collection of contemporary evidence supporting her claim. These documents are contained in "Representatives of Captain Joshua Huddy" (to accompany bill H.R. No. 935), House

of Representatives, 24th Congress, Second Session (Report No. 227), Louis Masur, *Rites of Execution* (New York: Oxford University Press, 1989), pp. 56–58.

48 William Franklin to Joseph Galloway, May 11, 1782, *DAR*, 19:298.

49 "Representatives of Captain Joshua Huddy," p. 35.

50 There are several secondary accounts: see Mayo, *General Washington's Dilemma* and David Fowler, " 'Loyalty Is Now Bleeding in New Jersey,' Motivations and Mentalities of the Disaffected," in *The Other Loyalists: Ordinary People, Royalism, and the Revolution of the Middle Colonies*, ed. Joseph S. Tiedemann, Eugene R. Fingerhut, and Robert W. Venables (Albany: State University Press of New York, 2009), pp. 45–77.

51 "Representatives of Captain Joshua Huddy," p. 23.

52 Heath, *Memoirs*, pp. 309–10.

53 Ibid., p. 310.

54 GW to Clinton, April 21, 1782, *FW*, 24:146–47.

55 William Willcox, ed., *The American Rebellion: Sir Henry Clinton's Narrative of His Campaigns, 1775–1782* (New Haven: Yale University Press, 1954), p. 359.

56 Sheila Skemp, *William Franklin: Son of a Patriot, Servant of a King* (New York: Oxford University Press, 1990), p. 261; Willcox, *The American Rebellion*, p. 360.

57 Clinton to Welbore Ellis, May 11, 1782, *DAR*, 21:72.

58 Willcox, *The American Rebellion*, pp. 359–61.

59 Franklin to Clinton, May 2, 1782, *DAR*, 21:62.

60 GW to Brigadier General Moses Hazen, May 18, 1782, *FW*, 24:263–64.

61 The surrender at Yorktown had not been "unconditional." Cornwallis's officers either had been paroled or had remained with their regiments (the Articles of Capitulation called for one officer to every fifty enlisted men) to be kept under the same conditions as those who departed on parole. Articles of Capitulation. Burgoyne's army had laid down its arms under a "Convention."

62 Capitulation, article 10.

63 Moses Hazen to GW, May 27, 1782, GWLC.

64 Ibid. Asgill was in fact nineteen.

65 Ibid.

66 James Gordon to Lincoln, May 27, 1782, BLP, reel 6.

67 GW to Moses Hazen, June 4, 1782, *FW*, 24:306.

68 *JCC*, 22:218.

69 GW to Brigadier General Elias Dayton, *FW*, 24:307.

70 Hamilton to Knox, June 7, 1782, *PAH*, 3:91–93.

71 Ibid.

Chapter Five

1 Clinton's had only recently received word that his resignation had been accepted. Welbore Ellis to Clinton, March 6, 1782, CPNAC.

2 Barnet Schecter, *The Battle for New York* (New York: Walker Books, 2002), pp. 204–18; Judith Van Buskirk, *Generous Enemies: Patriots and Loyalists in Revolutionary New York* (Philadelphia: University of Pennsylvania Press, 2002), pp. 21–43.

3   *Rivington's Royal Gazette*, May 8, 1782; *Pennsylvania Packet or the General Advertiser*, May 11, 1782.

4   Clinton to Major General Charles O'Hara, April 14, 1782, CPNAC.

5   Shelburne to Haldimand, April 22, 1782, *DAR*, 19:285; Haldimand to Clinton, April 28, 1782, in ibid., 19:317; John O. Dendy, "Frederick Haldimand and the Defence of Canada, 1778–1784" (Ph.D diss, Duke University, 1972), p. 230.

6   *New York Gazette and Mercury*, May 13, 1782.

7   L. F. S. Upton, *The Loyal Whig: William Smith of New York and Quebec* (Toronto: University of Toronto Press, 1969), p. 136.

8   William Willcox, *Portrait of a General: Sir Henry Clinton in the War of Independence* (New York: Knopf, 1964), p. 463; *Historical Memoir from 26 August 1778 to November 1783 of William Smith*, ed. W. H. W. Sabine (New York: Arno Press, 1971), p. 506.

9   Upton, *The Loyal Whig*, p. 118.

10 Ibid., p.120.

11 K. G. Davies, "The Restoration of Civil Government by the British in the War of Independence," in *Red, White and True Blue: The Loyalists in the Revolution*, ed. Esmond Wright (New York: AMS Press, 1976), pp. 111–34.

12 Smith to Germain, March 23, 1781, *DAR*, 19:275.

13 See Thomas Jones, *History of New York During the Revolutionary War* (New York: New York Historical Society, 1879), 2:126; L. F. S. Upton, "William Smith," *DCB* online; Smith fled New York with Carleton and eventually became chief justice of Quebec (Lower Canada).

14 Robertson to Jeffrey Amherst, December 8, 1781, in *The Twilight of British Rule in Revolutionary America: The New York Letter Book of General James Robertson*, ed. Milton Klein and Ronald W. Howard (Cooperstown: New York State Historical Association, 1983), pp. 231–33.

15 Shelburne to Carleton, April 4, 1781, *DAR*, 21:52–54.

16 Carleton to Washington, May 7, 1782, GWLC.

17 "stained the reputation of Britons" was deleted from the final letter Washington sent to Carleton, May 10, 1782, *FW*, 24:241n.

18 *JCC*, 22:263.

19 Paul H. Smith, "Sir Guy Carleton:, Peace Negotiations and the Evacuation of New York, *Canadian Historical Review*, 50 (1969), p. 254.

20 Sheila Skemp, *William Franklin: Son of a Patriot, Servant of a King* (New York: Oxford University Press, 1990), p. 262; GW to William Livingston, May 6, 1782, *FW*, 24:226–27.

21 Franklin to Joseph Galloway, May 11, 1782, *DAR*, 21:73.

22 Morgann to Shelburne, June 12, 1782, Shelburne Papers, Clements Library, University of Michigan.

23 For an analysis of attempts by the British to restore civil government during the Revolution, see Davies, "The Restoration of Civil Government by the British in the War of Independence," pp. 111–34.

24 William Willcox, ed., *The American Rebellion: Sir Henry Clinton's Narrative of His*

Campaigns, 1775–1782 (New Haven: Yale University Press,1954), p. 353; Germain to Clinton, January 23, 1779, in ibid., p. 398; extract of the minutes of a council of war held at New York, January 23, 1782, in ibid., pp. 593–94; Klein and Howard, *The Twilight of British Rule in Revolutionary America*, pp. 52–53.

25 Upton, *The Loyal Whig*, p. 138.

26 Skemp, *William Franklin*, p. 262.

27 Ibid., p. 261.

28 A transcript of the trial is printed in "Representatives of Captain Joshua Huddy" (to accompany bill H.R. No. 935), House of Representatives, 24th Congress, Second Session (Report No. 227).

29 Robertson to Carleton, June 18, 1782, CPNAC.

30 Transcript of the trial, p. 23.

31 Ibid., p. 37.

32 Carleton to GW, July 7, 1782, GWLC.

33 GW to Lieutenant Colonel John Laurens, July 10, 1782, *FW*, 24:422.

34 Carleton to GW, July 25, 1782, GWLC. In the letter Carleton refers to Chief Justice Frederick Smith—a likely clerical error.

35 GW to Carleton, July 30, 1782, *FW*, 24:441.

36 Instructions to Major General William Heath, August 3, 1782, in ibid., 24:456.

37 Carleton to GW, August 1, 1782, GWLC.

38 GW to Heath, August 3, 1782, *FW*, 24:458.

39 Carleton to GW, August 19, 1782, CWLC.

40 GW to President of Congress, August 19, 1782, *FW*, 25:40.

41 Ibid., p. 41.

42 Katherine Mayo, *General Washington's Dilemma* (New York: Harcourt, Brace, 1938), p. 212.

43 Lady Asgill to Comte de Vergennes, July 18, 1782, in ibid., p. 229.

44 Ibid.

45 Cornwallis to Carleton, August 4, 1782, CPNAC.

46 Vergennes to GW, July 29, 1782, in Mayo, *George Washington's Dilemma*, p. 231.

47 *The Life, Public Services, Addresses and Letters of Elias Boudinot*, ed. J. J. Boudinot (Boston: Houghton Mifflin, 1896), 1:248–51.

48 *JCC*, 23:715.

49 GW to Asgill, November 13, 1782, *FW*, 25:337. Some years later Asgill was quoted as accusing the Americans of holding him *in terrorem* by constructing a gallows outside his room so that he could preview his fate. Douglas Southall Freeman, *George Washington: A Biography* (New York: Charles Scribners' Sons, 1954), 6:64.

50 Carleton to Shelburne, June 18, 1782, *DAR*, 21.87.

51 Morgann to Shelburne, June 12, 1782, SPCL.

52 Ibid.

53 Ibid.

54 Morgann to Shelburne, May 10, 1782, Shelburne Papers.

55 Morgann to Shelburne, June 12, 1782, in ibid.

56 Franklin to Shelburne, March 22, 1782, in *Papers of Benjamin Franklin*, ed. Ellen Cohn et al. (New Haven: Yale University Press, 2004), 37:386; Shelburne to Commissioners, June 5, 1782, *DAR*, 21:77.

57 David Hancock, *Citizens of the World: London Merchants and the Integration of the British Atlantic Community, 1735–1785* (New York: Cambridge University Press, 1995), pp. 77–82; Charles R. Ritcheson, "To an Astonishing Degree Unfit for the Task: Britain's Peacemakers, 1782–1783," in *Peace and the Peacemakers: The Treaty of 1783*, ed. Ronald Hoffman and Peter Alberts (Charlottesville: University Press of Virginia, 1986), pp. 70–100.

58 *JCC*, 20:617, 651, 652; Richard B. Morris, *The Peacemakers: The Great Powers and American Independence* (New York: Harper and Row, 1965), pp. 214–15.

59 Laurens was sailing aboard the packet *Mercury*, which was also carrying secret dispatches, among them a draft treaty between the United States and the Netherlands. When the British read the treaty, it gave them an excuse to declare war on the Netherlands, sparking the Fourth Anglo-Dutch War. Laurens was released from parole in exchange for Cornwallis. *Papers of Henry Laurens*, ed. Philip Hamer et al. (Columbia: University of South Carolina Press, 1968–2003). 15: *passim.*

60 Morris, *Peacemakers*, pp. 260–64.

61 Shelburne to Commissioners for Restoring Peace, June 5, 1782, *DAR*, 21:79

62 Ibid., p. 80.

63 "Guy Carleton," *DCB* online.

64 Smith Diary, August 2, 1782, NYPL; Upton, *The Loyal Whig*, p. 139.

65 *New York Times*, June 11, 1904, quotes a letter of Sir Walter Scott to Robert Southey giving credence to the story. Simon Schama, *Dead Certainties* (New York: Knopf, 1991), pp. 17–18.

66 Upton, *The Loyal Whig*, p.139.

67 Ibid.

68 Captain William Feilding to Earl of Denbigh, August 10, 1782, in *The Lost War: Letters from British Officers During the American Revolution*, ed. Marion Balderston and David Syrett (New York: Horizon Press, 1975), p. 219.

69 William Heath to John Hancock, August 14, 1782, BPL, ms. 1182.

70 Carleton to Shelburne, August 14, 1782, *DAR*, 21:111.

71 Jonathan Williams to (?), September 28, 1782, BPL, ms. 1188.

72 Townshend to Carleton, October 27, 1782, *DAR*, 21:155.

Chapter Six

1 Clagdon to Gates, March 10, 1782, HGP, reel 13.

2 Lincoln to Knox, August 7, 1782, BLP, reel 9.

3 Quoted in David B. Mattern, *Benjamin Lincoln and the American Revolution* (Columbia: University of South Carolina Press, 1995), p. 129; E. Wayne Carp, *To Starve the Army at Pleasure: Continental Army Administration and American Political Culture, 1775–1783* (Chapel Hill: University of North Carolina Press, 1984), p. 209. Morris to Lincoln, May 7, 1782, *PRM*, 5:121.

4 GW to Morris, May 17, 1782, GWLC.

5 GW to Secretary of Foreign Affairs (Robert R. Livingston), May 22, 1782, *FW*, 24:271.

6 For a strategic view of the Revolution, see Piers Mackesy, *The War for America, 1775–1783* (Cambridge: Harvard University Press, 1964), particularly part 3, pp. 237–97. At France's urging, Spain declared war on Great Britain in 1779, while refusing to enter into a formal alliance with the United States. For its trouble France promised the return of Gibraltar, lost through the Treaty of Utrecht in 1713.

7 David Hannay, *Rodney* (reprint, Boston: Gregg Press, 1972), pp. 164–67; Mackesy, *War for America*, pp. 446–59.

8 GW to McHenry, September 12, 1782, *FW*, 25:150–52; Washington to Clinton, May 7, 1782, in ibid., 24:228.

9 GW to Livingston, June 5, 1782, in ibid., 24:315.

10 Charles M. Thompson, *Independent Vermont* (Boston: Houghton Mifflin, 1942), pp. 45–46.

11 Ibid., p. 105; Jere Daniell, *Colonial New Hampshire* (Millwood, VT: KTO Press, 1981), p. 137; Paul Wilderson, *Governor John Wentworth and the American Revolution* (Hanover, NH: University Press of New England, 1994), pp. 187–200.

12 GW to Philip Schuyler, October 26, 1775, *FW*, 4:46n.

13 GW to President of Congress, May 12, 1778, in ibid., 11:381.

14 Frank Smallwood, *Thomas Chittenden: Vermont's First Statesman* (Shelburne, VT: New England Press, 1997), p. 70.

15 Diary of William Smith, October 24, 1781, NYPL.

16 Haldimand to Clinton, April 28, 1782, *DAR*, 21:61.

17 Haldimand to Clinton, September 27, 1782, in ibid., 19:225; John O. Dendy, "Frederick Haldimand and the Defense of Canada, 1778–1784" (Ph.D. diss., Duke University, 1972), p. 241.

18 GW to Heath, December 15, 1781, GWLC.

19 GW to Joseph Jones, July 10, 1781, *FW*, 22:354.

20 GW to Chittenden, January 1, 1782, in ibid., 23:420–23.

21 GW to Joseph Jones, February 11, 1783, in ibid., 26:123.

22 *The Sinews of Independence: Monthly Strength Reports of the Continental Army*, ed. Charles H. Lesser (Chicago: University of Chicago Press, 1975), p. 224. The total army including those not fit for service numbered 10,500.

23 GW to Heath, May 8, 1782, *FW*, 24:232.

24 Heman Swift to Washington, May 4, 1782, GWLC; Washington to Swift, May 6, 1782, *FW*, 24:227–28; General Orders, May 12, 1782, in ibid., 24:249; James C. Neagles, *Summer Soldiers: A Survey and Index of Revolutionary War Courts Martial* (Salt Lake City: Ancestry, 1986), pp. 93, 143, 217; John A Nagy, *Rebellion in the Ranks: Mutinies in the American Revolution* (Yardley, PA: Westholme, 2008), p. 299.

25 Congress approved the first set of Articles of War on June 30, 1775. A second revised set was approved on September 20, 1776. Subsequent amendments were added. *JCC*, 2:111–22; *JCC*, 5:788–807; Charles P. Neimeyer, *America Goes to War: A Social History*

of the Continental Army (New York: New York University Press, 1996), pp. 134–135; Robert H. Berlin, "The Administration of Military Justice in the Continental Army During the American Revolution, 1775–1783" (Ph.D. diss., University of California, Santa Barbara, 1976), pp. 22–27.

26 *Thacher's Journal*, January 1, 1780, http://www.americanrevolution.org/thacher .html, accessed September 15, 2009.

27 GW to Colonel John Lamb, September 18, 1782 *FW*, 25:175.

28 *JCC*, 7:265–66.

29 James H. Edmondson, "Desertion in the American Army During the Revolutionary War" (Ph.D. diss., Louisiana State University, 1971), pp. 242, 250.

30 Neagles, *Summer Soldiers*, p. 34. Neagles's estimate comes from a sampling of surviving orderly books. While this methodology is hardly flawless, there is no reason to believe that his estimates are not within reason.

31 For examples of Washington's intercession to lessen punishment, see: GW to General Elias Dayton, May 18, 1782, *FW*, 24:264; GW to Colonel John Lamb, September 18, 1782, in ibid., 25:175; Berlin, "The Administration of Military Justice," p. 86.

32 Nagy, *Rebellion in the Ranks*, pp. 297–99. Nagy, pp. 299–301, also identifies twenty-six American naval mutinies.

33 Richard Miller, *In Words and Deeds: Battle Speeches in History* (Hanover, NH: University Press of New England, 2008), p. 1; Allen Bowman, *The Morale of the American Revolutionary Army* (Port Washington, NY: Kennikat Press, 1964), pp. 29–30; Neagles, *Summer Soldiers*, p. 37.

34 At the time, Washington had three aides assisting him: Jonathan Trumbull, Benjamin Walker, and David Humphreys. These three officers divided duties, but on this day Trumbull seems to have borne the lion's share of drafting letters. See *FW*, 24:271–80.

35 GW to Secretary of Foreign Affairs, May 22, 1782, in ibid., 24:271, 274; GW to Mathews, May 22, 1782, in ibid., 24:274–75.

36 General Order, May 22, 1782, in ibid., 279–80.

37 GW to Nicola, May 22, 1782, in ibid., 24:272–73.

38 http://www.amphil.org, accessed September 12, 2009.

39 *A Treatise of Military Exercise, Calculated for the Use of the Americans* (Philadelphia: Styner and Cist, 1776).

40 Ibid., title page.

41 Richard Haggard, "The Nicola Affair: Lewis Nicola, George Washington, and American Military Discontent during the Revolutionary War," *Proceedings of the American Philosophical Society* 146, no.2 (June 2002), p. 148.

42 *JCC*, 8:485.

43 Nicola to GW, May 21, 1782, GWLC.

44 Nicola to GW, May 22, 1782, in ibid. Nicola's previous "representation" has not been found.

45 Memoir, May 22, 1782, in ibid.

46 GW to Nicola, May 22, 1782, *FW*, 24:272–73.

47 Nicola to GW, May 23, 24, 28, 1782, GWLC.

48 Gordon to GW, September 24, 1788, and GW to Gordon, December 23, 1788, both in ibid.

49 Knox to Lincoln, May 29, 1782, KP, reel 8; Gilbert to his father, June 1, 1782, in John Shy, ed., *Winding Down: The Revolutionary War: Letters of Lieutenant Benjamin Gilbert of Massachusetts, 1780–1783* (Ann Arbor: University of Michigan Press, 1989), p. 59.

50 Letter from His Most Christian Majesty to Congress, October 22, 1781, *Pennsylvania Packet*, May 16, 1782.

51 This was a greater show of respect than Congress had extended to the commander in chief.

52 Charles Thomson provides a detailed description of the event. "Charles Thomson's Report on the Audience with la Luzerne," May 13, 1782, *LD*, 18:506–8.

53 Theodorick Bland to St. George Tucker, May 13, 1782, in ibid., 18:505.

54 GW to Villefranche, May 12, 1782, *FW*, 24:247.

55 *Thachers's Journal*, May 30, 1782.

56 Originally, the celebration was to be Thursday May 30, but it was postponed one day. General Orders, May 28, 29, 30, 1782, *General Orders of George Washington Issued at Newburgh on the Hudson, 1782–1783*, ed. Edward C. Boynton (Harrison, NY: Harbor Hill Books, 1973), pp. 22–23.

57 *Thacher's Journal*, June 1, 1782; Shy, *Winding Down*, pp. 58–59; General Orders, May 28, 29, 30, "A Programme for Conducting the Rejoicing on Friday, the 31st of May, 1782," in Boynton, *General Orders*, pp. 22–26.

58 *Thacher's Journal*, June 1, 1782.

59 Ibid.

60 Ibid.

61 Heath to GW, June 21, 1782, GWLC.

62 GW to Heath, June 22, 1782, *FW*, 24:370.

63 GW to Cary, June 15, 1782, in ibid., 24:347.

64 Lamb to General Heath, June 24, 1782, KP, reel 9.

65 William S. Baker, *Itinerary of General Washington from June 15, 1775, to December 23, 1783* (Philadelphia: J. B. Lippincott, 1892), p. 266; *Pennsylvania Gazette*, July 17, 1782.

66 Ibid.

67 Ibid.

68 Washington was fond of using this expression to describe the new nation. GW to Marquis de Chastellux, December 14, 1782, GWLC.

69 *Thacher's Journal*, July 4, 1782. A feu de joie was a running fire of guns.

70 Irwin Polishook, *Rhode Island and the Union, 1774–1795* (Evanston: Northwestern University Press, 1969), pp. 8–13.

71 E. James Ferguson, *The Power of the Purse: A History of American Public Finance, 1776–1790* (Chapel Hill; University of North Carolina Press, 1961), p. 152.

72 Varnum to GW, June 12, 1782, GWLC.

73 GW to Varnum, July 10, 1782, *FW*, 24:415–16. Although Washington had been away from camp for more than a week, he had responded to a variety of letters while traveling. He chose not to reply to Varnum until his return.

74 General Order, August 7, 1782, *FW*, 24;487–88.

75 GW had several spies on his payroll: see GW to Brigadier General David Forman, August 10, 1782, in ibid., 24:492–93.

76 http://www.mishalov.com/PurpleHeart, accessed October 15, 2009.

77 "Journal of Jean-Baptiste-Antoine De Verger," in The *American Campaigns of Rochambeau's Army, 1780, 1781, 1782, 1783*, trans. and ed. Howard C. Rice and Anne S. K. Brown (Princeton: Princeton University Press, 1972), 1:159.

78 Ibid., 1:165.

79 Ibid., 1:165n.

80 Ibid., 1:166.

81 *Thacher's Journal*, September 14, 1782.

82 Vaudreuil's fleet originally numbered thirteen ships of the line. The *Magnifique* ran aground and was lost in Boston Harbor. *Boston Evening Post*, August 17, 1782.

83 Pickering to Joseph Orne, August 18, 1782, Octavius Pickering, *The Life of Timothy Pickering* (Boston: Little, Brown, 1867), 1:369.

84 Rochambeau sailed to France via Providence. *Providence Gazette*, November 23, 1782. Verger, *Journal*, 1:170.

85 Ibid.

86 Pickering's reconnaissance was done during a particularly dry season. Although the site offered ample timber, he failed to notice that a good portion of the area was low ground. Fall and spring rains accompanied by melting snow would create problems. Conversation with Mike McGurty at Newburgh, April 16, 2010.

87 GW to Greene, October 17, 1782, *FW*, 25:267.

88 GW to Lincoln, October 2, 1782, in ibid., 25:282.

89 See, for example, Knox to Lincoln, July 15, 1782, KP, reel 9; Knox to John Lowell, October 8, 1782, KP, reel 10.

90 Gates to Morris, April (?), 1782, HGP, reel 13. This was a draft, and it is not certain that it was actually sent.

91 William Clagdon (?) to Gates, June 1, 1782, in ibid.; Gates to Morris, June 14, 1782, *PRM*, 5:409–10.

92 Morris to Gates, May 31, 1782, *PRM*, 5:301–2.

93 *LD*, 19:66n.

94 William Clagdon to Gates, April 13, 1782, HGP, reel 13.

95 *JCC*, 23:465.

96 Gates to GW, August 17, 1782, GWLC.

97 GW to Gates, August 27, 1782, *FW*, 25:68.

98 Gates to Elizabeth Gates, October 6, 1782, HGP, reel 13; seniority of command, *JCC*, 2:97.

99 Gates to Elizabeth Gates, October 6, 1782, HGP, reel 13.

100 Gates to Morris, October 25, 1782, in ibid.

101 Pickering to wife, October 31, 1782, PP, reel 4.

102 General Orders, October 28, 1782, *FW*, 25:303.

103 Quoted in Janet Dempsey, *Washington's Last Cantonment* (Monroe, NY: Library Research Associates, 1990), p. 46.

104 Knox to John Lowell, October 6, 1782, KP, reel 10.

Chapter Seven

1 Paul H. Smith, "Sir Guy Carleton: Peace Negotiations, and the Evacuation of New York," *Canadian Historical Review 50* (1969), p. 245.

2 Morgann to Shelburne, August 17, 1782, SPCL.

3 Ibid.

4 Shelburne to Carleton, June 5, 1782, CPNAC.

5 State of army under General Carleton, July 1, 1782, and B. G. John Campbell to Carleton, August 17, 1782, both in ibid.

6 Carleton to Townsend, October 29, 1782, *DAR*, 19:344.

7 For examples of intelligence reports from the field, see: "Intelligence Gentleman in Philadelphia to one in New York," October 16, 1782; "Information given by Mr. Cobb . . . ," January 5, 1783; "Intelligence," January 8, 1783 "Intelligence by Mr. Lewis of South Kingston, Rhode Island . . . ," January 11, 1783; "Intelligence by Joshua Mills and Thomas Burn," January 13, 1783; all in CPNAC.

8 Charles Moore, *The Northwest Under Three Flags* (New York: Harper and Brothers, 1900), p. 307.

9 Warrant, July 19, 1782, CPNAC.

10 For a long analysis of the political situation in Philadelphia, see Captain William Armstrong to Sir Guy Carleton, April 1, 1783, *Calendar of Manuscripts in the Royal Institution*, 4:1–7.

11 Intelligence report, January 1783, CPNAC.

12 Thomas Townshend to Carleton, August 14, 1782, *DAR*, 19:316. Charles Grey had previously served in America under General Sir William Howe. During the Philadelphia campaign (1777) he earned the nickname "No Flint Grey" when he ordered his men to remove the flints from their muskets so that no untoward shot would announce their presence. He was also accused of condoning atrocities against American troops at the so-called Paoli Massacre. Although unfounded, the charges stuck. The surprise is that the ministry would send him back to America at a time when making peace was more important than war. Paul David Nelson, *Sir Charles Grey, First Lord Grey* (Madison, NJ: Fairleigh Dickinson University Press, 1996), pp. 42–47, 64.

13 Paul H. Smith, "The American Loyalists: Notes on Their Organization and Numerical Strength," *William and Mary Quarterly*, Third series, 25 (1968), pp. 268–70.

14 Morgann to Shelburne, September 11, 1782, SPCL.

15 Quoted in Wallace Brown, *The Good Americans: The Loyalists in the American Revolution* (New York: Morrow, 1969), p.172.

16 Shelburne to Carleton, June 5, 1782, CPNAC; Shelburne to Carleton, February 18, 22, 1782, CPNAC.

17 Shelburne speaking in House of Lords, Fifteenth Parliament of Great Britain, Third Session (February 17, 1783), p. 70. Also quoted in *Scots Magazine* 45 (1783), p. 31.

18 Shelburne to Commissioners for restoring Peace (Secret), July 8, 1782, *DAR*, 21:89.

19 The orders for evacuation did not include St. Augustine. Carleton to Leslie, May 27, 1782, CPNAC.

20 This was the opinion of several subordinate officers. Captain William Feilding to Lord Denbigh, June 12, 1782, in Marion Balderston and David Syrett, eds., *The Lost War: Letters from British Officers During the American Revolution* (New York: Horizon Press, 1975), p. 215. Whether the Americans would have actually attacked seems unlikely; nonetheless, as a cautious commander Carleton had to assume the worst. Clinton left elaborate plans to defend New York. "Plan to Defend New York," May 29, 1782, CPNAC.

21 David Syrett, *Shipping and the American War, 1775–83* (London: Athlone Press, 1970), p. 17.

22 Ibid., p. 23.

23 Digby to Shelburne, September 13, 1782, *DAR*, 19:331.

24 Carleton to Shelburne, May 14, 1782, in ibid., 21:75; Syrett, *Shipping*, p. 236.

25 "State of Army Under Sir Guy Carleton," July 1, 1782, CPNAC.

26 The actual number eventually did reach over thirty thousand. See "Return of Loyalists Leaving New York," November 29, 1783, *DAR*, 21:225–26.

27 Wright to Carleton, July 6, 1782, CPNAC.

28 Leslie to Sir Henry Clinton, March 27, 1782, in ibid.

29 Captain William Feilding to Lord Denbigh, June 13, 1782, in Balderston and Syrett, *The Lost War*, p. 215.

30 For Carleton's relationship with Smith, see L. F. S. Upton, *The Loyal Whig: William Smith of New York and Quebec* (Toronto: University of Toronto Press, 1969), *passim*. Carleton arranged for Smith to receive payment for his services as chief justice and later secured the post of chief justice of Lower Canada (Quebec) for his friend.

31 Thomas Jones, *History of New York During the Revolutionary War* (New York: New York Historical Society, 1879), 2:262.

32 Canada, then consisting of present-day Quebec and Ontario, was under the command of Frederick Haldimand, who, while technically subordinate to Carleton, did all he could to assert his own independence. Shelburne to Haldimand, April 22, 1782, *DAR*, 19:285; Haldimand to Shelburne, July 17, 1782, in ibid., 19:313; Haldimand to Carleton, July 29, 1782, in ibid., 19:327; John O. Dendy, "Frederick Haldimand and the Defence of Canada, 1778–1784" (Ph.D. diss., Duke University, 1972), pp. 230–31.

33 Eventually, loyalists would settle in other provinces as well, but Nova Scotia took the vast majority. See "Return of Loyalists Leaving New York," *DAR*, 21:225–26.

34 Maya Jasanoff, *Liberty's Exiles: American Loyalists in the Revolutionary World* (New York: Knopf, 2011), pp. 147–75.

35 Quoted in Viola F. Barnes, "Francis Legge, Governor of Loyalist Nova Scotia, 1773–1776," *New England Quarterly* 4, no. 3 (1931), p. 445.

36 "Francis Legge," *DCB* online.

37 Carleton to Hamond, September 23, 1782, *DAR*, 19:336.

38 Theodore O. Barck, *New York City During the War for Independence* (reprint, Port Washington, NY: I. J. Friedman, 1966), p. 210; James S. MacDonald, *Memoir of Governor John Parr* (Halifax: Nova Scotia Historical Society, 1909), 14:49–57.

39 MacDonald, *Memoir of Governor John Parr*, p. 54.

40 Carleton to Leslie, May 23, 1782, CPNAC.

41 David Lee Russell, *The American Revolution in the Southern Colonies* (reprint, Jefferson, NC: McFarland, 1978), p. 316.

42 General Modecai Gist to Greene, August 27, 1782, *PNG*, 11:579–82.

43 James Thomas Flexner, *The Young Hamilton, A Biography* (Boston: Little, Brown, 1978), pp. 241, 255, 316.

44 GW to Greene, October 18, 1782, *FW*, 25:271; Christopher Ward, *The War of the Revolution* (New York: Macmillan, 1952), 2:840–42.

45 Washington to Greene, October 18, 1782, *FW*, 25:271.

46 Russell, *The American Revolution in the Southern Colonies*, p. 316.

47 Wayne to Greene, December 13, 1782, *PNG*, 12:290.

48 Ibid., pp. 290–92; Greene to Elias Boudinot, December 19, 1782, *PNG*, 12:301–4.

49 Contrary to Carleton's instructions, some British soldiers also carried away eight church bells from St. Michaels. A soon as he learned of the theft, Carleton demanded that the bells be returned. General Orders, January 28, 1783, CPNAC.

50 Russell, *The American Revolution in the Southern Colonies*, p. 317. Despite the fact that they had eagerly sought and accepted aid from Indian allies in the Carolinas and Georgia, in all of their plans for evacuation and later compensation the British made no attempt to assist these native loyalists.

51 John Sullivan, *Journals of the Military Expedition of Major General John Sullivan Against the Six Nations of Indians in 1779* (Albany: New York Secretary of State, 1885), p. 101.

52 Haldimand to Townshend, February 14, 1783, *DAR*, 21:155.

53 Haldimand to Lord North, June 2, 1782, in ibid., 19:404. Haldimand to Thomas Townshend, October 23, 1782, in ibid., 19:339.

54 Maclean to Haldimand, May 18, 1782, in ibid., 20:172.

55 North to Haldimand, August 8, 1783, in ibid., 19:426.

56 The Creek were actually a collection of several tribes but considered themselves a single people.

57 Spain joined the war in 1779 as an ally of France.

58 Browne to Carleton, April 28, 1783, CPNAC.

59 Jonathan Williams to (?), September 23, 1782, BPL 1188.

60 Digby to Carleton, October 18, 1782, CPNAC.

61 Feilding to Denbigh, August 10, 1782, in Balderston and Syrett, *The Lost War*, p. 219; Carleton to Haldimand, August 25, 1782, CPNAC.

62 Shelburne's expression, Shelburne to Carleton, June 5, 1782, CPNAC.

63 Robertson to Amherst, Milton Klein and Ronald W. Howard, eds., *The Twilight of British Rule in Revolutionary America: The Letterbook of General James Robertson* (Cooperstown: New York State Historical Association, 1983), p. 233.

64 Richard B. Morris, *The Peacemakers: The Great Powers and American Independence* (New York: Harper and Row, 1965), p. 294. The actual wording of the letter: "The principal points in contemplation were the allowance of independence to America upon Great Britain's being restored to the situation she was placed in by the treaty of 1763 and that a proper person should be sent to make a similar communication to M. de Vergernnes." Shelburne to Carleton and Digby, June 5, 1782, *DAR*, 21:78.

65 George III's "Warrant for Richard Oswald's First Commission for Negotiating Peace," July 25, 1782, *RDC*, 5:613; Morris, *Peacemakers*, pp. 295–96.

66 Adams to Jay, August 10, 1782, in John Adams, *Papers of John Adams*, ed. Gregg Lint et al. (Cambridge: Harvard University Press, 2006), 13:227. Volume 12 of this series focuses on Adams's diplomatic negotiation at The Hague.

67 Quoted in Morris, *Peacemakers*, p. 302.

68 *JCC*, 20:649.

69 In the original this passage was in capital letters. Jay to Morris, October 13, 1782, PJJ, 2:393.

70 Jay explains his position in a very long letter/report to Robert R. Livingston, November 17, 1782, in ibid., 2:366–452. He recounts his conversation with Oswald on pp. 380–84.

71 Morris, *Peacemakers*, p. 14.

72 Quoted in ibid., p. 300; Jay was in the class of 1764. Vardill took his degree in 1766. *Catalogue of Columbia College New York* (New York: E. B. Clayton, 1836), p. 21.

73 Morris, *Peacemakers*, p. 300.

74 Quoted in ibid., p. 310.

75 Quoted in ibid., p. 338.

76 Samuel Flagg Bemis, "Canada and the Peace Settlement of 1782–83," *Canadian Historical Review* 14 (1933), p. 276. Bemis makes the point that while the language was changed to give the appearance of recognition of American independence, some members of the cabinet took the view that such was not the case. Ibid., p. 277, 277n.

77 "Articles Agreed to Between the American and British Commissioners," October 8, 1782, in Wharton, *Revolutionary Diplomatic Correspondence*, 5:805–8.

78 Morris, *Peacemakers*, pp. 346–48. Had these boundary lines held in the final treaty, the United States would include today a portion of the province of New Brunswick as well as the southern part of Ontario province. Americans would have conceivably lost northern Michigan and the upper portion of Wisconsin.

79 Shelburne to Oswald, October 21, 1782, in Lord Edmund Fitzmaurice, *Life of William, Earl of Shelburne* (London: Macmillan Company, 1876), 3:283–86.

80 John Brooke, *The House of Commons, 1754–1790* (London: Oxford University Press, 1964), p. 303. Shelburne to Alleyne Fitzherbert, October 21, 1782, Fitzmaurice, *Life of William Earl of Shelburne*, 3:287.

81 Morris, *Peacemakers*, p. 361.

82 J. Hector St. John de Crevecoeur, *Letters from an American Farmer and Sketches of Eighteenth Century America* (New York: Penguin, 1986), p. 264.

83 Jay to Peter Van Schaak, September 17, 1782, PJJ, 2:344.

84 Since the states already ignored Congress in so many ways, it is hard to imagine that this body would have much influence over them in these matters.

85 http://avalon.law.yale.edu18th_century/prel1782.asp, accessed September 20, 2009. Appended to the treaty was a secret article that stipulated that should Great Britain have possession of West Florida (it had been taken previously by the Spanish), the border would be adjusted to favor the United States. Laurens had been released from the Tower of London in January 1782.

86 Vergennes to Luzerne, December 19, 1782, in Wharton, *Revolutionary Diplomatic Correspondence*, 6:151.

87 Benjamin Franklin to Vergennes, in ibid., 6:137–38. The passport is printed in ibid., 6:137n; Vergennes to Lucerne, December 19, 1782, in ibid., 6:151; Louis A. Norton, *Joshua Barney* (Annapolis, United States: Naval Institute Press, 2000), pp. 91–93.

88 Vergennes to Franklin, December 15, 1782, in Wharton, *Revolutionary Diplomatic Correspondence*, 6:140.

89 Franklin to Vergennes, December 17, 1782, in ibid., 6:144.

90 In 1780 Great Britain had also declared war on the Dutch Republic. Although Dutch money played an important role in supporting the Revolution, the military and mainly naval impact of Dutch participation was minimal. Friedrich Edler, *The Dutch Republic and the American Revolution* (Baltimore: Johns Hopkins University Press, 1911). See also *Papers of John Adams*.

91 *Journals of the House of Commons*, Fifteenth Parliament of Great Britain, Third Session (December 5, 1782–16 July 6, 1783), December 5, 1782.

92 Elkanah Watson, *Men and Times of the Revolution*, ed. Winslow C. Watson (New York: Dana, 1856), p. 203.

93 *Journals of the House of Commons*, Fifteenth Parliament of Great Britain, Third Session, p. 4.

94 Watson, *Men and Times*, p. 205.

Chapter Eight

1 Carleton and Digby to Washington, August 2, 1782, GWLC. Cornwallis was not actually confined. He was on parole; that is, he was free but not permitted to rejoin the army. Laurens to William Bell, September 1, 1782, in *Papers of Henry Laurens*, ed. Philip Hamer et al. (Columbia: University of South Carolina Press, 2002), 16:1–2.

2 Elkanah Watson, *Men and Times of the Revolution*, ed. Winslow C. Watson (New York: Dana, 1856) p. 205.

3 GW to Carleton, August 2, 1782, GWLC.

4 GW to President of Congress, August 5, 1782, *FW*, 24:466.

5 On April 19, 1782, the Dutch States General resolved that "Mr Adams shall be admitted and acknowledged in the quality of ambassador of the United States to Their High Mightiness." John Adams, *Papers of John Adams*, ed. Gregg Lint et al. (Cambridge: Harvard University Press, 2004), 12:422. Official notice did not reach Philadelphia until early September. Samuel Osgood to John Lowell, September 13, 1782, *LD*, 19:153.

6 Edmund C. Burnett, *The Continental Congress* (New York: W.W. Norton, 1964), pp. 350–51.

7 Georges Lemaître, *Beaumarchais* (New York: Knopf, 1949), pp. 177–78.

8 Louis W. Potts, *Arthur Lee: A Virtuous Revolutionary* (Baton Rouge: Louisiana State University Press, 1981), pp. 88–89.

9 Samuel Adams to Stephen Sayre, November 16, 23, in *Writings of Samuel Adams*, ed. Harry Alonzo Cushing (reprint, New York: Octagon Books, 1968), 2:56–61, 66–69.

10 *Letters of Dennys de Berdt, 1757–1770*, ed. Albert Matthews (Cambridge: J. Wilson and Son, 1911), p. 299.

11 Samuel Adams to Sayre, November 16, 1770, in *Writings of Samuel Adams*, 2:59.

12 *JCC*, 6:897. Lee replaced Thomas Jefferson, who declined the assignment.

13 For a summary of the feud, see Richard B. Morris, *The Peacemakers: The Great Powers and American Independence* (New York: Harper and Row, 1965), pp. 8–13 and Julian P. Boyd, "Death by a Kindly Teacher of Treason?" *William and Mary Quarterly*, third series (1959), pp. 165–87, 319–42, 515–50.

14 Instructions, June 15, 1781, *JCC*, 20:651–54.

15 Charles Thomson, "Notes of Debates," August 8, 1782, *LD*, 19:40. Jesse Root of Connecticut made a substitute motion to appoint a committee. Since the effect would be the same, Lee supported Root's motion and withdrew his own.

16 Madison to Edmund Randolph, August 15, 1782, in ibid., 19:59; Thomson, "Notes of Debates" August 8, 1782, in ibid., 19:44.

17 Robert Livingston to Franklin, September 5, 1782, *RDC*, 5:696–98.

18 *JCC*, 22:460n.

19 Ibid., 23:463; Thomson, "Notes of Debates," August 12, 1782, *LD*, 19:57.

20 Lincoln to Knox, August 12, 1782, KP, reel 9.

21 James Duane to Philip Schuyler, August 16, 1782, *LD*, 19:70.

22 Thomson, "Notes of Debates," August 12, 1782, in ibid., 19:58.

23 Morris to Ridley, August 6, 1782, *PRM*, 6:147. At the time, Ridley was in Holland negotiating a loan for the state of Maryland.

24 Charles Royster, *A Revolutionary People at War* (Chapel Hill: University of North Carolina Press, 1979), p. 23.

25 Merrill Jensen, *The Articles of Confederation: An Interpretation of the Social-Constitutional History of the American Revolution* (Madison: University of Wisconsin Press, 1970), pp. 56–57.

26 The terms *radicals* and *conservatives*, while appropriate in describing these points of view, were not necessarily contemporary terms. They are used here simply to make the distinction.

27 "Articles of Confederation," article 10, http://avalon.law.yale.edu/18th_century/art conf.asp, accessed October 19, 2009.

28 Jack N. Rakove, The *Beginnings of National Politics: An Interpretive History of the Continental Congress* (New York: Random House, 1979), p. 104.

29 For a detailed analysis of voting factions in the Congress, see Calvin Jillson and Rick K. Wilson, *Congressional Dynamics: Structure, Coordination, and Choice in the*

First American Congress, 1774–1789 (Stanford: Stanford University Press, 1994), pp. 167–286.

30 *JCC*, 19:112–13.

31 For a thoughtful analysis of the motivation behind those serving in the American cause, see Royster, *A Revolutionary People at War*, appendix, pp. 373–78.

32 John A Nagy, *Rebellion in the Ranks: Mutinies of the American Revolution* (Yardley, PA: Westholme, 2008), pp. 297–99.

33 Allen Bowman, *The Morale of American Revolutionary Army* (Port Washington, NY: Kennikat Press, 1964), pp. 24–25. Greene to William Greene, March 7, 1778, *PNG*, 11:301. Greene's numbers were likely exaggerated.

34 *FW*, 11:237.

35 Gates to Morris, April–May 10 (1782), *PRM*, 5:89.

36 Quoted in Terry Golway, *Washington's General: Nathanael Greene and the Triumph of the American Revolution* (New York; Henry Holt, 2005), p. 159.

37 GW to William Buchanan, February 7, 1778, *FW*, 10:427, 13:465.

38 Greene to GW, February 15, 1778, *PNG*, 11:285.

39 Paul Lockhart, *The Drillmaster of Valley Forge: The Baron Von Steuben* (New York: HarperCollins, 2008), pp. 95–117.

40 Theodoric Bland et al. to GW, November 1777, GWLC. In addition to Bland, the officers were M. Gist, Joseph Carvel Hall, Thomas Hartley, Robert Lawson, James Innes, John Taylor, and Henry Miller.

41 Theodoric Bland et al. to GW, November 1777, GWLC. These proposals were Cromwellian. After the British developed a professional army in the late seventeenth century following the Treaty of Ryswick, demands arose in Parliament for a reduction of the officer corps. To reward those who were being dismissed, Parliament agreed to half pay for life, thinking that it was only a temporary measure and would, as the officers died, eventually cease. The resumption of hostilities in 1702, however, resulted in the recall of officers from half-pay status, thus beginning a revolving door by which half pay became a permanent institution in the British army. Aside from the unintended consequence of permanency, this system created a class of half-pay soldiers who were inclined when not in service to turn to politics. As members of Parliament, they formed a strong pro-army clique. All of this was well known and detested in America. Hew Strachan, *Politics of the British Army* (New York: Oxford University Press, 1997), pp. 22–23; William H. Glasson, *Federal Military Pensions in the United States* (New York: Oxford University Press, 1918), p. 12.

42 "Remarks on Plan of Field Officers for Remodeling the Army," November 1777, *FW*, 10:125–26.

43 James Lovell to John Adams, January 13, 1778, John Adams, *Papers of John Adams*, ed. Gregg Lint et al. (Cambridge: Harvard University Press, 1983), 5:383–84.

44 Continental Congress Conference Committee to GW, December 10, 1777, GWLC. The British occupation of Philadelphia forced Congress to adjourn to York, Pennsylvania, where it met from September 30, 1777, to June 27, 1778.

45 Ibid.

46 GW to Elbridge Gerry, December 25, 1777, *FW*, 10:200–201.

47 James Lovell to Samuel Adams, January 13, 1778, *LD*, 8:580–81.

48 *JCC*, 10:285–86.

49 Connecticut Delegates to Jonathan Trumbull, May 18, 1778, in ibid., 8:708.

50 *JCC*, 11:502. For an analysis of the voting in Congress, see Jillson and Wilson, *Congressional Dynamics*, pp. 213–21.

51 *JCC*, 14:638–39.

52 Ibid., 14:779.

53 Ibid., 15:1337–38.

54 Ibid., 18:893.

55 Ibid., 18:897.

56 GW to President of Congress, October 11, 1780, *FW*, 20:158.

57 Ibid.

58 Members were elected by their state legislature.

59 Burnett, *Continental Congress*, pp. 406–27, 472.

60 *JCC*, 18:958–59.

61 Ibid., 21:1112.

62 Circular to the Governors of the States, May 16, 1782, *PRM*, 5:191.

63 Morris Diary, in ibid., 5:520.

64 *JCC*, 4:35; *JCC*, 6:912; January 6, 1776; October 30, 1776. For his views on money, see Pelatiah Webster, *To The Honourable The Legislatures of the Thirteen United States of America This Second Essay on Free Trade and Finance, Is Most Humbly Inscribed, August 20, 1779* (Philadelphia: Hall and Webster, 1779), p. 17.

65 Webster, *A Fourth Essay on Free Trade and Finance . . . , February 10, 1780* (Philadelphia: Hall and Sellers, 1780), p. 17.

66 Ibid., p. 15.

67 Ibid.

68 Webster, *Sixth Essay on Free Trade and Finance* (Philadelphia: T. Bradford, 1783), pp. 5, 12.

69 Ibid., p. 27.

70 Quoted in H. B. Learned, "Origins of the Superintendent of Finance," *American Historical Review* 10 (April 1905), p. 568.

71 Morris Diary, *PRM*, 5:520.

72 With the support of Henry Knox, officers of the Massachusetts Line had already petitioned the Massachusetts House and Senate for pay. Petition of Officers of the Massachusetts Line, July 1782, Knox to Lincoln, July 15, 1782, KP, reel 9.

73 *JCC*, 22:418.

74 Ibid., 22:423.

75 Thomson Notes, July 31, 1782, *LD*, 18:694.

76 Samuel Osgood to John Lowell, September 9, 1782, in ibid., 19:130.

77 Thomson Notes, July 31, 1782, in ibid., 18:694.

78 Ibid.

79 Thomson, "Notes of Debates," July 30, 1782, *LD*, 18:688.

80 Samuel Osgood to John Lowell, September 9, 1782, in ibid., 19:130.

81 Thomson Notes, July 31, 1782, in ibid., 18:695.

82 Morris Diary, *PRM*, 5:524n.

83 GW to Secretary at War, October 2, 1782, *FW*, 25:227–28.

84 Lincoln to GW, October 14, 1782, BLP, reel 6A.

85 Morris to GW, October 16, 1782, *PRM*, 6 (1984):604; For a similar view, see Alexander Hamilton to Lafayette, *PAH*, 3:191–93.

Chapter Nine

1 Although Philadelphia offered a closer point for debarkation, its proximity to New York, and location at the head of a long entrance via Delaware Bay, made it vulnerable to interference by the Royal Navy.

2 Lincoln to President of Congress, October 30, 1782, Papers of the Continental Congress, National Archives, no. 149, II, 105; David Mattern, *Benjamin Lincoln and the American Revolution* (Columbia: University of South Carolina Press, 1995), pp. 138–39.

3 Lincoln to President of Congress, October 30, 1782, Papers of the Continental Congress, no. 149, II, 105.

4 Madison to Edmund Randolph, October 29, 1782, *LD*, 19:322.

5 Lincoln to GW, November 22, 1782, GWLC.

6 Ibid.; *JCC*, 23:750. The recommendation did not cover the entire period of service, but if approved it would have set the precedent of state responsibility for army pay. See Robert Morris to President of Congress, December 3, 1782, *PRM*, 7 (1988):151n.

7 Morris Diary, November 30, 1782, in ibid., 7:136.

8 Morris to President of Congress, December 3, 1782, in ibid., 7:151.

9 Osgood to Lowell, September 9, 1782, *LD*, 19:130.

10 Knox to Lincoln, November 25, 1782, KP, reel 10.

11 Daniel Salisbury to Captain Simon Jackson, December 10, 1782, BPL, ms. 1199.

12 Kingston was the temporary state capital.

13 Massachusetts Line—Petition Vote and Proceedings, November 16, 1782. KP, reel 10.

14 Massachusetts Line, John Crane, from Braintree, Massachusetts, commanded the third artillery regiment. John Brooks was from Reading, Massachusetts, and commanded the Seventh Regiment. Hugh Maxwell was from Charlemont, Massachusetts, and Rufus Putnam was from Sutton, Massachusetts. Thacher was a regimental surgeon from Plymouth, Massachusetts. Fred Anderson Berg, *Encyclopedia of Continental Army Units* (Harrisburg: Stackpole Books, 1972), pp. 72–75; Robert K. Wright Jr., *The Continental Army* (Washington: Center for Military History, 1983), pp. 203–16.

15 Response of First Massachusetts, November 19, 1782, KP, reel 10.

16 Response of Tenth Regiment, November 19, 1782, and Response of Fifth Regiment, November 19, 1782, both in ibid.

17 Minutes of the meeting have not been found. It is simply reasonable to assume that the body did select a committee. It might also be speculated that the committee consisted of the three men who were elected to deliver the memorial to Congress.

18 *JCC*, 24:291.

19 "To the United States in Congress Assembled, the Address and Petition of the Officers of the Army of the United States," December 1782, in ibid., 24:291–93.

20 For McDougall's career, see Roger J. Champagne, *Alexander McDougall and the American Revolution in New York*. (Schenectady: Union College Press, 1975).

21 Instructions to the Committee from the Army, December 7, 1782, quoted in Champagne, *Alexander McDougall*, p.185.

22 GW to Jones, December 14, 1782, *FW*, 25:430.

23 Morris Diary, *PRM*, 7:226.

24 GW to Jones, December 14, 1782, *FW*, 25:430–31. Not only did Washington suffer the personal discomfort of not being able to travel home; he also endured financial difficulty. Four days after writing Jones, he had to borrow two thousand pounds from his friend George Clinton, the New York governor, to buy land near Mount Vernon. GW to Clinton, December 18, 1782, in ibid., 25:451–52.

25 Knox to Lincoln, December 20, 1782, KP, reel 10.

26 Madison's Notes on Debates, December 18, 1782, *LD*, 19:492.

27 Irwin Polishook, *Rhode Island and the Union* (Evanston: Northwestern University Press, 1969), pp. 81–101. See also resolution, *JCC*, 24:34.

28 Eliphalet Dyer to William Williams, January [10?], 1783, *LD*, 19:573.

29 Hamilton to John Laurence, December 12, 1782, *PAH*, 3:211–12. Laurence is not to be confused with John Laurens. *Biographical Directory of the United States Congress* (Washington: Government Printing Office, 1989). On July 22, with strong support from Alexander Hamilton and his father-in-law, Philip Schuyler, the New York Assembly called upon the Congress to call a "general Convention of the States" to revise the Articles of Confederation, particularly those sections dealing with fiscal affairs. Congress received the resolutions, assigned them to a committee, and there they languished and were never acted upon. *PAH*, 3:110–13.

30 McDougall to Knox, January 9, 1783, KP, reel 11; Champagne, *McDougall, p.* 186.

31 McDougall to Knox, January 9, 1783, KP, reel 11.

32 Morris Diary, December 31, 1782, *PRM*, 7:247.

33 The committee was composed of Phillips White (NH) Samuel Osgood (MA), Jonathan Arnold (RI), Oliver Wolcott (CT), Alexander Hamilton (NY), Silas Condict (NJ), Richard Peters (PA), John Dickinson (DE), Daniel Carroll (MD), James Madison (VA), Abner Nash (NC), and John Rutledge (SC). At the time, Georgia was not represented. Madison's Notes, January 6, 1783, *LD*, 19:539n; *Biographical Directory of the United States Congress*.

34 *JCC*, 11:502–3. Wolcott became chair in one of two ways: either he garnered more votes than anyone else when the committee was elected by the body, or he might have been elected by the members of the committee. In either case his election certainly sent a message. For committee structure in the Congress, see Calvin Jillson and Rick K. Wilson, *Congressional Dynamics: Structure, Coordination, and Choice in the First American Congress, 1774–1789* (Stanford: Stanford University Press, 1994), pp. 91–100.William H. Glasson, *History of Federal Military Pensions in the United States* (New York: Oxford University Press, 1918), pp. 10–11.

35 Samuel Osgood to John Lowell, January 6, 1782, *LD*, 19:543.

36 Madison's Notes, January 7, 1783, in ibid., 19:556.

37 Madison's Notes, January 10, 1783, in ibid., 19:571.

38 Hamilton to Clinton, January 12, 1782, *PAH*, 3:240–41.

39 Madison's Notes, January 10, 1783, *LD*, 19:571.

40 Madison's Notes, January 9–10, 1783, in ibid., 19:569.

41 Madison to Randolph, January 14, 1783, in ibid., 19:583.

42 Madison's Notes, January 13, 1783, in ibid., 19:579.

43 Ibid., pp. 579–81.

44 Head note, Morris to John Pierce, January 20, 1783, *PRM*, 7:330.

45 Madison's Notes, *LD*, 19:581; head note, Morris to Paymaster, January 20, 1783, *PRM*, 7:329.

46 "Observations on the Present State of Affairs," (January? 1783), *PRM*, 7:306.

47 Morris Diary, in ibid., 7:310.

48 To what degree the members of the committee, or Congress in general, were aware of this mission is uncertain. Morris was determined to keep the venture secret. Head note, Morris to John Pierce, January 20, 1783, in ibid., 7:328. Morris did keep Washington informed. Head note p. 328; "John Barry's Account of Proceedings on the *Alliance* and the *Duc de Lauzun*" and head note, both in ibid., 7:607–13.

49 "Observations on the Present State of Affairs," in ibid., 7:306.

50 Head note, Morris to Pierce, in ibid., 7:330.

51 Morris, Diary, in ibid., 7:315.

52 Head note, Morris to Pierce, in ibid., 7:330–31.

53 *JCC*, 24:83–92; Morris to President of Congress, January 24, 1783, *PRM*, 7:368. See also extensive notes accompanying the letter, pp. 361–71.

54 Madison's Notes, January 24, 1783, *LD*, 19:610.

55 Ibid.

56 Ibid.

57 Lee to Adams, January 29, 1783, *LD*, 19:630.

58 At first Hamilton knew little about public finance. In 1781 Washington was asked if Hamilton might be suited for the office of superintendent of finance. He responded, "How far Colonel Hamilton, of whom you ask my opinion as a financier, has turned his thoughts to that particular study I am unable to answer, because I never entered upon a discussion on this point with him." Washington to John Sullivan, February 4, 1781, *FW*, 21:181.

59 *JCC*, 24:93.

60 John Shy, ed., *Winding Down: The Revolutionary War Letters of Benjamin Gilbert* (Ann Arbor: University of Michigan Press, 1989), p. 67.

61 Head note, Morris to John Pierce, January 20, 1783, *PRM*, 7:327–37. This is an extraordinary footnote exemplary of the very best in documentary editing describing these circumstances.

62 Shy, *Winding Down*, p. 82.

63 McDougall and Ogden to Henry Knox, February 8, 1783, KP, reel 11.

64 Ibid.

65 There is no direct evidence for this "conspiracy," but the circumstantial evidence that follows convinces this writer that these men did concoct a plan. See also Richard Kohn, "The Inside History of the Newburgh Conspiracy: America and the Coup d'Etat," *William and Mary Quarterly*, third series, 27 (April 1970), pp. 187–220; Paul David Nelson, with a rebuttal by Richard H. Kohn, "Horatio Gates at Newburgh, 1783: A Misunderstood Role," *William and Mary Quarterly*, third series, 29 (January 1972), pp. 143–55; C. Edward Skeen, with a rebuttal by Richard H. Kohn, "The Newburgh Conspiracy Reconsidered," *William and Mary Quarterly*, third series, 31 (April 1974), pp. 273–98.

66 Nathanael Greene was also held in very high regard.

67 McDougall and Ogden to Knox, February 8, 1783, KP, reel 11.

68 Knox and Morris were well known to each other. They had served together the previous year in an unsuccessful attempt to work a prisoner exchange with the British. Mark Puls, *Henry Knox: Visionary General of the American Revolution* (New York: Palgrave, 2008), pp. 168–70.

69 Gouverneur Morris to Knox, February 7, 1783, KP, reel 11. Morris had a tendency toward the dramatic. On January 1, 1783, he wrote to John Jay: "The army may have swords in their hands . . . Depend on it, good will arise from the situation to which we are hastening . . . And although I think it probable, that much of convulsion will ensue, yet it must terminate in giving to government that power, without which government is but a name." Morris to Jay, January 1, 1783 in Jared Sparks, ed., *Life of Gouverneur Morris* (Boston: Gray and Bowen, 1832), 1:249.

70 Benjamin Walker to Edward Hand, February 14, 1783, GWLC.

Chapter Ten

1 GW to Baylies, January 8, 1783, *FW*, 26:22.

2 GW to Major General Arthur St. Clair, February 19, 1783, in ibid., 26:145–46.

3 GW to Howe, February 10, 1783, in ibid., 26:114.

4 The house had previously served as headquarters for Knox and is often referred to as Knox's Headquarters at Vails Gate. "Knox's Headquarters State Historic Site," State of New York Office of Parks and Recreation. Gates to Elizabeth Gates, January 17, 1783, HGP, reel 13.

5 Gates to Timothy Pickering, January 27, 1783, PP, reel 13. Mrs. Gates was indeed very ill. Gates to Elizabeth Gates, January 17, 1783, HGP, reel 1.

6 GW to Pickering, December 25, 1783, *FW*, 25:464–66.

7 Pickering to wife, January 19, 1783, PP, reel 1.

8 Knox to GW, September 10, 1782, KP, reel 9. Mark Puls, *Henry Knox: Visionary General of the American Revolution* (New York: Palgrave Macmillan, 2008), pp. 172–73.

9 GW to Knox, September 12, 1782, *FW*, 25:150n.

10 GW to Tilghman, January 10, 1783, in ibid., 26:29.

11 GW to Lund Washington, February 12, 1783, in ibid., 26:126–27.

12 Ibid., p.127. It may be at this point that Washington regretted a decision he made when appointed commander in chief. He declined to take a salary and asked only to be reimbursed for his expenses.

13 GW to John Augustine Washington, January 16, 1783, *FW*, 26:41–42.

14 Although Mary Ball Washington complained about her poverty, at her death in 1789 she owned lands, several slaves, and had very little debt. She also, curiously enough, left nearly everything to her negligent son George. Mary Ball Washington Will, May 20, 1788, GWLC.

15 GW to John Augustine Washington, January 16, 1783, *FW*, 26:42.

16 Ron Chernow, *Washington: A Life* (New York: Penguin, 2010), pp. 422–23.

17 GW to John Augustine Washington, January 16, 1783, *FW*, 26:43–44.

18 GW to Archibald Cary, June 15, 1782, in ibid., 24:347; Washington to Heath, February 5, 1783, in ibid., 26:97.

19 Alan Valentine, *Lord Stirling* (New York: Oxford University Press, 1969), p. 268.

20 Captain Richard Sill to Washington, January 14, 1783, and Marinus Willett to GW, February 19, 1783, both in GWLC.

21 Pickering to wife, January 3, 1783, PP, reel 1.

22 GW to Rittenhouse, February 16, 1783, *FW*, 26:136–37.

23 General Order, Newburgh, November 14, 1782, in ibid., 25:343.

24 James Dempsey, *Washington's Last Cantonment* (Monroe, NY: Library Research Associates, 1990), pp. 46, 54, 57, *passim*; see also GW to Joseph Jones, December 14, 1782, *FW*, 25:430–31.

25 Russell Bastado, comp., "Likenesses of New Hampshire War Heroes and Personages in the Collections of the New Hampshire State House and State Library," http://www.nh.gov/nhdhr/publications/warheroes/evansrev.html, accessed December 11, 2009; Robert K. Wright, Jr., *The Continental Army* (Washington: Center for Military History, 1983), pp.197–98.

26 General Orders, December 25, 1782, *FW*, 25:464; Gates's role in this project can be followed in Edward C. Boynton, ed., *General Orders of George Washington Issued at Newburgh on the Hudson, 1782–1783* (Harrison, NY: Harbor Hill Books, 1973), pp. 62–67.

27 GW to Rochefontaine, Service Certificate, August 19, 1783, GWLC. Following the establishment of the United States Army, President Washington appointed Rochefontaine commandant of the Corps of Engineers. United States Army Corps of Engineers, *History of the United States Army Corps of Engineers* (Washington: Corps of Engineers, 1998), p. 21. United States Army Corps of Engineers Web site, "Commanders of the Corps of Engineers," http://www.usace.army.mil/History/Pages/Commanders .aspx, accessed December 11, 2009.

28 Gates was deeply involved in the project. See Benjamin Tupper to Horatio Gates, January 8, 10, 25, 1783, and Tupper, Nelson, and Rochefontaine to General Horatio Gates (?), Estimate on Building Expense, January 1783. Nelson is not identified. He may have been a private contractor. See also Robert Oliver to Horatio Gates, January

16, 1783, HGP, reel 13. Tupper's regiment, the Sixth Massachusetts, disbanded on January 1, 1783. He was reassigned to the Tenth. Francis B. Heitman, *Historical Register of Officers of the Continental Army* (Baltimore: Genealogical Publishing, 1967), pp. 38–39.

29 State Historic Site. Although Rochefontaine's actual plans have not survived, sufficient contemporary descriptions of the building exist to make us fairly certain of its appearance. A reconstruction of the public building stands at New Windsor Cantonment, New York.

30 In 1757 David Fordyce's *Temple of Virtue* was published posthumously. This book by a popular Scottish professor of philosophy received wide notice and may have influenced Evans's choice of name.

31 Dempsey, *Washington's Last Cantonment*, p. 93.

32 Ibid., p. 96.

33 Ibid., p. 101.

34 General Orders, January 8, 1783, *FW*, 26:23.

35 A *feu de joie* was an impressive sequential firing of thousands of muskets. I am indebted to Mike McCurty for this description.

36 General Orders, January 29, 1783, *FW*, 26:75–76.

37 Dempsey, *Washington's Last Cantonment*, p. 106.

38 Ibid., p. 105.

39 After Orders, March 6, 1783, in Boynton, *General Orders of George Washington*, pp. 68–69.

40 Dempsey, *Washington's Last Cantonment*, p. 88; William Heath, *Memoirs of General William Heath by Himself*, ed. William Abbatt (New York: William Abbatt, 1901), p. 330.

41 Pickering to his wife, February 6, 1783, PP, reel 1.

42 Major General Gates's Orders, February 8, 1783, in Boynton, *General Orders of George Washington*, p. 67; Tupper to GW, May 2, 1783, GWLC.

43 Knox to McDougall, February 21, 1783, KP, reel 11.

44 James Thomas Flexner, *George Washington in the American Revolution*, 1775–1783 (Boston; Little, Brown, 1968), p. 203. Ron Chernow, *Alexander Hamilton* (New York: Penguin, 2004), pp. 73–74.

45 Hamilton to Philip Schuyler, February 18, 1781, *PAH*, 25:563–68.

46 Hamilton to GW, February (13), 1783, *LD*, 19:688–90. Some historians have suggested that Brooks carried both Morris's and Hamilton's letters. Given the dates, this seems unlikely.

47 For Brooks's role, see Richard Kohn, "The Inside History of the Newburgh Conspiracy: America and the Coup d'Etat," *William and Mary Quarterly*, third series, 27 (April 1970), p. 198n. Kohn's essay is the best analysis of the Newburgh Conspiracy.

48 Pickering to Gates, May 28, 1783, PP, reel 5.

49 Armstrong to Gates, April 29, 1783, HGP. Gates too was watching with great interest the "the political pot in Philadelphia." Gates to Richard Peter, February 20, 1783, in ibid., reel 13. It is possible that both Brooks and Hamilton were playing a double

game, with each, in his own way, warning Washington about the machinations in Congress and among his own command.

50 Knox to Morris, February 21, 1783, KP, reel 11. On the same day, he wrote a very similar letter to McDougall: Knox to McDougall, February 21, 1783, in ibid.

51 "Brutus" to Knox, February 12, 1783, in ibid., Kohn, "The Inside History," pp. 197, 197n.

52 Knox to McDougall, February 21, 1783, KP, reel 11.

53 See Kohn, "The Inside History," p. 204.

54 Diary of Robert Morris, February 13, 1783, *PRM*, 7:431.

55 Madison, Notes of Debates, February 20, 1783, *LD*, 19:719.

56 Madison to Edmund Randolph, February 25, 1783, in ibid., 19:733.

57 Madison, Notes of Debates, February 26, 1783, in ibid., 19:740.

58 Von Steuben to Knox, February 25, 1783, KP, reel 11.

59 On the evening of February 20, at a private dinner where nationalist sympathies ran high, Hamilton noted that "he knew Genl Washington intimately and perfectly, that his extreme reserve, mixed sometimes with a degree of asperity of temper both of which were said to have increased of late, had contributed to the decline of his popularity; but that his virtue, his patriotism and his firmness would it might be depended never yield to any dishonourable or disloyal plans into which he might be called; that he would sooner suffer himself to be cut into pieces." Madison, Notes of Debates, February 20, 1783, *LD*, 19:719.

Chapter Eleven

1 *JCC*, 23:726.

2 Madison, Notes, February 20, 1783, *LD*, 19:718.

3 Gates to Peters, February 20, 1783, HGP, reel 13.

4 Gates to his wife, January 17, 1783, in ibid.

5 Gates to GW, November 7, 1782, HGP, reel 13.

6 Gates to his wife, February 11, 1783, in ibid.

7 For a particularly critical view of Gates, see Dave R. Palmer, *George Washington and Benedict Arnold* (Washington: Regnery 2006), *passim*.

8 C. Edward Skeen, *John Armstrong Jr.* (Syracuse: Syracuse University Press, 1981), p. 3.

9 Pension Application of Banks (Barruck) Webb S40654, http://www.southerncampaign.org.pens40654, Maryland State Archives, Muster Rolls and Other Records of Service of Maryland Troops in the American Revolution, vol. 18, pp.155, 363, and 584. Accessed online October 12, 2009. Following the military practice of the time, it is possible that Richmond continued to act as an aide to Gates and stayed with him in Virginia and then accompanied him to New Windsor. Washington to Gates, August 27, 1782, *FW*, 25:68.

10 Official Register of the Officers and Men of New Jersey, http://www.njstatelib.org/ NJ; Francis B. Heitman, *Historical Register of Officers of the Continental Army* (Washington: Rare Book Publishing, 1914), p. 48; Information received from Library Society of the Cincinnati, typescript paragraph on back of photograph of portrait of

Richmond in library collection; Francis J. Sypher, Jr., *New York State Society of the Cincinnati Biographies of Original Members and Other Continental Officers* (Fishkill: New York State Society of the Cincinnati, 2004), p.15. Berg, p. 60; Wright, p. 167.

11 Speech of John Pope Hodnett given before United States Senate Committee on Education and Labor, May 21, 1886, Report 1313, 19th Congress, First Session, p. 39. Walter Stewart Orderly Book, online catalog description, American Philosophical Society. "Notes and Queries," *Pennsylvania Magazine of History and Biography* (1898), p. 382.

12 GW to von Steuben, February 18, 1783, FW, 26:143; Charles Willson Peale, "Mrs. Walter Stewart," Yale University Art Gallery, http://artgallery.yale.edu; obituary, "Walter Stewart," *Philadelphia Gazette and Universal Daily Advertiser*, June 6, 1796. Washington to Stewart, January 18, 1783, *FW*, 26:47.

13 The office of the inspector general had been created by Congress in February 1779. Congress appointed von Steuben to the post and granted considerable power to him directly and to his subordinates. *JCC*, 13:196; General Orders, July 5, 1781, GWLC.

14 The impact that the revolutionary experience had on young men such as the officers with Gates is examined in Stanley Elkins and Eric McKitrick, "The Founding Fathers: Young Men of the Revolution," *Political Science Quarterly* 76, no. 2 (June 1961), pp. 181–216.

15 After the war Stewart returned to Philadelphia, where he became a very successful merchant. He was a partner in ventures with Robert Morris and an investor in the bank of the United States as well as canals. He was also a holder of federal securities. Stewart obituary; Richard Kohn, "The Inside History of the Newburgh Conspiracy: America and the Coup d'Etat," *William and Mary Quarterly*, third series, 27 (April 1970), p. 205n; Forrest McDonald, *E. Pluribus Unum* (Boston: Houghton Mifflin, 1965), p. 27. For Stewart's views, see also Stewart to Gates, June 20, 1783, HGP, reel 13.

16 Gates to Armstrong, June 22, 1783, in George Bancroft, *History of the Formation of the Constitution of the United States* (New York: D. Appleton, 1883), 1:93.

17 Gouverneur Morris to Knox, February 7, 1783, *PRM*, 7:418.

18 Peters to Gates, March 5, 1783, HGP, reel 13.

19 GW to Jones, December 14, 1782, *FW*, 25:431.

20 Jones to Washington, February 27, 1783, *LD*, 19:746.

21 Hamilton to James Duane, September 6, 1780, *PAH*, 2:420; Broadus Mitchell, *Alexander Hamilton: Youth to Maturity, 1755–1788.* (New York: Macmillan, 1962), pp. 146–52. Hamilton had married the daughter of General Philip Schuyler, Gates's predecessor as commander of the northern army and an officer ill treated by Gates. He was firmly in the anti-Gates camp.

22 Although dated February 27, the letter did not leave Philadelphia until one or two days later. *LD*, 19:748n. Stewart's arrival came two days after the soldiers had lined up to get their weekly half crown. "The officers," however, according to Lieutenant Benjamin Gilbert, "got no pay as yet, and very little prospect of getting any at any period." Gilbert to his father, March 6, 1783, in John Shy, ed., *Winding Down: The Revolutionary War Letters of Lieutenant Benjamin Gilbert of Massachusetts, 1780–1783* (Ann Arbor: University of Michigan Press, 1989), p. 83.

23 GW to Hamilton, March 4, 1783, *FW*, 26:185. Brooks remains something of a mystery. See Gates to Pickering, May 19, 1783, and Pickering to Gates, May 28, 1783, both in HGP, reel 13. See Washington's comments about "the arrival of a certain Gentlemen from Phila in Camp." GW to Joseph Jones, March 12, 1783, *FW*, 26:213–16; GW to Hamilton, March 12, 1783, in ibid., 26:216–18.

24 GW to Hamilton, March 4, 1783, *FW*, 26:186.

25 For summaries and analysis, see Kohn, "The Inside History," *William and Mary Quarterly*, pp. 187–220; Paul David Nelson, with a rebuttal by Richard H. Kohn, "Horatio Gates at Newburgh, 1783: A Misunderstood Role," *William and Mary Quarterly*, third series, 29 (January 1972), pp. 143–55; C. Edward Skeen, "The Newburgh Conspiracy Reconsidered, with a Rebuttal by Richard H. Kohn," *William and Mary Quarterly*, third series, 31 (April 1974), pp. 273–98.

26 The evidence is clear that Armstrong was the principal author of the March 10 paper as well as the one on March 12. Logic suggests, however, that he sought advice from those around him, most likely including Richmond, Stewart, and Barber. To what degree he consulted Gates is uncertain. In addition to the officers mentioned, the names of Timothy Pickering and Dr. William Eustis, an army surgeon from Massachusetts, have been suggested as possibly being present. For evidence, most of it circumstantial, see: Pickering to wife, March 16, 1783, March 20, 1783, PP, reel 1; Gates to Armstrong, June 22, 1783. Bancroft, *History of the Formation of the Constitution of the United States of America*, 1:318; Pickering to Gates, May 28, 1783, HGP, reel 13. As the editors of the *PW* note (7:595–93h), there is a "discrepancy" in the surviving texts of the first "Address."

27 Pointed out to the author by Mike McGurty, historic guide, New Windsor Encampment, New York State Historic Site, during visit of April 16, 2010.

28 Armstrong's "Address" is printed in *JCC*, 24:295–97.

29 GW to Jones, March 12, 1783, *FW*, 26:214–15.

30 GW to Hamilton, March 12, 1783, in ibid., 26:216.

31 GW to Jones, March 12, 1783, in ibid., 26:215.

32 I am grateful to Michael McCurty for making this observation.

33 There is no documentary evidence to support this; however, given the previous roles these officers played and their closeness to Washington, it seems logical that their opinions would have been sought.

34 For Trumbull's service, see John W. Ifkovic, *Connecticut's Nationalist Revolutionary: Jonathan Trumbull, Jr.* (Hartford: American Revolution Bicentennial Commission of Connecticut, 1977), pp. 52–73.

35 *JCC*, 5:788–807. Article 1: "Whatsoever officer or soldier shall presume to use traitorous or disrespectful words against the authority of the United States in Congress assembled, or the legislature of any of the United States in which he may be quartered, if a commissioned officer, he shall be cashiered; if a non commissioned officer or soldier, he shall suffer such punishment as shall be inflicted upon him by the sentence of a court martial."

Article 3: "Any officer or soldier who shall begin, excite, cause or join, in any mutiny or sedition, in the troop, company, or regiment to which he belongs, or in any other troop or company in the service of the United States, or in any party, post, detachment of guard, on any pretence whatsoever, shall suffer death, or such other punishment as by a court martial shall be inflicted."

36 This, of course, is speculation, but given all that Washington knew and his suspicions of "old leven," he could have had little doubt that Gates's staff was involved.

37 General Order, March 11, 1783, *FW*, 26:208.

38 Since the report had been delivered more than a month before and its contents were well known, the officers must have thought that this summons was a bit late.

39 This distant attitude, of course, was precisely the behavior that had given rise to Hamilton's criticism.

40 GW to Jones, March 12, 1783, *FW*, 26:214; Washington to Hamilton, March 12, 1783, in ibid., 26:217.

41 GW to Jones, March 12, 1783, in ibid., 26:216.

42 Armstrong was certainly the principal author. Others may have helped, and again Gates must have been aware. See sources above as well as appendix 2, a statement by Rufus King concerning these events, in Charles R. King, ed., *The Life and Correspondence of Rufus King* (New York: G. P. Putnam, Sons, 1894), 1:621–22.

43 "To the Officers of the Army," *JCC*, 24:298–99.

44 While we cannot be certain about events at Hasbrouck House, it is clear from existing evidence that the daily routine was not altered. Trumbull was certainly involved, and it is not unlikely that Knox, Brooks, and perhaps others were consulted quietly.

45 The exact number present is uncertain; however, given Washington's orders that all general and field officers as well as a representative from each company be present, the total number could not have been less than one hundred.

46 I am indebted to Edward Lengel of the Washington Papers for confirming that this was the first time Washington addressed a general gathering of his officers in person.

47 Samuel Shaw to John Eliot, undated letter, probably May or April 1783, in Josiah Quincy, ed., *Journals of Samuel Shaw* (Boston: Wm Crosby and H. P. Nichols, 1847), pp. 103–4.

48 Ibid., p. 103.

49 Quotes from Washington's address are taken from Massachusetts Historical Society, *George Washington's Newburgh Address* (Boston: Massachusetts Historical Society, 1966).

50 I am grateful to Richard Miller, *In Words and Deeds: Battle Speeches in History* (Hanover, NH: University Press of New England, 2008) for providing a historical context within which to better appreciate this speech. For the "band of brothers" quote, see General Orders, April 6, 1778, *FW*, 11:224; GW to Anthony Wayne, September 6, 1780, in ibid., 20:2. He also used the quote after Newburgh. "Farewell Orders to the Armies of the United States," November 2, 1783, in ibid., 27:224.

51 Quincy, *Journals of Shaw*, p. 104. Some have suggested that Washington took his spectacles out earlier to read the "Address." This seems unlikely. The text of the Address at the Massachusetts Historical Society is in Washington's own hand. The script is large and quite legible. The "official copy of the Address is in the hand of Jonathan

Trumbull. It too is legible but in a much smaller hand. It is likely that Washington's personal copy of the Address is the one he read, while the Jones letter, written in a smaller and less familiar hand, is the one over which he stumbled. That he had not bothered to recopy the Jones letter in larger script may indicate that he decided only at the last moment to read it to the assembled officers, fearing that his speech had not had the desired effect. I am indebted to Mike Mccurty for this observation.

52 Schuyler to Stephen Van Rensselaer, March 17, 1783, in John Benson Lossing, *Life and Times of Philip Schuyler* (New York: Sheldon, 1873) 2:48.

53 In the Knox Papers there is a lengthy paper "B. Gen Rufus Putnam examination of certain anonymous paper March [14?] 1783." This paper appears to be a draft response to Armstrong's Address. If so, it supports the conclusion that Washington's response was a group effort and well planned. KP, reel 12.

54 *JCC*, 24:310

55 This too smacks of having been orchestrated. Before the Saturday meeting Putnam, apparently at Knox's request, prepared a lengthy analysis and rebuttal to the anonymous Address. "March [14?] 1783," KP, reel 12.

56 *JCC*, 24:310–11. J. A Wright to John Webb, March 16, 1783, *FW*, 26:229n. From this point on, Horatio Gates fades away. The next mention of him by the commander in chief is a simple reference in a General Order, April 16, 1783, in ibid., 26:328: "In the absence of Major General Gates Major Genl Heath will take the immediate command of the Army in this cantonment." Paul David Nelson, *General Horatio Gates* (Baton Rouge: Louisiana State University Press, 1976), pp. 276–77.

57 Pickering to his wife, March 16, 1783, March (20?), 1783, PP, reel 1.

58 Lossing, *Life and Times of Philip Schuyler*, 2:48.

59 Knox to McDougall, March 16, 1783, KP, reel 12.

60 Knox to Lincoln, March 16, 1783, BLP, reel 6A.

Chapter Twelve

1 *Boston Gazette*, March 24, 1783.

2 Arthur Lee to James Warren, March 12, 1783, *LMCC*, 7:77; Lee to GW, March 13, 1783, in ibid., 7:80.

3 GW to the President of Congress, March 18, 1783, *FW*, 26:229–32.

4 Ibid., p. 232.

5 *JCC*, 24:207. The deciding vote was cast by Eliphalet Dyer of Connecticut. A summary of this vote can be found in *PRM*, 7:395–96n. The vote on officers' pay may have actually taken place before Washington's letter was read. *LMCC*, 7:93n.

6 For a discussion of the issue, see *PRM*, 7:579–82n. The officers were to be paid "in money, or securities on interest at six per cent per annum." The value of the "securities" depended upon the ability of Congress to pay. *JCC*, March 22, 1783. Washington gave his own analysis of the situation. Washington to Bland, April 4, 1783, *FW*, 26:285–91.

7 *JCC*, 11:502; William H. Glasson, *Federal Military Pensions in the United States* (New York: Oxford University Press, 1918), p. 43.

8 *JCC*, 24:242.

9 Quoted in Janet Dempsey, *Washington's Last Cantonment* (Monroe, NY: Library Research Associates, 1990), p. 262.

10 Diary of William Smith, April 18, 1783, NYPL. I consulted both the manuscript diary (microfilm) as well as *Historical Memoir from 26 August 1778 to November 1783 of William Smith*, ed. W. H. W. Sabine (New York: Arno Press, 1971).

11 GW to the General Officers of the Army, April 17, 1783, *FW*, 26:328–29.

12 Dempsey, *Washington's Last Cantonment*, p. 162. Washington to President of Congress, April 18, 1783, *FW*, 26:330–34.

13 Edward C. Boynton, *General Orders of General Washington* (Harrison: Harbor Hill Books, 1973), pp. 78–80.

14 Several accounts of this occasion survive. None mention the presence of Washington.

15 Diary of Henry Sewall, April 19, 1783, MHS; John Armstrong to Gates, April 22, 1783, HGP, reel 13; Heath Memoirs, April 19, 1783. *The Complete Works of William Billings*, ed. H. N. S. Nathan and Richard Crawford (Boston: Colonial Society of Massachusetts, 1977), 2:244–55.

16 Armstrong to Gates, April 22, 1783, HGP, reel 13.

17 For soldiers' views, see Benjamin Gilbert to Father, June 6, 1783, in John Shy, ed., *Winding Down: The Revolutionary Letters of Lieutenant Benjamin Gilbert of Massachusetts, 1780–1783* (Ann Arbor, University of Michigan Press, 1989) pp. 106–7; Gilbert to Charles Bruce, June 10, 1783, in ibid., pp.107–8.

18 GW to Hamilton, April 22, 1783, *FW*, 26:351.

19 *JCC*, May 26, 1783.

20 Carleton to GW, April 6, 1783, *DAR*, 19:384.

21 Diary of William Smith, April 19, 1783, NYPL.

22 Ibid.

23 *New York Gazette*, September 29, 1783.

24 Carleton to Chevalier de Lavallette, April 16, 1783, CPNAC.

25 Carleton to Luzerne, March 19, 1783, in ibid. For a recent examination of prisoner of war treatment in the American Revolution, see Edwin C. Burrows, *Forgotten Patriots: The Untold Story of American Prisoners During the Revolutionary War* (New York: Basic Books, 2008).

26 Benjamin Lincoln denied that the Americans were preventing British prisoners from returning. With carefully chosen words he told Carleton "no prisoner is detained who wishes to return." Lincoln to Carleton, May 26, 1783, CPNAC.

27 Clinton to Benson, April 8, 1783, *PPGC*, 8:134–35.

28 Benson to Clinton April 17, 1783, in ibid., 8:141.

29 Ibid.

30 Ibid.

31 Ibid., p. 143.

32 Ibid., p. 144.

33 Livingston to Lafayette, May 1, 1783, in Stanley J. Idzerda, ed., *Lafayette in the Age of the American Revolution* (Ithaca: Cornell University Press, 1977), 5:128.

34 Scott to Clinton, April 19, 1783, *PPGC*, 8:148. Earlier Carleton himself had acknowledged that many Americans doubted his intent to depart. Carleton to Townshend, January 18, 1783, *DAR*, 19:366.

35 Thomas Townshend to Carleton, February 16, 1783, *DAR*, 21:156.

36 GW to Carleton, April 21, 1783, *FW*, 26:347.

37 Sabine, *Memoirs*, p. 584.

38 Carleton to GW, April 24, 1783, GWLC.

39 Christopher Ward, *The War of the Revolution* (New York: Macmillan, 1952), p. 617. Paul David Nelson, *Sir Charles Grey, First Earl Grey* (Madison, NJ: Fairleigh Dickinson University Press, 1996), pp. 41–46, 67–69.

40 A Journal of the Proceedings of H. M. S. *Perseverance*, ADM 51: Admiralty: Captains' Logs (1169–1853), British National Archives.

41 Smith later recounted the events of the meeting in his diary entry of May 9, 1983, NYPL. He refers to the smaller vessel as *Greyhound*. It was more likely *Viper*. J. J. Colledge, *Ships of the Royal Navy* (New York: Augustus Kelley, 1969), 1:244.

42 Journal of *Perseverance*, British National Archives.

43 Smith, Diary, May 9, 1783, NYPL. As chief of intelligence, Beckwith was the successor to the unfortunate Major John Andre.

44 Smith, Diary, May 9, 1783, NYPL.

45 Sabine, *Memoirs*, p. 585; Isabelle K. Savell, *Wine and Bitters* (New City, NY: Historical Society of Rockland County, 1975), pp. 5–56.

46 Sabine, *Memoirs*, p. 191.

47 Ibid., pp. 585–87.

48 Ibid., p. 585.

49 Ibid.

50 Ibid., p. 586.

51 Benjamin Quarles, *The Negro in the American Revolution* (Chapel Hill: University of North Carolina Press, 1961), pp. 163–67.

52 Proclamation by His Excellency Sir Henry Clinton," June 30, 1779, in *Royal Gazette*, July 28, 1779. This proclamation is frequently referred to as the Philipsburg Proclamation.

53 *PPGC*, 8:166; Sabine, *Memoirs*, p. 586.

54 General Order, April 15, 1783, CPNAC.

55 Carleton was true to his word and did keep a list. "Book of Negroes, April 23–November 30," CPNAC; see also http://www.blackloyalist.com/canadiandigi talcollection/documents/official/book_of_negroes.htm.

56 Washington to Daniel Parker, April 28, 1783, *FW*, 26:364.

57 "Substance of a Conference Between General Washington and Sir Guy Carleton," May 6, 1783, in ibid., 26:404.

58 GW to Harrison, May 6, 1783, in ibid., 26:401.

59 Carleton gave the order to withdraw from Westchester County on May 12, 1783. Carleton to Clinton, May 12, 1783, *PPGC*, 8:176.

60 Carleton to Clinton May 13, 1783, in ibid., 8:176.

61 GW to Commissioners, May 8, 1783, *FW*, 26:412–14.

62 Smith, Diary, May 9, 1783, NYPL.

63 Some have suggested that the nickname "Black Sam" belonged to an African Amer-
    ican. Evidence is lacking. I am grateful to Suzanne Prabucki, curator of Fraunces
    Tavern, for this information. Located at the corner of Broad and Pearl streets, the
    tavern was a favorite resort of British officers. Sabine, *Memoirs*, p. 271.

64 GW to President of Congress, May 8, 1783, *FW*, 26:411.

65 GW to Carleton, May 6, 1783, in ibid., 26:408–9; Clinton to Carleton, May 7, 1783,
    PPGC, 5:165–68.

66 Journal of *Perseverance*, May 8, 1783.

67 Sabine, *Memoir*, p. 588.

68 GW to President of Congress, May 8, 1783, *FW*, 26:411; Smith, Diary, May 9, 1783,
    NYPL.

69 Carleton at first wanted to provide an immediate answer, but Smith persuaded him to
    wait. Although the loyalists generally liked Carleton, they suspected that he, like
    other British officers, might be inclined to give the Americans concessions at loyalist
    expense. Smith wanted more time to properly consider the response to the letters.
    Smith, Diary, May 9, 1783, NYPL.

70 Despite legitimate suspicion that Carleton was feigning illness to avoid the meeting,
    the general seems to have been actually ill. Colonel William Bayard to Major John
    Beckwith, May 9, 1783, CPNAC; Washington to President of Congress, May 8,
    1783, *FW*, 26:411.

71 GW to Carleton, May 6, 1783, *FW*, 26:408–9.

72 Clinton to Carleton, May 7, 1783, *PPGC*, 8:165–68.

73 GW to Benson, Smith, and Parker, May 8, 1783, *FW*, 26:412–14; Sabine, *Memoir*,
    p. 588. Smith later married John Adams's daughter Abigail.

74 Sabine, *Memoirs*, p. 589.

75 Lord North to Carleton, April 19, 1783, DAR, 19:391. Also contributing to the deci-
    sion was the fact that Grey was reluctant to take command. *Guide To British Head-
    quarters Papers*, CPNAC, 4:v.

76 Sabine, *Memoirs*, p. 591.

77 Digby to Townshend, May 23, 1783, *DAR*, 19:396.

78 GW to Lafayette, May 10, 1783, *FW*, 26:421.

79 Knox to Washington, May 14, 1783, KP, reel 12.

80 Armstrong to Gates, May 9, 1783, HGP, reel 13. C. Edward Skeen, *John Armstrong,
    Jr. 1758–1843: A Biography* (Syracuse: Syracuse University Press, 1981), p. 19.

81 Christopher Richmond to Gates, May 29, 1783, HGP, reel 13.

82 GW to Knox, May 14, 1783, *FW*, 26:430.

83 Dempsey, *Washington's Last Cantonment*, p. 195.

84 GW to Lieutenant Colonel William Smith, May 15, 1783, *FW*, 26:433–35; Frank Griz-
    zard, *George! A Guide to All Things Washington* (Buena Vista, VA: Mariner, 2005), p.
    103.

85 Lieutenant Colonel Smith to GW, May 20, 1783, *FW*, 26:434n.

86 Mayeur to GW, March 2, 1783, GWLC.

87 GW to Smith, May 15, 1783, *FW*, 26:434.

88 Mayeur attended the general several times. See Mayeur to GW, July 1, 1783, July 16, 1783, GWLC; GW to Mayeur, July 16, 1783, *FW*, 27:67–68.

89 Madison to Edmund Randolph, May 13, 1783, *LD*, 20:248.

90 GW to Smith, May 21, 1783, *FW*, 26:449–50.

91 GW to Smith, May 15, 1783, in ibid., 26:435; GW to John Pintard, May 21, 1783, in ibid., 26:448; GW to Smith, May 21, 1783, in ibid., 26:449–50; GW to John Searle & Company, May 21, 1783, in ibid., 26:450–51; GW to Parker, June 18, 1783, in ibid., 27:20–21.

92 Marcus Hunemorder, *The Society of the Cincinnati: Conspiracy and Distrust in Early America* (New York: Berghahn Books, 2006), p. 14. That St. Louis was chosen as patron may be derived from the French Order of St. Louis (Ordre Royal et Militaire de Saint Louis) founded by Louis XIV in 1693. Several French officers who served in America were members of the order.

93 Society of the Cincinnati Web site, http://www.societyofthecincinnati.org, accessed July 25, 2009.

94 For development of this thesis, see Stanley Elkins and Eric McKitrick, "The Founding Fathers: Young Men of the Revolution," *Political Science Quarterly* 76, no.1 (June 1961), pp. 181–216.

95 Christopher Richmond to Gates, May 29, 1783, HGP, reel 13.

96 Conrad Wright, *The Transformation of Charity in Post-Revolutionary New England* (Boston: Northeastern University, 1992), pp. 13–47.

97 Osgood to Adams, December 14, 1783, *LMCC*, 7:416.

98 Aedanus Burke, *Considerations on the Society of the Cincinnati* (Hartford: Basil Webster, 1783), p. 4; Hunemorder, *The Society of the Cincinnati*, pp. 25–30.

Chapter Thirteen

1 General Orders, June 2, 1783, *FW*, 26:463–65. General Nathanael Greene furloughed the remnants of his army as well. Since the British had evacuated the South, his challenges were far simpler than those facing Washington. Benjamin Lincoln to Greene, May 28, 1783, *PNG*, 13:13–15, Greene to President of Congress Elias Boudinot, October 7, 1783, in ibid., 13:137.

2 Gilbert to Father, June 6, 1783, in *Winding Down: The Revolutionary War Letters of Lieutenant Benjamin Gilbert, 1780–1783*, ed. by John Shy (Ann Arbor: University of Michigan Press, 1989), p. 106.

3 Charles H. Lesser, ed., *The Sinews of Independence: Monthly Strength Reports of the Continental Army* (Chicago: University of Chicago Press, 1976), pp. 250–54.

4 Pickering to wife, June 5, 1783, and Pickering to Samuel Hodgdon, June 7, 1783, both PP, reel 34.

5 "Circular Letter to the States," June 8, 1783, *FW*, 26:483–96. Washington had sent several circular letters since 1777. His previous letters, however, had usually confined themselves to urging states to send forth supplies and soldiers.

6 See, for example, *Connecticut Courant*, September 9, 1783; *Vermont Gazette*, July 31, 1783; and *Salem Gazette*, July 24, 1783. This document, and Washington's "Farewell Address" delivered at the end of his presidency, may be his two greatest state papers.

7 Randolph to Madison, June 28, 1783, *FW*, 26:491n.

8 Howell to Nicholas Brown, July 30, 1783, *LD*, 20:484.

9 Stewart to Gates, June 20, 1783, HGP, reel 13; Virginia Delegates to Benjamin Harrison, July 27, 1783, *LD*, 20:466n.

10 Stephen Higginson to Samuel Adams, May 20, 1783, *LD*, 20:260, 266.

11 Boudinot to Governors, June 3, 1783, in ibid., 20:298.

12 Izard to Arthur Middleton, May 30, 1783, in ibid., 20:287. Armstrong's role in the mutiny is clouded. He may have conspired with the leaders, seeing a second Newburgh. The evidence is suggestive but inconclusive. Mary A. Y. Gallagher, "Reinterpreting the 'Very Trifling Mutiny' at Philadelphia in June 1783," *Pennsylvania Magazine of History and Biography* 119, nos. 1–2 (January–April 1995), p. 34. See also a curious reference to Armstrong in William Clagon to Horatio Gates, June 23, 1783, HGP, reel 13.

13 James Madison's Notes of Debates, June 21, 1783, *LD*, 20:351.

14 The memory of the Congress's flight because local authorities neglected to protect the members would be remembered in the new republic when the District of Columbia was created to be governed directly by Congress.

15 Armstrong to Gates, June (?), 1783, HGP, reel 13.

16 Instructions to Major General Robert Howe, June 25, 1783, *FW*, 27:35–36.

17 Benjamin Hawkins to Governor of North Carolina, June 24, 1783, *LMCC*, 7:199.

18 Eleazer McComb to Nicholas Van Dyke, June 30, 1783, *LD*, 20:379; Charles Thomson to Hannah Thomson, July 4, 1783, in ibid., 20:397.

19 GW to President of Congress, June 18, 1783, *FW*, 27:20. The trip apparently put a strain on Martha's health. GW to George William Fairfax, July 10, 1783, in ibid., 27:60.

20 GW to Schuyler, July 15, 1783, in ibid., 27:65.

21 GW to President of Congress, July 16, 1783, in ibid., 27:70; Washington's itinerary can also be followed in his expense account, George Washington's Family, August 5, 1783, Revolutionary War Accounts, Vouchers and Receipted Accounts, GWLC.

22 Franklin to Robert R. Livingston, April 27, 1783, www.yale.edu/franklinpapers. Accessed July 20, 2010.

23 Elizabeth Cometti, ed. and trans., *Seeing America and Its Great Men: The Journal and Letters of Count Francesco dal Verme, 1783–84* (Charlottesville: University Press of Virginia, 1969), p.12. For Washington's high opinion of the count, see GW to General John Sullivan, August 4, 1783, *FW*, 27:79 and note 24.

24 Cometti, *dal Verme*, p. 12.

25 GW to the Chevalier de Chastellux, October 12, 1783, *FW*, 27:190.

26 Ibid., p.189.

27 GW to Dr. Hugh Williamson, March 31, 1784, *FW*, 27:377–81.

28 Governor Clinton's nephew DeWitt would fulfill that promise with the building of the Erie Canal.

29 GW to Chastellux, October 12, 1783, *FW*, 27:190.

30 GW to Clinton, November 25, 1784, in ibid., 27:501; *The Papers of George Washington, Retirement Series*, Dorothy Twohig, et al., ed. (Charlottesville: University Press of Virginia, 1999), 4:485, 516, 524n.

31 GW to John Sullivan, August 4, 1783, *FW*, 27:79.

32 The trip was an ordeal, but the commander in chief came through well. Whatever impression he might have wished to leave on March 15 (that is, taking out his glasses), he proved he was physically fit.

33 Elias Boudinot to Washington, July 31, 1783, *LD*, 20:487.

34 GW to McHenry, August 6, 1783, *FW*, 27:82.

35 On the same day that he wrote to McHenry, Washington also wrote to Quartermaster General Timothy Pickering chastising him for spending too much time away from the army. GW to Pickering, August 6, 1783, in ibid., 27:81.

36 David Howell to Thomas G. Hazard, August 26, 1783, *LD*, 20:595.

37 McHenry to GW, August 11, 1783, in ibid., 20:538–39.

38 *JCC*, 24:494–95. Congress's statue never materialized. Virginia did better. On June 22, 1783, the House of Delegates resolved to "procure a marble statue of General Washington 'to be of the finest Marble and best Workmanship.'" As a result, Jean-Antoine Houdon's life-size statue stands today at the Virginia State Capitol.

39 Howell to Hazard, August 26, 1783, *LD*, 20:594.

40 During the Revolution Washington kept his headquarters at 169 locations. http:// gwpapers.virginia.edu/documents/revolution/itinerary/index.html. Accessed May 16, 2010. The widow's husband, Judge John Berrien, committed suicide by jumping into the nearby Millstone River on April 22, 1772. http://www.dennisberrien.com/StoriesJudgeJ.html. Accessed May 16, 2010.

41 Ibid.; Charles Thomson to Hannah Thomson, August 27, 1783, *LD*, 20:599.

42 http://www.dennisberrien.com/StoriesJudgeJ.html. Accessed May 16, 2010. Mrs. Berrien had apparently moved into her home in Princeton. *Independent Gazetteer*, November 11, 1783.

43 Charles Thomson to Hannah Thomson, August 27, 1783, *LD*, 20:599.

44 *JCC*, 24:521

45 Knox was particularly unhappy. His request for pay had been rejected by Benjamin Lincoln, the secretary at war, and Congress was slow in determining the status of the army at West Point. Knox to General Robert Howe, August 21, 1783, and Knox to R. T. Paine, August 22, 1783, both KP, reel 13. On the same day that he wrote to Lincoln, the secretary resigned his post. Knox to Benjamin Lincoln, August 1, 1783, BLP, reel 17. General Frederick Haldimand, the British commander in Canada, was uncooperative. Pickering to his wife, August 25, 1783, PP, reel 1; Knox to GW, August 26, 1783, KP, reel 13.

46 "Observations on an Intended Report of a Committee of Congress on a Peace Establishment, September 8, 1783," *FW*, 27:140–44; GW to James Duane, September 7, 1783, in ibid., 27:133–40.

47 GW to Duane, September 7, 1783, in ibid., 27:134.

48 GW to von Steuben, March 15, 1784, in ibid., 27:360.

49 GW to Hamilton, May 2, 1783, and "Sentiments on Peace Establishment," in ibid., 26:374–98.

50 GW to Morris, August 12, 1783, in ibid., 27:98.

51 Robert Dalzell and Lee Baldwin Dalzell, *George Washington's Mount Vernon: At Home in Revolutionary America* (New York: Oxford University Press, 1998), pp. 113–15.

52 GW to Parker, September 12, 1783, *FW*, 27:150. By Orange Town, Washington was most likely referring to the meeting at Tappan the previous May.

53 GW to Robert and William Lewis, September 6, 1783, *FW*, 27:132.

54 Monroe H. Fabian, *Joseph Wright: American Artist, 1756–1793* (Washington: National Portrait Gallery, 1985), pp. 22–38.

55 Thomson to GW, August 28, 1783, *LD*, 20:602.

56 Fabian, *Joseph Wright*, p. 45; Washington to Comte de Solms, January 3, 1784, *FW*, 27:291.

57 Hugh Howard, *The Painter's Chair: George Washington and the Making of American Art* (New York: Bloomsbury, 2009), pp. 13–14.

58 Elkanah Watson, *Men and Times of the Revolution* (New York: Dana, 1856), p. 139. While there is no doubt about the painting, there is some question as to whether Wright actually did a cast of Washington's face at Rockingham. The evidence seems to suggest that he did; in any case, the procedure described was common at the time and would have been the process used by Wright. Jean Antoine Houdon did a cast of Washington at Mount Vernon in 1785 using this process. Fabian, *Joseph Wright*, pp. 50–51n.

59 David Howell to William Greene, September 9, 1783, *LD*, 20:646.

60 Ibid., 647.

61 Ibid.

62 Franklin to Livingston, April 15, 1783, http://www.yale.edu/franklinpapers. Accessed July 20, 2010.

63 Charles Thomson to Hannah Thomson, October 13, 1783, *LD*, 21:52.

64 *JCC*, 25:701–2. Greene "retired" to a plantation in Georgia given to him by the state. He died there on June 19, 1786. There is no evidence that the cannon ever arrived. *PNG*, 13:171n.

65 GW to Morris, October 6, 1783, *FW*, 27:179; Patricia Brady, *Martha Washington: An American Life* (New York: Viking, 2005), pp. 143–44.

Chapter Fourteen

1 Quoted in "Guy Carleton," *DCB* online.

2 "Intelligence," F. Michaels to Major Beckwith, October 4, 1783, CPNAC.

3 Lord North to Carleton, December 5, 1783, *DAR*, 19:454.

4 Carleton to North, June 2, 1783, in ibid., 19:403–4.

5 Carleton to North, June 6, 1783, in ibid., 19:405; Lieutenant Colonel William Smith to GW, August 31, 1783, *FW*, 27:126n.

6 To "All Adherents to the British Government and Followers of the British Army Commonly Called Tories," August 15, 1783 (Poughkeepsie: Morton and Horner, 1783). "Brutus" was a common pen name often used by patriot writers.

7 Carleton to North, June 6, 1783, *DAR*, 19:405; Carleton to North, June 15, 1783, in ibid., 19:409; Carleton to North, June 21, 1783, in ibid., 19:411; Carleton to Clinton, July 25, 1783, and "Intelligence," August 11, 1783, both CPNAC; Carleton to Boudinot, August 17, 1783, DAR, 19:431; James Cook, "Information Before William Smith," September 16, 1783, CPNAC.

8 In this decision Carleton was supported by the government at home. North to Carleton, August 8, 1783, *DAR*, 19:426.

9 Smith to GW, July 15, 1783, GWLC.

10 Smith to GW, August 26, 1783, in ibid.

11 Ron Chernow, *Alexander Hamilton* (New York: Penguin, 2004), pp. 194–96.

12 Hamilton to Robert R. Livingston, August 13, 1783, *PAH*, 3:431–32.

13 *Rivington's Royal Gazette*, August 29, 1783. Some may have remembered the great fire of September 20–21, 1776, which destroyed a good part of the city. Although there is no evidence, suspicion of arson turned toward the American forces evacuating the city. Thomas Jones, *History of New York During the Revolutionary War* (New York: New York Historical Society, 1879), 2:120.

14 *New York Gazette*, September 29, 1783.

15 Carleton to North, July 11, 1783, CPNAC.

16 Richard B. Morris, *The Peacemakers: The Great Powers and American Independence* (New York: Harper and Row, 1965), pp. 435–37.

17 Ibid., p. 435.

18 Henry Laurens of South Carolina was also a commissioner, but at the time of the signing he was in London.

19 http://avalon.law.yale.edu/18th_century/paris.asp. Altogether the Treaty of Paris contained ten articles. A separate secret article, agreed to by the United States and Great Britain, gave to the latter additional territory in West Florida if "at the Conclusion of the present war" British forces were "in possession of West Florida."

20 Elbridge Gerry to John Adams, November 13, 1783, *LD*, 21:157; Samuel Osgood to Henry Knox, November 24, 1783, BLP, reel 7.

21 *Boston Evening Post*, November 1, 1783; *Newport Mercury*, November 1, 1783; *Providence Gazette*, November 1, 1783; *Pennsylvania Evening Post*, November 1, 1783.

22 "Farewell Orders to the Armies of the United States," November 2, 1783, *FW*, 27:222–27. In the "Farewell" Washington once again referred to a "band of brothers."

23 Although there is no direct evidence that Humphreys was on leave, I conclude this from the fact that between September 8 and November 7 Jonathan Trumbull Jr. seems also to have been absent. Washington's letters were drafted by his other secretaries, David Cobb and Benjamin Walker, *FW*, 27:144, 234.

24 "Farewell Orders," November 2, 1783, *FW*, 27:225.

25 http://gwpapers.virginia.edu/documents/revolution/itinerary/all.html.

26 GW to John Hancock, August 13, 1776, *FW*, 5:426–27.

27 General Orders, March 11, 1776, in ibid., 4:388.

28 *JCC*, 19:368; Washington to Varick, May 25, 1781, GWLC.

29 George Washington Papers: Provenance and Publication History, http://memory .loc.gov/ammem/gwhtml/gwabout.html; Tappan was Governor George Clinton's brother-in-law; Varick to Washington, July 19, 1781, GWLC.

30 GW to Parker, May 15, 1783, *FW*, 26:435.

31 GW to Howe, November 9, 1783, in ibid., 27:238.

32 Ibid.

33 Pickering to his wife, November 12, 1783, PP, reel 1.

34 "Address to His Excellency General Washington Commander in Chief of the Armies of the United States of America," November 15, 1783, GWLC.

35 *JCC*, 25:714

36 For a description of the tenor of debate over this issue, see Chares Thomson to Hannah Thomson, October 20, 1783, *LD*, 21:82–84 and same October 21, 1783, in ibid., 21:86–88. Kenneth R. Bowling, *The Creation of Washington, D.C. The Idea and Location of the American Capital* (Fairfax, VA: George Mason University Press, 1991), pp. 49–57. The date for reconvening proved to be absurdly optimistic. A quorum did not appear in Congress until January 14, 1784. Edmund C Burnett, *The Continental Congress* (New York: W.W. Norton, 1941), pp. 593–95.

37 GW to James Duane, November 15, 1783, *FW*, 27:241; "Orders Relating to the Withdrawal of the British Troops from the Various Parts in New York and Vicinity, Memoranda from Maj'r Beckwith," *PPGC*, 8:285–86.

38 For threats of violence, see Carleton to Clinton, November 19, 1783, *PPGC*, 8:282–83 and "Additional Information Concerning Evacuation Day Plots," November 18, 1783, in ibid., 8:284–85.

39 When American forces reoccupied Philadelphia in June 1778, Congress authorized Washington to secure the city. He gave the task to Benedict Arnold. *JCC*, 11:571; GW to Arnold, June 19, 1778, *FW*, 12:94–95.

40 Carleton to North, November 22, 1783, *DAR*, 19:451; Digby to North, November 25, 1783, in ibid., 19:452.

41 Elliott to Scott, November 17, 1783, and Elliott to Carleton, November 15, 1783, both CPNAC.

42 Timothy Pickering to Samuel Hodgdon, November 16, 1783, PP, reel 34.

43 Ibid.

44 Near 126th Street and Eighth Avenue—Frederick Douglass Boulevard.

45 Von Krafft's Journal, quoted in I. N. Phelps Stokes, *The Iconography of Manhattan Island* (reprint, New York: Arno Press, 1967), 5:1173.

46 Stokes, *Iconography*, 5:1172.

47 Ibid.

48 The "barrier" was located near the junction of the Bowery and Third Avenue. Ibid., 5:1173.

49 Carleton to GW, November 24, 1783, in Jared Sparks, ed., *Writings of George Washington* (Boston: American Stationers, 1835), 8:547.

50 "Orders to the Light Infantry of the American Army . . . from Orderly Book of Lt. Silas Morton," New York Historical Society.

51 James Riker, "Evacuation Day 1783" (New York: printed for the author, 1883), p 10. Washington rode two horses during the Revolution, Nelson (a sorrel) and Blue Skin. From this description it is likely that he was riding Blue Skin for his entrance into New York. The Papers of George Washington, http://gwpapers.virginia.edu/proj ect/faq/govern.html.

52 Stokes, *Iconography*, 5:1173.

53 Ibid., 5:1174.

54 Ibid., 5:1171.

55 Riker, "Evacuation Day," p. 10.

56 Ibid., p.14–16.

57 Given that Samuel Fraunces had spent the entire occupation in New York and that his tavern had been a well-known resort for British officers, some suspected his commitment to the patriot cause. Perhaps a bit nervous about his postwar future, Fraunces asked Washington for a letter testifying to his patriotism. Washington complied, writing, "You have invariably through the most trying Times, maintained a constant friendship and Attention to the Cause of our Country, and its Independence and Freedom." GW to Fraunces, August 18, 1783, *FW*, 27:111.

58 Riker, "Evacuation Day," pp. 18–19.

59 A reference to the French king.

60 In September 1783 Congress had ratified a treaty with Sweden, *JCC*, 25:613–14.

61 Orderly Book of Lieutenant Silas Morton, New York Historical Society.

62 Riker, "Evacuation Day," p. 20.

63 Ibid.

64 Broadside, December 2 1783, printed at the State Printing Office, no. 47, Hanover Square.

65 For a sample of addresses presented to Washington, see *FW*, 27:249–58.

66 Carleton to Washington, December 1, 1783, in ibid., 27:254n.

67 Benjamin Tallmadge, *Memoir of Col. Benjamin Tallmadge* (New York: Thomas Holman, 1858), p. 61.

68 Ibid., p. 63. There is some question as to whether or not Washington actually stayed at Fraunces. The evidence seems to support the conclusion that he was not a guest at the tavern. Fraunces Tavern curator to author, March 22, 2010; Benjamin Walker, December 27, 1783, Revolutionary War Accounts, Vouchers and Receipted Accounts 2, GWLC. This document is extremely difficult to read and interpret. Stuart Murray, *Washington's Farewell to His Officers* (Bennington, VT.: Images from the Past, 1999), pp. 226–27.

69 One New York officer not present was Alexander Hamilton.

70 Congress was no longer sitting in Philadelphia, so no representative to the body was present to greet Washington.

71 *Pennsylvania Packet*, December 9, 1783.

72 GW to James McHenry, December 10, 1783, *FW*, 27:266.

73 *Pennsylvania Packet*, December 23, 1783.

74 Howell to William Greene, December 24, 1783, *LD*, 21:227–28.

75 Ibid., p.228.

76 Hugh Williamson to William Blount, December 5, 1783, *LD*, 21:183.

77 Jefferson to Benjamin Harrison, December 17, 1783, in ibid., 21:205.

78 Ellery to Huntington, December 19, 1783, in ibid., 21:213.

79 *Annals of Annapolis* (Baltimore: Cushing, 1841) gives the arrival date as "Friday, the 17th December" (p. 209). Since Friday fell on the nineteenth, this appears to be an error.

80 Elihu Samuel Riley, *"The Ancient City": A History of Annapolis, in Maryland, 1649–1887* (Annapolis: Record Printing Office, 1887), p. 201.

81 GW to President of Congress, *FW*, 27:277–78.

82 *JCC*, 25:818–19. This may have been a parliamentary maneuver. Should the resolution not have passed, Ellery, as a member of the majority, could ask for reconsideration. Should he have voted yes and the motion lost, he could not ask for reconsideration.

83 Calvin Jillson and Rick K. Wilson, *Congressional Dynamics: Structure, Coordination, and Choice in the First American Congress, 1774–1789* (Stanford: Stanford University Press, 1994), pp. 139–42.

84 Julian Boyd, et al., ed., *The Papers of Thomas Jefferson* (Princeton: Princeton University Press, 1951), 6: editorial note, pp. 402–9. Boyd suggests that McHenry was, in his own words, "on a rack of suspense" by his upcoming marriage to Margaret Caldwell and that therefore he was of little use.

85 James Tilton to Gunning Bedford, December 25, 1783, *LD*, 21:232.

86 Later Mrs. James MacCubbin. William S. Baker, *Itinerary of General Washington from June 15, 1775, to December 23, 1783* (Philadelphia: J. B. Lippincott, 1892), p. 320.

87 Tilton to Bedford, December 25, 1783, *LD*, 21:232.

88 GW to von Steuben, December 23, 1783, *FW*, 27:283.

89 Burnett, *The Continental Congress*, p. 284.

90 Tilton to Bedford, December 25, 1783, *LD*, 21:232.

91 "Report of a Committee on Arrangements for the Public Audience," December 22, 1783 in Boyd, *The Papers of Thomas Jefferson*, 6:409; *JCC*, 25:837–38.

92 The speech was 341 words. "Address to Congress on Resigning His Commission," December 23, 1783, *FW*, 27:284–85. It is not clear from surviving accounts whether Washington read his speech or spoke from memory. He most likely read it. There is no mention of whether or not he was wearing glasses.

93 McHenry to Margaret Caldwell, December 23, 1783, *LD*, 21:221.

94 Ibid.

95 Ibid., 221.

96 Ibid.

97 Boyd, *Papers of Jefferson*, 6:407.

98 Washington and his companions may have stayed in Georgetown to await taking the ferry across the Potomac in the morning. Stanley Weintraub, *General Washington's Christmas Farewell* (New York: Free Press, 2003), pp. 165–66. Washington's precise homeward itinerary is unknown.

99 Jacky's widow, Eleanor Calvert Custis, had four children. After the death of her husband she lived for a time at Mount Vernon but then went to live at the Custis plantation, Abington, not far from Mount Vernon. Because she was not always in the best of health, the Washingtons agreed to care for her two youngest children, Nellie and Wash. Although they never formally adopted them, for all intents and purposes these two children became the Washingtons' adopted family. The widowed Eleanor remarried in the fall of 1783; her new husband was a local doctor, David Stuart. Patricia Brady, *Martha Washington: An American Life* (New York: Viking, 2005), pp.146–49. Ronald Reagan Washington National Airport occupies much of what was once Abington.

100 Quoted in Weintraub, *General Washington's Christmas Farewell*, p. 170.

101 GW to Charles Thomson, January 22, 1784, *FW*, 27:312.

102 Mount Vernon Web site, http://www.mountvenon.org/visit/plan/index.cfm/pid/355. Accessed June 25, 2010.

103 Ibid.

Epilogue

1 Samuel Osgood to John Adams, January 14, 1783, *LD*, 21:276–77.

2 Edmund C. Burnett, *Continental Congress* (New York: W.W. Norton, 1941), p. 593. Richard Beresford, for example, a South Carolina delegate, rose from his sickbed to attend.

3 *JCC*, 25:689–90.

4 GW to Benjamin Harrison, January 18, 1784, *GWCS* 1:57.

5 GW to Samuel Vaughan, January 14, 1784, in ibid., 1:45.

6 GW to William Hamilton, January 15, 1784, in ibid., 1:48.

7 GW to Mary Ball Washington, February 15, 1787, in ibid., 5:35.

8 Malcolm Freiberg, "The Reverend William Gordon's Autumn Tour of the Northeast," *New England Quarterly* 65 (September 1992), p. 470.

9 GW to Gordon, October 23, 1782, GWLC.

10 Gordon to GW, February 26, 1783, June 18, 1783, and August 13, 1783, in ibid.

11 GW to Gordon, May 8, 1784 *GWCS*, 1:377.

12 *JCC*, 27:427–28.

13 Merrill Jensen, *The New Nation: A History of the United States During the Confederation, 1781–1789* (New York: Alfred A. Knopf, 1965), p. 98. Gordon's work resulted in his *The History of the Rise, Progress, and Establishment of the Independence of the United States of America*, 3 vols. (New York: Samuel Campbell, 1794).

14 Morris to GW, April 17, 1785, *GWCS*, 2:507.

15 GW to Francis Hopkinson, May 16, 1785, in ibid., 2:562.

16 Pine to GW, December 16, 1785, in ibid., 3:460–61n.

17 Richard Henry Lee to GW, May 3, 1785, in ibid., 2:532.

18 Catherine Macaulay, *The History of England from the Accession of James I to That of the Brunswick Line*, 5 vols. (London: J. Nourse, 1763–83); GW to Richard Henry Lee, June 22, 1785, *GWCS*, 3:71.

19 GW to Knox, June 18, 1785, *GWCS*, 3:63.

20 GW to Knox, February 28, 1785, in ibid., 2: 399–400.

21 Thomas Stone to GW, January 28, 1785, in ibid., 2:297n.

22 Quoted in Kate Rowland, *The Life of George Mason, 1725–1792* (New York: G. Putnam's Sons, 1892), 2:93.

23 By this time Congress had moved to New York City.

24 GW to Lafayette, May 10, 1786, *GWCS*, 4:42.

25 GW to Fitzgerald, September 9, 1780, in ibid., 4:241–42.

26 Although signed by Dickinson, the report was written by Hamilton. *JCC, 30:677–*
80. James Madison was also present at Annapolis.

27 Ibid., 32:74.

28 GW to Randolph, March 28, 1787 *GWCS*, 5:113.

29 Knox to GW, March 19, 1787, in ibid., 5:95–98.

30 GW to Randolph, March 28, 1787, in ibid., 5:113.

31 *The Records of the Federal Convention of 1787*, ed. Max Farrand (New Haven: Yale University Press, 1911), 1:3–4.

32 Ibid., 1:4.

33 Morris to GW, October 30, 1787, *GWCS*, 5:400.

34 Ibid.

35 Pierce Butler to Weedon Butler, May 5, 1788, Max Farrand, ed., *The Records of the Federal Convention of 1787* (New Haven: Yale University Press, 1911), 3:302.

36 *Journal of the Senate of the United States*, April 6, 1789.

37 Thomson had taken the post at the First Continental Congress and did not resign until July 23, 1789.

38 Knox to GW, March 23, 1789, *The Papers of George Washington, Presidential Series* Dorothy Twohig, et al., ed. (Charlottesville: University Press of Virginia, 1987) 209.

39 Address to Charles Thomson, April 14, 1789, in ibid., 2:57n.

Manuscript Sources

Boston Public Library
American Revolution manuscripts
1152, 1182, 1188

British National Archives
ADM 51: Admiralty: Captains'
Logs (1169–1853)
ADM 52: Admiralty: Masters' Logs
(1672–1840)

Clements Library, University of
Michigan
Shelburne Papers

Library and Archives Canada
Carleton Papers (British Headquarters Papers/Microfilm)

Massachusetts Historical Society
Benjamin Lincoln Papers
Henry Knox Papers (microfilm)
Timothy Pickering Papers

New York Historical Society
Horatio Gates Papers

New York Public Library
Historical Memoir of the Province of
New York, 1780–83 (Smith Diary)
Orderly Book of Lieutenant Silas
Morton

Books and Journal Articles

Adams, John. *Papers of John Adams*. Ed., Gregg Lint et al. 15 vols., in progress. Cam-
bridge: Harvard University Press, 1977.
Adams, John. *The Works of John Adams*. Ed., Charles Francis Adams. 10 vols. Boston:
Little, Brown, 1850–56.

Adams, Samuel. *Writings of Samuel Adams*. Ed. Harry A. Cushing, 4 vols. Reprint, New York: Octagon Books, 1968.

Annals of Annapolis. Baltimore: Cushing, 1841.

Anthony, Walter C. *Washington's Headquarters, Newburgh, New York: A History of Its Construction and Its Various Occupants*. Newburgh: Newburgh Historical Society, 1928.

Baker, William S. *Itinerary of General Washington from June 15, 1775 to December 23, 1783*. Philadelphia: J. B. Lippincott, 1892.

Balderston, Marion, and David Syrett, eds. *The Lost War: Letters from British Officers During the American Revolution*. New York: Horizon Press, 1975.

Bancroft, George. *History of the Formation of the Constitution of the United States*. 2 vols. New York: D. Appleton, 1883.

Barck, Theodore. O. *New York City During the War for Independence*. Reprint, Port Washington, NY: I. J. Friedman, 1966.

Barnes, Viola. "Francis Legge, Governor of Loyalist Nova Scotia," 1773–1776," *New England Quarterly* 4, no. 3 (1931), pp. 420–47.

Barbé-Marbois, François. *Our Revolutionary Forefathers: The Letters of François Barbé-Marbois*. Trans. and ed., Eugene Parker Chase. New York: Books for Libraries, 1969.

Bayley, Rafael. *The National Loans of the United States from July 4, 1776, to June 30, 1880*. Washington: Government Printing Office, 1882.

Bemis, Samuel Flagg. "Canada and the Peace Settlement of 1782–83." *Canadian Historical Review* 14 (1933), pp. 265–84.

Billings, William. *The Complete Works of William Billings*. Eds. H. N. S. Nathan and Richard Crawford, 4 vols. Boston: Colonial Society of Massachusetts, 1977.

Boudinot, J. J., ed. *The Life, Public Services, Addresses and Letters of Elias Boudinot, LL. D. President of the Continental Congress*. 2 vols. Boston: Houghton Mifflin, 1896.

Bowling, Kenneth R. *The Creation of Washington, D.C. The Idea and Location of the American Capital*. Fairfax, VA: George Mason University Press, 1991.

Bowman, Allen. *The Morale of the American Revolutionary Army*. Port Washington, NY: Kennikat Press, 1964.

Bowman, Larry. *Captive Americans: Prisoners During the American Revolution*. Athens: Ohio University Press, 1976.

Boyd, Julian. "Death by a Kindly Teacher of Treason?" *William and Mary Quarterly*, third series, 16 (1959), pp. 165–87, 319–42, 515–50.

Boynton, Edward, ed. *General Orders of George Washington Issued at Newburgh on the Hudson, 1782–83*. Harrison, NY: Harbor Hill Books, 1973.

Brady, Patricia. *Martha Washington: An American Life*. New York: Viking, 2005.

Brooke, John. *The House of Commons, 1754–1790* London: Oxford University Press, 1964.

———. *King George III*. New York: McGraw-Hill, 1972.

Brookhiser, Richard. *Gentleman Revolutionary: Gouverneur Morris, the Rake Who Wrote the Constitution*. New York: Free Press, 2003.

Brown, Gerald. *The American Secretary: The Colonial Policy of Lord George Germain, 1775–78*. Ann Arbor: University of Michigan Press, 1963.

Brown, Wallace. *The Good Americans: The Loyalists in the American Revolution*. New York: Morrow, 1969.

Brumwell, Stephen. *Paths of Glory: The Life and Death of General James Wolfe*. Montreal: McGill-Queens University Press, 2005.

Buel, Richard. *In Irons*. New Haven: Yale University Press, 1998.

Burke, Aedanus. *Considerations on the Society of the Cincinnati*. Hartford: Basil, Webster, 1783.

Burnett, Edmund C. *The Continental Congress*. New York: W.W. Norton, 1941.

———. *Letters of Members of the Continental Congress*. 8 vols. Washington: Carnegie Institution of Washington, 1921–36.

Burrows, Edwin C. *Forgotten Patriots: The Untold Story of American Prisoners During the Revolutionary War*. New York: Basic Books, 2008.

Callahan, North. *Henry Knox*. New York: Rinehart, 1958.

Carp, E. Wayne. *To Starve the Army at Pleasure: Continental Army Administration and American Culture, 1775–1783*. Chapel Hill: University of North Carolina Press, 1984.

Champagne, Roger J. *Alexander Macdougall and the American Revolution in New York*. Schenectady: New York State American Revolution Bicentennial Commission in conjunction with Union College Press, 1975.

Chernow, Ron. *Alexander Hamilton*. New York: Penguin, 2004.

———. *Washington: A Life*. New York: Penguin, 2010.

Clinton, George. *Public Papers of George Clinton*. 10 vols. New York: Wynkoop Hallenbeck Crawford, 1900–1914.

College, J. J. *Ships of the Royal Navy*. 2 vols. New York: Augustus Kelley, 1969.

Columbia College. *Catalogue of Columbia College New York*. New York: E. B. Clayton, 1836.

Cometti, Elizabeth, ed. and trans. *Seeing America and Its Great Men: The Journal and Letters of Count Francesco dal Verme, 1783–84* Charlottesville: University Press of Virginia, 1969.

Dalzell, Robert, and Lee Baldwin Dalzell. *George Washington's Mount Vernon: At Home in Revolutionary America*. New York: Oxford University Press, 1998.

Daniell, Jere. *Colonial New Hampshire*. Millwood, NY: KTO Press, 1981.

Davies, K. G. *Documents of the American Revolution*. 20 vols. Dublin: Irish University Press, 1972–81.

———. "The Restoration of Civil Government by the British in the War of Independence." In *Red, White and the True Blue: The Loyalists in the Revolution*, ed. Esmond Wright. New York: AMS Press, 1976.

Dempsey, Janet. *Washington's Last Cantonment*. Monroe, NY: Library Research Associates, 1990.

Denny, Ebenezer. *Military Journal of Ebenezer Denny*. Philadelphia: Historical Society of Pennsylvania, 1859.

Dictionary of National Biography. 28 vols. London: Oxford Univesity Press, 1921–22.

Edler, Friedrich. *The Dutch Republic and the American Revolution*. Baltimore: Johns Hopkins University Press, 1911.

Elkins, Stanley, and Eric McKitrick. "The Founding Fathers: Young Men of the Revolution." *Political Science Quarterly* 76, no. 2 (June 1961), pp. 181–216.

Fabian, Monroe H. *Joseph Wright: American Artist, 1756–1793.* Washington: National Portrait Gallery, 1985.

Farrand, Max, ed. *The Records of the Federal Convention of 1787.* 3 vols. New Haven: Yale University Press, 1911.

Ferguson, E. James. *The Power of the Purse: A History of American Public Finance, 1776–1790.* Chapel Hill: University of North Carolina Press, 1961.

Fields, Joseph E., comp. *"Worthy Partner": The Papers of Martha Washington.* Westport, CT: Greenwood Press, 1994.

Fish, Hamilton. *George Washington in the Highlands.* Newburgh, NY: Newburgh News, 1932.

Fisher, Sydney. *The Struggle for American Independence.* 2 vols. Philadelphia: J. B. Lippincott, 1908.

Fitzmaurice, Lord Edmund. *Life of William, Earl of Shelburne.* 3 vols. London: Macmillan, 1875–76.

Flexner, James Thomas. *George Washington and the New Nation.* 4 vols. Boston: Little, Brown, 1965–72.

———. *The Young Hamilton, A Biography.* Boston: Little, Brown, 1978.

Ford, Corey. *A Peculiar Service.* Boston: Little, Brown, 1965.

Fowler, David. " 'Loyalty Is Now Bleeding in New Jersey,' Motivations and Mentalities of the Disaffected." In *The Other Loyalists: Ordinary People, Royalism, and the Revolution in the Middle Colonies*, ed. Joseph S. Tiedemann, Eugene R. Fingerhut, and Robert W. Venables, pp. 45–80. Albany: State University of New York Press, 2009.

Fowler, William M. *Empires at War: The Seven Years War and the Struggle for North America.* New York: Walker Books, 2005.

———. *William Ellery: A Rhode Island Politico and Lord of Admiralty.* Metuchen, NJ: Scarecrow, 1972.

Freeman, Douglas Southall. *George Washington: A Biography.* 7 vols. New York: Charles Scribners' Sons, 1948–57.

Franklin, Benjamin. *Papers of Benjamin Franklin.* Ed. Ellen Cohn et al. 39 vols. New Haven: Yale University Press, 1959–2008.

Freiberg, Malcolm, "The Reverend William Gordon's Autumn Tour of the Northeast." *New England Quarterly* 65 (September 1992), pp. 469–80.

Gallagher, Mary A. Y. "Reinterpreting the 'Very Trifling Mutiny' at Philadelphia in June 1783." *Pennsylvania Magazine of History and Biography* 119, nos. 1–2 (January–April 1995), pp. 3–36.

Gilbert, Benjamin. *Winding Down: The Revolutionary War Letters of Lieutenant Benjamin Gilbert of Massachusetts 1780–1783.* Ed. John Shy. Ann Arbor: University of Michigan Press, 1989.

Glasson, William H. *Federal Military Pensions in the United States.* New York: Oxford University Press, 1918.

Golway, Terry. *Washington's General: Nathanael Greene and the Triumph of the American Revolution.* New York: Henry Holt, 2005.

Gordon, William. *The History of the Rise, Progress and Establishment of the United States of America.* 3 vols. New York: Samuel Campbell, 1794.

Green, Nathanael. *The Papers of Nathanael Greene.* Ed. Richard Showman. 13 vols. Chapel Hill: University of North Carolina Press, 1976–2005.

Grizzard, Frank. *A Guide to All Things Washington.* Buena Vista, VA.: Mariner, 2005.

Haggard, Richard. "The Nicola Affair: Lewis Nicola, George Washington, and American Military Discontent During the Revolutionary War." *Proceedings of the American Philosophical Society* 146, no. 2 (June 2002), pp. 139–69.

Hancock, David. *Citizens of the World: London Merchants and the Integration of the British Atlantic Community, 1735–1785.* New York: Cambridge University Press, 1995.

Hannay, David. *Rodney.* Reprint, Boston: Gregg Press, 1972.

Harrison, S. A., *Memoir of Lieut. Col. Tench Tilghman.* Albany: J. Munsell, 1876.

Hawke, David. *Paine.* New York: Harper and Row, 1974.

Heath, William. *Memoirs of Major General William Heath by Himself.* Ed. William Abbatt. New York: William Abbatt, 1901.

Heitman, Francis B. *Historical Register of Officers of the Continental Army.* Washington: Rare Book Publishing, 1914.

Henderson, H. James. *Party Politics in the Continental Congress.* Lanham, MD: University Press of America, 1987.

Howard, Hugh. *The Painter's Chair: George Washington and the Making of American Art.* New York: Bloomsbury, 2009.

Humphreys, David. *Life of General Washington.* Ed. Rosemarie Zagarri. Athens: University of Georgia Press, 1991.

Hunemorder, Marcus. *The Society of the Cincinnati: Conspiracy and Distrust in Early America.* New York: Berghagn Books, 2006.

Idzerda, Stanley J., ed. *Lafayette in the Age of the American Revolution.* 5 vols. Ithaca: Cornell University Press, 1977.

Jasanoff, Maya. *Liberty's Exiles: American Loyalists in the Revolutionary World.* New York: Knopf, 2011.

Jay, John. *The Papers of John Jay.* Ed. Richard B. Morris. 2 vols. New York: Harper and Row, 1975.

Jefferson, Thomas. *The Papers of Thomas Jefferson.* 21 vols., in progress. Ed. Julian Boyd et al. Princeton: Princeton University Press, 1950–.

Jensen, Merrill. *The Articles of Confederation: An Interpretation of the Social-Constitutional History of the American Revolution.* Madison: University of Wisconsin Press, 1970.

Jillson, Calvin, and Rick K. Wilson. *Congressional Dynamics: Structure, Coordination, and Choice in the First American Congress, 1774–1789.* Stanford: Stanford University Press, 1994.

Jones, Thomas. *History of New York During the Revolutionary War.* 2 vols. New York: New York Historical Society, 1879.

Judd, Jacob. "Westchester County." In *The American Revolution Beyond New York City, 1763–1787*, ed. Joseph Tiedemann and Eugene R. Fingerhut, pp. 107–26. Albany: State University of New York Press, 2005.

Ketchum, Richard M. *Saratoga: Turning Point of the American Revolution War*. New York: Henry Holt, 1997.

———. *Victory at Yorktown*. New York: Henry Holt, 2004.

King, Charles R., ed. *The Life and Correspondence of Rufus King*. 6 vols. New York: G. P. Putnam Sons, 1894.

Klein, Milton, and Ronald W. Howard, eds. *The Twilight of British Rule in Revolutionary America: The New York Letter Book of General James Robertson*. Cooperstown: New York State Historical Association, 1983.

Knight, Betsy. "Prisoner Exchange and Parole in the American Revolution." *William and Mary Quarterly*, third series, 48 (April 1991), pp. 201–22.

Kohn, Richard. "The Inside History of the Newburgh Conspiracy: America and the Coup d'Etat." *William and Mary Quarterly*, third series, 27 (April 1970), pp. 187–220.

Lafayette, Marie Joseph Paul Yves Roch Gilbert Du Motier. *Marquis de Lafayette in the Age of the American Revolution*. Ed. Stanley Idzerda. 5 vols. Ithaca: Cornell University Press, 1977.

Laurens, Henry. *Papers of Henry Laurens*. Ed. Philip, Hamer, et al. 16 vols. Columbia: University of South Carolina Press, 1968–2003.

Lawler Jr., Edward. "The President's House in Philadelphia." *Pennsylvania Magazine of History and Biography* (January 2002), pp. 5–95.

Learned, H. B. "Origins of the Superintendent of Finance." *American Historical Review* 10 (April 1905), pp. 565–73.

Lemaître, Georges. *Beaumarchais*. New York: Knopf, 1949.

Lesser, Charles, ed. *The Sinews of Independence: Monthly Strength Reports of the Continental Army*. Chicago: University of Chicago Press, 1976.

Lewis, W. S. *The Yale Edition of the Horace Walpole's Correspondence*. 48 vols. New Haven: Yale University Press, 1937–83.

Lockhart, Paul. *The Drillmaster of Valley Forge: The Baron Von Steuben*. New York: HarperCollins, 2008.

Lossing, Benson. *Life and Times of Philip Schuyler*. 2 vols. New York: Sheldon, 1872–73.

Macauley, Catherine. *The History of England from the Accession of James I to That of the Brunswick Line*. 5 vols. London: J. Nourse, 1763–83.

MacDonald, James S. *Memoir of Governor John Parr*. Halifax: Nova Scotia Historical Society, 1909.

Mackesy, Piers. *The War for America, 1775–1783*. Cambridge: Harvard University Press, 1964.

Mackintosh, John P. *The British Cabinet*. London: Stevens and Sons, 1968.

Maier, Pauline. *The Old Revolutionaries: Political Lives in the Age of Samuel Adams*. New York: Knopf, 1980.

Masur, Louis. *Rites of Execution*. New York: Oxford University Press, 1989.

Mattern, David. *Benjamin Lincoln and the American Revolution*. Columbia: University of South Carolina Press, 1995.

Matthews, Albert. *Letters of Dennys de Berdt, 1757–1770*. Cambridge: J. Wilson and Sons, 1911.

Mayo, Katherine. *George Washington's Dilemma*. New York: Harcourt, Brace, 1938.

McCullough, David. *John Adams*. New York: Simon and Schuster, 2001.

McCusker, John J. *How Much Is that in Real Money?* Worcester: American Antiquarian Society, 1992.

————. *Money and Exchange in Europe and America, 1600–1775*. Chapel Hill: University of North Carolina Press, 1978.

McCusker, John J., and Russell Menard. *The Economy of British North America, 1607–1789*. Chapel Hill: University of North Carolina Press, 1991.

McDonald, Forrest. *E Pluribus Unum*. Boston: Houghton Mifflin, 1965.

Miller, Richard. *In Words and Deeds: Battle Speeches in History*. Hanover, NH: University Press of New England, 2008.

Mitchell, Broadus. *Alexander Hamilton: Youth to Maturity, 1775–1788*. New York: Macmillan, 1962.

Moore, Charles. *The Northwest Under Three Flags*. New York: Harper and Brothers, 1900.

Morgan, John Hill, and Mantle Fielding. *The Life Portraits of Washington and Their Replicas*. Philadelphia: printed for the Subscribers, 1931.

Morris, Gouverneur. *Life of Gouverneur Morris*, 3 vols. Ed. Jared Sparks. Boston: Gray and Bowen, 1832.

Morris, Richard B. *The Peacemakers: The Great Powers and American Independence*. New York: Harper and Row, 1965.

Morris, Robert. *The Papers of Robert Morris*. Ed. E. James Ferguson, et al. 9 vols. Pittsburgh: University of Pittsburgh Press, 1973–.

Murray, Stuart. *Washington's Farewell to His Officers*. Bennington, VT: Images from the Past, 1999.

Nagy, John A. *Rebellion in the Ranks: Mutinies in the American Revolution*. Yardley, PA: Westholme, 2008.

Neagles, James C. *Summer Soldiers: A Survey and Index of Revolutionary War Courts Martial*. Salt Lake City: Ancestry, 1986.

Neimeyer, Charles P. *America Goes to War: A Social History of the Continental Army*. New York: New York University Press, 1996.

Nelson, Paul David. *General Horatio Gates*. Baton Rouge: Louisiana State University Press, 1976.

————. "Horatio Gates at Newburgh: A Misunderstood Role, With a Rebuttal by Richard Kohn." *William and Mary Quarterly* third series, 29 (January 1972), pp. 143–58.

————. *Sir Charles Grey, First Lord Grey*. Madison, NJ: Fairleigh Dickinson University Press, 1996.

Nicola, Lewis. *A Treatise of Military Exercise*. Philadelphia: Styner and Cist, 1776.

Norton, Louis, A. *Joshua Barney*. Annapolis: United States Naval Institute Press, 2000.

Oberholtzer, Ellis P. *Robert Morris*. Reprint, New York: Burt Franklin, 1968.

Overton, Albert G., and J. W. W. Loose. "Prisoner of War Barracks in Lancaster Used During the Revolutionary War." *Journal of the Lancaster County Historical Society* 84 (1980), pp. 131–34.

Paine, Thomas. *Common Sense*. New York: Peter Eckler, 1918.

———. *The Crisis*. London: James Watson, 1835.

Palmer, Dave R. *George Washington and Benedict Arnold*. Washington: Regnery, 2006.

Peckham, Howard. *The Colonial Wars, 1689–1762*. Chicago: University of Chicago Press, 1964.

Pickering, Octavius. *The Life of Timothy Pickering*. 4 vols. Boston: Little, Brown, 1867–73.

Polishook, Irwin. *Rhode Island and the Union*. Evanston: Northwestern University Press, 1969.

Potts, Louis W. *Arthur Lee: A Virtuous Revolutionary*. Baton Rouge: Louisiana State University Press, 1981.

Puls, Mark. *Henry Knox: Visionary General of the American Revolution*. New York: Palgrave, 2008.

Quarles, Benjamin. *The Negro in the American Revolution*. Chapel Hill: University of North Carolina Press, 1961.

Rakove, Jack N. *The Beginnings of National Politics: An Interpretative History of the Continental Congress*. New York: Knopf, 1979.

Ranlet, Philip. *The New York Loyalists*. Knoxville: University of Tennessee Press, 1986.

Reuter, Frank T. "'Petty Spy' or Effective Diplomat: The Role of George Beckwith." *Journal of the Early Republic* 10 (Winter 1990), pp. 471–92.

Reynolds, Paul. *Guy Carleton: A Biography*. New York: Morrow, 1980.

Rice, Howard C., and Anne S. K. Brown, eds. and trans. *The American Campaigns of Rochambeau's Army, 1780, 1781, 1782, 1783*. 2 vols. Princeton: Princeton University Press, 1972.

Riley, Edward M. "St. George Tucker's Journal of the Siege of Yorktown, 1781." *William and Mary Quarterly*, third series, 5 (July 1948), pp. 375–95.

Riley, Elihu Samuel. *"The Ancient City": A History of Annapolis in Maryland, 1649–1887*. Annapolis: Record Printing Office, 1887.

Ritcheson, Charles R. "To an Astonishing Degree Unfit for the Task: Britain's Peacemakers, 1782–83." In *Peace and the Peacemakers: The Treaty of 1783*, ed. Ronald Hoffman and Peter Alberts, pp. 70–100. Charlottesville: University Press of Virginia, 1986.

Rowland, Kate. *The Life of George Mason, 1725–1792*. 2 vols. New York: G. P. Putnams Sons, 1892.

Royster, Charles. *A Revolutionary People at War*. Chapel Hill: University of North Carolina Press, 1979.

Russell, David Lee. *The American Revolution in the Southern Colonies*. Reprint, Jefferson, NC: McFarland, 1978.

Sabine, William H. W. *Historical Memoirs from 26 August 1778 to November 1783 of William Smith*. Reprint, New York: Arno Press, 1971.

Savell, Isabella K. *Wine and Bitters*. New City: Historical Society of Rockland County, 1975.

Schama, Simon. *Dead Certainties*. New York: Knopf, 1991.

Schecter, Barnet. *The Battle for New York*. New York: Walker Books, 2002.

Schenkman, A. J. *Washington's Headquarters at Newburgh*. Charleston: History Press, 2009.

Sellers, Charles C. *Charles Willson Peale*. New York: Charles Scribners Sons, 1969.

Shaw, Samuel. *Journals of Samuel Shaw*. Ed. Josiah Quincy, Boston: Wm. Crosby and H. P. Nichols, 1847.

Skeen, C. Edward. *John Armstrong Jr., 1758–1843: A Biography*. Syracuse: Syracuse University Press, 1981.

———. "The Newburgh Conspiracy Reconsidered With a Rebuttal by Richard Kohn." *William and Mary Quarterly*, third series, 31 (April 1974), pp. 273–98.

Skemp, Sheila. *William Franklin: Son of a Patriot, Servant of a King*. New York: Oxford University Press, 1990.

Smallwood, Frank. *Thomas Chittenden: Vermont's First Statesman*. Shelburne, VT: New England Press, 1997.

Smith, Paul H. "The American Loyalists: Notes on Their Organization and Numerical Strength." *William and Mary Quarterly*, third series, 25 (1968), pp. 259–77.

———. "Sir Guy Carleton: Peace Negotiations and the Evacuation of New York." *Canadian Historical Review* 50 (1969), pp. 245–64.

Stinchcombe, William C. *The American Revolution and the French Alliance*. Syracuse: Syracuse University Press, 1969.

Stokes, I. N. Phelps. *The Iconography of Manhattan Island*. 5 vols. Reprint, New York: Arno Press, 1967.

Strachan, Hew. *Politics of the British Army*. New York: Oxford University Press, 1997.

Sullivan, John. *Journals of the Military Expedition of Major General John Sullivan Against the Six Nations of Indians in 1779*. Albany: New York Secretary of State, 1885.

Sypher, Francis J. Jr. *New York State Society of the Cincinnati Biographies of Original Members and Other Continental Officers*. Fishkill: New York State Society of the Cincinnati, 2004.

Syrett, David. *Shipping and the American War, 1775–83*. London: Athlone Press, 1970.

Syrett, Harold, ed. *The Papers of Alexander Hamilton*. 27 vols. New York: Columbia University Press, 1961–87.

Tallamdge, Benjamin. *Memoir of Col. Benjamin Tallmadge*. New York: Thomas Holman, 1858.

Tarleton, Lieutenant Colonel Banastre. *A History of the Campaigns of 1780 and 1781 in the Southern Provinces of North America*. London: T. Cadell, 1787.

Thacher, Dr. James. *Military Journal, During the American Revolutionary War, from 1775 to 1783*. Hartford: Silas Andrus and Son, 1854. Also online: www.americanrevolution.org/thacher.html.

Thomson, Charles M. *Independent Vermont*. Boston: Houghton Mifflin, 1942.

Tiedemann, Joseph S. and Edward R. Fingerhut, eds. *The American Revolution Beyond New York City, 1763–1787*. Albany: State University of New York Press, 2009.

Tiedemann, Joseph S., Eugene R. Fingerhut, and Robert W. Venables, eds. *The Other*

Loyalists: Ordinary People, Royalism, and the Revolution in the Middle Colonies. Albany: State University of New York Press, 2005.

Tourtellot, Arthur B. "Rebels Turn Out Your Dead." *American Heritage Magazine* 21 (August 1970), pp. 147–52.

Uhlendorg, Bernhard A., ed. *Revolution in America: Confidential Letters and Journals 1776–1784 of Adjutant General Major Baurmeister of the Hessian Forces.* New Brunswick, NJ: Rutgers University Press, 1957.

United States Army Corps of Engineers. *History of the United States Army Corps of Engineers.* Washington: Corps of Engineers, 1998.

Upton, L. F. S. *The Loyal Whig: William Smith of New York and Quebec.* Toronto: University of Toronto Press, 1969.

Valentine, Alan. *The British Establishment.* 2 vols. Norman: University of Oklahoma Press, 1970.

———. *Lord Stirling.* New York: Oxford University Press, 1969.

Van Buskirk, Judith. *Generous Enemies: Patriots and Loyalists in Revolutionary New York.* Philadelphia: University of Pennsylvania Press, 2002.

Waite, Anthony. *Washington's Headquarters, the Hasbrouck House.* Albany: New York State Historic Trust, 1971.

Ward, Christopher. *The War of the Revolution.* 2 vols. New York: Macmillan, 1952.

Ward, Harry. *George Washington's Enforcers: Policing the Continental Army.* Carbondale: University of Southern Illinois Press, 2006.

Watson, Elkanah. *Men and Times of the Revolution.* Ed. Winslow C. Watson. New York: Dana, 1856.

Webster, Pelatiah. *To the Honourable the Legislatures of the Thirteen United States of America, This Second Essay on Free Trade and Finance, Is Most Humbly Inscribed, August 20, 1779.* Philadelphia: Hall and Webster, 1779.

Weinstraub, Stanley. *General Washington's Christmas Farewell.* New York: Free Press, 2003.

———. *Iron Tears.* New York: Free Press, 2005.

Wharton, Francis, ed. *The Revolutionary Diplomatic Correspondence of the United States.* 6 vols. Washington: Government Printing Office, 1889.

Wheatley, Henry B. *The Historical and Posthumous Memoirs of Sir Nathaniel William Wraxall.* 5 vols. London: Bickers and Sons, 1884.

Whiteley, Emily Stone. *Washington and His Aides de Camp.* New York: Macmillan, 1936.

Wilderson, Paul. *Governor John Wentworth and the American Revolution.* Hanover, NH: University Press of New England, 1994.

Willcox, William. *The American Rebellion: Sir Henry Clinton's Narrative of His Campaigns, 1775–1782.* New Haven: Yale University Press, 1954.

———. *Portrait of a General: Sir Henry Clinton in the War of Independence.* New York: Knopf, 1964.

Wright, Conrad. *The Transformation of Charity in Post Revolutionary New England.* Boston: Northeastern University, 1992.

Wright Jr., Robert K. *The Continental Army.* Washington: Center for Military History, 1983.

Ziegler, Philip. *King William IV.* New York: Harper and Row, 1973.

Washington's Writings

Abbot, William, ed., et al. *The Papers of George Washington. Confederation Series*. 6 vols. Charlottesville: University Press of Virginia, 1992–.

Chase, Philander D., ed. *The Papers of George Washington. Revolutionary War Series*. 20 vols., in progress. Charlottesville: University of Virginia Press, 1985–.

Fitzpatrick, John C., ed. *The Writings of George Washington*. 39 vols. Washington: Government Printing Office, 1931–44.

Jackson, Donald, ed., and Dorothy Twohig, assoc. ed. *The Diaries of George Washington*. 6 vols. Charlottesville: University Press of Virginia, 1976–79.

Sparks, Jared, ed. *The Writings of George Washington*, 12 vols. (Boston: American Stationers, 1834–1837).

Twohig, Dorothy, ed. *The Papers of George Washington. Presidential Series*. 15 vols., in progress. Charlottesville: University Press of Virginia, 1987–.

Dissertations

Berlin, Robert H. "The Aministration of Military Justice in the Continental Army During the American Revolution, 1775–1783." Ph.D. dissertation, University of California, Santa Barbara, 1976.

Dendy, John O. "Frederick Haldimand and the Defense of Canada, 1778–1784." Ph.D. dissertation, Duke University, 1972.

Edmonson, James H. "Desertion in the American Army During the Revolutionary War." Ph.D. dissertation, Louisiana State University, 1971.

Mintz, Max. "Gouverneur Morris: The Emergence of a Nationalist." Ph.D. dissertation, New York University, 1957.

Newspapers

Boston Evening Post

Boston Gazette

Connecticut Courant (Hartford)

Newport Mercury

New York Gazette and Mercury

New York Times

Parker's General Advertiser (London)

Pennsylvania Gazette (Philadelphia)

Pennsylvania Journal and Weekly Advertiser (Philadelphia)

Pennsylvania Packet (Philadelphia)

Providence Gazette

Rivington's Royal Gazette (New York City)

Sherborne Mercury (Dorset, United Kingdom)

Web Sites

"Articles of Capitulation," http://avalon.law.yale.edu/18th_century/art_of_cap_1781 .asp

"Articles of Confederation," http://avalon.law.yale.edu/18th_century/artconf.asp

Bastado, Russell, comp., "Likenesses of New Hampshire War Heroes and Personages in the Collections of the New Hampshire State House and State Library," http://www.nh.gov/nhdhr/publications/warheroes/evansrev.html

"Benjamin Franklin Papers," www.yale.edu/franklinpapers

Berrien, Judge John, www.dennisberrien.com/StoriesJudgeJ.html

"Book of Negroes," http://www.blackloyalist.com/canadiandigitalcollection/ documents/official/book_of_negroes.htm

"Commanders of the Corps of Engineers," http://www.usace.army.mil/History/ Pages/Commanders.aspx

Dictionary of Canadian Biography, http://www.biographi.ca/index-e.html

Grizzard, Frank E., "George Washington and the Society of the Cincinnati," http:// gwpapers.virginia.edu/articles/grizzard_2.html

Journals of the Continental Congress, http://memory.loc.gov/ammem/amlaw/lwjc.html

Letters of Delegates to Congress, http://memory.loc.gov/ammem/amlaw/lwdg.html

Official Register of Officers and Men of New Jersey, http://www.njstatelib.org/ NJ_Information/Digital_Collections/Digidox22.php

Purple Heart, http://www.thepurpleheart.com/

Society of the Cincinnari, http://www.societyofthecincinnati.org

Walter Stewart Orderly Book, American Philosophical Society, http://aps-pub.com/ mole/view?docId=ead/Mss.973.3.St4-ead.xml;query=;brand=default

"Mrs Walter Stewart," http://ecatalogue.art.yale.edu/detail.htm?objectId=59034

"Treaty of Peace," http://avalon.law.yale.edu/18th_century/paris.asp

"Washington's Headquarters," http://gwpapers.virginia.edu/documents/revolution/ itinerary/index.html

George Washington Papers at the Library of Congress, http://memory.loc.gov/am mem/gwhtml/gwhome.html

INDEX

Adams, John, 17, 21, 24, 25, 70, 81, 121,
    124, 130, 224
Adams, John Quincy, 24
Adams, Samuel, 16–17, 131
Addison (Armstrong), 180–84
Affleck, Edmund, 59
Albany, New York, 101–2, 212–14
Alexander, William, Lord Stirling, 54–55,
    163, 177
Allen, Ethan, 54–55, 89
Allen, Ira, 54–55
American Indians. *See* Native Americans
American Philosophical Society, 94
American Revolution
    British withdrawal following, 112–19,
        194–203, 222–24, 228–32
    continuation of, after Yorktown, 1–2, 10
    end of, 191–224, 228–32
    financing of, 23–28
    peace negotiations, 131–32, 189, 202–3,
        220, 224
    surrender at Yorktown in, 1–10
amnesty, for deserters, 33
Annapolis, Maryland, 12, 227–28,
    234–36, 241
Armstrong, John, 171, 176, 180–81, 184,
    203

Arnold, Benedict, 58, 110, 226
Articles of Confederation, 17–18, 77, 107,
    133, 153
Articles of War, 91–93, 97, 182
Asgill, Charles, 66, 67, 72, 78, 79
Asgill, Lady Theresa, 78–79
Associated Loyalists, 41–42, 64–65,
    73–75, 114

badge of merit, 103–4
Bahamas, 127
Barbé-Marbois, François, 24–25
Barber, William, 176, 177
Barney, Joshua, 127, 189
Barré, Isaac, 39
Bartlett, Josiah, 20
Bassett, Burwell, 11
Baylies, Hodijah, 159
Beckwith, George, 59–60, 110–11,
    198, 228
Benson, Egbert, 194–96, 199, 202
Berrien, Margaret, 216
Billings, William, 192
Bissell, Daniel, 104
Bland, Theodorick, 137
Board of Associated Loyalists. *See* Associated Loyalists

Bonetta, 7
Boudinot, Elias, 32, 79, 210, 214–17, 223
boundaries, of United States, 123–25
Brant, Joseph, 118
Britain. *See* Great Britain
British army
    morale of, 80
    surrender by, at Yorktown, 1–10
    withdrawal of, 112–14, 116–19,
        194–203, 222–24, 228–31, 232
British spies, 110
Brooks, John, 1, 149, 153, 155–58, 168,
    171, 187
Browne, Thomas, 119
Bunce, Jarold, 91
Burgoyne, John, 31, 46
Burke, Aedanus, 207
Burke, Edmund, 39–40
Butler, Pierce, 247
Butler, Richard, 211

Calvert, Eleanor (Nelly), 11, 12
Camden, South Carolina, 4
Canada, 46, 51, 62, 110, 113, 115–16, 223
Caribbean, 22, 87–88, 105, 127
Carleton, Sir Guy
    as British commander in North
        America, 47–52, 62, 67–86, 105,
        109–20, 191
    career of, 44–47
    end of war and, 193–203, 222–24,
        228–31, 232
    evacuation plan by, 112–14, 116–19
    loyalists and, 68, 73–75, 114–15,
        119–20, 203
    prisoners of war held by, 194
    as replacement for Clinton, 43–44
    Washington and, 71–73, 76–78,
        129–30, 194, 196–202, 271–73
Carlisle, Earl of, 50
Carlisle, John, 180–81
Carlisle Commission, 47
cartels, 31

Cary, Archibald, 101
central government
    nationalists and, 152
    need for strong, 22, 133, 141
    revenue source for, 134, 141
    Washington's urging for, 209–10,
        225
Challoner, Walter, 64
Charleston, South Carolina, 3, 23, 112,
    113, 114, 116–17, 200
Cherokee, 119
Chesapeake Capes, Battle of the, 2
Chew, Benjamin, 12
Chew House, 12, 19, 56
Chittenden, Thomas, 89, 90
"Circular Letter to the States"
    (Washington), 209–10
civil government, 74. *See also* Second
    Continental Congress
Clagdon, William, 86
Clark, Abraham, 143
Clinton, George, 70, 101, 152, 194–95,
    199, 201–2, 212, 223, 229–31
Clinton, Sir Henry
    as British commander in North
        America, 3–5, 32
    loyalists and, 42, 43, 65, 70
    prisoners of war and, 62, 65
    reputation of, in England, 41
    return to England by, 43–44, 68–70
    royal kidnapping plot and, 59–60
    slaves and, 200
    stepping down by, 67
    Yorktown defeat and, 9, 35
Cobb, David, 159
Combahee Ferry, 117
Common Sense (Paine), 28
Congress. *See* Second Continental
    Congress
Constitutional Convention, 246–47
Continental army
    condition of, 53–56, 69, 90–91, 108,
        110, 153–54, 164

Congress and, 134–44, 146–58, 168–71,
    174, 189–90, 211–12
deserters from, 7, 10, 32–33, 90, 93, 135
disbanding of, 190–93, 203–4, 208–9,
    225
discontent in, 28–29, 33, 55–56, 62, 91,
    97–100, 102, 106, 108, 110, 134–36,
    180–88, 193, 203, 211–12
fear of mutiny by, 1, 33, 55, 91, 97–98,
    110, 144, 154–57, 172
funding of, 27–28, 87, 145–46
memorial by, sent to Congress, 146–58
morale of, 27
officers in, 27–31, 33, 55, 96, 98, 103,
    134–40, 142–58, 174, 182, 190
payments to, 134–36, 145–58, 168,
    170–71, 178–79, 183–84, 189–91, 204,
    211–12
political promotions in, 30–31, 53
at Valley Forge, 18, 20, 56, 136
during winter, 18–19, 54–55, 106,
    159–60, 164–60
Continental Congress. See Second
    Continental Congress
Continental dollars, 18, 23–24
Conway, Henry Seymour, 41, 47
Copley, John Singleton, 52, 128
Cornell, Ezekiel, 31
Cornwallis, Lord Charles, 32, 35
    as commander during Revolution, 3–4
    release of, 129, 132–33
    reputation of, 41
    return to England by, 10
    surrender by, 1, 5–9, 42–43
    at Yorktown, 4–10
courts-martial, 10, 92
Crane, John, 54
Creek (native tribe), 119
Crisis, The (Paine), 28–29, 30
Cumberland, Duke of, 45
Custis, Daniel, 11
Custis, Daniel Parke, 11
Custis, Frances, 11

Custis, John (Jacky), 11
Custis, Martha (Patsy), 11

dal Verme, Count Francesco, 212–13
Dayton, Elias, 67
Deane, Silas, 14, 16–17, 20, 131
death penalty, 92
Declaration of Independence, 20
de Grasse, François-Joseph-Paul, 4–5, 9,
    10, 22, 88
Denny, Ebenezer, 5–6
de Noailles, Viscount de, 7
deserters, 7, 10, 32–33, 90, 93, 135
Dickinson, John, 234, 245–46
Digby, Sir Robert, 47, 68, 111, 113, 120
Duane, James, 144
DuBois, Tryntje, 57
Dundas, Thomas, 7
Dutch, 24, 127, 130, 154
Dyer, Eliphalet, 151

East Indies, 127
economy, during American Revolution,
    18, 23
Edwards, Stephen, 64
Eliot, George, 127
Ellery, William, 16, 235–37
Elliott, Andrew, 68, 197–99, 228
Ellis, Welbore, 44
Ellison House, 175, 177, 178, 180, 182, 184
England. See Great Britain
Evans, Israel, 9, 164–68
exports, 23

"Farewell Orders" (Washington), 225–26
"Farewell to His Officers" (Washington),
    232–33
Fielding, William, 84, 114
First Continental Congress, 14, 21
fishing industry, 23
fishing rights, 123, 124
floggings, 92
Florida, 117–19, 123, 127

Floridablanca, Conde de, 122
Fogg, Jeremiah, 118
Forbes, John, 176
Foreign Affairs department, 17
foreign loans, 24
Fortescue, Sir John, 4
Fort Independence, 53–54
Fort Pitt, 33
Fox, Charles James, 39, 48–49, 202–3
France
    Britain and, 82, 88, 111, 122–23
    financing of war by, 2, 23–27
    involvement of, in Revolution, 3, 4–5,
        22–27, 88, 104–6
    peace negotiations and, 121, 122,
        125–27, 131–32
Franco-American alliance, 52, 105, 110, 130
Franklin, Benjamin, 21, 25, 81–82, 121–27,
    131, 220, 224, 246
Franklin, William, 41–43, 64, 65, 68,
    73–75, 114
Franklin, William Temple, 126–27
Fraunces, Samuel, 201, 204–5
French and Indian War, 14, 81, 91, 176
Friendly Sons of St. Patrick, 19

Gálvez, Bernardo de, 119
Gates, Horatio, 86, 203
    on Congress, 136
    defeat at Camden, 4
    at Ellison House, 160, 165, 166
    role of, in mutiny plot, 173–85, 187
    treatment of, after defeat, 106–7
    Washington and, 107–8, 236
Gaylord, Ambrose, 91
George II, 45
George III, 2, 10, 35–39, 45, 47–49,
    72–73, 127–28, 172
Georgia, 4
Gérard, Conrad Alexandre, 25
Germain, Lord George, 35–38, 40, 42–47
German mercenaries, 52, 63, 113–14, 120
Gerry, Elbridge, 137

Gibbs, Caleb, 58
Gibraltar, 122, 127
Gilbert, Benjamin, 98, 208
Glover, John, 54
Gordon, James, 66–67
Gordon, William, 98, 242–44
Gorham, Nathaniel, 155
Graham, Catherine Macaulay, 244
Gray, Thomas, 83
Great Britain
    France and, 82, 88, 111, 122–23
    positions held by, after Yorktown, 1–2, 10
    reaction to Yorktown loss in, 35–41
    Spain and, 88, 122–23
    surrender by, at Yorktown, 1, 4–10
Greaton, John, 147
Greene, Nathanael, 4, 10, 20, 55–56, 92,
    94, 116–17, 136, 154, 161, 221
Green Mountain Boys, 89
Grenada, 127
Grey, Charles, 111, 197–98

Hague, The, 24, 130, 131
Haldimand, Frederick, 55, 69, 76, 90,
    110, 118, 119
half pay petition, 27, 137–44, 146, 149,
    152–58, 172, 179, 190, 210
Hamilton, Alexander, 49, 174
    Carleton and, 223
    Laurens and, 117
    Lippincott affair and, 67
    marriage of, 101
    national view of, 133, 152, 180
    officers' pay and, 146, 154, 156
    on state of union, 151
    Washington and, 168–71, 173, 179, 183
Hamond, Andrew Snape, 115–16
Hand, Edward, 187
Hanson, John, 15, 18
Hartley, David, 224
Hasbrouck House, 57–59, 86, 93–94,
    159–68, 179, 188, 203, 214
Hazen, Moses, 66

Heath, William, 53–55, 58, 60–62, 64, 76–77, 94, 108, 191
Higginson, Stephen, 210
Houdon, Jean-Antoine, 244
House of Burgesses, 14
Howard, Captain, 187
Howe, Bezaleel, 226–27
Howe, Richard, 47, 49–50
Howe, Robert, 160
Howe, Sir William, 19, 31, 47, 49–50, 211–12
Howell, David, 151, 210, 220, 234–35
Huddy, Joshua, 64–65, 67, 72–73, 75–76, 83
Hughes, Hugh, 56–57
Humphreys, David, 58, 159, 196, 225
Huntington, Samuel, 139

imports, 23
impost tax, 134, 143, 151, 210
independence
    as condition for ending war, 49–50, 80, 82, 121
    popular support for, 135
    recognition of, 122–23, 128, 172, 224
Independence Hall, 19, 130
Invalid Corps, 95
Iroquois, 118, 119
Izard, Ralph, 211

Jackson, Henry, 55
Jamaica, 88, 116
Jay, John, 24, 81, 121–24, 126, 224
Jefferson, Thomas, 2, 81, 237
Johnson, Samuel, 51
Jones, Joseph, 137, 150, 179–80, 183, 186
Jones, Thomas, 114
Judd, William, 140–42

Kentfield, Shem, 94
Knox, Henry, 54, 132, 168, 203–4
    discontent by, 55
    on discontent in army, 98, 108, 147

    entry into New York City by, 229–30
    Lippincott affair and, 67
    Morris and, 171
    mutiny plot and, 172–74, 187–88
    officers' memorial and, 147–48, 150, 157–58
    personal troubles of, 160–61
    promotion of, 30–31
Knox, Lucy, 160–61
Knyphausen, Wilhelm von, 68

Lafayette, Marquis de, 7, 9, 22, 49, 161, 163, 191, 196
Laurens, Henry, 81, 117, 121, 129
Laurens, John, 7, 117
Lauzun, Duc de, 35
Lee, Arthur, 16–17, 130–32, 156
Lee, Billy, 58, 239
Lee, Charles, 119
Legge, Francis, 115
legislative committees, 15–16
Leslie, Alexander, 114, 116–17
Life Guard, 58
Lincoln, Benjamin, 8, 17–22, 27, 30, 86–87, 132, 140–46, 188, 225
Lippincott, Richard, 64–67, 72–77
Liveried Companies of London, 40
Livingston, Robert R., 17, 19, 21, 26, 29, 121, 196
localism, 22
Louis Joseph Xavier François (Dauphin), 98–99
Louis XVI, 98
Lovell, James, 136, 137, 152
Lowell, John, 146–47
loyalists
    Carleton and, 68, 73–75, 111, 114–15, 119–20, 203
    compensation for, 124, 126, 224
    evacuation of, 52, 114–20, 222–23
    in New York City, 193, 222–23
    number of, 111
    retaliation against, 64–65, 222–23

loyalists (*continued*)
  skirmishes with, 55
  transport of, to Canada, 115–16
  treatment of, 7, 41–44, 70–71, 79–80,
    82–84, 111–12, 195, 201, 203, 224
Ludlow, Captain, 66–67
Luzerne, Chevalier de la, 24–27, 81,
  98–99, 194

Maclean, Allan, 118
Madison, James, 132–33, 143, 145–46, 154,
  172, 175, 180, 205
Marine department, 17, 18
Marion, Francis, 4
Massachusetts Line, 146–48
Mathews, John, 94
Maxwell, William, 177
Mayeur, Jean Pierre le, 204–5
McDougall, Alexander, 1, 18, 60–62, 149,
  151–57, 171–72, 187–88, 190, 232
McHenry, James, 88, 214–15, 237, 238,
  239
McKean, Thomas, 9
Mercer, Hugh, 176
Middleton, Sir Charles, 112
Mifflin, Thomas, 236, 239
military justice, 91–93
military pensions, 27, 137–44, 146, 149,
  152–58, 172
Minorca, 127
Mohawk River, 213–14
Monmouth Retaliators, 63, 64
Montserrat, 127
Moore House, 6, 7
Morgann, Maurice, 50–51, 72, 79–80,
  84, 109
Morris, Gouverneur, 19–21, 24, 121, 175
  on Constitutional Convention,
    246–47
  Knox's reply to, 171–72
  letter to Knox by, 157–58, 168, 174
  nationalist views of, 138–39
  on peace, 133

Morris, Robert, 107, 172, 189, 234, 246
  impost tax and, 134
  on payments to army, 137–41, 146,
    151–55, 156–57
  on peace, 144
  resignation by, 155–56
  as superintendant of finance, 17–20,
    23–29, 87
Morristown, 18
Morton, Silas, 231
Mount Vernon, 11, 12, 58–59, 161, 218–19,
  239–40, 242, 245
Muhlenberg, Frederick Augustus, 19
mutinies, 93, 97, 135, 150, 154, 156, 172,
  203, 211–12

national finance, 153
national government. *See also* central
  government
  under Articles of Confederation,
    17–18, 22
  lack of funds for, 22, 23
nationalists, 133–34, 138–39, 141–42,
  145–46, 171–72, 179, 189
Native Americans, 23, 118, 119, 217–18
navy, 18, 22
Navy Board, 112–13
Nelson, Thomas, 2, 10
"Newburgh Address" (Washington),
  185–88, 207
Newburgh encampment, 164–68, 174–88
New Hampshire, 89
New York, 89
New York City
  attack on, 22, 62
  British occupation of, 4, 23, 74, 89, 109
  condition of, at end of war, 223–24, 229
  devastation of, 68–69
  evacuation of British from, 112,
    194–203, 222–24, 228–32
  loyalists in, 41, 119–20, 193, 222–23
  trade in, 205
  Washington's entry into, 228–31

Nicola, Lewis, 94–98
North, Lord, 1, 36–40, 47–48, 202–3
North Carolina, 4
Nova Scotia, 115–16, 223

Ogden, Matthias, 1, 59–60, 149, 153–57,
    171, 187
O'Hara, Charles, 8
Order of Freedom, 206
Osgood, Samuel, 143, 145–47, 152, 207
Oswald, Richard, 81–82, 121–26

Paine, Thomas, 28–30
Paoli Massacre, 197–98
paper money, 18, 23–24
Paris, peace negotiations in, 120–28
Parker, Daniel, 202
Parker, Wyman, 91
Parliament
    Germain and, 36
    North government and, 38–39
    opposition to war in, 38–41, 44, 47
       49, 72
    peace negotiations and, 124, 127–28
Parr, John, 115–16, 223
Payne, Stephen, 75
peace negotiations, 120–28, 131–32, 189,
    202–3, 220, 224
Peale, Charles Willson, 12–13, 86
Penn, Richard, 19
Pennsylvania Line, 211–12
Penobscot, 112
pensions. See military pensions
Peters, Richard, 174–75, 179
Philadelphia, 12–13, 16, 18–19, 33–34,
    94, 151, 205, 234
Pickering, Timothy, 54–57, 87, 105–8, 160,
    166–68, 171, 187, 204, 208–9, 228–29
Pierce, John, 189
Pine, Robert Edge, 243–44
Pitt, William, 37, 45
political dissention, in Congress, 16–17
political power, 17

Powel, Elizabeth Willing, 12
Powel, Samuel, 12
Powel House, 12
prewar debts, 124, 126
Princeton, 18, 211–12, 227, 235
prisoners of war, 7, 31–32, 62–67, 194, 213
privateering, 23
promotions, political, 30–31, 53
property, confiscated from loyalists, 33
Purple Heart, 104
Putnam, Rufus, 186–87

Quebec, 45–46, 51

radicals, 133–34
Randolph, Edmund, 172, 210, 246
Rattlesnake, 9
Rendon, Francisco, 12
republicanism, 110
Revolutionary War. *See* American
    Revolution
Rhode Island, 101, 131, 151
Richmond, Christopher, 176–77, 203
Ridley, Matthew, 133
Rittenhouse, David, 163, 186
Robertson, James, 43–44, 65, 71, 75, 120
Rochambeau, General, 4, 5, 8, 10, 104–6
Rochefontaine, Stephen, 165–67
Rockingham, Marquis, 48, 49, 84
Rodney, Sir George, 87–88, 94
Rolle, Martha, 237
Root, Jesse, 142–44
Ross, Alexander, 7
Royal Navy, 2, 4, 10, 23, 88
Rutledge, Edward, 132–33, 154, 246
Rutledge, John, 132

Saintes, Battle of the, 88
Salisbury, Daniel, 147
Saratoga, battle at, 31
Savannah, Georgia, 112, 113, 116, 199–200
Schuyler, Elizabeth, 169
Schuyler, Philip, 101, 169, 186–88, 212–13

Scott, John Morin, 196, 199, 201
Second Continental Congress, 1, 15–16
  in Annapolis, 227–28, 234–36, 241
  under Articles of Confederation, 133
  attempts to reform, 17–18
  Continental army and, 134–44, 146–58, 168–71, 174, 183–84, 189–90, 211–12
  decline of, 15–18, 235, 245
  financial problems of, 2, 18, 22, 95–96, 130, 140, 156
  French and, 15–17
  inaction and indecision by, 2, 15–16, 133–34, 210–11
  meddling by, in war, 30–32
  news of peace settlement and, 132–33
  news of Yorktown victory delivered to, 9–10
  public opinion of, 110, 211
  relocation by, 211–12, 227–28, 235
  standing committees of, 16
  Washington and, 14–15, 18, 30–34, 78, 86–88, 96–97, 132, 144, 171–74, 179, 183–84, 190, 214–18, 235–39
Senegal, 127
Shaw, Samuel, 55, 185
Shelburne, Earl of, 48–52, 71, 79–85, 88, 109, 111–12, 120–24, 202
Shield, Benjamin, 62–63
shipbuilding, 23
slaves, evacuation of, by British, 199–201, 223
smallpox, 54
Smith, William, 43, 69–74, 76–77, 83–84, 114, 193, 197–99, 202–5
Society of the Cincinnati, 206–7
South Carolina, 3–4
Spain
  Britain and, 122–23
  control of Florida by, 119, 127
  involvement of, in Revolution, 24, 88, 122
  peace negotiations and, 127
spies, 110, 127

standing committees, 16
Stapleton, John, 194–95
states
  Congress and, 210–11
  disputes between, following war, 245
  lack of support from, 23–24, 26, 28, 30
St. Augustine, Florida, 113, 116–18
Stewart, Walter, 177–80, 183, 210
Stirling, Lord. See Alexander, William, Lord Stirling
Stormont, Lord, 36–37
Strachey, Henry, 124, 126
Sullivan, John, 118
Sumter, Thomas, 4
surrender ceremony, at Yorktown, 7–9
Surveillante, 35
Swift, Heman, 91

Tallmadge, Benjamin, 232, 233
Tappan Massacre, 198
taxation, 26, 29–30, 134, 140–42, 156, 210
Temple of Virtue, 165–68
Thacher, James, 7–8, 92, 99
Thaxter, John, 224–25
Thompson, Benjamin, 111
Thomson, Charles, 15, 19, 21, 212
Thurlow, Edward, 37, 48
Tilghman, Tench, 9, 19, 150, 159, 169
Tilton, James, 237–38
Tobago, 127
Tories. See loyalists
Townshend, Thomas, 85
trade
  during American Revolution, 23
  opening of, 205
  trans-Atlantic, 49, 123–24
Treasury department, 17
Treaty of Paris, 45, 123–28, 189, 199, 224–25, 241
Treaty of Utrecht, 115
Trenton, 18
Trumbull, Jonathan, Jr., 19, 58, 93–94, 159, 182, 188

Tupper, Benjamin, 165–68
typhus, 56
Tyson, John, 57

United States
    boundaries of, 123–25
    independence for, 128
    recognition of, 122–23, 130

Valley Forge, 18, 20, 56, 136
Vardill, John, 122
Varick, Richard, 58, 225, 226
Varnum, James Mitchell, 102–3
Vaudreuil, Marquis de, 105
Vaughan, Benjamin, 123
Vergennes, Comte de, 25, 78–79, 122,
    127, 224
Vermont, 54–55, 69, 89–90, 110
Verplanck's Point, 104–5, 106, 145
Versailles, 35
veterans, 95–96, 137–44
Villa de Penco, 3
Villefranche, Chevalier de, 99
Villeneuve, Cillart de, 35
Virginia, 4
von Steuben, Baron Friedrich Wilhelm
    Augustus, 108, 136, 161, 173, 177, 206,
    207, 212, 232

Walker, Benjamin, 58, 159
Walpole, Horace, 36
Walsingham, Lord, 36–37
War department, 17
Washington, George
    in Albany, 101–2
    appointment of, as commander in chief,
        14–16
    authority of, 181–82
    badge of merit and, 103–4
    Carleton and, 71–73, 76–78, 129–30,
        194, 196–202
    "Circular Letter to the States" by,
        209–10
    concerns of, over ending American
        Revolution, 1–2, 10, 87–89, 100–101
    Congress and, 14–15, 18, 30–34, 78,
        86–88, 96–97, 132, 144, 171–74, 179,
        183–84, 190, 214–18, 235–39
    at Constitutional Convention, 246–47
    documents of, 225–27, 234, 243
    end of war and, 191–93, 196–210, 212–21
    entry into New York City by, 228–33
    "Farewell Orders" by, 225–26
    "Farewell to His Officers" by, 232–33
    finances of, 218–19
    French and, 24–25
    in French and Indian War, 104–6, 176
    Gates and, 106–8
    Hamilton and, 168–71, 173, 180
    at Hasbrouck House, 57–59, 86, 93–94,
        159–68, 179, 181–88, 203–7, 214
    headquarters of, 56 59
    Heath and, 54
    Huddy murder and, 64–67, 72, 76–77
    Lincoln and, 145–46
    Lippincott affair and, 64–65, 72–78
    monument to, 215, 219–20
    on Native Americans, 217–18
    "Newburgh Address" by, 185–88, 207
    on payments to army, 27–28, 190
    pension issue and, 137–40
    personal troubles of, 161–64, 204–5
    in Philadelphia, 12–13, 18–19, 33–34, 234
    physical stresses on, 163–64
    as president, 247
    prisoners of war and, 31–32, 63
    reaction of, to officers' concerns, 150,
        181–88
    relationship with mother of, 11–12,
        162–63
    reputation of, 172, 179, 210, 225
    resignation by, 236–40
    retirement of, 217–19, 241–47
    as slaveholder, 200–201
    at Valley Forge, 136
    at Yorktown, 3–10

Washington, John Augustine, 162, 163, 242

Washington, Martha, 11, 12, 56, 102, 161, 203, 214, 216, 221, 237, 239–40

Washington, Mary Ball, 11–12, 162–63

Washington, Samuel, 161–62

Watson, Brook, 50–52

Watson, Elkanah, 127–28

Wayne, Anthony, 117

Webster, Pelatiah, 140–42

Wentworth, John, 89

western expansion, 213–14

West Indies, 9, 22, 69, 88, 111, 113

White, Philip, 63, 65

William Henry (prince), 59–60

Williamson, Hugh, 238

Wilson, James, 155

winter campaigns, 18–19, 54–55

Witherspoon, John, 132

Wolcott, Oliver, 152, 153

Wolfe, James, 45, 83–84

Wright, Joseph, 219–20

Wright, Sir James, 114

Yorktown
    American victory at, 1–10
    reaction to, in England, 35–41
    terms of surrender at, 7, 42–43

Young, Sir George, 40

A NOTE ON THE AUTHOR

William M. Fowler Jr. is Distinguished Professor of History at Northeastern University in Boston. Prior to that, for eight years he was director of the Massachusetts Historical Society. He is the author of *Empires at War: The French and Indian War and the Struggle for North America, 1754–1763, Jack Tars and Commodores: The American Navy, 1783–1815, The Baron of Beacon Hill: A Biography of John Hancock,* and *Samuel Adams: Radical Puritan.* He lives in Reading, Massachusetts